The Private Use of Tax-Exempt Bonds

Controlling Public Subsidy of Private Activity

THE URBAN INSTITUTE PRESS
Washington, D.C.

THE URBAN INSTITUTE PRESS
2100 M Street, N.W.
Washington, D.C. 20037

Library of Congress Cataloging in Publication Data

Zimmerman, Dennis.
The Private Use of Tax-Exempt Bonds: Controlling Public Subsidy of Private Activity/Dennis Zimmerman.

1. Securities, Tax-exempt—United States.   2. State bonds—United States.
3. Municipal bonds—United States.   I. Title.

UI6383.Z56	1990	343.7305'246—dc20	90-49016
			CIP

ISBN 0-87766-498-6 (alk. paper)
ISBN 0-87766-497-8 (alk. paper; casebound)

Urban Institute books are printed on acid-free paper whenever possible.

Printed in the United States of America.

9 8 7 6 5 4 3 2 1

Distributed by:
        University Press of America
4720 Boston Way   3 Henrietta Street
Lanham, MD 20706   London   WC2E 8LU   ENGLAND

THE URBAN INSTITUTE is a nonprofit policy research and educational organization established in Washington, D.C., in 1968. Its staff investigates the social and economic problems confronting the nation and government policies and programs designed to alleviate such problems. The Institute disseminates significant findings of its research through the publications program of its Press. The Institute has two goals for work in each of its research areas: to help shape thinking about societal problems and efforts to solve them, and to improve government decisions and performance by providing better information and analytic tools.

Through work that ranges from broad conceptual studies to administrative and technical assistance, Institute researchers contribute to the stock of knowledge available to public officials and private individuals and groups concerned with formulating and implementing more efficient and effective government policy.

Conclusions or opinions expressed in Institute publications are those of the authors and do not necessarily reflect the views of other staff members, officers or trustees of the Institute, advisory groups, or any organizations that provide financial support to the Institute.

To Mom and Dad
For love and lots of good advice

ACKNOWLEDGMENTS

This book could not have been written without the cooperation and encourgement of several institutions and many people. The Congressional Research Service (CRS) and the Library of Congress granted me a year's leave of absence, without which no manuscript would have been forthcoming. I am also indebted to the CRS for the freedom it has given me over the years to write about those public finance issues I have considered important to Congress, none of which have consumed more of my time than the ongoing saga of tax-exempt bonds. Of course, the views presented in this book are mine alone, and do not represent those of the Congressional Research Service or the Library of Congress.

The Urban Institute, particularly George Peterson, expressed interest in this project at an early stage. The Institute provided a home away from the CRS for my year's leave, and my experience there was rewarding. The Advisory Commission on Intergovernmental Relations (ACIR) greatly facilitated the survey of state experience with the bond volume cap by agreeing to make it a joint research project. My thanks to *Tax Notes, Municipal Finance Journal*, the National Tax Association–Tax Institute of America, and the Advisory Commission on Intergovernmental Relations for permission to reprint material from their publications; and last, but by no means least, the Internal Revenue Service for an interview that provided background for chapter 12, on "Administration and Enforcement."

Several people have read this manuscript in its entirety and provided me the benefit of their insight: Bruce Davie of the Office of Federal Tax Services of Arthur Andersen & Co., Washington, D.C., an economist with the U.S. House of Representatives Committee on Ways and Means during the 1980s when much of the tax-exempt bond legislation was being written; Chuck Vehorn of the International Monetary Fund, an economist with the General Accounting Office during those same years; Daphne Kenyon, Professor of Economics at Simmons College, Boston, an economist with the ACIR, the U.S. Department of the Treasury, and The Urban Institute during the 1980s; and Pearl Richardson, an analyst with the Congressional Budget Office. Others have read and commented on selected chapters of the book: George Peterson of the Urban Institute on chapters 2 through 11; Margaret Henry of the Ways and Means Committee and Eugene Steuerle of the Urban Institute on chapter 12; Michael Bell of Johns Hopkins University on chapter 13; Robert Ebel of the Advisory Commission on Intergovernmental Relations on chapters 1 and 15; Catherine Spain of the Government Finance Officers Association on chapter 15; and Felicity Skidmore of the Urban Institute on chapter 1.

I valued the comments of these people very much, and made many adjustments in the manuscript accordingly. But I by no means agreed with or responded to every comment and suggestion. If the reader finds something objectionable or wrong (analytically or factually) with this book's discussion, I have no doubt ignored the comments of one or more of these people. In other words, many thanks, but mistakes and errors of commission or omission are mine alone.

Finally, I talked with and received advice, suggestions, and material from other people and institutions too numerous to mention. To all of them, thank you for your cooperation and assistance.

CONTENTS

Tables

Figures

FOREWORD

Tax-exempt bonds are one component of a package of federal assistance to states and localities, a package the federal government reduced over the course of the 1980s. Tax-exempt bonds were intended to subsidize state and local infrastructure development such as roads, schools, and other "public good" projects, but have been increasingly used by states and localities for private as well as public use.

The last 20 years have seen numerous revisions of the Internal Revenue Code provisions concerning tax-exempt bonds, the purpose of which has been to ensure that state and local proceeds from these bonds do indeed contribute to the public good rather than to the "private" good of individuals and businesses. Dennis Zimmerman chronicles this legislative effort.

Tax-exempt bond laws are tricky to write and difficult to enforce. They represent one of the most explicit attempts the federal government has made to define public versus private purposes in statutory language, a problematic exercise indeed. Passage of these laws has to consider the rights and responsibilities of the federal government versus those of states, intergovernmental fiscal relations, the growing federal deficit, resource allocation, and tax equity. The story of the enactment of these laws provides an excellent example of what the author calls "the public policy process in all its messiness, one in which economic theory runs headlong into the realities of the political system with its multitude of conflicting economic interests and imperfect legislative process." Thus, it is not surprising that the author's intended audience includes not only the bond community, but also students of public policy and economics who, through analysis of this many-tendriled problem, might gain a better understanding of the complexities of federal tax policy.

This book continues a longstanding Institute interest in the tax-exempt bond market, including George Peterson's studies of the role of tax-exempt bonds in infrastructure finance, and studies by Peterson, John Weicher and John Tuccillo of the use of tax-exempt bonds by state governments to lower housing mortgage costs. While the viewpoints the author expresses about the private use of tax-exempt bonds and what should be done to regulate them are his, The Urban Institute supports the serious thought and objective research on which this book is based and the contribution it may make to the important subject of tax-exempt bond policy legislation and enforcement.

William Corham
President

Chapter One

PURPOSE, OVERVIEW, AND CONCLUSIONS

During the past two decades the issuance of tax-exempt bonds by state and local governments has been the subject of a running dispute within the family of American federalism. The first income tax law in the United States, in 1913, excluded from taxable income the interest income earned by holders of the debt obligations (bonds) of states and their political subdivisions. There the matter rested, with a few interludes of noisy talk but no action, for more than 50 years. Not until 1968 was the Internal Revenue Code (also referred to here as the Code) amended to limit the scope of the exemption. Since then the tax-exempt bond provisions of the Code have been amended many times, and were thoroughly overhauled by the Tax Reform Act of 1986. There is every reason to believe that further changes will also be made.

The legislative changes since 1968 reflect a profound clash of policy objectives between the federal and state-local government sectors. The federal government has been concerned that unfettered issuance of tax-exempt bonds erodes its income tax base, reduces economic output by misallocating the supply of scarce savings, distorts the equity of the income tax system, and involves the federal government unnecessarily in support of some state and local services. State and local governments naturally want to finance capital projects and short-term borrowing at the lowest possible cost. In addition, they have wanted to provide subsidized credit to private corporations, real estate developers, home buyers, college students, and charitable institutions, in order to promote local economic development, generate benefits to their constituencies, and advance other worthy objectives.

Some might say that a book about legislative efforts to control private use of tax-exempt bonds is fundamentally a book about greed. This is true. But more than that, it is a book about the immense difficulties representative governments face in writing legislation that successfully reconciles the benefits and costs of greed. Greed is economically valuable, the thread from which the cloth of a free market system is woven. By working hard, saving, and investing to increase their lifetime consumption, greedy individuals make everyone better off. In the absence of greed the U.S. economy would be in bad shape indeed. However, the pejorative flavor of greed comes from its undesirable effects, which work against free market goals. Cartels are formed, prices are fixed, environmental damage is ignored, entry into labor unions is restricted, and, yes, tax-exempt bonds are used for private purposes.

Impressive arguments have been mustered over the years to justify the subsidy of state and local capital formation represented by the interest exemption for tax-exempt bonds. It is, however, no easy task to write laws that prohibit self-interested individuals from using subsidies in ways that stray beyond the intent of the legislation. It should come as no surprise that state and local officials, underwriters, bond lawyers, state and local taxpayers, and other bond market participants have acted on their acquisitive impulses to push their use of the tax-exempt bond subsidy beyond legislative intent. The fact is, if any individual or governmental unit does not take advantage of the opportunities an imperfect tax law creates for using tax-exempt bonds for private purposes, the nature of our competitive economic system guarantees that other individuals and governmental units most certainly will. As Walt Kelly's Pogo said, "We has met the enemy, and it is us."

Twenty years of congressional effort to write boundaries into the tax law to effectively constrain market participants' behavior to the intent of the legislation, that is, to subsidize public capital formation, have not resolved this conflict. To develop effective legislation has been and remains extraordinarily difficult. Each major piece of tax legislation since 1980 has changed the tax-exempt bond rules in an atmosphere of intense lobbying by representatives of state and local governments. Administrations have usually urged Congress to tighten the rules. Representatives of the investment bankers and bond counsel whose livelihoods are determined by the volume of issuance enter into the legislative fray in a predictable but understandable way. The compromises reached have accomplished some federal objectives, but at the expense of significantly complicating the legitimate fiscal activities of state and local governments. Beyond the frustration of coping with ever-changing rules, state and local officials express genuine philosophical concern about whether the new rules conform to their understanding of traditional concepts of American federalism. In some instances state and local governments have challenged specific legislative acts in the courts.

I have four objectives in writing this book. First, I want to explain how private use of tax-exempt bonds is a predictable result of the economic incentives confronting bond market participants. Second, I want to demonstrate how the last 20 years of tax-exempt bond legislation have represented a reasonably consistent effort to manipulate these economic incentives. Third, I want to place these explanations within the context of the major public policy issues of the period. Some insights provided by economic theories in public finance and public choice proved to be helpful in these efforts. My fourth and final objective is to explore alternative methods of resolving the conflicting objectives of different levels of government.

A persuasive case is made that so long as any tax-exempt bonds are issued by state and local governments, there must be a set of federal rules to limit the volume of issuance. I am convinced of this, not because I am an economist employed by the U.S. Congress but because analysis of the alternative—unlimited issuance—demonstrates that the results would be untenable in both an economic and political sense. The conviction that there must be federal constraints on the power of state and local governments to issue tax-exempt bonds galls many state and local government officials, as well as many members of what is often called the "bond community." Since the clock cannot be wound back to pre-1968 law permitting unlimited issuance, a search for rules that merge federal objectives with state and local purposes in as simple and mutually beneficial a manner as possible should be worth the effort.

A brief digression is in order to tell the reader what this book is *not* about. It is not an in-depth analysis of tax-exempt bonds as a financial asset; of bondholders and bond issuers—those who make up the demand for and supply of tax-exempt bonds; or of how the bond market works—the roles of underwriters, bond counsel, credit rating agencies, and so forth. My treatment of these topics, which are covered in numerous other books about tax-exempt bonds, is limited to what is necessary for an informed discussion of my four principal objectives.

The book is divided into four parts, each of which is described next.

PART ONE: INSTITUTIONAL BACKGROUND

The three chapters in part 1 provide background information on tax-exempt bond policy. Chapter 2 explores the state and local sector's bond issuance experience in the 19th and first half of the 20th centuries. This history reveals problems similar in some respects to those encountered today: concerns with bond volume; the use of municipal debt to provide financial support for the private sector; and legislation to restrict volume and types of activities financed.

The legal framework within which the tax-exempt bond market functions is presented in chapter 3. The most important issue discussed is that of the long-standing claim of constitutional protection for tax exemption of state and local bond interest, an issue decided in 1988 when the U S. Supreme Court denied the claim. Although all bond market participants may not as yet have accepted the finality of the decision, it appears that the federal government's efforts over the last 20 years to tax the interest income on selected types of municipal bonds are legal. If these restrictions are to be reversed, it will be through economic and political rather than legal challenge. The chapter concludes with a brief discussion of the remaining legal framework affecting tax-exempt bonds—state constitutional and statutory restrictions on bond issuance, state and federal securities law, and other pertinent federal law.

Chapter 4 concludes part 1 with a discussion of the characteristics of the municipal bond market and market participants. Market characteristics discussed include the normal suspects—short versus long-term bonds, new issues versus refundings, revenue versus general obligation bonds, the federal revenue loss, and issuers (general government units, special districts, and authorities). The major insights from this discussion are the rapid growth in the federal revenue loss in the 1970s and 1980s, the increasing importance of revenue bonds as the preferred financing instrument, and the growing numbers of special districts and authorities that can issue tax-exempt bonds. These trends are noteworthy because special districts and authorities, rather than general governmental units, tend to issue most of the debt for private purposes, and most of this debt is issued as revenue rather than general obligation bonds.

The discussion of market participants includes state and local taxpayers, issuers, investors, underwriters, bond counsel, financial advisers, interest groups, and credit rating and bond insurance agencies. The discussion focuses on each participant's financial stake in the tax-exempt bond market. The present value of the interest exemption to state and local taxpayers and private beneficiaries from the tax-exempt bonds issued in any given year reached a peak of $48.6 billion in 1985, and was still $22.6 billion in 1988. Total issuance costs for underwriters, bond counsel, financial advisors, and others also peaked in 1985, at $5.2 billion, and fell to $2.1 billion in 1988. The ratio of total issuance costs to the present value of interest savings averaged a little more than 9 percent over the last two decades. These estimates indicate that the value of the interest exemption and the costs of obtaining that exemption are substantial and directly related to bond volume.

PART TWO: TAX-EXEMPT BONDS AND ECONOMIC POLICY

Tax-exempt bond legislation over the last 20 years reflects efforts to cope with five major areas of public policy: (1) intergovernmental fiscal relations—continual reassessment of the federal government's responsibility to provide financial assistance to state and local governments and the role of tax-exempt bonds as part of that package of intergovernmental assistance; (2) the budget and deficit—the sheer magnitude of the level and growth of the federal budget deficit has placed a premium in the 1980s on broadening the income tax base by reducing tax preferences (tax expenditures) that have long been a part of the tax system, of which none have a longer history than tax-exempt bonds; (3) resource allocation policy—growing awareness of the effect of non-neutral federal tax policy on the allocation of the scarce supply of savings among competing investments and its impact on economic output; (4) income distribution policy— concern that the distribution of the income tax burden by income class be such that everyone contributes meaningfully to the provision of public services; and (5) waste, fraud, and abuse—the American Lourdes where warm waters steeped in those well-known mineral salts called tax relief and service enhancements promise a miraculous cure for the true believer's pocketbook.

The influence of each of these policy concerns has ebbed and flowed as a factor in producing any year's tax-exempt bond legislation. But the enduring influence of all five issues is apparent when the municipal bond provisions of the tax code are studied carefully. Part 2, comprising chapters 5 through 8, addresses the first four policy issues, explaining the economics of each issue and its importance to tax-exempt bond policy.

By far the most attention is given to intergovernmental fiscal relations, because it brings not only the federal policy agenda into play but the state and local agenda as well. Chapter 5 indicates that a more restricted view of federal domestic program responsibilities has emerged over the last 10 years, a change that has been accompanied by reduced intergovernmental funding. This perspective on federal program responsibility is consistent with the economic justification for federal subsidy of state and local service provision. Federal subsidy is appropriate only when the service being provided generates collective benefits for federal taxpayers as well as for the state or local taxpayers in the jurisdiction providing the service. Since the tax-exempt bond subsidizes all state and local activities whether or not this criterion is satisfied, some federal control is suggested. The difficulty arises in trying to write legislation that applies this concept to particular activities.

The chapter closes with a discussion of three other policy issues that appear in the intergovernmental policy debate: the degree of budgetary control the federal government can exercise over the various types of intergovernmental assistance (grants, tax-exempt bonds, and state and local tax deductibility); the relative merits of each type of intergovernmental assistance in promoting economic efficiency, minimizing administrative costs, and maximizing the state and local subsidy per dollar of federal revenue cost; and the justification for restricting intergovernmental assistance to one factor of production, in particular to tax-exempt bonds for capital.

The federal government has dealt with budgetary control of tax-exempt bonds by restricting the types of services for which the exemption can be used and capping the annual dollar volume of bonds, thereby converting what amounts to an open-ended grant into a closed grant with budgetary control. The question remains, however, whether the U.S. Internal Revenue Service (IRS) is equipped to administer and enforce laws whose purpose is equivalent to that of a direct spending program.

None of the subsidy choices is clearly superior in terms of efficiency. When the objective is to stimulate all types of state and local spending, bonds have a role to play in promoting economic efficiency (ignoring their role in distorting factor prices), but are a poor second cousin to categorical grants when specific programs are to be targeted. Of course, bonds can be targeted to specific private activities, as the legislation in 1968 and the 1980s has increasingly done (see chapter 11), but administrative costs probably will have to rise if they are to be well targeted (see chapter 12). The tax subsidies probably entail lower administrative costs than grants, but undoubtedly achieve that by directing less of the subsidy to the desired groups. And none of the alternatives delivers a large share of the federal cost to increased state and local spending, although the tax-exempt bond share has improved, owing to the rate reductions enacted in 1986.

The case for subsidizing one factor of production, such as capital, depends upon whether that factor of production is underprovided relative to other factors. Several rationales can be put forth in support of such claims of underprovision of public capital: electoral pressures create a bias among officials for current spending; mobility creates a preference among taxpayers for current services; citizens underestimate the contribution capital services make to their welfare; and capital services have a larger spillover component than do current services. Evidence to back these rationales is scant.

Chapter 6 traces the history of the deficit and the role of tax policy, particularly the broadening of the income tax base, in restraining the growth of that deficit. It is clear that the tax-exempt bond provision of the Internal Revenue Code was not singled out for special treatment, but was one of many tax preferences enlisted in this effort. Chapter 7 demonstrates how the interest income exclusion distorts investment choices and causes the scarce supply of savings to be used for private investments that yield a lower rate of return than could have been earned in unsubsidized investments. This lowers the productivity of the capital stock and national income. In 1982, every $1,000 bond issued for private purposes would have had to generate approximately $10 in social benefits every year over the life of the bond to compensate for this lower national income; the comparable figure for 1989 is $8.30.

Chapter 8 discusses the role of tax-exempt bonds in allowing high-income taxpayers to escape the payment of income taxes. The data presented indicate that the concentration of tax-exempt interest income among the highest income classes has declined considerably since 1986, primarily owing to the flattening of the marginal tax rate schedule.

PART THREE: HISTORY AND ECONOMIC EVALUATION OF LEGISLATION

Few intergovernmental fiscal policy issues have proven to be as contentious and persistent as has the 20-year congressional struggle to restrict the tax exemption for those tax-exempt bonds that have at various times been labeled private-purpose, private-activity, and nongovernmental. The effort to control the volume of these private-activity bonds evolved into a struggle between two competing groups of public officials. The first group, composed primarily of Treasury Department officials and some members of Congress, wanted to restrict the use of tax-exempt bonds to the financing of traditional state and local capital projects such as highways, schools, and public hospitals. The second group, composed primarily of state and local officials, other members of Congress, and bond industry participants (e.g. underwriters and bond lawyers), wanted to continue the typical practice of using those bonds to finance activities provided by private entities in cooperation with the state and local sector, such as industrial park development, student loans, and housing. Almost every tax bill in the last two decades has addressed the issue, beginning with the Revenue and Expenditure Control Act of 1968 (Public Law 90-364) and continuing through the Omnibus Budget Reconciliation Act of 1989 (Public Law 101-239).

This protracted debate and its legislative history reflect the rough waters created by the sometimes cross-cutting currents of federal and state-local policy objectives. Part 3 of this book describes the legislative history and also explains the contradictory role of economics as a public policy tool. The persistence of this debate represents a failure of economists to translate a long-accepted theory of what constitutes a public good into practical guidelines for Congress to use in defining what activities serve a public purpose. But it is equally a triumph of economics. Contrary to assertions of state and local officials and the bond industry that this legislation has lacked a coherent rationale, it is clear that congressional efforts to control volume growth have focused on diluting the economic incentives that caused the growth.

Chapter 9 discusses the demand side of the market for tax-exempt bonds, that is, individual and corporate purchasers. The discussion is focused on the incentives that have been manipulated by tax legislation: the tax rate structure; the tax treatment of alternative tax shelters; the use of a minimum income tax on preference income; and the deductibility of commercial bank borrowing costs for the purchase of tax-exempt bonds. Chapter 10 discusses the supply side of the market for tax-exempt bonds, that is, state and local issuers. The discussion is focused on incentives in the Code that contribute to issuance of more than the socially desirable amount of bonds: confusion over public purpose definition; understatement of state and local taxpayer costs; overstatement of benefits to state and local taxpayers compared to federal taxpayers; reduction of the private sector's cost of capital; and electoral benefits to be garnered by state and local officials for providing conduit financing to private persons.

Chapter 11 discusses the legislation passed by Congress over the last 20 years to restrict bond issuance by manipulating incentives on both the demand and supply sides of the tax-exempt bond market. The discussion is organized into groups according to the economic incentive of each.

PART FOUR: SELECTED ISSUES IN TAX-EXEMPT BOND POLICY

The five chapters in the final part of the book use the framework and knowledge developed in the first three parts to analyze five issues important to future tax-exempt bond policy. Chapter 12 discusses the enforcement of the tax-exempt bond laws, a system that relies primarily on voluntary compliance. This topic is of particular interest for two reasons. First, some proposals for redefining public purpose would depend heavily upon the enforcement abilities of the Internal Revenue Service. And second, Congress has salvaged tax exemption for many private activities by turning them into social spending programs for targeted groups. Several actions might improve the administration and enforcement system: explicit congressional consideration in the tax writing process of the trade-off between more enforcement funding and more easily administrable tax-exempt bond laws; addition of the social goals of some bond provisions to the revenue goal criterion by which IRS managers are evaluated; use of the ultimate penalties for abuse—retroactive interest income taxation and blacklisting of issuers; and establishment of a small bond unit at the IRS whose sole purposes are to gather and analyze information on bonds and to report to the Treasury Department and Congress on the changes necessary to promote the social goals for which the bonds are issued.

Chapter 13 investigates claims that the past 20 years of congressional restrictions on the ability of state and local governments to issue tax-exempt bonds have contributed to the alleged decline in the nation's public capital formation, known popularly as infrastructure, and to the observed decrease in productivity. Exactly the opposite seems to be true: the financing of noninfrastructure projects with tax-exempt bonds raised interest costs on infrastructure financing and reduced state and local investment in infrastructure by an average annual amount from 1984 to 1986 of between $1.5 and $7.1 billion. The tax-exempt bond restrictions, to the extent they have succeeded in reducing the use of tax-exempt savings for non-infrastructure projects, have probably had some positive effect on state and local infrastructure spending and on the nation's productivity.

Chapter 14 investigates the role of tax-exempt bonds in fostering "municipal socialism," whereby the cost advantage of tax-exempt debt financing encourages municipalities to encroach on activities that can be performed adequately in the private sector. The discussion points to the focus in bond legislation on preventing private use of the public subsidy, and to the virtual absence of attention to preventing municipalities from producing private goods and using the profits to feed their general funds. A case study of the electric power industry is used to analyze the types of public goods rationalizations presented in chapter 5. The only provisions in the tax Code to address the incentives toward municipal socialism were enacted in 1987 to deal with public takeovers of investor-owned utilities, municipal purchase of rental housing outside its own political jurisdiction, and business enterprises of Indian tribal governments.

Chapter 15 reports the results of a survey of the states' 1989 experience with the private-activity bond volume cap. New issues of private-activity bonds in 1989 that were subject to the volume cap were 67 percent lower than the annual average of new issues of private-activity bonds from 1984 to 1986. The majority of states set aside portions of their cap allocations for local governments and for favored tax-exempt activities (most frequently housing and economic development). The volume cap is sufficiently large (or the list of exempt activities sufficiently restricted) that unused volume cap averages 36.3 percent of the volume cap in 41 of the 49 states in the survey. The average unused cap varies greatly by size of state: 56.7 percent for the 20 small states whose cap was a flat $150 million; 27.9 percent for the 21 large states whose cap was $50 per person. If an adjustment is made for the effect of 1989 financings that used volume cap carried forward from prior years, this unused cap could be reduced to as little as 30 percent of the volume cap for only 20 states.

In spite of these unused cap allocations, the states reported $6.0 billion of excess demand, projects that were denied or delayed cap allocations due to the unavailability of cap. Even more surprising, 62.9 percent of this excess demand was reported by states that reported unused volume cap. This may reflect the difficulties of making year-end transfers of unused cap between levels of government and among exempt activities that had received priority allocations; it may also reflect a desire to allow high-priority projects whose timing does not conform to the calendar year accounting for the volume cap to carry a current-year allocation forward rather than reassigning the unused volume cap to a lower priority project.

The states had several suggestions for improving the operation of the cap: allocate it among the states using criteria that reflect need and fiscal capacity better than population; remove environmentally oriented projects from the cap; allow carry-forwards to remain with the state for future allocation; and allow small rural states to use small-issue industrial development bonds (IDBs) for more than manufacturing.

The large unused cap in 1989 suggests that adding new activities to the list of exempt private activities is likely to increase the federal revenue loss, rather than increase competition for the available volume cap. This large unused cap suggests that this may be an opportune time to do one of two things if mortgage revenue bonds and small-issue IDBs are allowed to sunset in 1990. The first option has great appeal only to federal policymakers—reduce the size of the volume cap. The second option is to seize the moment to reallocate the volume cap, perhaps toward environmentally oriented projects. This option would have four advantages: unlike small-issue IDBs, environmental projects have a substantial element of collective consumption that meets the criterion for federal subsidy spelled out in this book (spillover of benefits across political jurisdictions); the federal subsidy would be redirected to state and local infrastructure, unlike housing and the private capital formation stimulated by small-issue IDBs, and, it is hoped, would help to arrest the slide in the nation's productivity; state and local officials are likely to support (or be less hostile to) such a change, since they seem to sense a substantial increased demand in the environmental area; and it would constitute a positive federal response to state and local complaints about the imposition of federal mandates (including those in the environmental area) without any corresponding federal financial support.

Chapter 16 discusses alternative means of accomplishing what the previous 20 years of legislation have tried to do—control bond volume and target it to socially desirable objectives. Are there better ways to accomplish these goals while allowing the state and local sector greater flexibility in choosing their projects? The recommendations of the Anthony Commission on Public Finance for redefining public purpose are critiqued, as are proposals to create a new tax-exempt category of "infrastructure" bonds and to require more state and local taxpayer financial responsibility in exchange for decreased federal controls. Finally, the allocation of volume cap among the states is compared to an allocation that considers interstate differences in need and fiscal capacity.

Efforts to redefine public purpose run up against an apparently insoluble dilemma. The nub of the problem is the desire of the public sector to enlist the aid of the private sector in providing public services, presumably because the private sector can accomplish the objective at lower cost. Set against this benefit is the unavoidable fact that private participation means that some federal benefit is being appropriated for the benefit of private persons, which creates an incentive for bond issuance to exceed the optimal amount, and can lead to costs that exceed society's benefits from the lower production costs of public services.

The current system of controls errs on the side of rejecting some projects with private participation that probably would serve a primarily public purpose. The proposals of the Anthony Commission would err on the side of accepting some projects with private participation that probably would serve a significant private purpose. The problem with switching to the commission's more permissive set of controls is the difficulty of administering and enforcing the rules that are devised to implement the controls. The current enforcement system is relatively mechanical and relies primarily on voluntary compliance. The proposed system would rely on interpretations of legally ambiguous economic terms such as *arm's-length negotiations* and *market prices*, and the potential gains to the private sector almost guarantee that considerable efforts would be expended to frustrate the intent of the legislation and tilt the system toward private gain. Another proposal would impose a requirement for general obligation issues in exchange for relaxation of federal controls. This proposal would probably open the door to tax-exempt debt financing for blue-chip private firms.

The solution may be to allow some relaxation of controls, but focus the list of exempt activities on infrastructure. As a first approximation, we might eliminate tax-exempt financing for small-issue IDBs, single-family housing, student loans, qualified redevelopment bonds, and some public utility services. These activities either do not serve as well as others to increase the nation's productivity and the size of the pie to be divided for our welfare, or generate insufficient public benefit spillovers to merit federal subsidy.

The volume cap has been successful in reducing the volume of private-activity bonds. Social benefits might be improved by allocating the cap according to measures of need and fiscal capacity. If the suggested activities were eliminated from the cap, the size of the cap could be reduced, state and local officials would have more incentive to allocate the scarce funds to those public/private partnerships weighted most heavily in the public sector's favor, and some federal controls might be relinquished.

CONVENTIONS USED IN THIS BOOK

The reader unfamiliar with tax-exempt bonds and economic jargon might be confused by several conventions I have adopted. It is, therefore, worth discussing them briefly. As with any topic subjected to in-depth treatment, the continual repetition of a term becomes monotonous. I therefore use the terms *tax-exempt bonds, state and local bonds,* and *municipal bonds* interchangeably to refer to state and local debt obligations whose interest income is exempt from federal income taxation. This is, of course, not literally correct. For example, in this book these three terms are meant to include state and local debt instruments with maturity of less than a year, even though these short-term instruments are usually referred to as notes rather than bonds. In contrast, the terms are not meant to include taxable debt instruments issued by state and local governments, even though taxables are also state and local bonds or municipal bonds. And the tax-exempt debt of municipalities is obviously much less than what this book calls municipal bonds.

Another term susceptible to misinterpretation is *public.* In this book, *public* is used in the context of economic theory. Public goods possess certain characteristics that cause at least a portion of the good to be consumed jointly or collectively. The importance of this use of the term is that the set of *public* goods and services is not necessarily identical to those being provided by the public sector. When the text refers to *public purpose,* the reference is confined to those goods and services possessing the characteristic of joint or collective consumption. This concept and its implications for tax-exempt bond policy are more fully developed in chapter 5.

As in any book dealing with intergovernmental relations, it is important to eliminate ambiguity in the use of the term *federal*. By far, *federal* is used most often in this book to refer to the national government. In those few instances where it is meant to refer to the multilevel governmental system, the wording of the sentence makes this clear.

Finally, a word about the variable use of "Conclusion" sections in the chapters. I purposely highlighted the conclusions of the chapters 2 to 16 in this first chapter. Combined with the table of contents, this should enable the reader to locate those chapters of most interest. Conclusion sections within chapters are omitted from chapters that are primarily descriptive or relatively short.

FOR WHOM IS THIS BOOK WRITTEN?

Every author should labor with a vision of the audience for whom he is writing, and I certainly have such a vision. In my mind's eye, the audience consists of far more than my fellow public finance economists, who will, I hope, find appealing my efforts to place fairly standard knowledge of the economics of tax-exempt bonds within the context of the public policy issues and legislative process of the period. This expanded audience includes the "bond community"— state and local officials, underwriters, bond counsel, interest groups, etc., who I hope will garner more of an appreciation (understanding may be a better word) for the economic incentives and conflicting public policy issues that have driven the last 20 years of bond legislation. This audience also includes students, both in public policy programs and applied economics courses, who I hope will see tax-exempt bonds as an example of the public policy process in all its messiness, one in which economic theory runs headlong into the realities of the political system with its multitude of conflicting economic interests and imperfect legislative process.

INSTITUTIONAL BACKGROUND: HISTORY, LEGAL FRAMEWORK, AND INDUSTRY CHARACTERISTICS

Chapter Two

HISTORY OF MUNICIPAL BONDS

The history of municipal bonds provides important background for the study of the last 20 years of tax-exempt bond legislation. The issues that concerned policymakers in the 19th and early 20th centuries are strikingly similar to those issues of concern to policymakers today: bond volume; the use of municipal debt to provide financial support for the private sector; and legislation to restrict volume and the type of activities financed. The major difference between then and now is the intergovernmental dimension—the issues primarily concerned the state and local sector until the adoption of the federal income tax in 1913, after which the exclusion of municipal bond interest income gave the federal establishment a budgetary stake in the issue.

WHY USE DEBT FINANCING?

Before turning to an historical overview, I want to dispense with the notion occasionally pushed by some guardians of the public purse that the issuance of state and local debt is synonymous with fiscal irresponsibility. In fact, the opposite is true—a government that eschews debt issuance is acting irresponsibly.

Since capital facilities provide services over a long period of time, it makes sense to pay for these facilities over a long period of time. This is particularly true for state and local governments. Their taxpayers lay claim to the benefits from these facilities by dint of residency and relinquish their claim to benefits when they move. Given the demands a market-oriented society places on labor mobility, taxpayers are reluctant to pay today for state and local capital services to be received in the future. The rational response of the state or local official concerned with satisfying the preferences of constituents is to match the timing of the payments to the flow of services, precisely the function served by long-term debt financing. Any attempt to pay for capital facilities "up front" is likely to result in a less than optimal rate of pubic capital formation.

State and local governments are also faced with the necessity of planning their budget for the year (or in some cases for two years). This requires a balancing of revenue forecasts against forecasts of the demand for services and spending. Not infrequently, the inevitable unforeseen circumstances that undermine any forecast cause a revenue shortfall that must be financed with short-term borrowing. In addition, even when the forecasts are met, the timing of expenditures may precede the arrival of revenues, creating the necessity to borrow within an otherwise balanced fiscal year. Finally, temporarily high interest rates that prevail at the time bonds are issued to finance a capital project may induce short-term borrowing in anticipation of a drop in rates.

Thus, state and local governments have good reasons to borrow funds. In fact, these reasons are so universally accepted that both taxpayers and the courts have acquiesced in the almost casual evasion of the 19th century legacy of unrealistically restrictive constitutional and statutory limitations on borrowing that are discussed later in this chapter.

DEBT ISSUANCE: 1800 to 1962

Prior to the beginning of the 19th century, most state and local capital improvements were modest and were financed with some combination of loans, sales of public lands, donations, subscriptions, lotteries, and current taxation. As the demand for public services grew, state legislatures approved the issuance of bonds for specific projects. Both states and localities began to issue bonds to finance internal improvements.

The data in table 2.1 indicate that, until the 1840s, states took the lead in issuing debt for capital facilities requirements. In 1840, outstanding state debt amounted to $175 million, compared to municipal debt of only $25 million. The depression of 1837 brought a rash of defaults to state debt issues and began the ascendance of municipalities as the primary borrowers for the state and local sector. By 1870, state debt had roughly doubled to $353 million, but local debt had outstripped state debt and grown to $516 million. Net state

Table 2.1 OUTSTANDING STATE AND LOCAL DEBT AND THE
NONGUARANTEED SHARE OF THAT DEBT: 1840–1962 ($ MILLIONS)

Year	Total Outstanding		Share of Total Nonguaranteed	
	State	Local		
1840	175	25	NA[a]	NA
1850	190	NA	NA	NA
1860	257	200	NA	NA
1870	353	516	NA	NA
1880	275	821	NA	NA
1890	211	926	NA	NA
1902	239	1,630	NA	NA
1912	346	3,476	NA	NA
1922	936	7,754	NA	NA
1932	2,374	15,216	NA	NA
1942	3,096	15,310	14.7	NA
1952	6,640	22,080	25.8	20.7
1962	21,612	55,931	52.3	32.0

Sources: Totals, 1840–1932, from Hillhouse (1936), p. 36; totals and shares, 1942–
62, U.S. Bureau of the Census, *Census of Governments*, various issues.
a. NA, not available.

issuance was negative during the next 30 years, reducing outstanding
state debt to $239 million in 1902. Local debt more than filled the
gap, breaking the billion dollar ceiling and rising steadily to $1,630
million by 1902.

Net state issuance turned positive in the 20th century, enabling
the outstanding stock of state debt to increase to $2,374 million by
1932. But this growth paled in comparison to that of municipal debt,
which increased to $15,216 million. The three decades following
1932 continued the rapid increase in outstanding debt of state and
local governments. By 1962 state debt had grown to $21,612 million
and municipal debt to $55,931 million.

USE OF DEBT FOR PRIVATE PURPOSES

The vast majority of outstanding state and local debt was issued for
internal improvements. Four factors were particularly important to
this growth. First was the continual growth in population; more
people meant more public capital. Second, the country faced a continual exodus of population from the farms to the cities. This growing
urbanization required municipalities to invest in such things as water

supply, streets, sewage disposal, and traffic control. Third, over this period education became more and more a primary public responsibility.

The fourth factor is the most interesting for the focus of this book, for it is here that the early use of debt for private purposes occurred. As the growing population filled up the eastern states and expanded westward, economic development opportunities abounded and created a demand for transportation facilities to tie the expanding country together and facilitate trade between its far-flung sections. The rapid evolution of science and technology caused the nature of this transportation network to change several times over the period, forcing economic obsolescence on many facilities long before their useful lives would have expired in a less technologically dynamic economy.

Many of the original state development efforts were devoted to such things as canal construction and plank roads. Government attention then switched to the arrival of the railroad. Eventually, the railroad was supplanted by the automobile and supplemented by the airplane. All of these changes necessitated, or at least elicited, state and local investments to facilitate their development.

This history of debt issuance is replete with examples of what has come to be called conduit financing—the issuance of bonds by a governmental unit and the use of the bond proceeds by or on behalf of a nongovernmental entity. The earliest examples are in the canal and turnpike building period of the early 19th century that began with Maryland and Ohio's successful borrowing to finance construction of the Chesapeake and Ohio Canal, followed by additional borrowing for canal construction in Pennsylvania, Indiana, Illinois, and Michigan.

Following the financial collapse of 1837, most state canal building programs came to a halt. Many of the bonds were ultimately forced into default as canals were never completed and generated no revenues. By 1842, nine states had defaulted on their debt—Mississippi, Florida, Arkansas, Indiana, Illinois, Michigan, Maryland, Pennsylvania, and Louisiana. Four of these states actually repudiated some of their debt—Arkansas, Florida, Michigan, and Mississippi. The states reacted by imposing constitutional restrictions on borrowing (discussed in the next section of this chapter).

But the nation and economy continued to grow, creating an incentive for municipalities to fill the continuing demand for public borrowing. Railroads were supplanting canals and turnpikes, and many towns were competing for the railroad lines. This usually entailed some sort of merging of public and private credit. Municipalities guaranteed railroad securities or issued municipal bonds and used the bond proceeds to purchase stock in the railroad company. During the 1830s the city of Baltimore, for example, loaned more than $4 million to the Baltimore and Ohio railroad, the Baltimore and Susquehanna Railroad, and the Susquehanna Canal, thereby increasing its outstanding debt from less than $1 million to more than $5 million (Studenski and Krooss 1952, 134).

The justification offered at that time for financial support of private enterprise has a familiar ring to today's student of private activity bonds and their use as a tool of public policy. An Alabama court ruled in 1854 that tax-supported bond financing legitimately

extends to the employment of all those means and appliances ordinarily adopted, or which may be calculated, to develop the resources of the state and add to the agrarian wealth and prosperity of the citizens; such, for example, as providing outlets for commerce, and opening up channels of intercommunication between different parts of the State. (*Stein v. Mayor etc. of Mobile*, 24 Ala. 591, 614 [1854])

In another case, the Tennessee Supreme Court approved support for conduit bonds based on the indirect benefits that enhance the commercial interest of a town (*Nichol v. Mayor etc. of Nashville*, 9 Humphreys [Tenn.] 252 [1848]).[1]

Another 19th century court opinion presaged part of the modern-day attack on private-activity bonds—that a state or local public purpose does not encompass a federal public purpose if the benefits from the state or local activity accrue entirely to the citizens of the issuing jurisdiction.[2] A federal judge commented (unfavorably) in 1859 on a similar rationale, except that in this case it was used to justify municipal aid to railroads when the state had already restricted state support:

The state being unwilling to involve herself in further debt, and risk a second insolvency, the scheme of city, county, and borough subscriptions was invented and put in practice. This had the appearance, if not the reality, of *greater justice and fairness than the original plan of state subscriptions; for the distant counties and boroughs, whose people were not benefited by a particular road, were not compelled to pay for making it, and only those who partook of the expected benefit would have to pledge their credit for the cost of its erection* [emphasis added]. (*Oelrich v. Pittsburgh*, Fed. Case No. 10442 [1859])

Another activity that attracted bonds to aid private enterprise in the 19th and 20th centuries was real estate speculation, of which the best-known episode occurred in Florida during the 1920s. But in some sense, the canal and railroad building of the 19th century discussed earlier were simply other, earlier, examples of real estate speculation.

Bonds, whether railroad aid, irrigation, drainage district or special assessment, have all too often been issued in aid of the real estate speculator and promoter, so much so that a large portion of all municipal debt difficulties could be summed up under the caption "real estate aid bond defaults." For example, only a tenuous legal distinction may be found between the old railroad aid bonds and the millions of improvement bonds issued during the 1920's. In the one case the bonds were directly in aid of private enterprise; in the other, the bonds legally and ostensibly were for a public purpose, although actually they were issued to enable a promoter to push his new properties, or a subdivider to open up a new subdivision. Fundamentally, real estate boom bonds have differed from railroad aid obligations only in that they have been subsidies to real estate speculators and promoters rather than to the railroad prototype of the sixties and seventies. (Hillhouse 1936, 67)

Localities, particularly in the Midwest, believed that their economic development would be severely constrained if they did not attract the railroad, and that their chances of attracting the railroad depended upon the provision of financial aid. Accordingly, jurisdictions often competed with each other to provide the best deal, often issuing bonds in excess of what the existing tax base could reasonably support, but anticipating the availability of stock dividends and an increase in land values and tax base brought on by the arrival of the railroad.

Unfortunately, bonds frequently were issued and stock purchased without the railroad ever coming to town. In other cases, financial aid encouraged overbuilding of railroad lines, causing many of them to fail or merge. In the absence of the railroad and stock dividends, the value of the town's land and tax base often proved inadequate to pay the principal and interest on the bonds. The depression of the 1840s caused taxpayers to begin to demand constitutional and statutory restrictions on municipal borrowing power. When a general financial collapse occurred in 1873, defaults increased in number, and some towns practiced outright repudiation. The result was a move to impose restrictions on municipal borrowing, although not to the degree that state borrowing was restricted 30 years earlier.

STATE AND LOCAL RESTRICTIONS ON DEBT ISSUANCE

Prior to 1840, most state constitutions did not refer to state borrowing, and the states were not restricted in matters of borrowing. The defaults and repudiations of the 1840s created a demand for permanent restrictions on the borrowing power of state legislatures. Although Rhode Island was the first state to impose restrictions, the New Jersey restriction of 1844 became the one emulated by most other states.

The legislature shall not, in any manner, create any debt or debts, liability or liabilities, of the state, which shall singly or in the aggregate with any previous debts or liabilities at any time exceed one hundred thousand dollars, except for purposes of war, or to repel invasion, or to suppress insurrection, unless the same shall be authorized by a law for some single object or work, to be distinctly specified therein; which law shall provide the ways and means, exclusive of loans, to pay the interest of such debt or the liability as it falls due, and also to pay and discharge its principal of such debt or liability within thirty-five years from the time of the contraction thereof, and shall be irrepealable until such debt or liability, and the interest thereon, are fully paid and discharged; and no such law shall take effect until it shall, at a general election, have been submitted to the people, and have received the sanction of a majority of the votes cast for and against it at such election; and all money to be raised by the authority of such law shall be applied only to the specific object stated therein, and to the payment of the debt thereby created. This section shall not be construed to refer to any money that has been or may be deposited with this State by the government of the United States. (Heins 1963, 8)

By the time of the Civil War, 19 states had adopted constitutional restrictions on the amount and purpose of state borrowing. Additional states in the South adopted restrictions during Reconstruction, and all states admitted to the Union since the Civil War have had some sort of constitutional restriction.

Following the financial collapse of 1873, many municipalities were subjected to constitutional and statutory restrictions on their borrowing. These restrictions usually entailed some combination of prohibitions against lending to private individuals or corporations, requirements to hold referenda before issuing bonds, and caps on the ratio of outstanding debt to assessed valuation.

Restrictions on state and local borrowing have persisted down to the present. The tables in the accompanying Appendix 2.A document state constitutional restrictions on state borrowing and state constitutional and statutory restrictions on local government borrowing as of 1986. One should not, however, be deceived by these restrictions, for they apply only to the issuance of general obligation (GO) debt that is backed by the full faith and credit of the issuing government.

The intention of the people in adopting the debt limitations . . . seems quite clear. These limitations were intended either to prohibit state borrowing for public improvements or to require public approval of this type of borrowing. Nonetheless, recent developments . . . have almost completely undermined the restrictive ability of constitutional debt limitations. (Heins 1963, 12)

In fact, the evasions of debt limitations seem to indicate a recognition that the capital needs of government have to be met, and that the debt limit legacy of the 19th century would prohibit governments from meeting these needs if the restrictions were not circumvented. Rather than incur the costs of a public campaign to alter the debt limits, legislators and other public officials have chosen to incur the higher interest costs inherent in issuing debt that lacks the backing of the public's taxing power.

DEVICES TO AVOID DEBT LIMITATIONS

Upon adoption of debt limitations, purchasers of new issues required assurance that the debt was being issued in compliance with these limitations. Public officials began to hire specialized attorneys who were knowledgeable about these limitations to assist them in issuing debt without violating the limitations. "Such attorneys provided an opinion that, notwithstanding the limitations imposed upon debt, the particular debt in question was valid and enforceable" (National Association of Bond Lawyers 1988, 21). These attorneys were the forerunners of today's bond counsel. Over the years, bond counsel and public elected officials, with the tacit approval of state and local taxpayers and the acquiescence of the court system, have developed several devices and institutions to evade the intent of these debt limitations.[3]

Special Districts

Upon exhaustion of its permissible debt, a municipality often creates a new government unit, called a special district, to perform a particular function such as the provision of park facilities or sewer services. The special district is a separate corporation whose debt is considered unrelated to the municipality's debt, even if the special district and municipality are coextensive and the district has the power to tax. Even if the district is held subject to the debt limitation, the permissible debt limit has been effectively doubled.

Special Funds

In many states, bonds payable from a "special fund" are not considered to fall within the constitutional limits on debt issuance. Debt service payments are restricted to monies deposited in a special fund, which cannot be supplemented by general funds of the issuer or tax levies. The source of the funds may be from special levies upon the land whose owners receive benefits from the constructed facilities (e.g., for sewer services) or from direct payments from individuals and businesses who receive services (e.g., for electricity). In theory, the property owners or the rate payers are the debtors, and the governmental unit simply acts as an agent for collecting money.

Public Authorities

The public authority, in effect a public corporation, borrows funds by issuing bonds and levies charges for its services sufficient to retire its debt. Upon retirement of the debt, the authority conveys the facilities to a traditional unit of government. An operating authority is actually a publicly owned business. It usually directs an enterprise such as a turnpike or airport that earns commercial revenue from private users. The authority is typically formed after a financial feasibility study indicates that revenues will be adequate to repay the debt. A building authority is very different. It has neither private customers nor independent revenue. Its basic functions are to issue the debt, build the facility, and lease the facility to a traditional governmental unit.

The operating authorities rely on nontax revenue sources, and their exclusion from debt limitation coverage is fairly clear. This is not the case with building authorities. The government's rental payments to the authority are, in effect, paid out of tax revenue. The exclusion of rental payments from debt limitations has been upheld "only upon tortured reasoning" (Morris 1967, 240). One source of the exclusion is that, in some states, rents are not debts as a matter of common law. A second source of the exclusion depends on the finding that an obligation that is contingent is not a debt and not subject to the debt limitation.

The premise of the exception is that since a lessee is obligated for rent only to the extent of use of the property, a lease is in the nature of a contingent obligation and constitutes an exception to the debt limitation. The lessee is therefore obligated only on an annual basis and not over a long term. (National Association of Bond Lawyers 1988, 23–24)

THE NATURE OF DEBT THAT EVADES STATE LIMITATIONS

With the exception of some special district debt, the debt issued using these devices does not pledge the full faith and credit of a governmental unit, and is therefore classified as revenue bonds, or nonguaranteed debt. The use of nonguaranteed debt has become increasingly popular in recent decades. The last two columns of table 2.1 document this growth. In 1942, tho first year for which data on state debt are broken down into GO and nonguaranteed components, nonguaranteed debt accounted for 14.7 percent of all outstanding debt. By 1962, that percentage had grown to 52.3 percent. The local share, not available until 1952, grew from 20.7 percent to 32.0 percent in 10 years. It is this nonguaranteed debt, not subject to volume and public activity restrictions at the state and local levels, that the federal government has attempted to restrict by denying tax exemption to its interest income.

Notes

1. These judicial opinions seem to suggest that any activity that increases investment, employment, and income is a legitimate candidate for public support. This is not very different from the argument used frequently today to justify continued tax exemption for private-activity bonds—that they increase federal revenue because they increase investment and employment. This issue is discussed in considerable detail in chapter 10.

2. This is the spillovers justification for intergovernmental aid, and is discussed in detail in chapter 5.

3. These special devices would have been created even if debt limitations did not exist. In some instances, it is efficient to provide some public services on a scale in excess of the area covered by some political jurisdictions. In such cases, it makes economic sense to create a special district or authority to serve a multijurisdictional area and avoid duplication of inefficient services (Sbragia 1983, 71).

CONSTITUTIONAL AND STATUTORY DEBT RESTRICTIONS

Tables in this appendix are reprinted with permission from Advisory Commission on Intergovernmental Relations (1989).

Table 2A.1 STATE CONSTITUTIONAL LIMITATIONS ON STATE BORROWING, 1986

State	Legislative Borrowing Power Limits — No Limitation	For Casual Deficits or Extraordinary Expenses Only	For Any Other Purpose	Referendum Required to Create Debt	Referendum Required to Exceed Limit	Exceptions to Limits — Limit May Be Exceeded: For Refunding	For Defense of State or Nation	For Other Purposes	Per Capita Total State Debt 1985
United States									$889.92
Alabama	X	$300,000(1)	(1)	(1)		X			805.73
Alaska				X		X(31)	X(2)	X(32)	10,925.34
Arizona		350,000				X	X(3)		214.59
Arkansas				X					349.60
California			$300,000		X(4)		X		609.01
Colorado		100,000	50,000		X(5)				470.59
Connecticut	X		(7)				X	X(6)	2,012.97
Delaware	X(8)	(10)					X		2,944.57
Florida			(9)	X(4)		X			441.18
Georgia			(10)			X			361.04
Hawaii			(11)				X		2,570.77
Idaho	X(12)	(13)			X(4)	X	X		626.12
Illinois		(15)	2,000,000	X(14)			X		848.48
Indiana		250,000					X		314.66
Iowa					X(4)		X	(33)	459.62
Kansas			1,000,000		X(4)		X	(34)	130.15

(continued)

Table 2A.1 STATE CONSTITUTIONAL LIMITATIONS ON STATE BORROWING, 1986 (continued)

State								
Kentucky	X(2)	500,000			X(4)	X	X	975.11
Louisiana					X	X	X(17)	1,806.44
Maine	X(3,35)	(16)	2,000,000			X	X(18)	1,052.06
Maryland						X	X(2,18)	1,159.17
Massachusetts	X(2)	(19)		(36)		X		1,734.96
Michigan	X(12)							649.64
Minnesota		(20)						835.35
Mississippi		1,000,000			X(4)	X		385.35
Missouri					X(4)			660.05
Montana	X(2)					X		901.34
Nebraska		100,000	(21)			X		640.14
Nevada								1,184.29
New Hampshire	X(3)		(22)		X(4,37)	X		1,983.21
New Jersey			(21)	(38)				1,767.37
New Mexico		200,000	(21)	(38)		X	X(39)	881.00
New York		(15)	(23)	X(4)		X	X(18)	1,819.45
North Carolina		2,000,000	(4)	X		X	X(18)	344.78
North Dakota		750,000				X	X	855.28
Ohio						X	X	763.59
Oklahoma		500,000		X(4)		X	X(40)	1,084.94
Oregon			50,000(24)	X(26)		X	X(25)	2,458.15
Pennsylvania						X	X(18)	614.97
Rhode Island			50,000		X	X	X(18)	2,907.15
South Carolina		(41)		X(27,4)		X	(42)	1,016.69
South Dakota		100,000				X		1,534.53
Tennessee	X(3)		(21)		X			401.80

State						
Texas	200,000		X		X(28)	317.20
Utah	X(3)				X	810.52
Vermont	(21)					1,658.72
Virginia	(28)	X(28)			X	581.30
Washington	(15)	(29,12)	X	X(28)	X	687.22
West Virginia	(15)	X	X		X	841.09
Wisconsin	(21)	(21)			X	936.77
Wyoming	(21)	X(30)			X	1,486.86

Notes

1—Governor authorizes debt up to $300,000. Specific bond issues are authorized by Constitutional amendment.

2—Requires approval by two-thirds of each house of legislature.

3—Requires approval by simple legislative majority.

4—Provision must be made for payment of interest and/or principal at time of borrowing.

5—Refers solely to receipts from 3-mill levy against state-assessed valuation for erection of state buildings.

6—May create additional debt for purposes of highway construction and improvement.

7—Debt is not to exceed 4.5 times the total tax receipts of the state during the previous fiscal year (statutory).

8—Requires approval by 75% of legislature.

9—Outstanding principal not to exceed 50% of total state tax revenue (excluding trust revenues) for two preceding fiscal years.

10—Debt service requirements may not exceed 10% of total revenue receipts, less refunds, in immediately preceding fiscal year in which debt is incurred.

11—General obligation bonds may be issued by the state when authorized by majority vote of the members to which each house of the legislature is entitled, provided that such bonds at the time of issuance would not cause the total amount of the principal and interest payable in the current or any future fiscal year, whichever is higher, on such bonds and on all outstanding general obligation bonds to exceed 18.5% of the average of the general fund revenues of the state in the three fiscal years preceding such issuance.

12—Requires approval of 60% of legislature.

(continued)

Table 2A.1 STATE CONSTITUTIONAL LIMITATIONS ON STATE BORROWING, 1986 (continued)

13—In an amount not to exceed 15% of state appropriations for the fiscal year to meet deficits caused by emergencies of failures of revenue; such debt to be repaid within one year of the date it is incurred.

14—Alternative to 60% of the legislature.

15—May borrow for this purpose but no maximum specified.

16—Temporary loans may not exceed 10% of the amount appropriated for general and highway fund purposes or 1% of the total valuation of the State of Maine, whichever is less.

17—The legislature is authorized to insure debt for specified purposes (mortgage loans for industrial, manufacturing, fishing and agricultural enterprises—up to $90 million; for house acquisition and/or improvements of the two tribes on the Indian reservations—up to $1 million; for resident Maine veteran mortgage loans—up to $4 million; and revenue bonds of the Maine School Building Authority—up to $6 million) and may authorize the issuance of state bonds if it becomes necessary to make payments on such insured debt.

18—For tax or revenue anticipation loans.

19—Short-term cash flow borrowings of less than one year which are limited to 15% of undedicated revenue received by the state during the preceding fiscal year, borrowing for the state's qualified school bond loan program, and transportation bonds pledging taxes on fuels sold for transportation purposes.

20—Bonded indebtedness cannot be in excess of 1.5 times the sum of all revenue collected in the state during any one of the four preceding fiscal years, whichever year might be greater.

21—Not to exceed 1% of assessed valuation of all property subject to taxation as shown by preceding general assessment.

22—Limitation of 1% of total annual appropriation.

23—Creation of debt limited to two-thirds the amount by which the state's outstanding indebtedness has been reduced during the preceding biennium.

24—Debt created for rehabilitation and acquisition of forest lands may not exceed 3/16 of 1% of the cash value of all state property taxed on ad valorem basis.

25—Debt created for forest lands may not exceed 3/16 of 1% of market value of all state property taxed on ad valorem basis. May be exceeded for road construction and maintenance with limits set by percent of assessed value.

26—Referendum not required for capital projects specifically itemized in a capital budget if such debt will not cause the amount of all net debt outstanding to exceed 1.75 times the average of the annual tax revenues deposited in the previous five years.

27—Referendum not required for debt created for "ordinary purposes of state government." Any referendum requires two-thirds approval.

28—Limitation for casual deficit in terms of state income and sales tax revenues for the preceding year. Limitation on general obligation debt backed by full faith and credit for capital projects in terms of average annual state income and sales tax revenue for the three prior fiscal years, subject to a simple majority of each house and referendum on projects. Self-liquidating debt with backing of full faith and credit may be issued without referendum if approved by 2/3 majority of each house of the legislature, subject to the limitation of the annual average income and retail sales revenue for the three preceding fiscal years. No limit on debt obligations to which full faith and credit is not pledged or committed.

29—Aggregate debt contracted shall not exceed that amount for which principal and interest payments in any one fiscal year would require the state to expend more than 9% of its average general state revenues for the three immediately preceding fiscal years.

30—Referendum required for creation of debt in excess of amount of taxes for current fiscal years.

31—Only debt outstanding on 1/3/59 when Constitution became effective.

32—A simple legislative majority may authorize debt to meet natural disasters.

33—By judicial interpretation, obligations issued in anticipation of and paid from tax revenues in the same General Assembly biennial period are not considered debt under the Iowa constitutional limitation.

34—State may issue revenue bonds for state highways, flood control, and water resources.

35—Every law authorizing a state debt must provide for discharge of principal within 15 years.

36—Requires approval by two-thirds of each house of the legislature and a majority of the electors voting thereon at any general election, except for short-term borrowing, qualified school bond loan bonds, and transportation bonds pledging fuel taxes.

37—Voter approval not required for refinancings resulting in debt service savings which are to be applied to payment of principal.

38—For over $200,000.

39—Not to exceed 1% of assessed valuation of all property subject to taxation as shown by preceding general assessment.

40—State Industrial Finance Authority may issue up to $90 million of general obligation bonds for industrial loans.

41—Limited to 5% of prior year general fund revenue.

42—Can be exceeded for nonrecurring purposes by two-thirds vote of both houses.

Source: ACIR staff with the assistance of state attorneys general and other state officials.

Table 2A.2 STATE CONSTITUTIONAL AND STATUTORY LIMITATIONS ON LOCAL GOVERNMENT POWER TO ISSUE GENERAL OBLIGATION LONG-TERM DEBT, 1986

State and Types of Local Government	Citation	Rate Limit		Provisions for Exceeding Limit	Remarks
		Percent	Applied Against		
Alabama					
Counties	C-S	5	LAV	None	[1]Many exceptions are provided by constitutional amendment and statutes applicable to individual local governments.
Municipalities	C-S	20[1]	LAV	None	
Alaska	C	No Limits	No Limits	M[1]	[1]General obligation debt may be authorized only for capital improvements.
Arizona					
Counties	C	6	EAV	M[1]	[1]But in no case to exceed 15% of equalized assessed valuation.
Municipalities	C	6	EAV	M[2]	[2]Up to 20% additional for water supply, sewers, and lighting, and for the acquisition and development of land or interest therein for open space preserves, parks, playgrounds and recreational facilities.
School Districts	C	6	EAV	M[1] [3]	[3]Unified school districts may become indebted to an amount not exceeding 30% of the taxable value within the district.
Arkansas					
Counties	None	No Limits[1]	No Limits[1]	NA	[1]Limited only as to the maximum allowable property tax rate for debt service.
Municipalities	None	No Limits[1]	No Limits[1]	NA	[2]By permission of State Board of Education limit may be raised not to exceed 13% of total assessed valuation.
School Districts	S	15	LAV	[2]	
California					
Counties	C	No Limits[1]	No Limits[1]	2/3 vote	[1]Limited only in that general obligation bonds must be approved by a 2/3 vote of those voting in a local election.
Municipalities	C	No Limits[1]	No Limits[1]	2/3 vote	
School Districts	C	No Limits[1]	No Limits[1]	2/3 vote	
Colorado					
Counties and School Districts	None	NA	NA	NA	[1]Chartered and home rule municipalities may establish their own limits.
Municipalities	S[1]	NA	NA	NA	
Connecticut	None	No Rate Limitations[1]	No rate Limitations[1]	NA	[1]Debt restricted to 2.25 times the latest tax receipts. This limit can be increased for certain purposes (e.g., sewers, school building projects and urban renewal projects). Certain kinds of debt (e.g., water supply, gas, electric, and transit) are excluded from this limit.
Delaware					
New Castle County[1]	S	3	LAV	None	[1]Requires 75% approval of County Council.
Sussex County[2]	S	12	LAV	None	[2]Requires 80% approval of County Council.
Kent County[3]	S	12	LAV	None	[3]Requires 5/7 approval of County Levy Court.
Florida	None	No Limits	No Limits	NA	

					Footnotes
Georgia:					
Counties	C	10	NA	LAV	[1]Local school systems which are authorized by law on June 30, 1983, to incur debt in excess of 10% may continue to do so.
Municipalities	C	10	NA	LAV	
School Districts	C	10[1]	NA	LAV	
Hawaii					
Counties	C	15	None	LAV	
Idaho					
Counties	C	No Limits[1]	None	No Limits[1]	[1]Debt incurred in any year cannot exceed revenue for fiscal year without approval by a 2/3 majority of the voters on the issue.
Municipalities	C	2	None	MV	
School Districts	C	2	None	MV	
Illinois					
Counties	S	2.875[1]	None	EAV	[1]With specified exceptions.
Municipalities	S	8.625[1],[2]	None	EAV	[2]Does not apply to home rule municipalities which set own limits.
School Districts	S	13.8a.[3]	None	EAV	[3]K-12 Special Districts Townships.
Special Districts	S	2.875[1]	None	EAV	
Townships	S	2.875[1]	None	EAV	
Indiana					
Counties	C	2	None	LAV	
Municipalities	C	2	None	LAV	
School Districts	C	2	None	LAV	
Townships	C	2	None	LAV	
Iowa					
Counties	C	5	None	MV[1]	[1]By judicial interpretation.
Municipalities	C	5	None	MV[1]	
School Districts	C	5	None	MV[1]	
Kansas					
Counties	S	3[1]	None	LAV	[1]Debt incurred for county hospitals, refunding, and for sanitary sewer improvements is excepted from limit.
Municipalities	S	30[2]	None	LAV	[2]City of Olathe has a limit of 35% until June 30, 1990. Bonds issued by a city for municipal utilities or street improvement are not included in computing total bonded indebtedness.
School Districts	S	14[3]	4	LAV	[3]Bonds issued without an election, but with written approval of the State Board of Education (not to exceed $20,000) are not included
					[4]With approval of State Board of Education and voters of school district.
Kentucky					
Counties	C	2[1]	None[2]	MV	[1]Plus 5% for roads.
Municipalities	C	3 to 10[3]	None[2]	MV	[2]Unless emergency public health or safety should require.

(continued)

Table 2A.2   STATE CONSTITUTIONAL AND STATUTORY LIMITATIONS ON LOCAL GOVERNMENT POWER TO ISSUE GENERAL OBLIGATION LONG-TERM DEBT, 1986 (continued)

State and Types of Local Government	Citation	Rate Limit		Provisions for Exceeding Limit	Remarks
		Percent	Applied Against		
Kentucky (cont'd)					
School Districts	C	2	MV	None[2]	[3] 1st and 2d-class cities, and 3d-class cities with more than 15,000 population, 10%; 3d-class cities with less than 15,000 population and 4th-class cities and towns, 5%; 5th and 6th-class cities and towns, 3%.
Louisiana					
Parishes (counties)	S	10	LAV	None	
Municipalities	S	10	LAV	None	
School Districts	S	25	LAV	None	
Maine					
Counties	None	No Limits	No Limits	NA	[1] Including school purposes, storm or sanitary sewer purposes, energy facility purposes or municipal airport purposes.
Municipalities[1]	C-S	15	LAV	None	
Maryland					
Counties (chartered)	S	15	LAV	[1]	[1] A maximum of 25% of local assessed valuation is allowed for sewerage and sanitation treatment facilities bonds.
Counties (nonchart.)	None	No Limits	No Limits	NA	
Municipalities	None	No Limits	No Limits	NA	
Massachusetts					
Counties	S	No Limits[1]	EAV	None	[1] Each county bond issue is subject to state legislative authorization.
Municipalities	S	5[2]	EAV	[3]	[2] Debt incurred for certain purposes is excepted (for example, 10% for water supply).
School Districts	S	2.5[2]	EAV	[3]	[3] An additional 5% for towns and 2.5% for cities with approval of the emergency finance board.
Counties	C	10[4]	EAV	None	[4] Voter approval required for issuance of unlimited (as opposed to limited) general obligation bonds pledging full faith and credit.
Michigan					
Municipalities	C-S	10[1 2 3]	EAV	None	[2] Includes cities, villages, and charter townships.
					[3] Plus 0.375% in cities and 0.25% in villages for relief of victims of fire, flood, or other disaster.
School Districts	C-S	15[1 4]	EAV	None	[4] Intermediate districts, 1/9 of 1% for limited tax bonds without vote of electors; other districts, 5% for limited tax bonds without vote of electors; no limit on, or voter approval required for, qualified school bonds. Community colleges, 1.5% on first $250 million EAV plus 1% of excess over $250 million EAV for limited tax bonds without vote of electors. Voter approval is not required for limited tax bonds regardless of outstanding voter-approved bonded indebtedness for energy improvement and asbestos removal projects for intermediate and other school districts.

Minnesota					
Counties	S	7.33	EAV	None	[1]Limitation does not apply to 1st-class cities (St. Paul, Minneapolis, Duluth) which are limited to 1.67% of market value or 3.33% of market value if the city charter authorizes debt in excess of the 1.67% limit.
Municipalities[1]	S	7.33	EAV	None	[2]Independent school districts in 1st-class cities are limited to 2.75% of LAV, after authorization by 2/3 vote of city governing body.
Townships	S	7.33	EAV	None	[3]Where at least 20% of the local tax base consists of railroad property (which is exempt from local taxation) special provisions apply.
School Districts	S	10[2]	MV[3]	None	
Mississippi					
Counties	S	10[1 2]	LAV	None	[1]15% until September 30, 1987.
					[2]15% for debt incurred to repair flood damage to roads and bridges.
Municipalities	S	10[1 3]	LAV		[3]15% for debt incurred for water, sewer gas, electric and special improvements.
School Districts	S	20	LAV	4	[4]25% if pupil total increased over 50% in last five years.
Missouri					
Counties	C-S	5	EAV	2/3[1]	[1]Additional 5%.
Municipalities	C-S	5	EAV	2/3[1 2]	[2]Cities may incur an additional 10% for streets and sanitation and/or for waterworks and electric plants, but total debt outstanding cannot exceed 20%. In addition, cities, incorporated towns and villages within any county which has less than 400,000 population may issue industrial development bonds up to 10% of EAV.
School Districts	C-S	10	EAV	None	
Montana					
Counties	S	11.25[1]	EAV	1	[1]Plus 27.75% plus a variable percent of new production taxes for buying land and school buildings and an additional 12.5% plus a variable percent of new production taxes for building jails.
Municipalities	S	28[2]	EAV	2	[2]Plus 55% for water and sewer debt.
School Districts	S	45	EAV	None	
Nebraska	None	No Limits	No Limits	NA	
Nevada					
Counties	S	10	EAV	None	[1]Some variation authorized.
Municipalities	S	30[1]	EAV	None	
School Districts	S	15	EAV	None	
New Hampshire					
Counties	S	2	LAV	None	[1]Ten percent for cooperative school districts.
Municipalities	S	1.75	EAV	None	
School Districts	S	7[1]	EAV	None	
New Jersey					
Counties	S	2	EAV	1	[1]Approval of State Local Finance Board.
Municipalities	S	3.5	EAV	1	[2]Varies from 1.5 to 4% depending upon grade level of School Districts instruction.
School Districts	S	2,3	EAV	4	[3]Eight percent in cities of first class; 6% for 2d class cities in excess of 80,000 population.
					[4]Approval of State Local Finance Board, Commissioner of State Department of Education, and referendum.

(continued)

Table 2A.2 STATE CONSTITUTIONAL AND STATUTORY LIMITATIONS ON LOCAL GOVERNMENT POWER TO ISSUE GENERAL OBLIGATION LONG-TERM DEBT, 1986 (continued)

State and Types of Local Government	Rate Limit			Provisions for Exceeding Limit	Remarks
	Citation	Percent	Applied Against		
New Mexico					
Counties	C	4	LAV	None	[1]May contract debt in excess of limitation for construction or purchase of a water or sewer system.
Municipalities	C	4	LAV	None[1]	
School Districts	C	6	LAV	None	
New York					[1]Excludes the five counties comprising New York City.
Counties[1]	C	7[2]	MV	None	[2]Except Nassau County where the limit is 10%.
Cities, Towns, Villages	C	7[3]	MV	None	[3]Ten percent for New York City, and 9% for other cities over 125,000 population, including debt for school purposes. The 7% limit for all other municipalities excludes school debt.
School Districts	C-S	5 to 10[4]	MV	3/5[5]	[4]Five percent for school districts in cities under 125,000 population; statutory limit of 10% of current full valuation for non-city school districts with assessed valuation over $100,000. No limit for non-city school districts with assessed valuation under $100,000. [5]Subject to approval by 60% of the voters, the State Board of Regents and, in the case of school districts in cities under 125,000 population, the State Comptroller.
North Carolina					[1]All debt must be approved and the bonds marketed by the Local Government Commission, a state agency.
Counties	S	8[1]	LAV	M[2]	[2]The constitution requires voter approval of all general obligation, long-term debt incurred in excess of 2/3 of net debt reduction in the preceding fiscal year with limited exceptions.
Municipalities	S	8[1]	LAV	M[2]	
North Dakota					[1]Additional debt may be incurred for waterworks, up to 4%.
Counties	C	5	EAV	None	[2]Additional 3%.
Cities	C	5[1]	EAV	2/3[2]	[3]Additional 5%.
School Districts	C	5	EAV	M[3]	
Ohio					[1]Voter approval required for indebtedness in excess of 1% LAV. Net indebtedness shall never exceed 3% of first $100,000,000 of taxable value plus 1.5% of taxable value in excess of $100,000,000 and not in excess of $300,000,000, plus 2.5% of taxable value in excess of $300,000,000.
Counties	S	1	LAV	M	[2]Voter approval required for indebtedness in excess of 5.5% LAV. Net indebtedness shall never exceed 10 1/2% LAV.
Municipalities	C-S	10.5[2]	LAV	None	[3]Subject to voter approval.
Townships	S	2[3]	LAV	M	[4]No vote for up to 1%; vote required for 1 to 3%; over 4% (and up to 9%) vote required and prior approval of Tax Commissioner and State Superintendent of Public Instruction. Over 9%, must also be a special needs school district.
School Districts	S	4	LAV	4	

Oklahoma					
Counties	C	5¹ ²	LAV	None	¹Amount incurred in any year may not exceed revenue for the year, except by a 3/5 majority vote.
Municipalities	C	10¹ ²	LAV	None	²By majority vote can authorize debt to secure and develop industry. Tax may not exceed 5 mills.
School Districts	C-S	5¹	LAV	3/5³	³Additional 5%.
Oregon					
Counties	S	2	MV	None	¹0.55% for grades K-8; 0.75% for grades 9-12; 1.5% for community college or area education district.
Municipalities	S	3	MV	None	
School Districts	S	1	MV	None	
Pennsylvania					
Counties	S	1	—	M	¹Limitation applied against borrowing base defined as average revenues of unit for the three fiscal years prior to incurring debt; counties—300% of borrowing base, municipalities—250%, school districts—100%.
Municipalities	S	1 ²	—	M	²For Philadelphia, the limit is 13.5% of locally established assessed value with up to 3% without referendum (by constitution).
School Districts	S	1	—	M	
Rhode Island					
Municipalities	S	3	LAV	None	
South Carolina					
Counties	C	8¹	LAV	None	¹Numerous specific exceptions.
Municipalities	C	8¹ ²	LAV	None	²Where two or more municipalities overlap, or school districts overlap, aggregate limit is 15%.
School Districts	C	8¹ ²	LAV	None	
South Dakota					
Counties	C	5	EAV	M¹	¹Up to an additional 10% (18% for cities over 8,000 population) for specified purposes.
Municipalities	C	5	EAV	M¹	
School Districts	C	10	EAV	¹	
Tennessee	None	No Limits¹	No Limits¹	NA	¹Except that industrial building bonds are limited to 10% of assessed valuation, and require a 3/4 majority in referendum.
Texas					
Counties	C-S	1	LAV	None	¹Limit on taxing authority for debt repayment is generally $.80 per $100 LAV.
Municipalities	C-S	1	LAV	None	²Limit on taxing authority for debt repayment is $1.50 per $100 LAV for general law cities and generally $2.50 per $100 LAV for home rule cities.
School Districts	C-S	10	LAV	None	
Utah					
Counties	C	2¹	MV²	None	¹Debt incurred in any one year may not exceed amount of taxes raised for the year without a simple majority approval of the electorate (property taxpayers).
Municipalities	C	4¹	MV²	3	²By judicial interpretation.
School Districts	C	4¹	MV²	None	³1st and 2nd class cities are granted an additional 4%, 3rd class cities and towns an additional 8% debt for construction of water, lights, and sewer facilities.
Vermont					
Municipalities¹	S	10²	LAV	None	¹There are a few exceptions specified in the state statutes.
					²The statutory limit is "10 times the grand list of the municipal corporation." The "grand list" is 1% of the locally assessed valuation.

(continued)

Table 2A.2 STATE CONSTITUTIONAL AND STATUTORY LIMITATIONS ON LOCAL GOVERNMENT POWER TO ISSUE GENERAL OBLIGATION LONG-TERM DEBT, 1986 (continued)

	C-S	Limit	Basis	Provisions
Virginia				
Counties	C-S	No Limits[1]	No Limits[1]	NA
Municipalities[2]	C-S	10	LAV	None
Washington				
Counties	C	5[1]	LAV	1
Municipalities	C	5[1]	LAV	1
School Districts	C	10[2]	LAV	2
West Virginia				
Counties	C-S	5	LAV	None
Municipalities	C-S	5	LAV	None
School Districts	C-S	5	LAV	None
Wisconsin				
Counties	C-S	5[1]	EAV	None
Municipalities	C-S	5[1]	EAV	2
School Districts	C-S	5[3]	EAV	3
Wyoming				
Counties	C-S	2	EAV	None
Municipalities	C	2[1]	EAV	[1]
School Districts	C	10	EAV	None

Virginia
[1]By referendum.
[2]Including counties that elect to be treated as cities.

Washington
[1]Debt incurrence that would bring total above 1.5% subject to approval by 60% majority vote, but in no case may it exceed 5%. However, an additional 5% is authorized for municipally owned utilities.
[2]Debt incurrence that would bring total above 1.5% subject to approval by 60% majority vote, but in no case may it exceed 5%. However, a constitutional amendment authorizes an additional 5% for "capital outlays."

Wisconsin
[1]No more than 4% for county buildings or 1% (by sole action of the county board) for highways.
[2]Municipalities operating schools, except Milwaukee, may incur an additional 10% for school purposes.
[3]Ten percent for school districts offering no less than grades 1-12 and which are eligible for highest level of state aid ("integrated" districts).

Wyoming
[1]Additional 4% authorized for sewer construction.

Note: This table deals only with limitations that affect generally the amount of general obligation debt in counties, municipalities, and school districts can issue. In a number of states, general obligation debt issued for specified purposes is excluded from the general rate limitations either by constitutional or statutory provisions. In addition, specific debt limitations are often imposed under special districts. No attempt has been made to treat the exceptions or the special district limitations because of their great variety. Also excluded from this table are provisions that set maximum interest rates or time periods for which bonds may be issued.

*C—State's constitution, S—statutes, C-S—both.
**Percentage debt limitations are generally applied against property values.
MV—Full or market value.
LAV—Locally established assessed value or state established assessed value in case of state assessed property such as utilities.
EAV—State equalized assessed value.
***M—A simple majority (a favorable majority of 50% plus one of all votes subject to counting on the question); where more than a simple majority is required, the required percentage is entered. These provisions are other than by amendment of the constitution or statutes.
NA—not applicable.

Source: ACIR staff with the help of state attorneys general or other state officials.

Chapter Three

INTERGOVERNMENTAL TAX IMMUNITY
AND LEGAL FRAMEWORK

Although this book's focus is on the economics of tax policy that denies tax exemption to some municipal bonds, it would be remiss to ignore the legal framework within which bonds are issued, and particularly the claim that the economics of this issue is irrelevant.

Until 1988 it was asserted by many that any taxation of interest income derived from municipal bonds is unconstitutional because the exemption is protected by the Tenth Amendment and the doctrine of intergovernmental tax immunity, notwithstanding that the U.S. Congress for 20 years beginning in 1968 had been declaring some state and local bonds to be taxable. The issue appears to have been settled by a 1988 decision of the U.S. Supreme Court that rejected this claim of constitutional protection for the interest income exclusion. Some contend, however, that the decision was flawed, and others seek an amendment to the U.S. Constitution that would provide the constitutional protection recently denied. Thus, the aftermath of this legal issue is likely to remain with us for the foreseeable future.

HISTORY OF INTERGOVERNMENTAL TAX IMMUNITY

The usual place to begin a discussion of the doctrine of intergovernmental tax immunity is with Justice John Marshall's famous 1819 decision in *McCulloch v. Maryland* and the even more famous phrase from that decision that "the power to tax involves the power to destroy" (17 U.S. 316, 431 [1819]).[1] The issue in *McCulloch* was whether a state could tax an instrumentality of the federal government, the Bank of the United States. The Court held that such a tax would undermine the supremacy clause of the Constitution. Although the *McCulloch* decision would presumably still be relevant to a case involving a discriminatory tax levied on state or local government obligations, it does not seem relevant to the question of whether or not Congress can extend a generally applicable income tax to income received as interest on state and local bonds. The more appropriate place to begin this short history is with the Civil War income tax and the *Day* case to which it gave rise.

The Civil War Income Tax and the *Day* Case

America's first experience with income taxation came during the Civil War. As enacted in 1861, the Civil War income tax was a paragon of simplicity. Initially it was a 3 percent tax on income in excess of $800 from "whatever source derived," except that interest on U.S. government securities was taxed at 1½ percent. There was no exemption for interest on state and local government securities, but state and local taxes were deductible.

This tax is important to the intergovernmental tax immunity doctrine's history because of the *Day* case. Day was a state judge who successfully argued that the United States could not tax the salaries of judicial officers of a state (*Collector v. Day*, 11 Wall. 113 [1871]). The case was one of several that developed the doctrine that taxes could not be imposed on income received pursuant to a contract with a government because such a tax was equivalent to a tax on the government, either federal or state, itself.

The *Pollock* Case

In 1894 a federal income tax was reenacted modeled generally after the Civil War tax. The measure was quickly judged to be unconstitutional in *Pollock v. Farmers Loan & Trust Co.* (157 U.S. 492 [1895]). The principal issue was the constitutional requirement that any direct tax be apportioned among the states. But this tax also provided an exclusion for interest on U.S. government obligations and not those of state or local governments. The Supreme Court decision went beyond the apportionment issue and held that the 1894 act was also unconstitutional because it included interest on state and local obligations in the tax base: "The tax in question is a tax on the power of the States and their instrumentalities to borrow money, and consequently repugnant to the constitution." In *Pollock* the Court referred to the decision in the *Day* case and also the *McCulloch* decision, even though the latter decision had nothing to do with immunity of state instrumentalities from taxation by the federal government.

During the process of congressional passage and state ratification of the Sixteenth Amendment, which removed the barrier to federal income taxation imposed by the apportionment clause, assurances were given and hopes expressed that there was no intention to tax interest on state and local government obligations (Buenker 1964). The assurances and hopes were given and expressed despite the plain language of the amendment, which gave the federal government the power to tax income "from whatever source derived." The income tax of 1913, which followed ratification of the Sixteenth Amendment in February of that year, reflected the political consensus of the day. The statute specified that interest on state and local government bonds was to be exempt.

Secretary Mellon's Argument

The income tax was not yet 10 years old when Treasury Secretary Andrew Mellon launched an attack on tax-exempt bonds. Writing to the chairman of the House Ways and Means Committee on April 30, 1921, he urged the elimination of all tax-exempt bonds.

I suggest for the consideration of Congress that it may also be advisable to take action by statute or by Constitutional amendment, where necessary, to restrict further issues of tax-exempt securities. It is now the policy of the federal government not to issue its own obligations with exemptions from federal surtaxes and profits taxes, but States and municipalities are issuing fully tax-exempt securities in great volume. It is estimated that there are outstanding, perhaps, ten billion dollars of fully tax-exempt securities. The existence of this mass of exempt securities constitutes an economic evil of the first magnitude. The continued issue of tax-exempt securities encourages the growth of public indebtedness and tends to divert capital from productive enterprise. Even though the exemptions of outstanding securities cannot be disturbed, it is important that future issues be controlled or prohibited by mutual consent of the State and federal Governments (Mellon 1924, 141–42)

Roosevelt's Bond Proposals

On April 25, 1938, President Franklin D. Roosevelt sent a message to Congress calling for passage of a statute that would tax interest on newly issued state and local government securities. His main concern was with the fairness issue. "A fair and effective progressive income tax and a huge perpetual reserve of tax-exempt bonds could not exist side by side," (in U.S. Congress 1939, 1). The message covered more than municipal bonds. The president also called for taxation of salaries paid by state and local governments. A month later the Supreme Court held in Helvering v. Gerhardt (304 U.S. 405 [1938]) that the salaries of engineers of the Port of New York Authority were subject to federal income tax, effectively overturning the Day decision. The next Congress dealt with the salary issue by prohibiting any retroactive taxation of state and local salaries.

In arguing for the president's proposal before the Ways and Means Committee, Under Secretary of the Treasury John Hanes presented detailed evidence of the distributional effects of tax exempt bonds. In passing, he indicated that Presidents Warren Harding, Calvin Coolidge, and Herbert Hoover had all urged the discontinuance of tax-exempt securities. Representatives of state and local governments, as might be expected, argued for continuing the use of tax-exempt bonds. Mayor Fiorello La Guardia of New York City, representing the National Conference of Mayors, summed up their position by saying that "this exemption of State and municipal securities is just a part of our scheme of government, a part of the whole fabric of our financial structure" (U.S. Congress 1939, 309).

Nothing came of President Roosevelt's proposal. A few years later, in the midst of fiscal planning for World War II, Secretary of the Treasury Henry Morgenthau urged the Congress to eliminate tax exemption not only for newly issued obligations but for outstanding issues as well. He argued that the increased tax rates necessary to finance the war would generate unjustifiable windfalls for current holders of tax-exempt securities and provide an avenue of tax avoidance for those who would otherwise be subject to high wartime tax rates. Congress ignored this proposal too, choosing once again to respond to the urgings of state and local officials (Maxwell 1946, 374).

Nowhere in the debate over tax-exempt bonds during the first 30 years of the income tax was there any discussion of limitations on their use. The arguments were for or against these bonds in their entirety. Not until after World War II was any policy concern expressed about particular uses of tax-exempt bonds.

The Emergence of IDBs

As discussed in the preceeding chapter on the history of municipal debt, extensive use was made of debt financing for private banks, canals, railroads and a few other ventures in the 19th and early 20th centuries. Several of these ventures ran into financial difficulties during periods of recession. When called upon to pay debt service out of taxes rather than the receipt of dividends and increased property values as originally anticipated, several governments defaulted, and there were some outright repudiations. In reaction, most state constitutions were amended or, in the case of new states, drafted to prevent the extension of state credit to private persons. Thus, the use of what is now often called conduit financing fell into disuse.

The first modern industrial development bonds (IDBs) were issued by the state of Mississippi in 1936, and represented a reversion to the financing practices of the canal- and railroad-building period in American history. Only a few other southern states followed the Mississippi example and issued IDBs prior to World War II, and their issuance was slow to pick up after the war.

Congressional Restrictions on the Use of Tax-Exempt Bonds

The simple one-sentence exemption of interest on state and local obligations contained in the 1913 Internal Revenue Code and not modified until 1968 served American notions of fiscal federalism well for more than 50 years, only because there was no widespread use of tax-exempt bonds for private purposes or the earning of arbitrage profits. The first congressional reaction to the issuance of IDBs did not occur until the development of the Internal Revenue Code of 1954. During markup in the Ways and Means Committee, an amendment was agreed to that eliminated the use of bonds to build factories or other facilities that would then be leased to private firms. As then Deputy to the Secretary of the Treasury (in charge of tax policy), Dan Throop Smith wrote after the event, "The organized outcry was so great that the action was rescinded in less than a week. . . ." (1961, 61). The Ways and Means Committee *Calendar* (1954), however, shows that the provision passed the House, was not in the Senate bill, and was dropped in conference. More than a decade passed before an essentially similar provision was enacted into law.

In 1968 Congress began the process of curtailing the issuance of tax-exempt bonds. The first step was to limit the use of IDBs and the next year to limit the issuance of arbitrage bonds. The evolution of this restrictive legislation is reviewed in part 3 of this book, but it is appropriate here to note the pattern followed. The technique has been to define the "bad" use of tax-exempt bonds, typically followed with a list of exceptions, rather than to define the "good" uses. Although the *South Carolina* decision (discussed next) frees Congress from any lingering doubts about the constitutionality of its efforts to define "good" and "bad" bonds over the last two decades, there are both economic and political reasons to expect continuing restrictions rather than the outright prohibition of tax-exempt bonds.

The *South Carolina* Case

The state of South Carolina brought its case to the Supreme Court on original jurisdiction in reaction to the registration provision contained in the Tax Equity and Fiscal Responsibility Act of 1982. This provision required bonds to be issued in registered, as opposed to bearer, form as a precondition for tax exemption.[2] The plaintiff, joined by the National Governors' Association, charged that the provision was constitutionally invalid under the Tenth Amendment and the doctrine of intergovernmental tax immunity.

Justice William Joseph Brennan, delivering the 7–1 opinion, responded by indicating that "States must find their protection from Congressional regulations through the national political process, not through judicially defined spheres of unregulable State activity." *South Carolina v. Baker* (485 U.S. 505, [1988]). To judge from reactions quoted in the press, this part of the decision was widely expected. It is consistent with a number of recent decisions, including *Garcia v. San Antonio Metropolitan Transit Authority* (469 U.S. 528 [1985]), holding that federal rules regarding overtime pay applied to state and local government as well as private employers.

The Court surprised those who had been following the case by going beyond the narrow issue of the registration requirement's efficacy to address the intergovernmental tax immunity doctrine. Many state and local government officials have, over the years, taken the position that this doctrine, articulated most famously in the Court's decision in the *Pollock* case of 1895, prevented the federal government from taxing interest on state and local government bonds either entirely or more certainly in the case of "public purpose" bonds. These officials have been joined, and indeed cheered on, by bond lawyers and underwriters. Speaking for the Court, Justice Brennan settled the matter.

We see no constitutional reason for treating persons who receive interest on governmental bonds differently than persons who receive income from other types of contracts with the government, and no tenable rationale for distinguishing the costs imposed on States by a tax on State bond interest from the costs imposed by a tax on the income from any other State contract. (*South Carolina v. Baker*, 485 U.S. 505, [1988])

REACTION TO SOUTH CAROLINA

As soon as the Court's decision hit the news wires, there was a brief period of falling prices and uncertainty in the secondary market for tax-exempt bonds. But calm was soon restored after it became clear to market participants that the decision did not alter the status of outstanding bonds or even newly issued securities. The substantive law had not been changed. In a press release later that day, Chairman Dan Rostenkowski, of the Committee on Ways and Means, said, "There is no reason to believe that today's decision will either prompt or deter future Congressional action." Senator Lloyd Bentsen, chairman of the Senate Committee on Finance, was quoted as saying, "The fact is the exemption for general obligation bonds is extremely popular in the Congress. There's a strong feeling that the federal government should not interfere with those bonds."

Some strong reactions did come from representatives of state and local governments. The executive director of the National League of Cities, Alan Beals, was quoted as saying, "Local government officials throughout the United States are angered and disgusted by the unrelenting assault by the Congress and by the executive branch on the activities and revenue systems of our cities, towns and States." Virginia Rutledge, the president of the Government Finance Officers Association said, "My fear is that Congress takes this as a green flag to get into any and all State and local activity. This will renew and strengthen interest in a constitutional amendment to guarantee tax exemption for State and local bonds."

In fact, the reaction of those who oppose any taxation of municipal bond interest has taken two tacks. First, a number of states and various regional organizations have mounted a campaign to adopt a constitutional amendment that would overturn *South Carolina* and protect the tax exemption for state and local bonds. As of January 1990, legislatures in Utah, Oklahoma, New Mexico, Idaho, North Dakota, South Carolina, and Texas (listed in chronological order of adoption) had passed resolutions urging Congress to adopt the following amendment:

The Congress shall not have the power to lay and collect taxes on income representing interest on obligations issued by or on behalf of the several states and their political subdivisions to raise revenues for governmental undertakings and operations for a public purpose or, to finance property owned and operated by governmental entities for a public purpose.

This article shall not restrict the power of the Congress to exclude from taxation income or other amounts derived from other obligations issued by or on behalf of the several states or their political subdivisions.

In the second approach, some suggest that the majority opinion in the *South Carolina* decision "is flawed because it reaches beyond the statute at issue without considering the drastic effects this decision will have on a state's power to borrow" (Trujillo 1989, 148). The claim that the decision reached beyond the statute is based upon the view that the primary effect of registration was to increase issuance costs, and that the Court had previously held in both *Garcia* and *Helvering v. Gerhardt* that "Federal taxation, which merely results in higher costs for state and local governments, is not adequate evidence that a state's sovereignty is threatened" (Trujillo 1989, 166). In contrast, it is claimed, the 1986 Tax Act does more than increase operating costs—it interferes with a state's powers to borrow and self-govern.[3]

Legal disagreements aside, students of federalism see the writing on the wall and are preparing to adapt to a new intergovernmental policy environment.

... the question of whether issuing tax exempt bonds is a sovereign right of the states or a privilege they are accorded by the Congress has been settled. Immunity is not a right under the Tenth Amendment. The doctrine of intergovernmental tax immunity has been officially replaced by principles of taxation that accord superior powers to the national government .... Not only is the future of intergovernmental fiscal policy certain to be changed, but the basic character of the political partnership will in all likelihood be affected as well (Wrightson 1989, 51–52)

THE REMAINDER OF THE LEGAL FRAMEWORK

In addition to the necessity to conform to federal tax law (if the interest income is to be exempt from federal income tax), municipal bonds must be issued in conformance with a host of state constitutional and statutory restrictions, local ordinances, and securities laws. This section provides brief discussions of the nontax legal framework, based largely upon detailed discussions in National Association of Bond Lawyers (1988).

State Constitutional and Statutory Restrictions

Every municipal debt issue must be checked for compliance with a state's constitution and statutes that authorize or limit the issuance of debt obligations. Details of these restrictions as of 1986 are presented for each state in Appendix 2.A to chapter 2. In some instances, compliance at time of issue can prove inadequate if laws not directly related to municipal bonds turn out to be unconstitutional (in violation, for example, of voting rights, equal protection, and due process laws).

Most states have some requirement that a public purpose must be served by a debt issue and bar use of public credit for private purposes. It is, of course, true that what satisfies a public purpose at the state level is likely to change over time as state interests and political coalitions develop and new cases are adjudicated.[4] A wide variety of other issues may arise to complicate any given bond issue, such as: the use of bond proceeds to benefit religious entities; taxation without representation; unauthorized delegation of legislative powers to authorities or agencies; encroachment on private enterprises; and granting of special privileges. In addition, issues concerning taxpayer protection (bond interest rate ceilings, tax levy limits, referenda requirements) and bondholder protection frequently arise.

Securities Law

The municipal securities market is subject to regulation from both federal and state securities law. Although municipal bonds are exempt from federal registration requirements in the Securities Act of 1933 and the Securities Exchange Act of 1934, they are not exempt from the antifraud provisions of these acts. In addition, municipal securities brokers and dealers are regulated by the Municipal Securities Rulemaking Board, which was created by a 1975 amendment to the 1934 act.

Several events in the last two decades—the city of New York's fiscal crisis in the mid 1970s, the Washington Public Power Supply default in the mid 1980s, and the arbitrage-driven transactions that were rushed to market in the mid 1980s and eventually collapsed, becoming known as the "Matthews and Wright" scandal after the underwriting firm that originated many of the deals—have caused the judiciary to review the applicability of the antifraud provisions to municipal bonds. These pressures have caused the Securities and Exchange Commission (SEC) to increase the disclosure requirements for underwriters of state and local bonds. In June 1989, the SEC adopted rule 15c2-12, which requires underwriters of issues in excess of $1 million to review the near-final official statement from the issuer for its accuracy and completeness of key representations regarding the securities, prior to bidding for or purchasing the securities; and to send a copy of the final official statement to potential customers for a specified period after underwriting is completed (after which such official statements will be available from a newly created central repository).[5]

State regulation of municipal securities began with Kansas legislation in 1911. By the onset of the Great Depression, almost all states had enacted some regulation of the municipal market. The focus of these laws is to use some combination of three requirements to protect investors from fraud: prohibition of specified fraudulent practices by market participants; registration of persons and entities selling or offering securities; and registration of securities prior to public offering. All states exempt from registration both GOs and those revenue bonds whose proceeds are used directly by a municipality.

The Securities Acts Amendments of 1975 created the previously mentioned Municipal Securities Rulemaking Board as an independent, self-regulatory rulemaking body for municipal brokers and dealers, but not issuers. Its purpose is to prevent fraud, promote fair markets, and protect investors and the public interest. Although its rules have the force of law, it has no inspection or enforcement powers, and must rely for these functions on the Securities and Exchange Commission, the National Association of Securities Dealers, and federal banking agencies.

Other Federal Law

A bond issue may at times also run afoul of other federal statutes beyond the tax and securities law. This is most likely to occur in the areas of antitrust and environmental law. The antitrust law may occasionally place the bond issuance activities of a state or local government in conflict with federal prohibitions against anticompetitive behavior. In addition, some projects contemplated at the state or local level may violate environmental laws such as The Wild and Scenic Rivers Act of 1968, the National Historic Preservation Act, and the Endangered Species Act; or social laws such as the Civil Rights Act of 1964, the Rehabilitation Act of 1975, and the Age Discrimination Act of 1975.

Notes

1. Much of this section is adapted from Davie and Zimmerman (1988). The purpose here is to trace the general outlines of the dispute, not to provide an exhaustive treatment of the legal aspects of the immunity doctrine.

2. Section 310(b)(1) of the Tax Equity and Fiscal Responsibility Act of 1982 (TEFRA) required that all bonds be issued in registered form. As a result, section 103(j) of the Internal Revenue Code of 1954 denied tax-exempt status to state and local government obligations not issued in registered form. (The provision became section 149(a) of the 1986 Code when the tax-exempt bond provisions were recodified by the Tax Reform Act of 1986.) Direct penalties were not imposed on states and localities but, rather, the holder was subjected to the loss of tax exemption. This had the effect, of course, of inducing issuers to comply.

The legislative history of TEFRA indicated that the registration provision was viewed as a compliance issue. Concerns were expressed that under prior law bearer bonds were used to evade gift and estate taxes. Evasion of the capital gains tax on tax-exempt bonds was particularly easy when they were bearer bonds. Another concern was the use of bearer bonds in money laudering schemes. There had been reports in the press, based on criminal and securities law investigations, of suitcases full of cash being exchanged for portfolios of bearer municipal bonds. (On May 16, 1988, the firm of E. F. Hutton was fined $1 million in a money laundering case dating back to the 1982–84 period involving such bonds see *Washington Post*, May 17, 1988, C2). Those engaged in illicit activities were more than willing to pay the implicit tax of a low yield in return for freedom from any obligation to report the interest income on tax returns. But even this last refuge of scoundrels has been closed. The 1986 act requires that all tax-exempt interest be reported on returns.

3. This distinction seems somewhat artificial. The essence of the tax exemption is to reduce borrowing costs, which is certainly a cost of governmental operation. In addition, the decision may affect the "power" to borrow at tax-exempt rates, but it in no way prevents states from issuing taxable bonds. It appears the primary alteration in their borrowing powers is to make them more costly.

4. The issue of how a public purpose is defined, and how this definition is likely to vary between federal and state-local levels of government, is addressed in detail in chapter 5.

5. For a thorough discussion of the new SEC rule on municipal disclosure and its implications for issuers and underwriters, see John Petersen (1989a, 1989b).

Chapter Four

CHARACTERISTICS OF MUNICIPAL BONDS AND MARKET PARTICIPANTS

Having examined the early history of municipal bonds and the long-running legal dispute over intergovernmental immunity, some background on the modern municipal bond market is desirable. The tax-exempt market is composed of issuers who supply bonds and investors who demand bonds, plus a variety of individuals and institutions whose jobs are to bring the two sides of the market together.[1]

A central theme of this book is that much of the growth in the modern municipal bond market is a natural product of the economic incentives created for market participants by the tax law. State and local officials see benefits to be garnered in excess of their taxpayers' costs; underwriters, bond lawyers, financial advisors, and the insurance industry see fees to be earned; private business sees a lower-cost alternative to debt financing than is available from the private capital market; investors see a way to shelter their income from federal, and sometimes state and local, income taxation; and the interest groups staffed by marketers of public policy expertise see wages and visions of policy influence.

Many books have been written detailing the basic characteristics of tax-exempt bonds and market participants (e.g., Moak 1970, Public Securities Association 1987). The discussion here is restricted to an overview of those tax-exempt bond characteristics and the motivations of market participants that are particularly important to the central issues of this book. Market participants are described, the function of each is explained, and, where possible, some idea of the magnitude of their financial stake in the tax-exempt bond market is provided.

SHORT-TERM VERSUS LONG-TERM BORROWING

State and local governments must borrow money for long and short periods of time. Long-term debt instruments are usually referred to as bonds, and carry maturities in excess of one year. Short-term debt instruments are usually referred to as notes, and carry maturities of 12 months or less.[2] If the notes are to be paid from specific taxes due in the near future, they are called tax anticipation notes (TANS); if from anticipated intergovernmental revenue, they are called revenue anticipation notes (RANS); and if from long-term borrowing, they are called bond anticipation notes (BANS). Tax anticipation notes and revenue anticipation notes are often grouped together and referred to as tax and revenue anticipation notes (TRANS).

Table 4.1 displays the volume of long-term and short-term borrowing from 1965 to 1988. (Note that the data in this chapter refer to the volume of debt issued in a year, unlike the historical data in chapter 2 that referred to the stock of outstanding debt). Long-term borrowing dominates state and local debt activity in most years, with

Table 4.1 VOLUME OF SHORT- AND LONG-TERM TAX-EXEMPT BONDS: 1965–88 ($ MILLIONS)

Year	Short-term	Long-term	Long-term Share (%)
1965	6,537	11,084	62.9
1966	6,524	11,089	63.0
1967	8,025	14,288	64.0
1968	8,659	16,374	65.4
1969	11,783	11,460	49.3
1970	17,880	17,762	49.8
1971	26,281	24,370	48.1
1972	25,222	22,941	47.6
1973	24,667	22,953	48.2
1974	29,041	22,824	44.0
1975	28,973	29,326	50.3
1976	21,905	33,845	60.7
1977	21,349	45,060	67.9
1978	21,642	46,215	68.1
1979	20,897	42,261	66.9
1980	26,485	47,133	64.0
1981	34,443	46,134	57.3
1982	43,390	77,179	64.0
1983	35,849	83,348	69.9
1984	31,068	101,882	76.6
1985	19,492	204,281	91.3
1986	21,526	150,972	87.5
1987	20,270	105,523	83.9
1988	22,602	117,011	83.8

Sources: Bond Buyer (1989 and earlier years).
Note: Long-term volume contains refunding issues.

the long-term share peaking in 1985 at over 90 percent of the market. Most of the legislation discussed in this book is devoted to the economic issues raised by long-term borrowing. The few exceptions are noted as they occur.

REVENUE, GENERAL OBLIGATION, AND LEASE RENTAL BONDS

Another way to cut the tax-exempt bond market is to classify bonds in terms of the security provided to the bondholder. General obligation (GO) bonds pledge the full faith and credit of the issuing government. The issuing government makes an unconditional pledge of its powers of taxation to honor its liability for interest and principal repayment. Revenue bonds, or nonguaranteed debt, pledge only the earnings from revenue-producing activities, most often the earnings from the facilities being financed with the revenue bonds. Should these earnings prove to be inadequate to honor these commitments, the issuing government is under no obligation to utilize its taxing powers to finance the shortfall. Some revenue bonds have begun to be issued with credit enhancements provided by insurance or bank letters of credit that guarantee payment upon such a revenue shortfall.

GO and revenue bonds are sometimes further differentiated by the degree of security,[3] but this simple two-part division is adequate for the issues to be raised in this book. The first two columns to the right of the stub in table 4.2 display the breakdown between long-term GO and revenue bonds from 1965 to 1988. The long-term market has been and continues to be dominated by revenue bonds, that is, by nonguaranteed debt. During the 1960s, revenue bonds constituted less than 40 percent of long-term bond volume; during the 1970s the revenue bond share crept into the 50 percent to 65 percent range; and beginning in 1979 this share settled into the high 60s and low 70s, achieving a high of 73.1 percent in 1988. Most of the legislation discussed in this book concerns state and local use of revenue bonds.

All tax-exempt interest income attributable to state and local governments does not appear in the form of bonds. They may engage in installment purchase contracts and finance leases for which the portion of the installment or lease payment representing the vendor's interest payments is tax exempt. For example, computer equipment or road building equipment could be purchased from a vendor using

Table 4.2 VOLUME OF LONG-TERM TAX-EXEMPT DEBT: GENERAL
OBLIGATION (GO), REVENUE, AND REFUNDING BONDS, 1965–88
($ MILLIONS)

	Long-term Bond Volume			Refunding Bonds	
Year	GOs ($)	Revenue ($)	Revenue Share ($)	Share of Long-term ($)	(%)
1965	7,445	3,639	32.8	789	7.1
1966	7,013	4,076	36.8	221	2.0
1967	9,192	5,090	35.7	174	1.2
1968	9,611	6,763	41.3	138	0.8
1969	8,047	3,413	29.8	51	0.4
1970	11,803	5,959	33.5	56	0.3
1971	16,241	8,129	33.4	453	1.9
1972	14,121	8,820	38.4	1,569	6.8
1973	12,827	10,126	44.1	1,235	5.4
1974	13,031	9,793	42.9	582	2.5
1975	15,003	14,323	48.8	934	3.2
1976	16,916	16,929	50.0	3,515	10.4
1977	17,887	27,173	60.3	9,587	21.3
1978	17,894	28,321	61.3	9,284	20.1
1979	12,615	29,646	70.1	1,872	4.4
1980	16,347	30,786	65.3	1,649	3.5
1981	13,988	32,146	69.7	1,192	2.6
1982	23,276	53,903	69.8	4,044	5.2
1983	22,584	60,764	72.9	13,048	15.7
1984	27,508	74,374	73.0	11,390	11.2
1985	55,287	148,994	72.9	57,867	28.3
1986	45,555	105,417	69.8	56,063	37.1
1987	30,867	74,656	70.7	38,490	36.5
1988	31,502	85,509	73.1	36,591	31.3

Sources: Bond Buyer (1989 and earlier years).

a lease agreement or an installment sales contract, under which the
monthly payments to the vendor include repayment of the vendor's
interest expense in borrowing the money to purchase the equipment
being leased or purchased. This interest income of the vendor is tax
exempt. Such transactions are often referred to as municipal leasing.

A variation on revenue bonds has recently attained a degree of
popularity—lease rental revenue bonds and certificates. An authority or nonprofit corporation issues bonds, builds a facility with the
proceeds, and leases the facility to a municipality. Security for the
bonds or certificates is based on the lease payments. When the bonds
are retired, the facility belongs to the lessee (the municipality). An
advantage to this type of arrangement is that many states' constitu-

tional and statutory definitions do not consider this type of financing to be debt because the lease payments are annual operating expenses based upon appropriated monies.[4]

The leasing technique has also been used to provide tax-exempt funds to nonprofit organizations. A municipality issues the bonds for the construction of a facility that is leased to a nonprofit hospital or university. Again, security for the bonds is based on the lease payments. Little information is available on the magnitude of tax-exempt leasing activity. The Treasury Department's forthcoming report on 1987 bond volume required by the Tax Reform Act of 1986 will provide the first comprehensive report on this type of financing.

NEW-ISSUE VERSUS REFUNDING BONDS

Long-term tax-exempt bond issues can also be broken down between new issues and refunding issues. New issues represent bonds issued to finance new capital facilities. Refundings usually are made to replace outstanding bond issues with bonds that carry lower interest rates or other favorable terms. As such, the refunding issue usually does not add to the stock of outstanding bonds or the capital stock. The proceeds of the refunding bonds are used to pay off the remaining principal of the original bond issue, which is retired. Advance refunding bonds, however, do add to the outstanding stock of bonds without adding to the stock of capital. Advance refunding bonds are issued prior to the date on which the original bonds are refunded, so that for a period of time there are two bond issues outstanding to finance the same capital facilities.

The last two columns of table 4.2 show the dollar value of refunding issues and their share of total long-term bond volume. The share varies widely, depending to a great extent on changes in the relative magnitudes of taxable and tax-exempt interest rates. The share grew rapidly during two brief periods—1976 to 1978, when $9.3 billion of refundings in 1978 represented 20.1 percent of long-term issues; and 1984 to 1986, when $56.1 billion of refundings in 1986 represented 37.1 percent of the long-term market.

THE TAX EXEMPTION PRIVILEGE

The volume of bonds over the last 10 years indicates the existence of a robust market for raising public sector capital. Without such a market, the state and local sector would be subject to intermittent service disruptions and a continual suboptimal level of capital formation. Since the state and local sector is an important component of each citizen's economic life, national welfare would suffer.

The federal government has not chosen to stand idly by and hope for the best in the public capital market. It has encouraged this market by granting the debt instruments of state and local governments a unique privilege—the exemption of interest income from federal income taxation. Even after the *South Carolina* decision (see chapter 3), there has been no effort in Congress to eliminate this exemption for traditional municipal bonds.

To investors with federal marginal tax rates of 28 percent, the tax savings from this exempt interest income make them indifferent to a taxable corporate bond yielding 10 percent before tax and 7.2 percent after tax versus a tax-exempt bond of equivalent risk yielding 7.2 percent both before and after tax.[5] The state or local government can raise capital from this taxpayer at a 2.8 percentage points (280 basis points) lower interest cost than can a corporation. Thus, this interest exemption has the effect of reducing the interest rate on state and local bonds.

The magnitude of this interest rate differential is summarized by the yield ratio—the interest rate paid on municipal bonds divided by the interest rate paid on corporate bonds of equivalent risk. Table 4.3 lists the average yield on Aa-rated municipal and corporate bonds from 1970 to 1989 and calculates the yield ratio for each year. The ratio fell to a low of 0.62 in 1979 and achieved a high of 0.76 from 1985 through 1987. The lower the yield ratio, the greater the interest savings to state and local governments compared to the interest rates they would have to pay if they financed with taxable debt. As the ratio rises toward 1, state and local borrowing costs approach the level of taxable bond interest rates.

These variations in the cost of state and local borrowing relative to the cost of taxable borrowing depend upon the demand for and supply of both tax-exempt and taxable bonds. Demand depends upon the number of investors, their wealth, and their alternative tax shelter opportunities. Supply depends upon the desire of the state and local sector for capital facilities and their ability to engage in conduit financing (issuing state or local government bonds and and passing the proceeds through to businesses or individuals for their private use). Almost all of the factors that influence demand and supply are affected by federal tax policy. When the federal tax policy elephant twitches, the municipal bond market reacts.

Table 4.3 YIELDS ON TAX-EXEMPT AND CORPORATE BONDS OF
EQUIVALENT RISK AND THEIR YIELD RATIO: 1970–89

Year	Tax-Exempt Yield	Corporate Yield	Tax-Exempt/ Corporate
1970	6.28	8.32	0.75
1971	5.36	7.78	0.69
1972	5.19	7.48	0.69
1973	5.09	7.66	0.66
1974	6.04	8.84	0.68
1975	6.77	9.17	0.74
1976	6.12	8.75	0.70
1977	5.39	8.24	0.65
1978	5.68	8.92	0.64
1979	6.12	9.94	0.62
1980	8.06	12.50	0.64
1981	10.89	14.75	0.74
1982	11.31	14.41	0.78
1983	9.17	12.39	0.74
1984	9.88	13.31	0.74
1985	8.93	11.82	0.76
1986	7.16	9.47	0.76
1987	7.39	9.68	0.76
1988	7.49	9.94	0.75
1989[a]	7.16	9.57	0.75

Source: Moody's Investors Service (1990 and earlier years). Aa-rated bonds.
a. Based on 9-month average.

THE FEDERAL REVENUE LOSS

The direct cost to the federal government of this interest exclusion
for state and local government is the foregone tax revenue. Consider
the 28 percent marginal tax rate investor who purchases a 7.5 percent
tax-exempt 20-year term bond with a face value of $1,000. Each year
for 20 years this taxpayer receives $75 interest income. Each year
the federal government foregoes collecting $100 × (0.28) = $28 of
revenue, because the revenue loss is based upon the yield the taxpayer foregoes (in this case, the 10 percent taxable bond yield) to
buy the municipal bond.[6]
   The loss of federal revenue on the outstanding stock of tax-exempt
bonds is estimated separately by the Treasury Department's Office
of Tax Analysis and the Joint Committee on Taxation. The Treasury
Department's estimates for the last 10 years are displayed in table
4.4.[7] Because they are based upon the outstanding stock of tax-exempt bonds, it takes time for some legislative changes to show up

Table 4.4 FEDERAL REVENUE LOSS ON THE OUTSTANDING STOCK OF TAX-
EXEMPT BONDS, 1980–89

Year	Revenue ($ billions)
1980	7.697
1981	9.800
1982	11.435
1983	13.775
1984	16.080
1985	18.170
1986	21.305
1987	22.215
1988	21.800
1989	20.915

Sources: Office of Management and Budget. *Special Analyses: Budget of the United States Government*, various fiscal years.
Note: Average annual rate of growth, 1980–87: 15.14%.

in these data. The losses grew at an annual rate slightly in excess of 15 percent from 1980 through 1987. As the restrictions of the Tax Reform Act of 1986 began to take hold (owing to rate reductions and volume restrictions), the revenue loss declined slightly for the first time to $21.8 billion in fiscal year (FY) 1988, and is projected to decline slightly in 1990 to $21.2 billion.

These revenue losses represent calculations of the anticipated change in tax revenue that would result from eliminating the tax preference for tax-exempt bonds, and as such have been controversial. It has been argued that these estimates are too high because they depend critically upon the assumption that a change in the use of tax-exempt bonds does not change the economy's debt/equity ratio or any of the real variables in the economy, such as the share of savings and the level of gross national product (GNP) and taxable income.[8]

For example, the revenue estimates in table 4.4 assume that the elimination of tax-exempt debt would be replaced by taxable debt.[9] This ignores the possibility that a substantial portion of the tax-exempt debt could be replaced with corporate equity. Were this the case, the revenue in the table would be overstated because corporate equity is a partially taxed rather than a fully taxed asset, which implies that some of the revenue loss would not be recouped. A related aspect of this problem concerns efforts to control the use of tax-exempt bonds for private purposes. The revenue loss from these "private activity" bonds assumes that none of these activities would be financed with general obligation debt if private activity financing were terminated. This might be true for some activities such as mortgage revenue bonds, but activities such as solid waste disposal might well be so financed. If tax-exempt financing of these activities continued, the revenue loss would not be recouped.[10]

It is also argued that the revenue estimating procedure ignores the macroeconomic effects of the bond activity: savings are increased, investment is increased, economic activity is increased, and federal tax revenue is generated to offset the direct revenue loss from the bonds. One way to look at this question is to ask Which of the many federal programs or subsidies, many of which interact, should be credited with the stimulative impact of federal budget and tax policy? The answer is none, since the stimulative effects would be badly overestimated if each individual program or provision had its "reflow" effects attributed to it. No one tax or spending program can be viewed as the marginal determinant of fiscal policy (Toder and Neubig 1985). This issue is addressed in more detail in chapter 10.

ISSUERS

States, Indian tribes, U.S. possessions (U.S. Virgin Islands, Puerto Rico, American Samoa, and Guam), the District of Columbia, and political subdivisions of these entities can issue tax-exempt bonds. These entities also create special districts and dependent agencies, authorities, and corporations that can issue bonds. Some of these created entities issue bonds "on behalf of" the states and their political subdivisions, frequently for the benefit of nonprofit organizations (charitable, educational, and other charitable organizations that qualify for tax exemption under section 501(c)(3) of the Internal Revenue Code).

States, Indian Tribes, Possessions, and Their Political Subdivisions

A political subdivision is generally defined as possessing at least one of three characteristics of sovereignty: the power to tax; the power of eminent domain; and police power. The U.S. Bureau of the Census (1988b) identified 83,236 governmental units in 1987. The states and general-purpose local governments (county, municipal, township) numbered 38,983. The remaining units were limited-purpose local governments, including 14,721 school districts and 29,532 special districts.

This book's focus is on the use of revenue bonds for private activities. General-purpose units of government and school districts that have access to the full range of local taxing power tend to issue GO bonds.[11] Special districts tend to issue revenue bonds. Most of these districts have no access to property taxation (56.5 percent), and must rely for the financing of their debt service on some combination of fees and charges (24.1 percent), special assessments and earmarked taxes (16.4 percent), and lease payments, reimbursements, and so forth (30.4 percent).

These special districts have been the fastest growing portion of the government sector for the last three decades. Between 1962 and 1987 special districts grew by 61.2 percent, from 18,323 to 29,532, while all other local governments (excluding school districts) grew by only 2.0 percent over the same time period, from 38,185 to 38,933.

What functions do these special districts serve? Table 4.5 provides information on the number and growth of special districts by function between 1977 and 1987 (1977 is the last year the Census Bureau's disaggregation by function is comparable to 1987). The largest increases occurred in the areas of health (38.3 percent), libraries (41.6 percent), housing and community development (43.9 percent), and

Table 4.5 NUMBER OF SPECIAL DISTRICTS, BY FUNCTION: 1977–87

Function	1987	1977	Percentage Change
Single-function districts			
Natural resources	6,360	6,596	−3.6
Fire protection	5,070	4,187	21.1
Housing and community development	3,464	2,408	43.9
Water supply	3,060	2,480	23.4
Cemeteries	1,627	1,615	0.7
Sewerage	1,607	1,610	−0.2
Parks and recreation	1,004	829	21.1
Libraries	830	586	41.6
Hospitals	783	715	9.5
Education	713	1,020	−30.1
Highways	621	652	−4.8
Health	484	350	38.3
Airports	369	299	23.4
Other[a]	1,489	896	66.2
Multifunction districts	2,051	1,720	19.2

Source: U.S. Bureau of the Census (1988b, 1978).
a. Includes parking facilities, water transport and terminals, solid waste disposal, gas, electric and public transit utilities, industrial development, and mortgage credit.

"other" (66.2 percent).[12] The "other" category includes some of the functions that will prove of particular interest to this tax-exempt bond discussion—parking facilities, water transport and terminals, solid waste disposal, gas, electric, and public transit facilities, industrial development, and mortgage credit.

When, however, one turns to the debt issues of these districts, the reported debt does not seem very important. Table 4.6 displays the outstanding debt of special districts in 1986 by size of debt. Of the 29,532 districts, 40.5 percent reported no debt and 33.4 percent did not report. Of the remaining 26 percent, over two thirds, or 18.8 percent, reported less than $2 million of outstanding debt, while only 0.6 percent reported $50 million or more.

Clearly, many of these special districts are not engaged in the issuance of public debt for financing major capital facilities, but, in the words of Walsh (1978, 354) "are little more than methods of collecting earmarked taxes for fire protection, sanitation, mosquito control, and so forth." Based on surveys of each state's own counts of public authorities as of 1972, Walsh concluded that only 5,000 to 6,000 of the 24,000 special districts were public authorities with independent managing and borrowing powers. The situation does not seem to have changed by 1987.

On Behalf of Issuers: Dependent Agencies

So who are the organizations that issue the revenue bonds? The answer is that they are an unknown number of authorities and government corporations that the Census Bureau classifies as dependent agencies of other units of government, that is, of states, counties, municipalities, or townships. For the Census Bureau, this "depen-

Table 4.6 SPECIAL DISTRICTS BY DEBT SIZE: 1986

Debt-Size Group ($ millions)	Number	Percentage
Total	29,352	100
$50 or more	175	0.6
$25 to less than $50	165	0.6
$5 to less than $25	850	2.9
$2 to less than $5	960	3.3
less than $2	5,560	18.8
None	11,965	40.5
Not reported	9,857	33.4

Source: U.S. Bureau of the Census, (1988b).

dent" status seems to be based upon the lack of independent taxing powers, ignoring the importance of "access to private money markets and to revenue-producing monopoly services . . . as a source of independent financial power" (Walsh 1978).

These agencies issue bonds "on behalf of" the units of government that gave them life. They are either "constituted authorities" specifically authorized by state law to issue bonds for a public purpose on behalf of political subdivisions of a state,[13] or corporations formed under general state nonprofit corporation law [14] But for the purposes of this text, these dependent agencies perform the same function as the special districts—they are vehicles by which the state and local sector issue nonguaranteed tax-exempt debt that is not constrained by constitutional and statutory restrictions. In fact, their lack of independent taxing authority makes them ideal instruments for this purpose.

As noted by E. J. Rossant in the foreword to a book on government corporations (Walsh [1978], xi):

It was about ten years ago that the trustees of the Twentieth Century Fund first took note of a proliferation of public authorities and public corporations in the New York metropolitan area. Further examination revealed that the phenomenon was not merely local but statewide and even nationwide. State and local governments were resorting to the authority device to perform an increasing number of important functions, including regional transportation development, housing development, natural resource management, and economic development.

On Behalf of Issuers: Nonprofit Organizations

An early decision of the U.S. Supreme Court predating the enactment of the Internal Revenue Code, *Dartmouth College v. Woodward* (17 U.S. 518 [1819]), confirmed the legality of government support for charitable organizations that were providing services to the public. The original Internal Revenue Code, in conformance with this principle, exempted from taxation virtually the same organizations now included under section 501(c)(3). In addition to their tax-exempt status, these institutions were permitted to receive the benefits of tax-exempt bonds.

In theory, the 366,071 (in 1985) nonprofit organizations that qualify as 501(c)(3)s are potential users of tax-exempt bonds, although it is likely that the vast majority never use the privilege (Internal Revenue Service 1985). A 501(c)(3) organization must achieve either political subdivision or "on behalf of" status in order to be the issuer of tax-exempt bonds. In practice, due to the specialized expertise necessary to bring bonds to market, bonds to benefit 501(c)(3) organizations are usually issued through a constituted authority or corporation created by a state or one of its political subdivisions. The actual procedures vary from state to state, depending upon each state's constitutional and statutory requirements. Some states form different agencies to issue bonds for different functions—one for nonprofit organizations in the health care area, one for the education area, one for libraries, etc. Other states form fewer agencies or authorities to issue bonds for nonprofits covering a variety of functional areas.

Issuers' and Private Users' Benefits

The benefits to issuers and private users are determined primarily by the volume of tax-exempt bonds issued each year and prevailing interest rates. The dollar volume of long-term debt from 1970 to 1988 is presented in table 4.7, column 2. Volume increased from $17.8 billion in 1970 to a high of $204 billion in 1985, an average annual rate of growth of 14.6 percent. The Deficit Reduction Act of 1984 and the Tax Reform Act of 1986 reversed this trend, and bond volume declined to $150.9 billion in 1986 and $105.5 billion in 1987, bringing the 22-year annual average growth rate down to a still-robust 9.7 percent. Volume rose in 1988 to $117.0 billion.

A substantial portion of this volume comes from refundings of outstanding bond issues, which add relatively little to interest savings because they replace other issues.[15] Column 3 subtracts refundings to obtain the volume of new long-term bond issues. Column 4 presents the spread between the interest rate paid on Aa-rated corporate and tax-exempt bonds. Column 5 contains estimates of the present value of the interest savings over the liftime of the bonds issued in that year to state and local taxpayers and to private businesses and individuals who managed to obtain access to tax-exempt financing. The estimates assume that, in the absence of tax-exempt financing, all the bonds would have been issued at the taxable interest rates prevailing in that year and that the average maturity of every bond issue is 17.5 years. The state and local social discount rate is assumed to be 80 percent of the tax-exempt borrowing rate.[16]

The numbers in column 5 represent the difference between interest cost of the bond volume in column 3 issued at taxable interest rates and the interest cost of this bond volume issued at tax-exempt rates, discounted at the social discount rate. The magnitude of the interest

Table 4.7 PRESENT VALUE OF INTEREST SAVINGS TO MATURITY ON EACH
YEAR'S LONG-TERM TAX-EXEMPT BOND VOLUME, 1970–88
($ MILLIONS)

Year	Long-term Volume ($)	Long-term New Issues ($)	Yield Spread (%)	Interest Savings to Maturity ($)
1970	17,762	17,706	2.04	4,148
1971	24,370	23,917	2.4?	6,647
1972	22,941	21,072	2.29	5,621
1973	22,953	21,718	2.57	6,410
1974	22,824	22,242	2.80	7,152
1975	29,326	28,392	2.40	7,826
1976	33,845	30,330	2.63	9,161
1977	45,060	35,473	2.85	11,610
1978	46,215	36,931	3.24	13,742
1979	42,261	40,389	3.82	17,719
1980	47,133	45,484	4.44	23,193
1981	46,134	44,942	3.86	19,923
1982	77,179	73,135	3.10	26,037
1983	83,348	70,300	3.22	25,997
1984	101,882	90,492	3.43	35,646
1985	204,281	146,414	2.89	48,595
1986	150,972	94,909	2.31	25,178
1987	105,523	67,033	2.29	17,629
1988	117,011	80,420	2.45	22,628

Sources: Tables 4.1–4.3 and author's calculations.
Note: Interest savings—present value in the year issued of the interest savings over
the life of new-issue bonds. Assumes 17.5-year average maturity, Aa yield spread,
and a state and local social discount rate equal to 80 percent of the tax-exempt rate.

savings is driven by bond volume, the level of interest rates, and the
yield spread. For example, the 44 percent interest cost increase in
1985 was attributable primarily to the 62 percent volume increase
and to a small reduction in the social discount rate caused by a 10
percent decrease in the tax-exempt yield (see table 4.3). These effects
swamped the influence of a yield spread that fell from 3.43 to 2.89
percentage points. In contrast, interest costs in 1981 decreased by
more than 26 percent, even though new-issue bond volume decreased by only 1 percent. The decrease is attributable to a 13 percent
decrease in the yield spread and to the higher social discount rate
caused by a 35 percent increase in the tax-exempt yield (see table
4.3). The present value of interest savings on tax-exempt bonds issued in 1988 exceeds $21 billion. Clearly, the tax exemption is worth
a considerable amount to state and local taxpayers and to private

businesses and individuals who can take advantage of conduit financing.

It is important here to emphasize the difference between the estimates in tables 4.4 and 4.7. The estimates in table 4.4 represent the federal government's revenue loss (the cost to federal taxpayers) on all bonds outstanding at a specific time, calculated as this outstanding stock times the taxable interest rate times the average marginal tax rate of bondholders. The estimates in table 4.7 are the interest savings over the life of the bonds (the benefits to state and local taxpayers and private users of the bonds) issued in any given year, and are calculated as just described. The interest savings have a different pattern over time and are considerably higher than the revenue loss estimates for several reasons: they depend upon annual volume, which changes more rapidly than does the outstanding stock of bonds; the interest savings are not reduced by the marginal tax rate of taxpayers; and the social discount rate is assumed to be lower than the market discount rate.

MUNICIPAL FINANCE INDUSTRY AND ISSUANCE COSTS

Many people in the financial services industry make their living by providing services that facilitate the bringing together of the suppliers of bonds (issuers) and the purchasers of bonds (investors). The compensation received by these providers is known as issuance costs, and consists of fees paid to underwriters, financial advisers, bond counsel, credit rating agencies, paying agents, accountants, printers, and advertisers. This section discusses the first four of these providers and provides some data about the magnitude of their fees. The section also discusses the increasingly important role of bond insurers, whose fees are not at this time considered part of issuance costs.

Underwriters

Many municipal bond issues are purchased directly by commercial banks for their own or a small consortium of correspondents' portfolios, particularly in the case of small lots issued by small governmental units. But the great bulk of the bond volume is issued in amounts too large for private placement, and these issues are usually purchased by investment bankers, often grouped together in syndicates, for resale to individuals and institutional investors.

These purchases may be either competitive or negotiated. In a competitive sale (often required by state law for GO issues), the issuer invites the underwriting community (usually several underwriting syndicates) to make bids to purchase the bonds at an interest cost based on their judgment of market conditions. The issuer chooses the most attractive offer. The syndicate then attempts to resell the bonds, and its profit depends upon how accurate it was in forecasting market conditions. The competition among underwriters should produce the lowest underwriting fees. In 1988, $21.2 billion of bonds were issued competitively.

For a negotiated sale, often the underwriting choice for lesser-known issuers or for very complicated issues, the issuer chooses an underwriting syndicate to work with, usually after formal presentations from many groups. The underwriter not only attempts to produce the lowest interest cost on the bond issue but also performs many other functions for the issuer in helping to structure the issue. The underwriter has control of the issue, and may choose to market the issue entirely by itself or sell off part of the issue to other underwriters. In 1988, negotiated long-term bonds totaled $95.7 billion. The negotiated sale allows more flexibility in timing to conform to market conditions.

The underwriter's fees are dependent upon the underwriter's spread, which is the difference between the price at which the underwriter sells the bonds to investors and the price it pays the issuer for the bonds. Estimates from a survey conducted by the Financial Markets Research Center (FMRC, 1989), State University of New York, indicate that in 1988 underwriter's spread was the largest component of issuance cost, ranging from 48.3 percent of total issuance costs for issues of $5 million or less to 87.6 percent for issues of $75 million or more. Table 4.8 presents the cost of underwriter's spread in dollars and as a percentage of issue size for 1988. Underwriter's spread increased from an average of $35,000 on issues of $5 million or less to an average of $1.96 million on issues of $75 million or more. As a percentage of issue size, underwriter's spread declined from 1.31 percent to 0.99 percent.

Financial Advisers

The decision to issue a bond requires many decisions, decisions that often depend upon information that the issuers' employees are poorly

Table 4.8 COMPONENTS OF ISSUANCE COST, IN DOLLARS AND
PERCENTAGES OF BOND PROCEEDS, 1988

	Size of Bond Issue ($ millions)					
	$5 or Less	$5 to $10	$10 to $25	$25 to $50	$50 to $75	$75 or More
Underwriter's spread						
$ thousands	35.4	83.4	180.9	362.5	560.2	1962.5
% bond proceeds	1.31	1.25	1.06	1.03	0.92	0.90
Financial adviser						
$ thousands	14.3	21.8	32.9	29.9	32.1	63.5
% bond proceeds	0.63	0.31	0.02	0.09	0.05	0.04
Bond counsel						
$ thousands	11.5	17.9	37.2	59.2	56.6	81.9
% bond proceeds	0.47	0.24	0.04	0.16	0.09	0.06
Moody's rating						
$ thousands	3.4	5.2	6.8	8.3	11.5	15.8
% bond proceeeds	0.15	0.07	0.04	0.02	0.02	0.01
Standard & Poor's rating						
$ thousands	4.3	5.7	6.9	9.4	10.6	15.2
% bond proceeds	0.16	0.08	0.04	0.03	0.02	0.01

Source: Financial Markets Research Center (1989), exhibit 3.
Note: Components of issuance cost not shown include independent audit, notice of
sale and official statement, and other items.

prepared to provide, particularly among the smaller issuers. Financial advisers are frequently hired to provide this expert advice.

A project financed with revenue bonds usually requires both an engineering report and a financial feasibility study to project the revenue stream and how this stream may vary with the future course of the economy. The terms of the bond must be determined, including the nominal interest rate, the maturities and debt payment schedule, date of sale, and special provisions such as calls. Special provisions may need to be incorporated to increase the attractiveness of the instrument to a particular segment of the potential pool of purchasers. Many of these decisions depend upon thorough knowlege of those groups who purchase tax-exempt bonds and upon the ability forecast the future course of interest rates and the economy in general.

Table 4.8 also presents the cost of financial adviser fees in dollars and as a percentage of issue size. Financial adviser fees increased from an average of $14,300 on issues of $5 million or less to an average of $93,500 on issues of $75 million or more. As a percentage of issue size, the fees declined from 0.63 percent to 0.04 percent.

Bond Lawyers

The attractiveness of tax-exempt bonds as a financial asset is almost entirely dependent upon qualification for tax exemption. It is the responsibility of bond lawyers to certify that the bonds conform to the various state and federal laws on tax exemption, securities laws, and any other laws that may affect the legality of the bond issue, both in terms of the ability of state and local governments to issue the bonds and the ability of purchasers in the states to purchase the bonds.

Bond counsel is the term usually given to those bond lawyers who must render opinions on tax exemption. At the federal level, this means ensuring that the conditions of issuance satisfy the relevant sections of the Internal Revenue Code, the regulations pertaining to the Code, and a variety of other United States statutes that lie outside the tax Code. In addition, all states and some local governments stipulate a variety of constitutional and statutory requirements that must be fulfilled before these debt obligations can legally be considered enforcable obligations of the issuing governments.

The underwriter's counsel performs a different function. The underwriter is primarily interested in being able to market the bonds it has just purchased from the governmental issuer to a variety of investors interested primarily in receiving tax-exempt income. The bond counsel has certified that the bonds meet federal and state law regarding tax exemption. In addition, underwriter's counsel must make certain of compliance with Securities and Exchange Commission (SEC) rule 15c2-12 (adopted in June 1989), which imposes disclosure requirements on underwriters of issues in excess of $1 million (see the discussion in chapter 3). In addition, most states have a variety of laws and regulations regarding financial disclosure that must be satisfied by the issuers of a financial liability before commercial banks and other financial institutions, insurance companies, and trusts can purchase the liability. It is the responsibility of underwriter's counsel to provide an opinion certifying that financial disclosure is adequate to ensure the legal marketability of the instrument in any given state.

Table 4.8 shows that bond counsel fees varied from $11,500 on issues of $5 million or less to $81,900 on issues of $75 million or more. These costs represent a decreasing share of bond proceeds, ranging from 0.47 percent of the smallest issues to 0.06 percent of the largest issues.

Credit Rating Agencies

Issuers of most major bond offerings seek a rating of credit worthiness from one of the two major rating agencies, Moody's Investors Service or Standard & Poor's Corporation. Issuers of many of the largest offerings seek ratings from both agencies. A GO issue's rating depends upon numerous factors, including the economic and tax base of the issuing government, the professionalism and efficiency of its management, and its existing debt obligations. A revenue bond's rating depends upon the financial resources of the user of the bond proceeds. Thus, a revenue bond for a nonprofit hospital or a conduit bond for a private firm is rated according to the expected success of the hospital or the financial condition of the private firm, rather than according to the condition of the political subdivision that issued the bond or created the authority that issued the bond. An economic analysis is performed that encompasses the demand for the service to be provided, the costs and efficiency of the operator, and the degree of competition in the industry.

Table 4.8 presents the average rating fees for both Moody's and Standard and Poor's that were reported for the bonds in the FMRC sample. They exhibit the same pattern as the other issuance costs, increasing in dollar value by issue size and decreasing in percentage terms. The Moody's and Standard & Poor's ratings cost an average of $3,400 and $4,300, respectively, for the smallest issues and increased to $15,800 and $15,200, respectively, for the largest issues. These amounts represented 0.15 and 0.16 percent, respectively, of the smallest issues' bond proceeds and 0.01 percent of the largest issues' proceeds.

Bond Insurers

A bond insurer promises to pay principal and interest if the issuer of the debt is unable to fulfill its obligations. Bond insurance serves to reduce the interest costs of issuers, increase the security of investors, and improve the liquidity of the secondary market for municipal bonds. Most bond issues are not insured, and most that are insured are GOs. Four or five firms dominate the municipal bond insurance industry.

Total Issuance Costs

The object here is to generate a series on total issuance costs to get some idea of the financial returns to the financial services industry from the tax-exempt bond market. It is thus necessary to obtain an estimate of the average issuance cost per bond issue. Every bond issue does not use every financial service. For example, large issues may not use a financial adviser and small issues may not use a credit rating agency or underwriters. Since the cost reported for each of these services in table 4.8 is based upon only those issues that report using the service, adding the data across services would overstate average issuance costs.

The U.S. General Accounting Office (GAO) (1989, 20) reports that issuance costs on private-activity bonds (which are all revenue bonds) in 1985 ranged from 3.4 percent of bond proceeds on issues of $5 million or less to 2.2 percent on issues of $75 million or more. This is undoubtedly an overstatement of issuance costs for all types of bonds prior to 1987. The FMRC reports that issuance costs on revenue bonds issued in 1988 were at least 0.5 percent higher than on general obligation bonds (both competitive and negotiated). Applying this differential to the 1985 GAO data suggests that issuance costs on GO bonds in 1985 may have ranged from 2.9 percent to 1.7 percent. After averaging across size classes, total issuance costs presented in table 4.9 for years prior to 1987 are calculated using issuance costs of 2.7 percent for revenue bonds and 2.2 percent for GO bonds.

After 1986, issuance costs paid out of tax-exempt bond proceeds were restricted by law to 2 percent of bond proceeds.[17] The FMRC data report that the 1988 issues reporting expenses for underwriter's spread had total issuance costs ranging from 1.13 percent of bond proceeds on the smallest issues to 2.71 percent on the largest issues. This issuance cost decline is consistent with the observed decrease in underwriter's spreads, the major component of issuance costs, from about $25 per thousand of bond proceeds in 1982 to about $16 in 1988 (U.S. General Accounting Office 1989, 24). Based upon this information, the estimates in table 4.9 for post-1986 assume average issuance costs of 1.8 percent.

The 1965–85 period was, of course, a time of rapidly increasing bond supply that strained the capacity of the market makers—fertile conditions for rising fees in parts of the financial services industry. Accordingly, total issuance costs climbed fairly steadily, reaching a peak of $5.2 billion in 1985 when bond volume mushroomed in anticipation of the Tax Reform Act of 1986. The situation has now

Table 4.9 ESTIMATED TOTAL ISSUANCE COSTS ON LONG-TERM TAX-
EXEMPT DEBT, 1965–88 ($ MILLIONS)

Year	Issuance Costs	Year	Issuance Costs
1965	262	1977	1,127
1966	264	1978	1,158
1967	340	1979	1,078
1968	394	1980	1,191
1969	269	1981	1,176
1970	421	1982	1,967
1971	577	1983	2,137
1972	549	1984	2,613
1973	556	1985	5,239
1974	551	1986	3,848
1975	717	1987	1,899
1976	829	1988	2,106

Sources: Table 4.3 and author's calculations.
Note: Prior to 1987, assumes issuance costs were 2.7 percent of bond proceeds for revenue bonds and 2.2 percent for GOs; after 1986, assumes 1.8 percent for all bonds. See text for detailed explanation.

changed, as the decreased volume from the 1986 act left the industry with excess capacity. Underwriters and bond lawyers have been leaving the business, and issuance costs have apparently declined to an average level below the 2 percent ceiling imposed by the 1986 act on private-activity and nonprofit bonds. Total issuance costs fell to $1.9 billion in 1987, but have rebounded above $2.1 billion in 1988 with the recovery in bond volume. Even at this lower level of volume, the financial stakes are sizable. This is a large market that was considerably larger not long ago. It should come as no surprise that its participants lobby the federal government for minimal restrictions on the tax-exempt bond market.

Total Issuance Cost Compared to Present Value of Interest Savings

A comparison of the issuance costs on each year's long-term bond volume from table 4.9 with the present value of beneficiaries' interest savings to maturity on each year's new-issue long-term bond volume from table 4.7 provides some idea of how the federal government's costs are distributed among market participants.[18] In figure 4.1, the ratio of issuance costs to interest savings for bonds issued in a year ranges from a low of 5.1 percent in 1980 to a high of 15.3 percent in 1986. The average for the 19-year period is 9.3 percent.

Figure 4.1 RATIO OF TOTAL ISSUANCE COSTS TO PRESENT VALUE OF
INTEREST SAVINGS ON NEW LONG-TERM BOND ISSUES, 1970–88

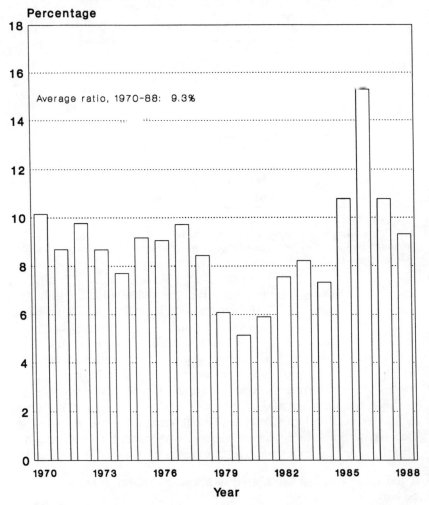

Sources: Tables 4.7 and 4.9.

INVESTORS

Tax-exempt bonds are purchased primarily by households, commercial banks, property and casualty insurance companies, and open-
end bond funds. All of these investors are motivated primarily by
the tax-exempt interest. These investors tend to move in and out of

the municipal bond market as their need for sheltering income from taxation rises and falls and the tax treatment of the interest income changes.

The first panel of table 4.10 displays the share of bonds outstanding held by these investors for five-year intervals from 1965 to 1985 and for 1986 through 1988. The second panel displays the change in dollar value of debt holdings for the last three years in the table. Notable in these data is the decline of the share held by commercial banks since the Tax Reform Act of 1986 (note the large decrease of almost $30 billion per year in their net holdings in 1986, 1987, and $21.1 billion in 1988), the increase in the share held by households starting in 1986 (from 31.6 percent in 1986 to 39.8 percent in 1988), the rise of the bond funds (money market and mutual funds) from a zero percent share in 1965 to 19.0 percent share in 1988 (essentially surrogates for household holdings), and the relative stability of the property and casualty insurance companies' share. Although these property and casualty insurance companies are now at their historical share of holdings, they may soon find themselves buying less

Table 4.10 INVESTORS' SHARES OF OUTSTANDING TAX-EXEMPT BONDS, 1965–88, AND CHANGES IN INVESTORS' HOLDINGS SINCE TAX REFORM ACT

Share of Total Debt Outstanding

Year	Total Debt Outstanding ($ billion)	Household	Commercial Banks	Property and Casualty Insurance	Mutual and Money Market Funds
1965	100.3	36.3%	38.7%	11.3%	0.0%
1970	144.4	31.9%	48.6%	11.8%	0.0%
1975	223.8	30.4%	46.0%	14.9%	0.0%
1980	350.3	24.8%	42.6%	23.0%	1.8%
1985	658.4	33.9%	35.1%	13.2%	10.6%
1986	689.2	31.6%	29.4%	13.3%	18.7%
1987	723.7	39.0%	24.0%	13.1%	18.3%
1988	760.0	39.8%	20.1%	15.6%	19.0%

Change in Total Debt and Net Holdings ($ billions)

1986	30.8	− 16.4	− 28.5	15.7	59.3
1987	34.5	43	− 29.1	23.8	3.1
1988	36.3	20.5	− 21.1	24.3	12.2

Source: Federal Reserve System (1988).
Note: Other holders of tax-exempt debt and their share of the outstanding stock in 1988 are: nonfinancial corporate business—1.6%; state and local governments—1.4%; savings and loan & mutual savings banks—0.4%; life insurance companies—1.5%; and brokers and dealers—1.0%.

as the alternative minimum tax is increased (Davie 1989). In short, the market for municipals is becoming increasingly dominated by direct holdings of households and their holdings in the bond funds.

INTEREST GROUPS

One of the fastest growing industries in Washington, D.C., is the group that keeps track of the federal government's activity and attempts to influence the course of that activity. This industry is usually referred to as *government relations offices* and/or *lobbyists*. *Interest groups* is another name frequently attached to such organizations. The municipal bond industry is by no means short of such representation.

Issuers' Groups

The state and local governments have a host of organizations representing their interests. The most visible of these groups on tax-exempt bond issues is the Government Finance Officers Association (GFOA), which represents the interests of cities and towns on financial matters. The National League of Cities is also very active in this area, although it relies on the GFOA for much of its technical bond support. The National Association of State Treasurers has become actively involved in the federal legislative process, and has been the moving force behind the effort to provide constitutional protection from federal taxation of interest income on tax-exempt bonds. The National Association of State Budget Officers and the National Governors' Association are both active supporters of tax-exempt bonds on behalf of the state governors. The counties have weighed in through their organization, the National Association of Counties. Less continually involved in the bond issue are the National Conference of State Legislatures, on behalf of state legislatures, and the United States Conference of Mayors, on behalf of the cities.

These state and local-funded groups have not spoken with a uniform voice on the tax-exempt bond market. Some groups have been supportive of some federal efforts to restrict the use of bond proceeds for certain types of private activities, while others have asserted the inalienable right of state and local officials to determine all questions of eligibility. In addition, many cities and states retain private lawyers and public relations or lobbying firms to represent their interests in Washington whenever tax-exempt bonds become an issue. For example, a city desiring to build a sports stadium may, in the past, have hired a law firm to present its case to the appropriate congressional audience.

Activity or Industry Groups

A second type of tax-exempt bond support group clusters about bonds for certain types of activities and industries. For example, the National Council of State Housing Finance Agencies and the Association of Local Housing Finance Agencies are aggressive supporters of bonds for multifamily rental housing. The Council of Industrial Development Bond Issuers is an active proponent of bonds for the purpose of economic development. The National Association of Housing and Redevelopment Officials is supportive of both housing and economic development activities. The American Public Power Association is interested in tax-exempt bonds for government owned electric utilities. Various nonprofit groups are vitally interested in maintaining the exemption for 501(c)(3) entities.

Finance Groups

The finance part of the industry has been very active in support of most types of tax-exempt bonds, regardless of activity, through the work of the Public Securities Association, which is funded by the finance industry. In addition, the bond lawyers are represented by the National Association of Bond Lawyers and the bond lawyers subcommittee of the American Bar Association. Bond insurers have recently formed the Association of Financial Guarantors.

Notes

1. An alternative approach would be to consider the market in terms of the demand for and supply of loanable funds. In this context, the issuers of bonds would be demanding credit from savers and would be on the demand side of the market, and the buyers of bonds would be supplying savings to the state and local sector and would be on the supply side of the market.

2. "While notes are generally regarded as short-term obligations and many municipal credit analysts will label any tax-exempt security with a maturity of one year or less as a note, there is no clear industry-wide consensus as to how long an obligation can

remain outstanding and still be classified as a note. A number of states have statutes which define permitted length of maturity. At Moody's, however, the method of payment and purpose are equally or even more important criteria than length of maturity" (Moody's Investors Service 1987, 18).

3. Distinctions are drawn between bonds issued by jurisdictions with access to a fully developed tax base and those issued by jurisdictions whose tax base is limited to a specified tax source or maximum tax rate. these are both general obligation bonds (GOs) in the sense that each jurisdiction's full taxing powers back the bonds. In addition, bonds secured by a special tax or fee, but in case of inadequate revenue also secured by full faith and credit, are GOs. See Moak (1970) and Moody's Investors Service (1987)

4. These examples of municipal leasing activity represent but a small part of the creative methods that have been devised to take advantage not only of tax-exempt financing but at times to also obtain some of the benefits from tax preferences available to the private sector in the form of accelerated depreciation and the investment tax credit. These financing arrangements have been referred to at various times as the true lease, tax-exempt lease, lease-purchase agreement, sale-leaseback, leveraged lease, leveraged sale-leaseback, and service contracts. These techniques had several advantages compared to long-term debt financing: not subject to debt ceilings or voter approval, avoidance of some issuance costs associated with bond issuance (e.g., legal fees and preparation of official statements), and flexible maturity for expensive but short-lived assets (e.g., automobiles and other equipment). For a brief discussion of these techniques, see Petersen and Forbes (1985), pp., 31–33. More comprehensive coverage is available in Vogt and Cole (1983).

5. Comparisons are sometimes made between the yields on tax-exempt bonds and securities of the Federal government. Such comparisons are less than ideal for several reasons. When trying to identify the influence of differential taxation on tax-exempt yields, part of the observed yield differential would reflect a risk differential because the Treasury security is inherently a less risky asset than is a tax-exempt bond. And the yield on Treasury securities was greatly influenced in the 1980s by its attractiveness to foreign investors.

6. It is not true, of course, that the municipal purchaser's preferred alternative is always a taxable bond. There exists an entire range of financial and real assets with different yield, risk, and degree of preferential taxation. The decision about preferred alternatives is critical to estimates of the revenue loss from tax-exempt bonds. For a discussion of this issue, see Galper and Toder (1981) and Kormendi and Nagle (1981).

7. These estimates are derived by summing the revenue loss estimates for each activity listed in the tax expenditures budget. Technically, this is incorrect because each activity's revenue loss is calculated in isolation, and there are interaction effects (Neubig 1989). Nonetheless, without an estimate of the interaction effects' impact on revenue loss, the summing employed here provides the best available order of magnitude.

8. See Kenyon (1989) for a summary of the controversy over revenue estimation for tax-exempt bonds.

9. This does not mean that the estimates assume that the people who held tax-exempt debt now hold taxable debt. Rather, it is assumed that the former holders of tax-exempt bonds switch to somewhat less preferentially (partially) taxed assets, whereas some of the former holders of these partially taxed assets switch to the newly created fully taxed debt. Thus, the estimates do account for revenue changes attributable to a lower average marginal tax rate.

10. The argument can get even more subtle. Many jurisdictions continue to finance some public capital facilities that are eligible for tax-exempt debt financing with tax revenue. They could easily increase their proportion of debt financing for these ac-

tivities and use the tax financing for the facilities that have been ruled ineligible for tax-exempt financing. Kenyon (1989, 28) discusses this possibility in the context of publicly owned utilities.

11. This is not to say that general governmental units do not issue revenue bonds, for they do. But for a variety of reasons, including state constitutional and statutory restrictions, they are far more likely to create a special district to issue this type of debt.

12. The education special districts, which experienced a decrease of 30.1 percent, are primarily school building authorities enmeshed in the consolidation movement of the nation's public schools.

13. These authorities must satisfy six criteria. They must be: authorized by specific state statute; for a public purpose; and a governing body controlled by political subdivision. They must have power to acquire, lease, and sell property and issue bonds. Their earnings cannot benefit private persons. And titles to bond-financed property must revert to the political subdivision upon dissolution.

14. These corporations must meet five criteria: they must be for public purposes and not organized for profit; their earnings must not benefit private persons; the political entity must have an interest in the corporation while the debt is outstanding and must obtain full legal title to the property when the debt is retired; and the political subdivision must have approved its bond issue.

15. Advance refundings would, of course, increase interest costs during the relatively brief period prior to retirement of the original issue being advance refunded.

16. Interest savings are overstated because, in fact, all these bonds would not be issued if taxpayers or private users had to pay taxable bond rates. Clark and Neubig (1984) and Auten and Chung (1988) reported the average maturity of private-activity bonds in 1983 and 1986 to be 17.5 years. The issue of the appropriate social discount rate has long been controversial. For a discussion of whether a discount rate lower than the state and local borrowing rate should be used, see Lind (1982).

17. The 1986 act includes the following items as part of the 2 percent limit on issuance costs: underwriter's spread; counsel fees; financial adviser fees; rating agency fees; trustee fees; paying agent and certifying and authenticating agent fees; accountant fees; printing costs; costs of the public approval process; and costs of engineering and feasibility studies. Bond insurance premiums and other credit enhancement fees are not counted as issuance costs subject to the 2 percent limit.

18. The denominator of this ratio includes the issuance costs of refunding issues. The numerator does not include the interest savings on refunding issues. It is not clear whether this biases the results, because it is not clear whether the refunding issue's interest savings would be larger or smaller than the interest savings on the retired bond issue. This would depend primarily on the yield spread applicable to the two bond issues. Refunding issues were unusually large shares of the market in 1976–78 and 1985–88.

Part Two

TAX-EXEMPT BONDS AND ECONOMIC POLICY

Chapter Five

INTERGOVERNMENTAL FISCAL
RELATIONS

Perhaps the policy area affected most by tax-exempt bond legislation is intergovernmental relations. The federal revenue loss from municipal bonds ($20.9 billion in 1989, from table 4.4) amounted to 12 percent of total federal intergovernmental assistance; and an even more impressive 20 percent if grants-in-aid designated for pass-through to individuals (e.g., Medicaid and Family Assistance Program) are removed from the intergovernmental assistance base. In contrast, tax-exempt bonds are a minor part of the federal income tax. The revenue loss from these bonds amounted to about 4 percent of income tax revenue in 1989.

The tax-exempt bond legislation of the last 20 years is best understood and evaluated if placed in the context of what was a very dynamic intergovernmental policy. This chapter provides that context. First, the economic rationales for federal intergovernmental assistance are described. Although there is theoretical support and guidance for a federal responsibility to provide financial assistance to state and local governments, the implementation of that responsibility is sufficiently subjective to allow for a wide range in the level and breadth of federal financial support. Second, the chapter briefly reviews the last 30 years of federal financial assistance, indicating that the range of support has varied. Intergovernmental policy has evolved from a relatively broad view of federal domestic program responsibilities in the 1960s and 1970s to an increasingly narrower view of those responsibilities. This changing philosophy has been accompanied by reductions in federal funding for all types of intergovernmental assistance. The chapter closes with discussions of three other issues that appear periodically in the intergovernmental policy debate: the extent to which the federal government can control the budget cost of the different types of intergovernmental assistance; the relative merits of each type of assistance in promoting economic efficiency, minimizing administrative costs, and maximizing the state and local subsidy per dollar of federal revenue cost; and the justification for restricting intergovernmental assistance to one factor of production—in particular, to tax-exempt bonds for capital.

THE ECONOMIC CASE FOR FEDERAL SUPPORT OF STATE-LOCAL SERVICES

As mentioned in the discussion of intergovernmental tax immunity in chapter 3, there are, or at least the federal government behaves as if there are, "good" and "bad" bonds. Although many claim that congressional disallowance of tax exemption for some activities represents ad hoc decisions motivated solely by federal revenue considerations, the last 20 years of federal efforts to define a public purpose or a private activity can be rationalized on the basis of public goods theory.

One hesitates to suggest that the political community in the nation's capital consciously incorporates the abstract theories of economists into their policy deliberations, but there is ample evidence that such abstractions occasionally seep by osmosis through the public policy membrane to make a small contribution to the decision-making process. For example, the tax-exempt bond legislation of the last 20 years seems a good illustration of Keynes's dictum: "The ideas of economists and political philosophers . . . are more powerful than is commonly understood. . . . Practical men, who believe themselves to be quite exempt from any intellectual influences, are usually the slaves of some defunct economist" (Keynes 1936).[1] The next section of the chapter cites instances when intergovernmental funding changes have been justified on the basis of the type of concepts presented in this section.

The intellectual parentage of federal efforts to limit use of tax-exempt bonds can be explained in two easy steps. First, one must understand the reasons why a state or local government intervenes in the operation of the private market and provides public services. Second, one must understand that federal financial support of this intervention requires that the benefits of the public services provided extend beyond the boundaries of the state or local government to federal taxpayers more generally.

The Decision to Intervene in Private Markets

A good that requires public provision is known as a pure public good and possesses two essential characteristics: (1) consumption cannot be denied to those unwilling to pay for the good (like national defense, which once provided can be consumed whether or not an individual pays for it); and (2) one person's consumption of the good does not prevent another person from using it (again, like national defense). If these characteristics are present, this pure public good cannot be provided at a profit, and the private sector has no incentive to produce an adequate amount of the good. The benefits from these goods are consumed collectively, or jointly.

Beyond producing pure public goods, there may be reasons for public intervention in the market for a good that is produced by the private sector. This is because the private sector may not produce the "correct" amount of the good at the "correct" price. There may be some costs (such as pollution from manufacturing activities) or benefits (such as good citizenship from education) associated with production of the good that are imposed on or enjoyed by society as a whole, and for which the decisions of private producers and consumers do not account. These external costs and benefits provide justification for some intervention by the public sector in the production and consumption decisions of the private sector. In effect, the "external" portion of the good's benefits or costs are consumed collectively, or jointly.

A special case of the private sector not producing the correct amount of a good is monopoly. By dint of being the sole producer of a good, either due to peculiar cost characteristics in an industry or coercive behavior, the monopolist maximizes its profits by producing less than the socially desirable amount of the good.[2] It is necessary for the public sector to regulate the monopolist's production to assure the socially desirable output.

One can conclude from this very brief discussion of the economic justification for public intervention in private markets that there exists a spectrum of, for want of a better word, "publicness." The public sector must decide how much of society's resources should be devoted to producing those goods all of whose benefits are consumed collectively; otherwise, the decision will be to produce none of them. In contrast, those goods, some of whose benefits are consumed collectively and some privately, will be produced by the private sector in some amount, but not necessarily in the socially desired quantities. In neither case does this mean the public sector must physically produce the good—it can contract with the private sector to produce the quantity agreed upon through the public decision-making process. It is this latter category of quasi-public goods that creates the difficult decisions about public intervention with tax-exempt bond financing.

The Importance of Spillovers

The decision about public sector intervention is further complicated in the context of the federal system of government in the United States. Since external costs and benefits exist with many privately produced goods and services, taxpayers in a state or a local region often judge public provision or financial support of private provision of a particular good to be justified. This does not, however, necessarily justify federal financial support for this state or local decision. In fact, from an economic perspective, federal support should only be provided to those state and local public services that are likely to be underprovided by state and local governments.

Such underprovision results from the spillover of benefits among jurisdictions. The sheer number of state and local political jurisdictions implies that any one jurisdiction is likely to have a geographic reach that fails to encompass all individuals and businesses who benefit from its public services. Thus, some of the collective consumption benefits spill over the border of a taxing jurisdiction, such as in the case of redistributive welfare programs, some educational services, or environmental projects. Collective consumption benefits from providing such goods exceed the benefits to taxpayers in the providing jurisdiction. Because many taxpayers are unlikely to be willing to pay for services received by nonresidents, it may be desirable for a higher level of government (which does receive tax payments from the spillover beneficiaries) to subsidize their consumption in order to induce state and local governments to provide the proper, that is, larger, amount.[3]

Thus, federal financial support of a state and local service is only justified if a portion of the benefits from state or local provision accrues to taxpayers who reside outside the state or local area providing the service.[4] If such spillovers do not exist, then federal financial support for state and local provision simply has the effect of redistributing income geographically, which may not be the intent of the subsidy.

In consequence, an economic case can be made for federal financial support of some state and local services and for the denial of such support to other state and local services. Some services make economic sense and are "good" because a federal interest is served. Others do not make economic sense and are "bad" because there is no justification for public provision of the service provided or because only local benefits are produced. Applying the reasoning to particular cases, however, raises a host of measurement problems that are addressed later in this book.

INTERGOVERNMENTAL ASSISTANCE: THE POLICY RECORD

Tax-exempt bonds are but one of several vehicles by which the federal government provides financial support to state and local governments. Grants-in-aid have long provided direct assistance both for current services and for particular types of public capital formation such as highways, mass transit facilities, water treatment plants, hospitals, and the like. Most major state and local taxes have also been deductible from federal taxable income. Deductibility provides indirect assistance to state and local governments: after-federal-tax incomes of taxpayers are increased and the after-federal-tax cost of a state and local tax dollar is decreased, both of which presumably make state and local taxpayers willing to pay additional state and local taxes. This section provides a brief overview of federal spending on the three types of aid and then discusses each one separately in more detail.

These three major types of federal assistance have been funded at very different levels. Table 5.1 provides data on federal government costs from 1980 to 1989. Grants-in-aid is by far the largest category of assistance. Grant-in-aid outlays rose from $91.5 billion in 1980 to an estimated $123.6 billion in 1989. The federal government exercises some control over the spending of grant monies, ranging from very specific purposes (categorical grants) to less specific purposes (block grants). General revenue sharing (GRS) is listed as a subcategory of grants-in-aid because the terms of its provision (for unspecified purposes) were very different from other grants-in-aid. GRS was the smallest type of assistance, and was eliminated during the decade. The foregone federal revenue from state and local tax deductibility was $20.5 billion in 1980, it rose above $32.2 billion in 1985, and declined to $27.7 billion after the Tax Reform Act of 1986 terminated sales tax deductibility, reduced tax rates, and lowered

Table 5.1 COST OF FEDERAL FINANCIAL ASSISTANCE TO STATE AND LOCAL
GOVERNMENTS, BY TYPE OF ASSISTANCE, CURRENT DOLLARS:
1980–89 ($ BILLIONS)

Type of Aid	1980	1985	1989	Percentage Change, 1980–89	
				Nominal	Real[a]
Grants-in-aid	91.5	105.9	123.6	35.1	−9.4
General revenue sharing	6.8	4.6	0.0		
Tax-exempt bonds	7.7	18.2	20.9	171.7	82.5
Tax deductibility	20.5	32.2	27.7	35.2	−9.3
Tax-exempt bond share of total costs (%)	6.1	11.3	12.1		

Sources: Office of Management and Budget (1989); and Office of Management and
Budget, *Special Analyses: Budget of the United States Government*, various years.
a. Real percentage changes are calculated using the deflator for "total outlays" that
appears in Office of Management and Budget, "Deflators for 1990 Budget," Jan. 4,
1989.

the proportion of taxpayers who itemize. The foregone revenue from
tax-exempt bonds was $7.7 billion in 1980 and rose to $20.9 billion
by 1989.

Several things are noteworthy in these data. First, the share of
federal intergovernmental assistance costs attributable to tax-exempt
bonds doubled over the decade, from 6.1 percent to 12.1 percent.
Second, foregone revenues from municipal bonds grew by 171.7
percent during the decade, compared to 35 percent increases for
grants-in-aid and tax deductibility. Third, when the substantial price
increases that occurred during the decade are taken into account,
bonds represent the only source of intergovernmental assistance that
experienced positive real growth, a very substantial 82.5 percent. In
contrast, grants-in-aid and deductibility both suffered negative real
growth of 9.4 and 9.3 percent, respectively.

Tax-Exempt Bonds

State and local use of tax-exempt bonds grew rapidly from the mid
1960s through the first half of this decade. The first panel of figure
5.1 traces the growth in long-term tax-exempt bond volume from
1965 to 1987. Volume rose from $11.1 billion in 1965 to a peak of
$204.3 billion in 1985, before falling to $98.7 billion by 1987. The
annual growth rate between 1965 and 1985 was a remarkable 14.6
percent.

Figure 5.1 LONG-TERM TAX-EXEMPT BOND VOLUME, 1965–87: ACTUAL AND ADJUSTED FOR INFLATION AND STATE-LOCAL SIZE

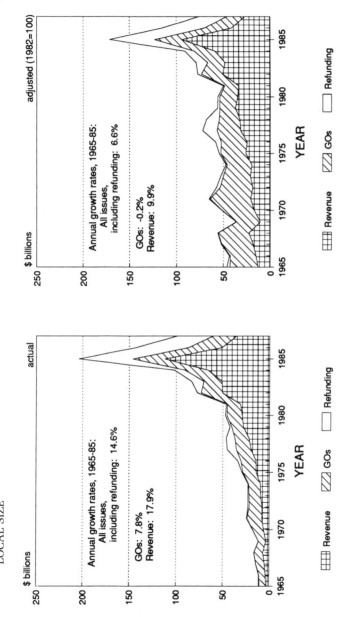

Source: *The Bond Buyer* (1988).

Note: Revenue and general obligation (GO) bonds are net of refunding issues.

This rapid growth did not escape the attention of Congress or Treasury Department officials. Aside from the revenue loss, concern was expressed that an increasing proportion of this federal financial assistance was being used for conduit financing, in which a state or local governmental entity issued bonds and passed the proceeds through to businesses and individuals for their private use. Witness President Ronald Reagan's concern when presenting his tax reform proposal in 1985:

Increasingly, however, State and local governments have used their tax-exempt financing privilege to obtain funds for use by nongovernmental persons .... The revenues lost as a result of tax-exempt nongovernmental bonds represent an indirect Federal subsidy program, based in the tax code, and thus significantly free of the scrutiny that attaches to direct Federal expenditures. In many cases, the issuer of nongovernmental bonds would not spend its own revenues to support the activities that are Federally subsidized through tax-exempt nongovernmental bonds. (Executive Office of the President 1985, 283)

Activities being financed included: student loans and mortgages for owner-occupied and multifamily rental housing; facilities for sports events, convention and trade show centers, airports, docks, wharves, parking, sewage and solid waste disposal, utility services, air and water pollution control, and industrial parks; and virtually any activity using a bond issue of less than $1 million for the acquisition, construction, or improvement of land or depreciable property.

Similar concerns were expressed by Congress when explaining the reasons for adoption of the bond provisions of the Tax Reform Act of 1986:

Congress was concerned with the large and increasing volume of tax-exempt bonds being issued under prior law .... Congress recognized the important cost savings that tax-exempt financing could provide for State and local governments, in a period marked by reductions in direct Federal expenditures for such purposes. To the extent possible, Congress desired to restrict tax-exempt financing for private activities without affecting the ability of State and local governments to issue bonds for traditional governmental purposes. (Joint Committee on Taxation 1987b, 1151)

The growth of private-use bonds is difficult to document because data on bond volume by private use was not collected until 1983. One way to get a rough approximation is to divide bond volume between its general obligation (GO) and revenue components. Almost all GO bonds are issued to support what has come to be termed

public purposes.[5] Almost all bonds issued to finance what have come
to be called private activities are issued in the revenue bond form,
although many activities considered to satisfy public purposes are
also financed with revenue bonds.[6]

The first panel of figure 5.1 also provides a rough idea of the
growing importance of revenue bonds, and thus to some extent of
bonds issued for private activities. Those bond issues (both GO and
revenue) that represent refundings of pre-existing bond issues (usually to take advantage of lower interest rates) are subtracted from
total volume, and the remaining bond volume used to finance new
capital facilities is divided between GOs and revenue bonds. These
original-issue revenue bonds (the checkered area in figure 5.1) grew
at an annual rate of 17.9 percent from 1965 to 1985, while original-
issue GOs (the lined area in the figure) grew at a much more modest
7.8 percent rate. Thus, the type of bond (revenue) issued for private
activities was growing much more rapidly than the type (GO) normally used to finance traditional public-purpose activities. It must,
however, be reiterated that some activities considered to be public
purpose are financed with revenue rather than GO bonds.

Of course, one would expect tax-exempt bond volume to grow in
order to accommodate growth in the size of the state and local sector
and the effect of inflation. For that reason, the second panel of figure
5.1 adjusts the bond volume data for the effects of inflation and
population growth. These adjustments cut the annual growth rate of
total volume by more than half, to a rate of 6.6 percent. Decomposing
this growth rate by type of bond shows that revenue bonds grew in
real terms at a 9.9 percent annual rate, whereas GOs actually had a
very small negative growth rate over the 20-year period of -0.2 percent. Clearly, these data indicate that revenue bonds were responsible for the expanding municipal debt market. And private activities
are invariably financed with revenue bonds.

An alternative and also less-than-precise view of the bond volume
issued for selected private activities is available for a shorter time
period, 1975 to 1986. The data in table 5.2 from 1975 to 1982 are
from the Joint Committee on Taxation (1983). The private-activity
volume data cover only seven private activities (but probably 90
percent of all private-activity bond volume): single-family housing,
multifamily housing, veterans' housing, small-issue industrial development, private hospitals, student loans, and pollution control.
These private activities accounted for an increasing share of total
long-term bond volume, rising from 20.6 percent in 1975 to 53.6
percent in 1980. The data in table 5.2 from 1983 to 1986 come from

Table 5.2 PRIVATE-ACTIVITY BOND VOLUME FOR SELECTED PRIVATE
ACTIVITIES, AS A PERCENTAGE OF TOTAL BOND VOLUME, 1975–86
($ BILLIONS)

	Private Activity ($)	Share of Total Volume (%)
1975	6.2	20.6
1976	8.4	24.0
1977	13.1	27.9
1978	15.8	32.2
1979	21.6	51.1
1980	29.4	53.6
1981	27.4	48.5
1982	44.0	51.7
1983	49.9	71.0
1984	65.8	72.7
1985	99.4	67.9
1986	17.2	20.0

Sources: Data for 1975–82, from Joint Committee on Taxation (1983); 1983–86 private-activity data from Auten and Chung (1988); 1983–86 new issue volume for share calculation from The Bond Buyer's (1989). Joint Committee data do not include data for such private activities as ports, airports, sports or convention facilities, industrial parks, and the local furnishing of electicity or gas. Auten and Chung data are comprehensive.

Auten and Chung (1988) and are derived from reports filed with the Treasury Department for every private-activity bond issue. These data include all activities classified by the tax law as private. By 1984, private-activity bond share of new issue long-term bond volume was 72.7 percent.

Congress reacted to the growth of revenue bonds for private activities by imposing a series of limitations on the issuance of bonds for private activities beginning with the Revenue and Expenditure Control Act of 1968 and culminating in the Tax Reform Act of 1986. These limitations included attempts to define what constituted a private-activity bond that would be taxable (based upon governmental/nongovernmental use of the proceeds and the presence of trade or business property as security backing for the bonds); a string of exceptions that allowed private-activity bonds issued for certain activities to remain tax exempt (refer back to the list of private activities enumerated at the beginning of this section); restrictions on arbitrage profits; and volume caps on those private-activity bonds that were favored with continued tax exemption.

By 1986, private-activity bond volume had fallen to 20 percent. This precipitous drop was attributable primarily to the acceleration of bond issuance in 1985 in anticipation of forthcoming restrictions (the original House bill was to be effective on December 31, 1985), and to some of the provisions adopted in the Tax Reform Act of 1986, particularly the volume cap. The revenue savings to the federal government from the 1986 act were estimated by the Joint Committee on Taxation to start at a mere $78 million in 1988 and to grow to $716 million by 1991.

Grants-in-Aid

The 1960s and 1970s saw the most extensive increases in federal assumption of domestic responsibilities since the depression years of the 1930s. As might be expected, this period was marked by substantial increases in the federal intergovernmental assistance devoted to implementing these responsibilities in a federal system of government. Grant outlays more than tripled during the 1960s, from $7.1 billion in 1961 to $24.1 billion in 1970; and almost quadrupled in the 1970s, to $91.5 billion in 1980. A brief review of the earlier period is helpful to an understanding of current policy.[7]

Approximately 160 grant programs were authorized in 1962, and another 379 in 1966. They included what is today the largest grant program, Medicaid, which was enacted in 1966 as an addition to the entitlement programs created by the Social Security Act of 1935. The 1960s also witnessed the first funding for compensatory education of the disadvantaged. In the 1970s, large increases were made primarily in grants to local governments for economic development, local public works, public service employment, and antirecession fiscal assistance.

Efforts were made in the 1970s to simplify the grant structure by replacing numerous categorical grants (for specified programs) with a general revenue-sharing grant and six special revenue-sharing programs. The General Revenue Sharing (GRS) program and three of the special revenue-sharing programs (community development, comprehensive employment and training, and law enforcement assistance) were enacted as block grants. Nonetheless, authorization continued for many of the categorical programs that were supposed to be replaced by these block grants.

The Nixon administration's efforts to reduce expenditures included an attempt to impound funds for some categorical programs, primarily for wastewater treatment and highway construction grants.

The Congressional Budget and Control Act of 1974, however, required the executive branch to ask Congress for permission to withhold appropriated funds. As a result, little progress was made in controlling grant outlays.

By 1979 both the Carter administration and Congress questioned the national benefit from the proliferation of grant programs. As a result, the first large cutbacks occurred that year: the elimination of the antirecession fiscal assistance and local public works programs; a reduction in wastewater treatment and public service employment grants; and discontinuance of the state portion of GRS and a refusal to adjust the nominal dollars in the local government portion of GRS for inflation.

At this point the Reagan administration rode in from the West with an agenda that included reassessment of federal responsibility for a broad range of domestic programs. Its conceptual crystal ball revealed that the federal government was providing financial support for a host of services that either should be provided by state and local governments or stripped of public support and returned to the private sector. The administration's New Federalism plan of 1981 sought to implement this philosophy, proposing increased reliance on states, local governments, and the private sector for the financing of domestic programs.

Although much of this proposed realignment of responsibilities between the states and the federal government did not take place, the decade of the 1980s was marked by a reduction in grants-in-aid funding and a change in the structure of grants-in-aid. This reduction in grants-in-aid funding is best understood in the context of the entire U.S. budget.

Total U.S. budget outlays expanded from $590.9 billion in 1980 to $1137.0 billion in 1989, an increase of 92.4 percent. When corrected for inflation, this increase is reduced to 29.1 percent. The allocation of this growing public budget was unevenly distributed among the major budget functions listed in table 5.3. The most rapidly growing portion of the budget during this period was the "net interest" category. The burgeoning deficit caused inflation-adjusted net interest payments to grow by 111.7 percent. The other major budget categories that exhibited real growth over this period were "national defense/international affairs" (41.3 percent) and "direct payments for individuals" (27.8 percent).

In contrast to these three categories, outlays for the other two major budget functions decreased in real terms. "Grants to state and local governments" increased in current dollars from $91.5 billion in 1980

Table 5.3 U.S. BUDGET OUTLAYS BY SELECTED CATEGORIES OF
EXPENDITURE: 1980–89, CURRENT DOLLARS ($ BILLIONS)

Category of Spending	1980	1985	1989	Percentage Change, 1980–89 Nominal %	Percentage Change, 1980–89 Real[a] %
Total U.S. budget outlays	590.9	946.3	1137.0	92.4	29.1
National defense/ international affairs	146.7	268.9	309.0	110.6	41.3
Direct payments for individuals	245.6	377.5	468.0	90.6	27.8
Interest (net)	52.5	129.4	165.7	215.6	111.7
Grants to state and local governments	91.5	105.9	123.6	35.1	− 9.4
For individuals	31.9	48.1	66.5	108.5	39.9
For states	59.6	57.8	57.1	− 4.2	− 35.7
All other federal outlays	54.6	64.6	70.7	29.5	− 13.1

Source: Office of Management and Budget (1989).
a. Real percentage increases are calculated using the deflator for "total outlays" in Office of Management and Budget, 1989, "Deflators for 1990 Budget," Jan. 4.

to $123.6 billion in 1989, while "all other federal outlays" increased over this period from $54.6 billion to $70.7 billion. When adjusted for inflation, these figures represent decreases of 9.4 percent for "grants to state and local governments" and 13.1 percent for "all other outlays."

A 9.4 percent reduction in real spending spread over a decade does not seem like a sea change in federal intergovernmental policy. But to appreciate fully the change in federal policy toward the state and local sector, the "grants to state and local governments" category must be broken down further. The Office of Management and Budget divides this category into two types: payments for state and local programs (labeled "for states" in the table), and payments for individuals (labeled "for individuals" in the table). This distinction emphasizes that some grants provide cash or in-kind benefits to identifiable individuals—through Medicaid and the Family Assistance Program, for example. Other grants provide funding for state and local programs that in a sense benefit all state and local taxpayers—such as highway construction and environmental cleanup programs or General Revenue Sharing.

The component of "grants to state and local governments" that is channeled to individuals contains transfer-type (pro-poor) activities of the Federal government that are similar to the nongrants category in table 5.3 called "direct payments for individuals." The primary difference between the transfer-type activities included in the "grants to state and local governments" category and those in the "direct payments" category is that, for one reason or another, the degree of financial and administrative responsibility varies between the levels of government.[8]

These two categories have, in fact, fared reasonably well in the 1980s. Table 5.3 shows that the "for individuals" componont of "grants to state and local governments" grew in constant dollars by 39.9 percent, compared to 27.8 percent for "direct payments for individuals." Thus, in a sense, the effort to evaluate changes in federal responsibility to provide financial support for state and local service provision should be based upon the "for states" component of the "grants to state and local governments" category in table 5.3.

This "for states" component in table 5.3 decreased in real terms by 35.7 percent. Clearly, the two grant components did not suffer uniformly during the 1980s. Those that represented the federal contribution for the needier members of society continued to grow in real terms. Those that represented federal payments for programs considered primarily to be state and local responsibilities experienced large negative real growth, a number whose magnitude suggests a serious redirection of intergovernmental policy.

Not only was the level of grants-in-aid reduced, but efforts were made to alter their structure.[9] Smaller categorical programs were merged into block grants. Direct payment of grant monies to local governments was largely eliminated, although some of the funding was rechanneled to the states. A federal commitment was made to provide a "safety net" (income maintenance and social services) and support for elementary and secondary education, but with increasing state participation. And transportation grants were increased while funds for other programs were reduced. As a result of all this activity, grant programs decreased from 534 in 1981 to 422 in 1987, with a corresponding increase in block grants from 4 to 13.[10] The Federal government seemed to be sweetening its reduced financial commitment with a greater willingness to allow state and local governments to utilize greater discretion in the allocation of grant monies.

State and Local Tax Deductibility

The major state and local nonbusiness taxes for general purposes—income, general sales, excises, and real and personal property—were deductible from the federal income tax base upon its adoption in 1913.[11] Two categories of state and local taxpayer payments were not allowed to be deducted: user charges such as those for sewer and water services, as well as special fees for the use of facilities, such as recreational and cultural facilities; and special assessments for property improvements, such as construction of sidewalk and drainage systems. Only two changes were made to these arrangements prior to the 1980s. The Revenue Act of 1964 eliminated the deduction for motor vehicle operators' license fees and state and local excise taxes, other than on gasoline. The Revenue Act of 1978 eliminated the deductibility of the gasoline excise tax. These changes were justified on the basis of removing encouragement for consumption of socially undesirable products (primarily cigarettes and alcohol), simplifying the tax structure, or acknowledging the essential nature of the tax as a user charge (motor vehicle license fees and gasoline excise taxes).[12]

Thus, while tax-exempt bonds and grants-in-aid have been the center of attention at the intergovernmental party, dancing every dance as it were, the big three general-purpose state and local taxes remained wallflowers until invited onto the dance floor in the mid-1980s. Just as the 1980s saw a decrease in grants-in-aid, so was the intergovernmental assistance provided through deductibility ultimately subjected to a cutback. The Reagan tax reform proposal of May 1985 suggested elimination of the deduction for all state and local taxes.

The deduction for State and local taxes may also be regarded as providing a subsidy to State and local governments, which are likely to find it somewhat easier to raise revenue because of the deduction. A general subsidy for spending by State and local governments can be justified only if the services which State and local governments provide have important spillover benefits to individuals in other communities. The existence of such benefits has not been documented. (Executive Office of the President 1985, 64)

Elimination of all deductible taxes was expected to generate between $33 and $40 billion revenue each year from 1987 to 1990. After considerable debate, the Tax Reform Act of 1986 terminated the deduction only for nonbusiness general sales taxes. Elimination of the sales tax deduction was expected to generate between $4.5 and $5.0 billion revenue per year from 1988 through 1991.

FEDERAL BUDGETARY CONTROL OF
INTERGOVERNMENTAL ASSISTANCE

The discussion here of the economic rationale for intergovernmental assistance suggests that there is a priori justification for denying federal financial support for every dollar of public service provided by state and local governments, because many of these services provide minimal or no benefits to federal taxpayers. If this is the case, it is desirable to put the decision about the budgetary cost of the subsidy in the hands of the federal government.

Grants-in-Aid

In this regard, financial support provided in the form of grants-in-aid is very different from the two tax subsidies. The major types of grants are specific (categorical), which facilitates federal conditions and control on state and local performance, and block, which increases the programmatic latitude of the recipients. More important for the purposes here, the grants may be open-ended or closed. If the federal government appropriates a given amount for a grant, and this amount determines the matching ratio of state-local funds, the grant is closed; the federal budgetary cost is fixed and controlled. If, however, the matching ratio is set and the federal contribution is determined by the amount of state and local spending, the grant is open-ended.[13]

Most federal grants have historically been closed, particularly those for the state and local programs portion of grants-in-aid (see table 5.3). The major exceptions have been the public assistance programs that have historically been open-ended, such as Medicaid and the Family Assistance Program that appear in the "for individuals" portion of grants-in-aid (see table 5.3). The uncertainty these open-ended grants impose on federal budget policy has been a source of considerable friction, and Congress has moved in recent years to control and cap these programs.

Tax-Exempt Bonds and Tax Deductibility

Tax-exempt bonds and state and local tax deductibility are, in effect, the equivalent of open-ended matching grants for the entire spectrum of state and local services. The federal government loses its ability to control its budget (defined as the sum of its direct expenditures and the tax revenues foregone from preferential treatment of some sources and uses of income). The federal government has attempted to deal with this problem for tax-exempt bonds by enacting a series of restrictive measures to control the types of services for which the exemption can be used and to cap the dollar volume of certain types of bonds that can be issued in any year. This suggests that it is possible, in principle, to tinker with the tax-exempt bond law and convert what amounts to an open-ended grant into a closed grant with budgetary control. The question remains, however, as to whether the Internal Revenue Service (IRS), whose primary responsibility is to collect revenue, is equipped to administer and enforce a host of laws and regulations whose purpose is to allocate scarce spending (the foregone revenue) among a plethora of claimants. This issue is discussed more fully in chapter 12.

EFFICIENCY OF INTERGOVERNMENTAL ASSISTANCE

The discussion to this point has focused on the cost of intergovernmental assistance to the federal government. Another issue appears in policy discussions of tax-exempt bonds—the contention that they are not a very efficient subsidy instrument. Care must be taken when using the term *efficient*, for it means different things to different people. To an economist, economic efficiency in this context means ensuring that intergovernmental assistance adjusts prices and marginal costs so that producers' and consumers' decisions allocate resources "efficiently." To a program manager, administrative efficiency means making certain that administrative costs are kept to a minimum. To others, *efficency* may mean transfer efficiency, whereby a subsidy is structured so that the greatest possible share of federal costs go to the intended recipients. Each of these "efficiencies" is discussed in turn.

Economic Efficiency

If the object of the federal government's intergovernmental assistance is correction of state and local underspending due to externalities and spillovers, spending is encouraged by lowering the cost of the underprovided services in proportion to the external benefits. Given these cost adjustments, economic efficiency is maximized by allowing state and local governments maximum flexibility to adjust to the change in relative prices by exercising their decentralized decision making.

The type of subsidy instrument should depend on how broadly based is the state and local underspending. If underspending is present in equal proportion·across all types of state and local programs, then unconstrained assistance such as revenue sharing, tax deductibility, and tax-exempt bonds may be appropriate. The choice among them ought to be based upon such considerations as the magnitude of the underspending, which, if it is not great from the federal perspective, might suggest revenue sharing (which imposes a limit) rather than tax deductibility or tax-exempt bonds (which are open-ended commitments); and whether the underspending is focused on a particular factor of production, which, if capital is the underutilized factor, might suggest tax-exempt bonds or a capital-constrained revenue-sharing program (the likelihood of capital underspending is discussed later in this chapter). If the underspending is specific to one or two functions, then a categorical grant or tax-exempt financing restricted to the relevant function may be considered, but tax deductibility is out.

Administrative Efficiency

When Congress creates intergovernmental assistance programs, it is establishing spending priorities in conformance with its own view of social objectives. Accomplishing these goals often requires fairly specific restrictions on how these dollars are to be spent and substantial administrative guidelines and reporting requirements to ensure compliance with federal objectives. The state and local perspective is different, stressing that needs and priorities vary greatly across the 50 states, and within the states across very different kinds of local governments. Restrictions and administrative guidelines reduce state and local officials' flexibility to take diverse needs into account when establishing spending priorities, and chew up dollars that could be spent on direct provision of public services.

Administrative costs are greatest for grants. Categorical aid, almost by definition, generally is accompanied by mandates to provide special services, reporting requirements to ensure compliance, and other provisions requiring minimum service levels or maintenance of effort. From the state and local perspective, categorical grants have high administrative costs. As for block grants, although claims have been made of an efficiency advantage (relative to categorical grants) of up to 25 percent, a more conservative figure offered by organizations representing the states is a block grant advantage relative to categorical grants of about 10 percent (Osbourn 1981). Additional but unspecified savings are generally ascribed to the even less restrictive General Revenue Sharing program (U.S. General Accounting Office 1982).

Administrative costs for tax deductibility and tax-exempt bonds are a largely unexplored area, but are almost surely considerably lower per dollar of foregone federal revenue than for any type of grant. The Internal Revenue Service does not disaggregate its administrative and enforcement costs by individual provisions that appear on form 1040, such as the itemized deduction for state and local taxes. Withheld state and local taxes are recorded on wage earners' W-2 forms, and the 1040 is computer checked at a very low cost per return. Undoubtedly, the administrative costs for tax deductibility are very small per dollar of foregone federal revenue compared to any type of grant.

Information on tax-exempt interest income did not even appear on tax returns until 1987. The IRS has relied primarily on private bond counsel for voluntary compliance with the tax-exempt bond laws, and its small enforcement effort has been reactive to external information received about abusive bond deals (this is discussed more thoroughly in chapter 12). The administrative costs for tax-exempt bonds are also likely to be very low per dollar of foregone revenue compared to any type of grant.

Transfer Efficiency

Tax-exempt bonds have long been plagued with the allegation that the federal government's revenue loss exceeds the reduction in state and local borrowing costs, thereby making bonds an inefficient method for transferring money from the federal to state and local governments. This is true, but its importance is overstated for two reasons. First, this "transfer inefficiency" was greatly reduced by the lowering of the marginal tax rate schedule that occurred in 1986. And, second, it is also true that grants-in-aid and state and local tax deductibility do not convert every dollar of grant or revenue loss into an increase in state and local budgets. This section begins by explaining the nature of this transfer inefficiency and its reduction that occurred in 1986.

A taxpayer with marginal tax rate t who can purchase a corporate (taxable) bond with an interest rate equal to r_c will earn an after-tax return equal to $r_c(1 - t)$. He or she will be indifferent between purchasing this corporate bond and a tax-exempt bond of equivalent risk yielding r_m, where $r_m = r_c(1 - t)$. In effect, the taxpayer has traded the higher yield on the corporate bond for the absence of tax on the interest income on the municipal bond. This implicit tax is $t = (r_c - r_m)/r_c$. The taxable bond yield foregone by the taxpayer $(r_c - r_m)$ just equals the tax revenue foregone (tr_c) by the federal government on the taxable bond yield.

If the marginal tax rate that clears the municipal bond market and establishes the differential between taxable and tax-exempt bond yields is equal to t_m, any bond purchaser whose marginal tax rate exceeds t_m $(t_x > t_m)$ saves taxes on foregone taxable bond income $(t_x r_c)$ that exceed the value of the foregone taxable bond yield. The taxpayer earns a windfall, that is, he or she receives a higher yield on the municipal bond than was necessary to induce him or her to purchase the bond. What this means is that the federal revenue loss $(t_x r_c)$ is greater than the reduced borrowing costs of state and local governments $(r_c - r_m)$.

This can be seen by comparing the federal revenue loss and the reduction in state and local borrowing costs, where t_m is the market clearing tax rate, t_x is the average marginal tax rate of municipal bondholders, and S is the stock of municipal debt:

$$t_x r_c S > t_m r_c S \qquad (5.1)$$

The federal revenue loss is on the left-hand side of the equation— the stock of municipal debt times the interest income the taxpayer would have earned in a taxable bond times the average tax rate of municipal bondholders. The value of the tax subsidy to state and local governments is on the right-hand side of the equation, and is calculated in the same way except that the relevant tax rate is that which clears the municipal bond market.[14]

The transfer efficiency of tax-exempt bonds is calculated by dividing the reduction in state and local borrowing costs by the federal revenue loss, which reduces to the ratio of t_m/t_x. It is not difficult to obtain a ballpark estimate for this ratio. Prior to the 1986 tax reform, individual tax rates ranged to 0.5 and the corporate rate to 0.46. Assuming the average household marginal tax rate of municipal bondholders was 0.38, and the household and corporate shares of municipal debt (from table 4.10) were 0.517 and 0.483, respectively, a weighted average tax rate of municipal bondholders was 0.42. If the market clearing rate was 0.24 (see the yield ratios in table 4.3), the transfer efficiency of municipal bonds prior to the 1986 tax reform was 0.57.

The 1986 tax reform reduced and flattened the individual progressive rate structure and reduced the corporate tax rate, eliminated the deductibility of bank interest expense for most municipal bond purchases, and instituted an alternative minimum tax on all corporate tax-exempt interest income. All of these changes acted to reduce the differential between t_x and t_m (some by decreasing the share of municipal bonds held in corporate portfolios). As a result, the transfer efficiency of tax-exempt bonds increased to about 0.80.[15] Thus, although tax reform may have had an adverse impact on the supply of bonds and damaged state and local claims to intergovernmental immunity, it did succeed in making the bonds a more attractive intergovernmental subsidy alternative to grants-in-aid.

I turn now to the second issue, a demonstration that none of the available subsidy instruments succeeds in transferring anywhere close to 100 percent of the federal cost to increased state and local services. The transfer efficiency of grants depends in some sense on how one defines the issue. If the objective is to provide dollars to state and local decision makers, by definition every dollar of federal grants goes to state and local governments as fiscal assistance. In this sense the transfer efficiency of grants-in-aid is 1. But this approach seems unnecessarily mechanical and ignores any state and local responses to the receipt of the grant dollars. Taking a broader perspective, the objective can be viewed as the increase of state and local spending.

This latter perspective acknowledges that the recipient government has the option of using the grant funds for the intended purpose or substituting the funds for state and local tax effort and reducing its own tax levies. Government is viewed as nothing but a veil for state and local taxpayers, who ultimately decide how to divide the federal funds between private and public consumption (between tax relief/debt reduction and public expenditure increases). The trade-off between these two options differs according to whether the structure of the grant program changes only taxpayer income (a grant not requiring matching funds) or also alters the relative prices of public and private consumption (a grant requiring matching funds).

An extensive literature investigates the extent to which state and local governments substitute grant dollars for their own tax effort. Excellent surveys of this literature have been done by Gramlich (1977), Inman (1979), and the U.S. Department of the Treasury (1985). Gramlich breaks grants into three categories: open-ended matching grants that affect taxpayer incomes and prices; closed-ended matching grants that affect taxpayer incomes and prices; and closed-ended lump-sum grants that affect only taxpayer incomes. The lump-sum grants, of which GRS was the primary example, experience the greatest proportion of grant dollars used for state and local tax reduction. Surprisingly, the proportion of GRS dollars siphoned off for tax relief was not nearly so great as consumer theory suggested it should be. If one takes the income elasticity of demand for public goods to be approximately 10 percent, and if taxpayers perceive the monetary consequences of GRS clearly through the governmental veil, tax reduction should have been about $0.90 on the dollar. But empirical estimates of tax reduction's share ranged from about $0.60 to more than $0.90, implying that the increase in state and local spending ranged somewhere between $0.40 and less than $0.10 per dollar.[16] This text uses a mid-range estimate of 0.20 for the transfer efficiency of GRS—about $0.20 of a lump-sum grant dollar is spent on providing state and local services and $0.80 is spent on tax relief.

Studies of open and closed-ended matching grants indicate, on average, a smaller proportion of substitution for tax reduction, with the proportion depending on the presence of effort-maintenance provisions (restrictions that attempt to prohibit substitution of state and local tax reduction for spending). Although there is no generally accepted number for the spending response, its magnitude has declined as more and more studies have been completed. Gramlich's 1982 study suggested that categorical grants with an average matching rate of 20 percent generated additional state and local spending of $0.38.[17] In other words, on the average, $0.62 of every grant dollar appears as a reduction in state and local spending.

The deductibility of state and local nonbusiness taxes from the federal income tax base provides financial assistance to state and local taxpayers in a very different way than does grants-in-aid. Deductibility reduces the after-federal-tax price (cost) of state and local taxpayers' tax dollar and increases their after-federal-tax income. Both the lower price and higher income cause taxpayers to desire a higher level of state and local services, and to increase their willingness to pay higher state and local taxes. The extent of this increase in state and local taxes and spending depends upon the sensitivity of itemizers' demand for public services to these changes in their tax price and income, and on itemizers' success in making the political process reflect their changes in demand. Thus, just as every dollar of federal grants-in-aid does not appear as an increase in the state and local budget, the effect of the deductibility subsidy on state and local spending is also less than federal revenue loss figures for deductibility that appear in table 5.1.

Early estimates of the transfer efficiency of tax deductibility were made by Noto and Zimmerman (1983) and Kenyon (1984). Noto and

Zimmerman used assumptions that tended to maximize the spending response: that the itemizer controlled the political decision on spending level; and that spending was responsive to price changes (a price elasticity of demand equal to −0.5). Using an early-1980s estimate of the itemizer's marginal tax rate of 0.34, deductibility reduced the price of a state and local tax dollar from $1.00 to $0.66, a 41 percent reduction in price. This implied a 20.5 percent increase on that portion of spending financed with deductible taxes. Thus, every dollar of state and local tax deductions cost the federal government $0.34 in revenue and raised state and local spending by $0.205. The transfer efficiency of tax deductibility was approximately 0.60; $0.40 of every dollar of federal revenue loss was not received by state and local governments. Thus, using very generous assumptions to maximize the state and local spending response, deductibility seems to fare well compared to grants-in-aid.

Deductibility's transfer efficiency worsened after the Tax Reform Act of 1986. Statutory tax rates were lowered, thereby lowering the price reduction on deductible taxes. And the percentage of taxpayers who itemize was reduced, thereby reducing the share of taxpayers who receive a price reduction. Both of these changes made taxpayers desire a lower level of public spending and taxation.[18] Incorporating these changes into the estimates reduces the transfer efficiency of deductibility.

This discussion assumes that itemizers' average marginal tax rate falls to 0.24, costing the federal government $0.24 for every dollar of deductible taxes. Now, however, relax the assumption that itemizers control the political process and allow nonitemizers to have an equal vote. If 60 percent of state and local taxpayers do not itemize (and have a tax price of 1.0 compared to 0.76 for itemizers), the weighted tax price for all taxpayers is 0.9. This implies a percentage price reduction of 10.0 percent, and an increase of spending financed with deductible taxes of 5.0 percent. Thus, every dollar of state and local tax deductions costs the federal government $0.24 in revenue and raises state and local spending by $0.05. The transfer efficiency of tax deductibility is approximately 0.21; $0.79 of every dollar of revenue loss is not received by state and local governments.

Comparable types of estimates have not been made for tax-exempt bonds. But surely the state and local sector's demand for capital formation is not perfectly elastic. Spending on capital formation is unlikely to have increased by the amount of the foregone federal tax revenue, and the 0.80 post-1986 tax-exempt bond transfer efficiency discussed earlier is obviously an overestimate. None of the subsidy instruments manages to translate every dollar of Federal cost into higher state and local public service spending.

A CAPITAL SUBSIDY AND FACTOR PRICE DISTORTION

Political acceptance that the economic justification (the spillover test) for federal subsidy of some state and local activities is satisfied is not equivalent to justification of subsidy provision via tax-exempt bonds. Although the focus of this book is not to question the tax exemption for municipal bonds (for which political support seems solid) but, rather, its use for certain activities (for which political support is sometimes weak), it is worth taking a moment to spell out the tenuous conceptual basis for this form of subsidy. In effect, the tax-exempt bond lowers the price of capital relative to the price of other factors of production such as labor and operating costs.[19] In public finance terms, the interest exemption appears to "distort" factor prices.

In the face of this distortion, can it make sense to provide financial support in the form of a capital subsidy for debt instruments? It might if capital services are underprovided relative to current services. One can muster several arguments for why state and local budgets might favor current services and underspend on capital formation, thereby rationalizing a subsidy such as tax-exempt bonds that alters the relative prices of state and local factors of production.

Electoral Pressures: A Bias for Current Spending?

The first possibility arises from the incentives facing state and local officials. These officials want to get reelected, and the electoral process may induce them to favor spending that produces immediate benefits to constituents. The only evidence of such a bias seems to be as a response to cyclical factors—many observers have noted that tightening of budgets tends to generate efforts to maintain current services in the short run by scrimping on capital replacement and maintenance (National Council on Public Works Improvement 1988). But a cyclical phenomenon such as this is not a basis for justifying a permanent structural subsidy for capital spending.

Does Mobility Create a Preference for Current Services?

Second, citizens in a mobile society may be reluctant to spend on long-lived assets at the local level because they expect to move before these assets produce benefits. Although it is undeniably true that U.S. society is extremely mobile, two other factors would have to occur for this to be an important factor. The time pattern of repayment on the bonds used to finance capital facilities would have to be accelerated relative to the time pattern of services provided by the capital facilities. This is certainly possible, as one indicator of a mismatch (but by no means a conclusive one)—bond maturity—is sometimes shorter than the actual productive life of the physical capital. But even if this were the case, citizens would have to be sufficiently sophisticated about the financial aspects of public capital formation to be aware of the mismatch.

Is There Capital Services Illusion?

Third, citizens may simply be unaware of the contribution capital spending makes to their consumption of current services. Such a result implies that taxpayers suffer from some sort of fiscal illusion, that is, that they do see the economic world clearly. The idea that people suffer from "money" illusion or "tax" illusion has a long history in the economics literature, so it is not outlandish to suggest that taxpayers may misperceive the relationship between capital spending in prior years and consumption of current services.

Do Capital Services Have More Spillovers?

And fourth, it may be that some capital services have a larger spill-over component than do current services, and are thus more likely to be underprovided. For example, access to such services as garbage collection and fire protection can be easily restricted to residents. But denying nonresidents access to such things as parks, libraries, and pollution abatement may entail prohibitively large transaction costs.

Any or all of these four factors could produce a tendency for the state and local sector to in effect use too high a discount rate when evaluating what some call infrastructure projects. If this were the case, a federal subsidy of capital goods acquired by state and local governments need not result in a misallocation of resources in every case, contrary to Treasury Secretary Andrew Mellon's argument in the 1920s.

CONCLUSIONS

A more restricted view of federal domestic program responsibilities has emerged over the last 10 years, a change that has been accompanied by reduced intergovernmental funding. This perspective on federal program responsibility is consistent with the economic justification for federal subsidy of state and local service provision. Federal subsidy is appropriate only when the service being provided generates collective benefits for federal taxpayers as well as for the state or local taxpayers in the jurisdiction providing the service. Since the tax-exempt bond subsidizes all state and local activities whether or not this criterion is satisfied, some federal control is suggested. The difficulty arises in trying to write legislation that applies this concept to particular activities.

The federal government has attempted to deal with the problem of budgetary control of tax-exempt bonds by enacting a series of restrictive measures to control the types of services for which the exemption can be used and to cap the dollar volume of bonds that can be issued in any given year. Thus, it is possible, in principle, to tinker with the tax-exempt bond law and convert what amounts to an open-ended grant into a closed grant with budgetary control. The question remains, however, whether the Internal Revenue Service, whose primary responsibility is to collect revenue, is equipped to administer and enforce laws whose purpose is equivalent to that of a direct spending program.

No form of intergovernmental assistance is clearly superior in terms of efficiency. When the objective is to stimulate all types of state and local spending, bonds have a role to play in promoting economic efficiency (ignoring their role in distorting factor prices), but are a poor second cousin to categorical grants when specific programs are to be targeted. Of course, bonds can be targeted to specific private activities, as the legislation in 1968 and the 1980s has increasingly done, but administrative costs probably will have to rise if they are to be well targeted. The tax subsidies probably entail lower administrative costs than grants, but undoubtedly achieve that by directing less of the subsidy to the desired groups. And none of the alternatives delivers a large share of the federal cost to increased state and local spending, although the tax-exempt bond share has improved due to the rate reductions enacted in 1986.

The case for subsidizing one factor of production, such as capital, depends upon whether that factor of production is underprovided relative to other factors. Several rationales can be summoned in support of such claims of underprovision of public capital, but evidence to support these rationales is scant: electoral pressures create a bias among officials for current spending; mobility creates a preference among taxpayers for current services; citizens underestimate the contribution capital services make to their welfare; and capital services have a larger spillover component than do current services.

Notes

1. Discussions of what constitutes a public purpose can be found as early as Adam Smith's *Wealth of Nations*. Some suggest that the formalization of modern public goods theory began with Paul Samuelson's 1954 article on the pure theory of public expenditures. The systematic application of public goods theory to the federal budget process can be found in public finance texts beginning with Richard Musgrave (1959). One of the early and thorough discussions of the spillover rationale for intergovernmental assistance is provided by Break (1967, 71–77).

2. In technical terms, the monopolist maximizes profits at the output where marginal revenue equals marginal cost rather than the output at which price equals marginal cost. The result is that consumers attach a greater value to their last unit of consumption from the monopoly producer (measured by the price they pay) than to their last unit of consumption from nonmonopoly producers (measured by the monopolist's marginal cost, that is, what the monopolist has to pay for the resources it hires away from other producers). Consumer welfare can, therefore, be increased by decreasing the output of (and shifting resources from) nonmonopoly producers whose production is valued by the consumer at the monopolist's marginal cost and increasing the output of (and shifting resources to) monopoly producers whose production is valued at the monopolist's price.

3. In fact, taxpayers are often likely to be unwilling to provide services to resident nontaxpayers, a situation worsened by the existence of fiscal disparities among jurisdictions. The per-person tax base varies substantially from state to state, requiring taxpayers in one state to make a greater tax effort (pay a higher tax price) than taxpayers in another state in order to provide equivalent public services. The desire to reduce this unequal tax-base wealth and its potential effect on the provision of basic services in different states is often cited as a "fiscal disparities" justification for federal subsidy of the state and local sector

4. Although the Reagan revolution has questioned the legitimacy of most grants to state and local governments, the necessity for federal support fo public assistance programs has been recognized. This is attributable to the fact that a much greater proportion of the collective consumption benefits from transfer programs spill over state and local political boundaries than is true for most other public services.

5. Major exceptions to this conclusion are veterans' housing bonds issued primarily in California, Oregon, and Texas, and some industrial development bonds issued by the state of Maine. The 1986 volume for veterans' housing bonds was $0.34 billion in California, $1.053 billion in Oregon, and $0.967 billion in Texas.

6. Some revenue bonds are actually retired from earmarked tax revenues, such as

motor fuel taxes used to finance highway construction, or lease payments financed by annual appropriations, which are equivalent to interest and debt redemption payments for public buildings and jails constructed by state agencies and leased to the state.

7. A more detailed discussion of this background is available in Miller (1988).

8. For example, Food Stamp benefit levels are set and financed by the federal government, and the program is classified in the "direct payments for individuals" category. Aid to Families with Dependent Children benefit levels are set and partially financed with state funds, and the program is classified in the "grants to states" category. The federal share of benefit levels in 1987 ranged from 50 percent in 11 states to 78.5 percent in 1 state.

9. This discussion of structure is based upon Nathan et al. (1987) and Miller (1988). The Reagan administration proposed a 25 percent cut in these programs. Funding for the merged programs as approved by Congress averaged about 12 percent below the total for the prior year for all programs placed in the block. These cuts ranged from zero for the energy assistance block grant to a 34 percent cut in the cummunity services block grant.

10. An additional five proposals for block grants were defeated during this period. Even though block grants were replacing categoricals, the proportion of funds distributed through categorical programs continued to increase, accounting for 87 percent of total grants in 1988 compared to 79 percent in 1980. (See Advisory Commission on Intergovernmental Relations 1987, 1–2.)

11. In the Income Tax Act of 1861, state and local taxes and federal taxes were the only deductions specifically allowed.

12. For more complete discussions of the history and rationales for deductibility, see Brazer (1959) and Noto and Zimmerman (1983).

13. Revenue sharing is not discussed here because it served a different function than did traditional grants-in-aid. General revenue sharing (GRS) was predicated on a belief that the federal government had an interest in seeing that standard state and local functions were provided at some base level, and that the federal government's tax-raising ability was superior to that of state and local governments. In other words, the motivation was not underprovision due to spillovers but, rather, to a mismatch between local needs and revenue-raising ability. (See Maxwell and Aronson 1977, 71.)

14. The state and local interest savings are $(r_c - r_m)S$, the difference between taxable and tax-exempt rates times the stock of debt. Referring back to the expression for the implicit tax rate, cross multiplication shows that $r_c - r_m = t_m r_c$.

15. This estimate uses household and corporate holding shares of 0.643 and 0.357 from table 4.10, and assumes the average tax rate for households is 0.28 and the market clearing tax rate is 0.24.

16. The difference between the high estimates of the GRS impact on state and local spending and the estimate suggested by consumer theory was labeled the "flypaper effect," because it suggested that money sticks where it hits. See Oates (1979) and Courant, Gramlich, and Rubinfeld (1979). Gramlich's (1982) study of President Reagan's 1982 New Federalism proposal suggested a short-term increase in spending from unconstrained grants of $0.04 per dollar and a long-term response of $0.18.

17. Rymarowicz and Zimmerman (1988) suggested that both states and local governments behaved in the 1980s in a manner consistent with grant substitution by substituting their own tax effort for reduced grant dollars. From 1980 through 1986, in response to reduced grants-in-aid, the states' own-source revenue increase in excess of inflation was sufficient to reduce the federal contribution ratio by $9.21 per $100

of own-source revenue; the comparable ratio for local governments was $1.92 per $100 of own-source revenue.

18. The deductibility of sales taxes was also eliminated. This would also work to reduce the effect of deductibility on state and local spending but not necessarily on the transfer efficiency of the remaining deductible taxes. Rough estimates of the effect of these three tax reform changes on the level of state and local spending by state have been made by Kenyon (1988). The reduction in tax costs from deductibility was estimated to have raised state and local spending in 1982 an average of 3 percent above what it would otherwise have been. This increase in spending was expected to decline to about 1 percent in 1987. This suggests a small reduction in state and local spending from the Tax Reform Act of about 2 percent. In only two states (Utah and Colorado) was the decline estimated to be as high as 3 percent.

19. This is not literally true in all cases. If money is borrowed to pay for current expenses such as salaries and supplies, the price of these factors is also reduced. Generally, state and local statutes and regulations, as well as the risk avoidance behavior of investors, prevents such borrowing for noncaptial expenses. But the New York City fiscal crisis in the late 1970s illustrates the ability of elected officials to circumvent such hurdles when faced with difficult budgetary problems.

20. Money illusion suggests that people feel better off when their incomes rise, even though real income has not risen due to price increases. Tax illusion suggests people are not aware, due to such things as income tax withholding and indirect sales and excise taxes, of the share of their income being paid in taxes.

Chapter Six

THE BUDGET AND THE DEFICIT

Although chapter 5 illustrated that the federal effort to reduce support for tax-exempt bonds in the 1980s was entirely consistent with evolving intergovernmental policy, there can be no doubt that the escalating federal budget deficit in the 1980s heightened concerns about federal tax expenditures and played an important role in the desire of the nation's policymakers to curb the growth of municipal bonds. This desire to increase revenues by restricting bond issuance was clearly expressed by Congress in justifying the bond provisions in each successive round of tax legislation.

Congress was concerned with the volume of tax-exempt bonds used for private activities. . . . The increasing volume of private activity bonds has also caused mounting Federal revenue losses. (Joint Committee on Taxation 1982, 98–99)

*   *   *

Congress was concerned with the large and increasing volume of tax-exempt bonds being issued under prior law. The effects of this increasing volume included . . . mounting revenue losses. (Joint Committee on Taxation 1987b, 1151)

This chapter places tax-exempt bond legislation in the context of the growing federal budget deficit and federal efforts to control the deficit. The history of the deficit is traced and its origins explored. The role of tax policy, particularly the broadening of the income tax base, in restraining the growth of the deficit is examined. And finally, the relative importance of tax-exempt bonds as a source of income tax base broadening and deficit reduction is discussed.

OUTLAYS, RECEIPTS, AND DEFICITS: 1965–1988

As noted in table 5.3, interest on the federal debt was the most rapidly growing component of the federal budget in the 1980s, rising in real terms by 111.7 percent, almost triple the 41.3 percent growth of the second fastest-growing budget component, national defense and international affairs. This growth is attributable to the mushrooming budget deficit that began in the late 1970s and continued with a vengeance in the 1980s.

The history of revenues, outlays, and the deficit is illustrated in figure 6.1. One source of the deficit problem of the 1980s can be traced to the period of the late 1960s and early 1970s.[1] As spending for the Vietnam war declined from 1968 to 1973, the inevitable deficit that appears in time of war declined from 3.0 percent to 1.2 percent of gross national product (GNP). But some of this "peace dividend" was used to fund expansions in social programs, primarily Social Security and Medicare. In effect, services for the elderly and disabled were improved, and these improvements were funded by cutting military spending. But these improvements also represented long-term commitments that would require additional funding, and reduced military spending was clearly not a long-term option for this funding.

By the late 1970s, when defense spending bottomed out at 4.7 percent of GNP, there was general consensus that defense preparedness was inadequate and that defense spending must be increased substantially. At the same time, the increased long-term commitments for social programs made early in the decade required continued funding increases. For a time, the dilemma was solved by inflation and bracket creep that raised individual and corporate tax revenues, which managed to keep the deficit as a percentage of GNP below 3.0 percent from 1977 through 1981.

Two factors shattered this short-term fix. First, the Reagan administration, intent on reestablishing the muscle of the U.S. military, arrived in Washington and convinced Congress to accelerate the buildup of military spending, from the 3 percent real growth proposed by the Carter administration to 9 percent. Some of this increased military spending was to be paid for by decreased domestic spending, but disagreement between the president and Congress over the nature of the cuts caused the actual magnitude of these budget savings to be smaller than projected.

Second, the tax revolts that hit the state and local sector in the late 1970s arrived in Washington with the Reagan administration. Federal receipts peaked in 1981 at 20.1 percent of GNP, fueled by inflation and bracket creep in the progressive individual income tax. The response was the Economic Recovery Tax Act of 1981, which cut individual marginal tax rates and the effective tax rates on most

Figure 6.1 FEDERAL RECEIPTS, OUTLAYS, AND DEFICIT, 1965–89

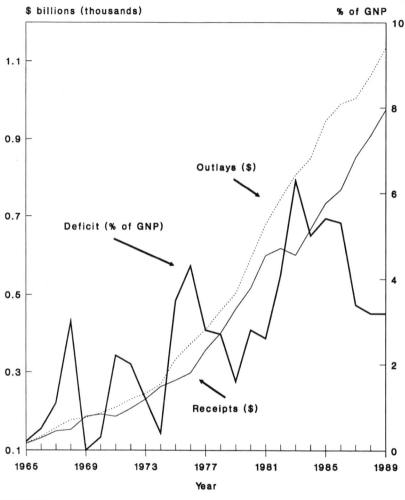

Source: Office of Management and Budget (1989).
Note: Budget ran a small surplus in 1969 of 0.3% of GNP.

capital income. It was expected that the supply-side effects of these cuts would unleash entrepreneurial spirits and stimulate growth, thereby lowering receipts to a healthy but not oppressive 19 percent of GNP. Unfortunately, while the supply-side response never materialized, a recession did, and receipts actually fell to 18.1 percent of GNP in 1983 and 1984.

The result of all this was a ballooning deficit, rising from slightly more than $40 billion in 1979 to $208 billion in 1983. This increased the deficit as a percentage of GNP from a manageable 1.6 in 1979 to 6.3 in 1983. The picture did not improve substantially through 1986, when the deficit stood at $221 billion, 5.3 percent of GNP.

Such large deficits in the absence of war and the presence of prosperity raise disturbing problems. Future economic growth is affected, as the high volume of public borrowing necessary to fund the deficit crowds out private investment and retards growth in the private capital stock. The economy is also vulnerable to the whims of international financial markets that provide much of the savings to fund this debt. Should international lenders' views about the future prosperity of the U.S. turn pessimistic, they would demand much higher compensation for purchasing Treasury securities. These higher interest rates would raise outlays on interest payments, force reductions in other budget spending, and retard private capital formation. In addition, as the share of the budget devoted to interest payments grows, the ability of the U.S. to deal with unexpected budget emergencies is increasingly compromised. Finally, it is a dangerously constraining legacy to leave to our children, particularly when we know they will be whipsawed by the large size of our age cohorts relative to theirs, making it economically difficult for them to support established social programs during their prime wage-earning years and simultaneously making it politically difficult to reduce that support.

TAX-EXEMPT BONDS AS A REVENUE RAISER

Recognition of the problem and its potential consequences led not only to efforts to constrain the growth in some categories of budget outlays but also to reduce what Leonard (1986) refers to as "quiet" or nonappropriated spending. It is the "quiet" spending made through the income tax system that is of primary interest here. The Tax Equity and Fiscal Responsibility Act of 1982 (TEFRA), the Deficit Reduction Act of 1984 (DRA), and the Tax Reform Act of 1986 (TRA) all acted to broaden the income tax base, that is, to close what are variously called loopholes, tax preferences, or incentives for capital formation and other socially desirable activities.

Once broadening the income tax base became part of the political agenda, it was inevitable that tax-exempt bonds would receive serious consideration. If one is looking for revenue, it makes sense to go after the big revenue losers. Table 6.1 lists the 11 largest estimated revenue losers in 1983, chosen from those tax provisions officially classified as tax expenditures during the base-broadening period of the 1980s. The largest revenue loss in this list is generated by the net exclusion of pension contributions and earnings from current

Table 6.1 TAX EXPENDITURES RANKED BY MAGNITUDE OF REVENUE LOSS
IN 1983 AND THEIR CONTRIBUTIONS TO DEFICIT REDUCTION
FROM TAX REFORM IN THE 1980S ($ MILLIONS)

Provision	1983 Revenue Loss	Contributions to Deficit Reduction
Net exclusion of pension contributions and earnings	56,900	TEFRA (1,844), DRA (70), TRA (21,036)
Deduction of nonbusiness state and local taxes	26,080	TRA (10,873)
Investment tax credit	21,245	TEFRA (5,018), DRA (148), TRA (77,313)
Deduction of mortgage interest on owner-occupied houses	20,800	Reduced by Revenue Act of 1987
Capital gains (other than on timber, agriculture, iron ore, and coal)	15,335	DRA (83), TRA[a]
Exclusion of employer contributions for medical insurance premiums and medical care	15,270	
Old age survivors' insurance benefits for retired workers	14,035	Reduced by Social Security Act Amendments of 1983
Exclusion of interest income on state and local bonds	13,775	TEFRA (863), DRA (−663), TRA (199)
Deduction of charitable contributions	12,140	DRA (−180)
Accelerated depreciation	11,530	TEFRA (29,890), DRA (148), TRA (−7,900)
Deduction of interest on consumer credit	9,215	TRA (11,391)

Sources: Office of Management and Budget, *Special Analyses: Budget of the United States Government, Fiscal Year 1985* (Washington, D.C.: U.S. Government Printing Office, 1984); and Joint Committee on Taxation (1982, 1984, 1987b).
Notes: TRA—Tax Reform Act of 1986; DRA—Deficit Reduction Act of 1984; TEFRA—Tax Equity and Fiscal Responsibility Act of 1982. Numbers in parentheses represent the provisions estimated three-year contributions to tax revenues. A negative number signifies a revenue loss from the legislation.
a. Revenue gain was counted as part of gain from tax rate reduction.

taxation, and was estimated to cost almost $57 billion in fiscal year 1983. The smallest revenue loser in this group is the deduction of interest on consumer credit, estimated to cost $9.2 billion in FY 1983. The exclusion of interest on tax-exempt bonds ranks eighth on the list, estimated to cost $13.8 billion in FY 1983.

The last column of table 6.1 provides a summary of the contribution each of these tax expenditures (loopholes, tax preferences, or socially desirable incentives) made to deficit reduction from the three major tax acts of the 1980s, based upon the revenue gain estimates of the Joint Committee on Taxation.[2] The tax act(s) that pruned the revenue loss is cited, with the provision's estimated three-year contribution to tax revenues listed in parentheses. Thus, the numbers in the last column, representing a three-year summation, are sometimes larger than the estimated revenue loss for 1983.

It is clear from table 6.1 that tax-exempt bonds were not singled out for special attention. Seven of the 11 provisions were affected adversely by these three tax acts, and an eighth (old age survivors' benefits for retired workers) was altered to produce revenue by the Social Security Act Amendments of 1983. If the table were extended to incorporate the Revenue Act of 1987, the mortgage interest provision would also show a small contribution to deficit reduction. The Revenue Act of 1987 denied the deductibility of mortgage interest payments made on the portion of any mortgage in excess of $1 million. The only major tax expenditures to escape the decade unscathed are the exclusion of employer contributions for medical insurance premiums and medical care. The deduction for charitable contributions actually enjoyed a slight increase in its preferences, due to changes made in the DRA.

Nor were tax-exempt bonds the primary contributor to deficit reduction. The biggest contributions came from the corporate side of the income tax system in the form of reductions in accelerated depreciation benefits for investments in equipment and structures and the elimination of the investment tax credit for equipment. The estimated three-year revenue gain from accelerated depreciation adjustments made by TEFRA was $29.9 billion; the gain from the elimination of the investment tax credit made by the TRA was $77.3 billion. Another large contributor was capital gains, which the 1986 act taxed at the same rate as ordinary income. No estimate of revenue gain is available for capital gains, because the Joint Committee on Taxation allocated the revenue gain to the marginal tax rate reduction made by the act.

Tax expenditures for pensions also contributed continually to deficit reduction during the decade. All three tax acts took a bite, with the TRA providing an estimated three-year revenue gain of about $21 billion. The TRA also made substantial hits on: the deduction of consumer interest, raising a projected $11.4 billion over three years; and state and local governments, raising an estimated $10.9 billion over three years from elimination of the deduction of general sales taxes and $199 million from restrictions on tax-exempt bonds. The estimate of the bond contribution to revenue is very low because the Joint Committee did not foresee as large a drop in bond volume as did the Treasury Department, and much of the revenue gain from the provisions was expected to accrue in the out years when the volume cap takes hold and restricts bond issuance.

Notes

1. Much of this section is based upon a discussion of deficit history and its origins in Minarik and Penner (1988).

2. The revenue gain estimates and some of the rankings would be different if Treasury Department estimates were used. In addition to judgments about the economic effects of some changes, every tax reform that entails multiple changes in the tax law requires that decisions be made about "stacking" of the provisions. For example, do you calculate the revenue gain from the taxation of capital gains at the pretax reform rates or the posttax reform rates? The Treasury Department and the Joint Committee on Taxation do not always agree on either the stacking order or the appropriate behavioral assumptions, both of which can affect the estimates. See Kenyon (1989) and Neubig (1989) for dicussions of these issues.

Chapter Seven

RESOURCE ALLOCATION

Chapter 5 discussed the federal government's concern with the proper allocation of resources between the public and private sectors. Federal concern extends beyond intersectoral resource allocation, however, to a desire to maintain a "level playing field" for private investment decisions. This means that, when capital markets operate properly, all potential private investments face a cost of acquiring capital that differs only by the risk premium that savers associate with investment in different activities.[1]

As documented in chapter 5, tax-exempt bonds have been used increasingly by state and local governments for nontraditional activities, to the extent that Congress in 1986 finally labeled bonds used for many of these activities "private-activity" bonds. One commentator characterized the issue in the following way: "States and localities have stretched their imaginations to find new ways to use tax-exempt bonds. They have defined for themselves a "social banker" function, in which they borrow large sums of money at tax-exempt rates, then relend the funds at below-market rates for politically popular purposes" (Peterson 1984, 233).

Such behavior interferes with the maintenance of a level playing field in the allocation of scarce savings among the many competing potential private investments, and has been responsible for a substantial degree of unintended nonneutral taxation of private investments. This interference has been cited repeatedly by Congress as justification for legislative efforts to curtail the use of tax-exempt financing for private purposes.

The availability of tax-exempt financing for exempt activities and other private activities causes distortions in the allocation of scarce capital resources. The ability to obtain a lower cost of borrowing creates a bias in favor of investment in those activities. In effect, those favored activities are subsidized at the expense of other activities. Thus, the effect of the subsidy is that the allocation of capital investments is based upon government decisions rather than their relative economic productivity. (Joint Committee on Taxation 1982, 99)

*   *   *

... Congress determined that the availability of tax-exempt financing for certain types of projects had tended to encourage investment in such projects independent of the economic value of the project. Such financing was, therefore, diverting investment capital from more productive uses. (Joint Committee on Taxation 1984, 931).

This chapter first discusses the benefits of a level playing field (neutral taxation) for choosing among private investments, and the conditions under which it may be desirable for the federal government to tilt the playing field in favor of particular types of private investments. This is followed by a discussion of the use of tax-exempt bonds for subsidy of private investment and its implications for the nation's welfare. The chapter then provides some estimates of the extent to which tax-exempt bonds have distorted private investment choices, and the costs this has imposed on the country.

NEUTRAL TAXATION OF CAPITAL INCOME—THE LEVEL PLAYING FIELD

If capital markets are operating perfectly, the private market will allocate the available supply of savings among activities (assets, businesses) until the rate of return on the marginal investment in any one activity equals the rate of return that can be earned in the best alternative investment opportunity. Thus, the capital market assures society that scarce savings are not being wasted on investments in one activity that generate a lower return than is available in another activity. This maximizes national income and the size of the pie available for consumption.

This does not, of course, mean that the federal government should never intervene in the private capital market and lower the cost of capital for an investment in one type of activity compared to investments in other activities. As noted in the discussion of market intervention for public goods in chapter 5, the private sector does *not* consider the effects of external benefits and costs when calculating the marginal rate of return on its investments. If external benefits are present, the actions of the private capital market in allocating savings to equalize marginal private returns will generate underinvestment in those activities that produce the external benefits; if external costs are present, there will be overinvestment in those activities that produce the external costs.

One solution is to tilt the playing field by reducing the cost of capital for private investments that generate external benefits. This reduction increases the private rate of return on investments in these activities generating external benefits. The increased rate of return induces the private capital market to reallocate savings to these activities and away from the activities with lower marginal private rates of return. The increased investment in these externality-generating investments drives down their marginal private rates of return, whereas the decreased investment in other activities raises their marginal private rates of return. This process continues until the marginal private rates of return are equalized and national welfare, measured as the sum of national income and the external benefits, is maximized.

The federal government has been very active in tilting the playing field for investments in all sorts of activities, using both the corporate and individual income taxes.[2] Investments in oil and gas exploration have long been favored by the tax code through the depletion allowance and the expensing of intangible drilling costs; investments in owner-occupied housing have been and continue to be favored by allowing the deduction of home ownership expenses (mortgage interest and property taxes), while permitting the exclusion from the tax base of the imputed income from the home; and appreciating assets such as timber have been favored by the special treatment of capital gains. Numerous other examples of investments that have benefited from subsidized capital costs are readily available. In theory, all of these subsidies were provided to satisfy some public policy objective.[3]

TILTING THE PLAYING FIELD WITH TAX-EXEMPT FINANCING

Disregard, for a moment, arguments that the capital cost subsidies provided to private investments are misguided and counterproductive, and assume instead that the subsidies are socially desirable and of the proper size to adjust for external benefits. Now consider tax-exempt bonds, which were intended to be used to subsidize the cost of capital for public capital formation. Private capital formation was not expected to be favored with the below-market debt financing costs available from tax-exempt bonds (refer to the discussion in chapter 5 and the yield ratios presented in table 4.3). Although this view of the intent of the bond provision is subjective and inconsistent with some special provisions in the bond portion of the tax code, it conforms to the general thrust of tax-exempt bond policy over the last 20 years.[4] This perspective suggests two things.

First, unanticipated access to below-market debt financing for some private investment implies that any reallocation of savings from the private to the public sector is too small because the cost of capital for public investments relative to private investments is too high (because the private cost of capital is lowered by its access to tax-exempt borrowing). Some of the supply of savings seeking tax-exempt income that ought to be allocated to public capital formation is being allocated to the private sector.

Second, access to tax-exempt financing is dependent upon states and localities, and they differ widely both in their willingness to act as conduits and in their sophistication in doing so. Thus, the use of tax-exempt financing is not available to all firms and all activities on an equal basis. An unintended distortion has been introduced into the private cost of capital. Access to tax-exempt debt financing by the private sector directs resources toward those projects fortunate enough to have such access and causes the marginal returns among investments in different types of activities to be unequal. The level playing field has been tilted without the corresponding increase in social benefits to compensate society.

EFFECT ON INVESTMENT CHOICES AND NATIONAL INCOME

Questions arise as to whether this distortion is sufficiently large to affect investment choices, and, if so, what the distortion costs the economy. How much does the ability to use tax-exempt financing reduce the cost of capital for private investments compared to those investments that do not have access to such financing?

The rental cost of capital is denoted as c:

$$c = r^* + d, \qquad (7.1)$$

where r^* is the pretax real rate of return and d is the economic depreciation rate.

In the presence of taxes the rental cost is:

$$c = (R + d)[1 - uz(1 - xk) - k]/(1 - u), \qquad (7.2)$$

where R is the real aftertax discount rate of the firm making the investment, u is the corporate income tax rate, k is the rate of the investment tax credit, x is the basis adjustment for the investment tax credit, and z is the present value of depreciation deduction per dollar of investment.

Two factors in equation (7.2) require more explanation. First, the real aftertax discount rate R is:

$$R = f_1[r_m(1-u)-p] + f_2[r_t(1-u)-p] + (1-f_1-f_2)r_e, \qquad (7.3)$$

where r_m is the yield (interest rate) on tax-exempt (state and local) bonds, r_t is the nominal yield on corporate taxable bonds, r_e is the real return on equity, f_1 and f_2 are the shares of the investment financed with tax-exempt debt and taxable debt, and p is the anticipated inflation rate. In effect, R provides the rate the firm must pay for its selected mix of financing. The estimates presented here assume every investment is 50 percent equity financed $(1 - f_1 - f_2) = 0.50$, with different proportions of tax-exempt (f_1) and taxable debt (f_2) summing to 50 percent.

The second factor to discuss in equation (7.2) is z, the present value of depreciation deductions per dollar of investment. The value of z for assets financed with taxable debt or equity is characterized by a declining balance formula that allows for a switch to straight-line depreciation:

$$z = [a/(rT+a)][1+[ae^{-(r(a-1)T/a+a-1)}]/(rT)]$$
$$- [ae^{-(rT+a-1)}]/(rT), \qquad (7.4)$$

where a is the rate of declining balance (e.g., 2.0 for 200 percent declining balance), T is the tax life for depreciation, and r is the nominal aftertax discount rate (that is, $r = R + p$).

Prior to the enactment of TEFRA in 1982, assets (both equipment and structures) could be depreciated over relatively short periods of time at relatively rapid rates of 150 percent and 175 percent declining balance. Since then, asset lives have been lengthened, while depreciation rates for equipment have been increased to 200 percent declining balance and rates for structures have been decreased to straight line. In addition, beginning with TEFRA of 1982, the tax-exempt bond-financed portion of an investment must use the straight-line depreciation formula, and with TRA of 1986, longer asset lives:

$$z = (1 - e^{-rT})/(rT) \qquad (7.5)$$

The taxation of capital income was changed in many other ways over the decade: marginal individual and corporate tax rates were reduced, capital gains were taxed as ordinary income, and the investment tax credit for equipment was eliminated. For these reasons, table 7.1 presents the effect of tax-exempt financing on capital costs for both 1982 and 1989. The estimates assume that the investment is representative of the U.S. capital stock in terms of the shares of equipment, structures, and research and development (R&D) spending (both tangible and intangible). The values of all parameters are specified in the appended table to this chapter (table 7A.1) and reflect a variety of sources such as *Moody's Investors Service* (1990) and *Council of Ecomimc Advisors* (1990).

The first panel of table 7.1 shows the rental cost of capital for investments in 1982 and 1989, using various percentages of tax-exempt financing ranging from 0 percent to 50 percent.[5] The first two rows in this panel contain the rental cost of capital estimates, and the second two rows contain the percentage change in the rental cost due to the switch from taxable debt financing to tax-exempt debt financing. In 1982, an investment financed 50 percent with tax-ex-

Table 7.1   EFFECT OF TAX-EXEMPT FINANCING ON COST OF CAPITAL FOR PRIVATE INVESTMENTS AND ON NATIONAL INCOME AND PRODUCTIVITY OF THE CAPITAL STOCK, 1982 AND 1989

	Share of Tax-Exempt Financing					
	0.00	0.10	0.20	0.30	0.40	0.50
Effect on Capital Costs						
Rental cost of capital	(cents per dollar of investment)					
1982	13.18	12.95	12.73	12.51	12.29	12.07
1989	16.31	16.15	15.98	15.82	15.65	15.48
Percentage reduction in rental cost due to tax-exempt financing						
1982	NA[a]	1.75%	3.41%	5.08%	6.75%	8.42%
1989	NA	0.98%	2.02%	3.00%	4.05%	5.09%
Effect on National Income						
Pretax real return	(cents per dollar of investment)					
1982	5.14	4.94	4.74	4.54	4.34	4.14
1989	8.60	8.44	8.27	8.11	7.94	7.77
Percentage reduction in pretax return due to tax-exempt financing						
1982	NA	3.89%	7.78%	11.67%	15.56%	19.46%
1989	NA	1.86%	3.84%	5.70%	7.67%	9.65%

a. NA, not applicable.

empt bonds enjoyed a capital cost reduction from 13.18 cents per dollar to 12.07 cents per dollar, equivalent to an 8.42 percent reduction in price. In 1989, capital cost was reduced from 16.31 cents per dollar to 15.48 cents per dollar, a 5.09 percent reduction. Clearly, these reductions are large enough to motivate investors to go to the considerable trouble necessary to interact with state and local governments to arrange for tax-exempt financing. The tilt of the playing field is substantial.

What does this mean for the economy? Some insight can be gained by looking at the pretax real rate of return implied by these cost of capital estimates. The pretax real return is the rental cost of capital minus the economic depreciation rate ($r^* = c - d$ from equation 7.1), and represents what an investment contributes to the national income. Estimates of the pretax real return are presented in the first two rows of the second panel of table 7.1.

One can interpret the results in two ways. First, assume that these investments serve no public purpose, that they represent the use of bonds for truly private purposes. If this is the case, in the absence of tax-exempt financing, an investor found it necessary to earn a real return of at least 5.14 cents per dollar in 1982 and 8.60 cents per dollar in 1989 to make it worthwhile to invest in a project. With tax-exempt financing of 50 percent of the investment, the investor found it profitable to invest in a project that earned as little as 4.14 cents per dollar in 1982 and 7.77 cents per dollar in 1989. The acceptable rate of return compared to a project with no tax-exempt financing declined by 19.46 percent in 1982 and 9.65 percent in 1989, according to the percentage changes presented in the last two rows of the second panel of table 7.1. In effect, access to tax-exempt financing directed the scarce supply of savings into investments that yielded considerably lower rates of return than could have been earned by using the savings for unsubsidized investments. The productivity of the capital stock was lowered and national income decreased by the lower rates of return earned on the subsidized investments.[6]

Second, assume these investments do serve some pubic purpose. The data in table 7.1 tell us the value we would have to place on the social benefits from these private investments to keep national welfare from falling. For a project with 50 percent tax-exempt financing in 1982, social benefits would have had to equal at least 19.46 percent of the pretax real return on an unsubsidized investment, and 9.65 percent in 1989. In 1982, this meant that every $1,000 bond issued for private purposes would have had to generate approximately $10 in social benefits every year over the life of the bond; in 1989, the comparable amount of social benefits per year would have been $8.30.[7]

Notes

1. Claims that capital markets do not operate properly, that they are not "perfect, are widespread. It has been suggested that the market discriminates against: small relative to large businesses (a frequent justification for the Small Business Administration's activities); inner city relative to other urban or suburban investments (a frequent justification for the Urban Development Action Grant program or the Enterprise Zone proposal); or numerous other dichotomies of investment that one can conjure. An extensive literature discusses the possibility of discrimination in captial markets. For a recent investigation of the topic with regard to mortgage lending, see Bradbury, Case, and Dunham (1989).

2. For a summary of the effects of preferential taxation of corporate and individual income on rates of return and effective tax rates, see Gravelle and Zimmerman (1984).

3. Obviously, the desirability of these subsidies has been and continues to be a contentious issue. Some claim that they serve a limited social purpose and are therefore wasteful, while others contend that they improve resource allocation and increase national welfare. A set of papers that discuss these issues and quantify the effects on the allocation of resources appears in Harberger and Bailey (1969).

4. Nothing in this area is ever definitive. Clearly, there are members of Congress and other policymakers who feel it is good policy to allow private investments to take advantage of the tax exemption privilege, and Congress has legislated access to such funding for certain private activities. The discussion in this section simply suggests that these are the exceptions that prove the rule.

5. Many projects have used 75 percent to 100 percent tax-exempt financing. The estimates are restricted to 50 precent for two reasons. First, firms are charged nominal interest on a fixed nominal sum, rather than real interest on an inflation-indexed sum. This gives the investor a growing equity interest in the investment over its lifetime as the real value of the debt declines relative to the asset value. Second, the lower the equity share, the higher the risk premium probably required to make an investment profitable to undertake. This higher risk premium would ameliorate the decline in the rate of return caused by the higher tax-exempt financing share.

6. Not every investment financed with tax-exempt bonds imposed losses equivalent to those discussed here. Investors pick off projects from those with the highest to the lowest returns. Thus, some projects probably provided returns almost as high as those available with unsubsidized projects. If this were true, the total loss of national income would be a weighted average of the difference between the unsubsidized return and the various subsidized returns.

7. In 1982, the unsubsidized pretax real return was 5.14 percent, which yields $51.40 on a $1,000 bond. Social benefits must equal at least 19.46 percent of that return, or $10.00; in 1989, the unsubsidized pretax real return was 8.60 percent, which yields $86.00 on a $1,000 bond. Social benefits must equal at least 9.65 percent of that return, or $8.30.

PARAMETER ESTIMATES FOR RENTAL
COST OF CAPITAL

Table 7A.1 VALUES OF PARAMETERS FOR ESTIMATES IN TABLE 7.1

Parameter	1982	1989
Corporate tax rate	0.46	0.34
State-local bond yield	0.095	0.0738
Corporate bond yield	0.125	0.1005
Real return on equity	0.07	0.0883
Anticipated inflation rate	0.06	0.0456
Depreciation values and investment tax credit		
Equipment		
T	4.5	7 (13 for portion financed with tax-exempt debt)
d	0.15	0.15
a	1.5	2.0
k	0.1	0.0
x	0.5	NA[a]
Public utility structures		
T	13	NA
d	.03	NA
a	1.5	NA
k	0.1	NA
x	0.5	NA
Other structures		
T	15	31.5
d	.03	0.03
a	1.75	NA
k	0.0	0.0
x	0.0	NA

Sources: Moody's Investors Service (1990), Council of Economic Advisors (1990), and author's calculations.

Note: For 1989, calculations use same parameter values for public utility structures as for other structures. Meaning of parameters appears in text of chapter 7.

a. NA, not applicable.

Chapter Eight

TAX EQUITY

The fourth policy issue that has played a part in the evolution of tax-exempt bond legislation over the last 20 years is the distribution of the tax burden by income class. This continues a long-standing concern with the equity aspects of tax-exempt bonds. Witness the comments of Secretary of the Treasury Andrew Mellon (1924):

It is also necessary to bear in mind that in the long run all of these public debts, whether the debts of States and their political subdivisions or of the Federal Government itself, as well as the taxes which must be imposed to meet them, fall upon but one body of taxpayers, and that the apparent advantage of borrowing by States and cities at the expense of the Federal revenues is illusory, since any temporary advantages thus obtained will have to be paid for by the Federal Government at the expense ultimately of the great body of taxpayers. This is particularly true of tax-exempt securities, for their effect is to provide a refuge from taxation for certain classes of taxpayers, with correspondingly higher taxes on all the rest in order to make up the resulting deficiency in the revenues. (160–61)

The breadth and intensity of feelings about high-income taxpayers' use of tax-exempt bonds to escape their social duty as taxpayers was never greater than during the depths of the Great Depression. Growing unemployment and decreasing public budgets produced bread lines sufficiently long that people beyond the usual circle of public officials and financial market sophisticates began to question the sources of declining tax collections. Cowboy humorist and social critic Will Rogers was one who in 1935 identified tax-exempt bonds as a prime suspect:

See there is a bill in congress to do away with tax exempt bonds, thats the best bill of all of em. The way it is a man could have a million dollar income from tax free bonds, own no property or nothing else, and not pay one cent of tax. And its all lawful. If they can make all these bonds pay tax they will be doing one of the most fair share the wealth plans there is.

It was put in so that a town or a state, or the government could sell more
bonds than it ought to. (Day 1949, 387)

Such views have some grounding in experience. If one ignores or
dismisses as of little value the social objectives of the interest income
exclusion that were discussed in chapter 5, one is left with the conclusion that tax-exempt bonds are, from the federal perspective, little
more than a vehicle for investors to shelter a portion of their income
from federal income taxation. There have even been a few cases of very
wealthy individuals who considered payment of any federal income
tax so distasteful that they invested all of their wealth in tax exempt
bonds, even though it can easily be shown that investors' after-tax rate
of return can be increased by investing a portion of their wealth in
higher-yielding assets that generate taxable income sufficient to absorb
allowable exemptions, deductions, and exclusions (Bailey 1974).

This thread of distributional justice has never disappeared from
the tax-exempt bond debate, and appeared in the explanation Congress gave for its adoption of the bond provisions of the Tax Reform
Act of 1986: "Congress was concerned with the large and increasing
volume of tax-exempt bonds being issued under prior law. The effects
of this increasing volume included . . . the ability of higher-income
persons to avoid taxes by means of tax-exempt investments . . . ."
(Joint Committee on Taxation 1987b, 1151).

This chapter begins with a discussion of the change in the federal
tax burden by family income that occurred from 1977 to 1985. The
effective tax rate data show that the tax burden of the highest-income
families declined over this period, while the tax burden of the lowest-
income families increased. This trend heightened concerns over the
distributional effects of the federal tax system and the possible contribution of tax-exempt bonds to these changes. Data are then presented
on the distribution of tax-exempt bond interest income before and after
the Tax Reform Act of 1986. These data illustrate that the concentration
of tax-exempt interest income among the highest-income classes declined considerably after 1986. The chapter concludes with a discussion of how difficult it is to interpret the equity implications of these
data.

EFFECTIVE TAX RATES BY FAMILY INCOME,
1977 AND 1985

Congressional Budget Office estimates for 1977 and 1985 of effective
federal tax rates (the ratio of taxes to family income) for quintiles

and the top 5 percent of the population are presented in figure 8.1. The federal taxes include individual and corporate income taxes, social insurance taxes, and excise taxes.[1] The lowest quintile's (the poorest 20 percent of the population's) effective tax rate rose from 9.5 percent to 10.6 percent, an increase of 11.5 percent. The highest quintile's (the richest 20 percent of the population's) effective tax

Figure 8.1 EFFECTIVE FEDERAL TAX RATES, POPULATION RANKED BY
INCOME, 1977 AND 1985: LEVELS AND PERCENTAGE CHANGE

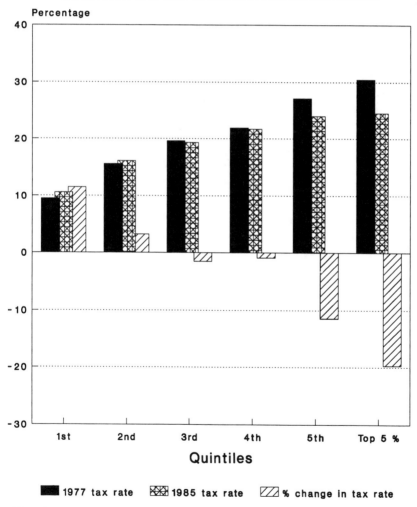

Source: Congressional Budget Office (1987).

rate declined from 27.1 percent to 24.0 percent, a decrease of 11.4 percent. The richest 5 percent of the population's effective tax rate declined from 30.5 percent to 24.5 percent, a decrease of 24.5 percent.

These changes in effective tax rates by income class are not all attributable to federal tax policy. Three factors are responsible: changes in the tax law alter the relationship between income and taxes; changes in the tax law induce people to change their economic behavior, which changes the level and distribution of income; and incomes change for reasons independent of changes in the tax law. But whatever the cause, it is clear that the tax burden of the highest-income taxpayers, expressed as a porcentage of family income, declined over the 1977 to 1985 period, while that of the lowest-income taxpayers increased over the period. As the most preferentially taxed of all assets available to investors, and one for which supply was increasing rapidly during the 1977 to 1985 period (see figure 5.1), tax-exempt bonds surely played a role in this changing picture.

THE DISTRIBUTION OF INTEREST INCOME FROM TAX-EXEMPT BONDS

As discussed in more detail in chapter 9, higher-income families with high tax rates are expected to be the primary purchasers of tax-exempt bonds. It is these individuals who find the after-tax rate of return on the bonds to be higher than on alternative partially and fully taxed assets of equivalent risk. But the greater the supply of bonds, the farther down into the marginal tax rate schedule issuers will have to dip to find buyers for the last bond issued, which in turn means some bonds will be purchased by families with incomes below the highest levels. The fact that some buyers have relatively low marginal tax rates means that those purchasers with higher marginal tax rates earn interest income on their tax-exempt bond purchases in excess of the amount necessary to induce them to purchase the bonds. These excess earnings of high tax-bracket taxpayers have often been described with the pejorative term *windfall.*

Tracking the change in the distribution of tax-exempt interest income is not easy. Prior to 1987 when taxpayers had to begin reporting their tax-exempt interest income, the federal tax authorities collected no information on the tax-exempt interest income earned by each taxpayer. Data on the income class distribution of this interest income had to be obtained from other sources. For example, the U.S.

Department of the Treasury started with the estimate of total interest paid by state and local governments that is reported in the National Income and Product Accounts. The Federal Reserve System's *Flow of Funds* (1988) estimate of the percentage of tax-exempt debt held by individuals was used to calculate the share of this interest income received by individuals.[2] This interest income was then distributed among individuals using estimates of asset holdings by income class derived from the Federal Reserve System's Survey of Consumer Finances (Avery, Elliehausen, and Kennickell 1988).

Unfortunately, the Treasury estimates are not available. The cross-hatched bars in figure 8.2 represent each income class's share of total tax-exempt interest income received in 1983 as reported by the Survey of Consumer Finances. Each respondent's household income was adjusted to 1987 price levels before being classified by income class.[3] The lined bars represent each income class's share of tax-exempt interest income received in 1987 and classified by 1987 AGI class. The data are from the tax-exempt interest income reported on the 1987 income tax return as required by the Tax Reform Act of 1986. If one were to evaluate the two distributions at face value, a substantial change seems to have occurred—every income class below $100 thousand had a larger share of total tax-exempt interest income in 1987 than it did in 1985. For example, middle-income taxpayers in the two income classes ranging from $30,000 to $75,000 increased their combined share of tax-exempt interest income from 19.8 percent to 29.4 percent. The highest-income taxpayers, those in the two income classes above $100,000, decreased their combined share of tax-exempt interest income from 70.8 percent to 46.1 percent.

The changes implied by the 1987 data seem excessive for two reasons. First, the total reported interest income in some classes seems very high. For example, the average tax-exempt interest in the $50,000–$75,000 class is slightly over $8,000. This suggests that the average taxpayer in that class holding tax-exempt bonds, if yields were 8 percent, has a tax-exempt bond portfolio somewhat in excess of $100,000. Even more remarkable, returns with negative AGI have average tax-exempt interest of more than $20,000, with implied holdings of $250,000. These numbers suggest that sizable numbers of wealthy individuals with high economic incomes are lowering their AGI and taxes by taking advantage of tax shelters, including tax-exempt bonds. Second, if the distribution of interest income has changed this much, it implies an enormous amount of secondary market activity as bond holdings were reshuffled among income classes.

Figure 8.2 SHARE OF TAX-EXEMPT INCOME EARNED BY DIFFERENT INCOME
            CLASSES, 1983 AND 1987

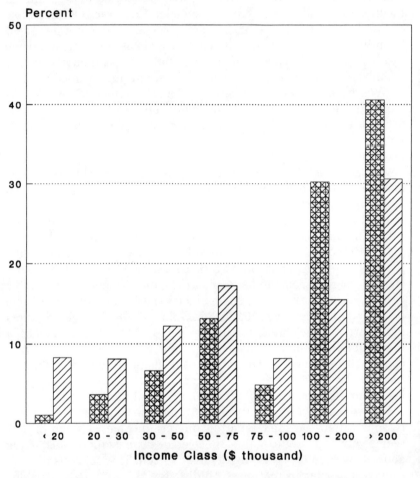

Source: Federal Reserve System (1983); Internal Revenue Service (1989).

The tax law and financial markets did change in ways that were
expected to shift tax-exempt interest income toward lower-income
classes, but probably not to the extent reflected in these data. Measurement problems probably overstate the extent of the change. The
tax law and financial market issues are dealt with here first. The
reduction of the top marginal tax rate from 50 percent to 28 percent

made investment in tax-exempt bonds in 1987 attractive equally to taxpayers with a much broader range of incomes than was true in 1986 and earlier years. The 28 percent marginal tax rate in 1987 applied to joint returns with taxable income in excess of $29,750 ($17,850 for single returns), whereas in 1985 the 50 percent tax rate applied to joint returns with taxable income in excess of $175,250 ($88,270 for single returns).[4] (See chapter 9 for a more detailed discussion of the importance of marginal tax rates to the investment decision.)

These rate changes occurred at the same time that the development of mutual funds made it easier and less expensive for individuals to invest in small amounts of tax-exempt bonds, and other changes in the tax law reduced the attractiveness of tax-exempt bonds to commercial banks and caused banks to decrease their holdings of tax-exempt bonds. The result was that conditions were right for the stock of tax-exempt bonds to become much more heavily concentrated in individual portfolios during the 1980s (see table 4.10 and chapters 9 and 11).

Two measurement problems cause the shift in tax-exempt bond holdings toward lower income classes shown in figure 8.2 to be overstated. First, the amount of bonds held by taxpayers in lower-income classes in 1983 may be underestimated. 1983 asset holding data from the Survey of Consumer Finances does not capture the increased importance that mutual funds had attained by 1985 as investors in tax-exempt bonds. Second, the amount held by taxpayers in lower-income classes in 1987 may be overestimated. Imprecise reporting instructions may have caused low-income taxpayers (who tend to complete their own tax returns) to report tax deferred income such as individual retirement account interest as well as tax-exempt income.

WHAT DOES IT ALL MEAN?

The equity implications of these data are tough to interpret. Those who object to tax-exempt bonds because of their impact on equity cannot be pleased with the evidence presented in figures 8.1 and 8.2, which suggest that although the tax benefits associated with tax-exempt bonds are more equally distributed among income classes since passage of the Tax Reform Act of 1986, the overall federal tax burden of the highest-income classes has decreased while that of the lower income classes has increased. It appears that the battle has been won but the war has been lost.

This is a good illustration of the danger of focusing on any particular tax provision as a basis for evaluating the tax system's equity. Tax-exempt bonds seem to be a particularly subversive foe to fairness because they can be used to reduce the statutory tax rate to zero. But the equity objectives of the society are not expressed in the statutory marginal tax rate structure of the individual income tax. This was illustrated eloquently by Pechman (1977), who described how each income class's access to exemptions, deductions, exclusions, credits, deferrals, and so forth, generated a substantial difference between each income class's 1976 statutory and effective tax rates. The statutory rate for all joint taxpayers in 1976 was 30.6 percent, but the effective rate was 12.4 percent. For joint taxpayers in the $200,000 to $500,000 class, the rates were 64.5 and 32.7 percent, respectively.

It is simply not realistic to view the statutory rate structure of 1976 as an expression of society's equity norms at that time. If that were so, what can possibly account for the discrepancy between the statutory and effective rate structure produced by an open and representative political system such as ours? Given that the effective rate structure is society's desired norm, one can expect that any effort to alter tax-exempt bonds on equity grounds is likely to be countered by adjustments in other tax preferences that leave the overall pattern of effective tax rates relatively unchanged.

Others have attacked on entirely different grounds the equity implications to be gleaned from data such as those presented in figure 8.2. The text here picks up the discussion from the section on transfer efficiency in chapter 5 and adopts the notation used there. Mussa and Kormendi (1979) maintain that the high incidence of bond holdings by high-income taxpayers is irrelevant to equity concerns because most of the tax benefits that supposedly accrue to those purchasers whose marginal tax rate exceeds the market-clearing tax rate are actually taxed away by inflation. They argue that the excess of the purchasers' tax benefits over their foregone before-tax return on taxable bonds is actually taxed away because the tax system taxes nominal rather than real returns on capital. The *effective* market-clearing tax rate for tax-exempt bonds is thus actually much higher than t_m.

Consider a 28 percent taxpayer choosing between a taxable bond yielding 10 percent before tax and a municipal bond of equivalent risk yielding 7.2 percent. In an economy with anticipated inflation of $p = 5.0$ percent, the anticipated real yield on the taxable bond is

5 percent before tax. This taxpayer is subject to a tax of 2.8 percent, leaving an after-tax nominal return of 7.2 percent and an after-tax real return of 2.2 percent. Because the tax applies to the nominal yield, a substantial part of the anticipated real yield has been taxed away. The effective tax rate, including inflation, is 56 percent rather than 28 percent $[t_m r_c/(r_c - p)]$. This argument suggests that the portion of the federal revenue loss not going to state and local governments is not entirely a windfall gain to high-income taxpayers and that the gain is smaller than it was thought to be.

The two arguments just presented have distributional implications for those whose concern with tax-exempt bonds is the inequity of allowing high-income taxpayers to earn unwarranted windfall gains. The first argument suggests that the gains are not as concentrated among high-income taxpayers as one might think and that other changes in the tax system have counteracted the bond changes, and the second argument suggests that the windfall gains are not as large as one might think.

Notes

1. For detailed explanations of the methodology that produced these estimates, including tax incidence assumptions, see Congressional Budget Office (1987).

2. Another estimation method for tax-exempt interest income earned by individuals utilized the Federal Reserve Board's *Flow of Funds* data on individual holdings of tax-exempt bonds, data on annual new issues and refundings, and a weighted average yield for bonds issued in each year.

3. These estimates were provided by the Division of Research and Statistics, Board of Governors, Federal Reserve System.

4. The top marginal rate was actually 33 percent, due to the phase out of the benefits of the 15 percent marginal tax bracket and the personal exemptions for taxpayers above a certain taxable income.

Part Three

HISTORY AND ECONOMIC EVALUATION
OF TAX-EXEMPT BOND LEGISLATION

Chapter Nine

ECONOMIC INCENTIVES AND DEMAND

The volume of tax-exempt bonds issued every year is a product of the interaction of investors' desire to purchase (demand) the bonds at various prices and state and local governments' desire to issue (supply) bonds at various prices. Federal legislative changes have sought to manipulate both the demand for and supply of tax-exempt bonds in order to restrict bond volume. Some legislation has, at times inadvertently, shrunk the tax benefits associated with the purchase of tax-exempt bonds, thereby reducing investor demand and causing the quantity of bonds issued to decline; other legislation has, usually intentionally, reduced the incentives for issuers to float new issues, thereby inducing state and local governments to issue fewer bonds no matter the size of the tax benefits earned by investors.

Although this book focuses on the legislation that has intentionally manipulated incentives on the supply side of the market, the discussion here begins with the characteristics of the income tax structure that affect the demand for bonds. Demand for tax-exempt bonds, as noted in chapter 4, is primarily driven by the income tax considerations of those seeking to place their savings in assets offering the best combination of return and security. The current chapter discusses the roles of individual and corporate investors; the effect of progressive marginal tax rate schedules; the influence of alternative tax shelters; the use of a minimum income tax on preference income; the deductibility of commercial bank borrowing costs for the purchase of tax-exempt bonds; and nontax factors affecting corporate demand, particularly commercial banks and insurance companies.

The discussion of the demand side of the market proceeds from the perspective of the income tax system as it existed prior to the enactment of federal legislation beginning in the late 1960s that changed some of these incentives. Compared to 1989, this was a time of high marginal and corporate income tax rates and a progressive individual marginal rate structure ranging from 14 percent to 70 percent.

THE DEMAND SCHEDULE

The exclusion of interest income on state and local bonds from federal income taxation reduces the interest rate on tax-exempt bonds relative to the rate on taxable bonds of equal maturity. The value of this subsidy to the state and local sector fluctuates over time and is usually summarized by the ratio of the yield on tax-exempt bonds to the yield on taxable bonds. When this yield ratio declines, the value of the subsidy increases because the state and local sector's borrowing cost for new issues falls relative to its borrowing cost if it has to issue taxable debt. When the ratio rises, the value of the subsidy declines.

The yield ratio is determined by the factors that influence the demand for and supply of tax-exempt bonds. On the demand side, investors with marginal tax rate of t will compare the after-tax return on a taxable bond, $(1 - t)r_c$ where r_c is the pretax return, with the return on a tax-exempt bond of equivalent risk and maturity, r_m. The yield ratio (r_m/r_c) is equal to $(1 - t_m)$, as determined by the marginal investor's marginal tax rate. I deal here with the influence of marginal tax rates.

The demand for tax-exempt bonds is labeled "Demand" in figure 9.1, where the horizontal axis represents the quantity of bonds issued and the vertical axis measures the marginal tax rate that equates the returns on tax-exempt and taxable bonds. The demand for tax-exempt bonds of investors with the highest marginal tax rate that prevailed in the late 1960s, $t = 70$ percent for individuals, is labeled AB. If all tax-exempt bonds can be sold to these investors, r_m will be small compared to r_c, and the yield ratio will be low. If the supply of bonds to be sold exceeds the amount investors in the highest tax bracket are willing to purchase, it becomes necessary to attract individual investors who have lower marginal tax rates. The demand for tax-exempt bonds of individuals with marginal tax rates ranging down to 48 percent is labeled BC.[1] Issuers must offer a higher r_m to attract these investors, causing the yield ratio to be higher.

If the supply of bonds has still not been exhausted, it becomes necessary to sell to a corporate sector that has a 48 percent marginal tax rate. The corporate sector's demand is labeled CD in figure 9.1. To attract corporate buyers, issuers must offer a still higher r_m, causing the yield ratio to be higher still. Finally, the supply of bonds may have to be sold to individual investors with marginal tax rates

Figure 9.1 DEMAND AND SUPPLY OF TAX-EXEMPT BONDS (1968 TAX RATES)

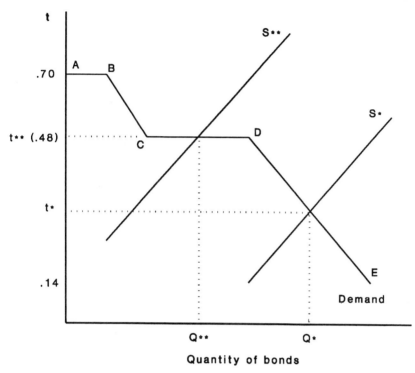

below 48 percent, whose demand is labeled *DE*. The tax-exempt rate r_m will again rise and the yield ratio will go up still higher.

Given this demand curve, the market-clearing marginal tax rate and the yield ratio are determined by the supply schedule of tax-exempt bonds. Other things equal, the greater the volume to be sold, the higher will r_m have to be to attract investors further down in the marginal tax brackets, the higher will be the yield ratio, and the smaller will be the federal subsidy of state and local borrowing costs.[2] If issuers decide to bring a relatively large volume of bonds to market at any given price, the supply curve is shifted right, the market clearing tax rate is relatively low, and the yield ratio and state and local borrowing costs are relatively high. This situation is depicted as the intersection of the demand and S^* curves in figure 9.1, with quantity Q^* of bonds issued at marginal tax rate t^*. If issuers decide to bring a relatively small volume of bonds to market at any given price, the supply curve is shifted left, the market clearing tax rate is relatively high, and the yield ratio and state and local borrowing costs are relatively low. This situation is depicted as the intersection of the Demand and S^{**} curves in figure 9.1, with quantity Q^{**} of bonds issued at marginal tax rate t^{**}.

POSITIONING OF THE DEMAND SCHEDULE

The positioning of the demand curve is affected by changes in the tax structure and a variety of other economic factors. The remainder of the chapter is devoted to a discussion of these factors.

Marginal Tax Rate Structure

A change in the individual marginal tax rate schedule changes the relationship between the tax-exempt bond return, r_m, and the after-tax return on the taxable bond, $(1 - t)r_c$. If the tax rate schedule is lowered, investors at each individual marginal tax rate (all segments of the demand curve except CD—see figure 9.1) find that the after-tax return on taxable bonds has risen relative to tax-exempt bonds. (If the rate structure were increased, all the directional movements would be exactly the opposite to these.) In effect, the untaxed income provided by tax-exempt bonds becomes less attractive relative to the taxable income provided by other assets. The horizontal portion of the demand curve representing each tax bracket's desired purchases of tax-exempt bonds shifts down and is shortened. Some individuals in the BC segment of the demand curve may now have marginal tax rates less than the 48 percent corporate rate, moving them to the DE segment and sliding the corporate segment CD to the left.

In effect, the portions of the curve representing the demand of individuals shift down along the supply curve. If the supply and demand curves intersected to the right of CD prior to the change in the individual rate structure, or if the intersection after the tax change has moved from the CD segment to the DE segment, issuers must market bonds to investors with lower marginal tax rates, the yield ratio will increase, and state and local borrowing costs will increase.[3] The quantity of bonds issued will decrease.

If the corporate tax rate is lowered, the CD segment of the demand schedule is shortened and lowered. Some individuals move from the DE segment of the schedule to the BC segment as their marginal tax rates move above the new corporate rate. This slides the now-shortened CD segment to the right. If the demand and supply schedules intersect on or to the right of the *CD* segment prior to and after the tax change, issuers must market bonds to investors with lower marginal tax rates, the yield ratio will increase, and state and local borrowing costs will increase. The quantity of bonds issued will decrease.

Deductibility of Commercial Bank Interest Expenses

An important tax provision that affects corporate demand for tax-exempt bonds is the ability of commercial banks, when calculating their taxable income, to deduct the interest they pay to depositors to obtain funds that are subsequently used to purchase tax-exempt bonds. Deduction of interest expenses on funds used to purchase tax-exempt bonds is not permitted to individuals. The theory of an income tax is that one should be able to deduct the expenses incurred in earning income, provided the income is included in the tax base. Since interest on tax-exempt bonds is excluded from the tax base, expenses are not deductible in the calculation of taxable income.

Deductibility of interest expenses enables commercial banks to avoid taxes on income from non-tax-exempt bond sources that would otherwise be taxable. This has the effect of increasing the return on tax exempts and increasing commercial bank demand for tax-exempt bonds. In terms of figure 9.1, the *CD* portion of the demand curve associated with the corporate sector is lengthened relative to what it would be in the absence of deductibility. The demand curve from segment *CD* on down shifts to the right. If the supply curve prior to deductibility intersected the *DE* portion of the demand curve but after deductibility intersects the now-lengthened *CD* portion of the demand curve, issuers can market bonds to investors with higher marginal tax rates, the yield ratio will decrease, and state and local borrowing costs will decrease. The quantity of bonds issued will increase.

Alternative Tax Shelters

Although characterization of the investor's portfolio decision as a choice between two financial assets simplifies the expositional task, the fact is that investors balance the expected returns from these financial assets with the expected returns from a variety of preferentially taxed real and financial assets, including such diverse choices as common stock, real estate, equipment leasing, and timber growing. A change in the degree of preferential taxation of these alternative assets will also change investors' demand for tax-exempt bonds in all or some marginal tax brackets.

An increase in the degree of preferential taxation of real assets will decrease the demand for tax-exempt bonds of some investors, both corporate and individual. In terms of figure 9.1, this will shorten some or all portions of the demand schedule, shifting it to the left. If the supply schedule prior to the tax change intersected the CD or DE portions of the demand schedule and after the tax change now intersects the DE portion, issuers must market tax-exempt bonds to investors with lower marginal tax rates. The yield ratio will increase, and state and local borrowing costs will increase. The quantity of bonds issued will decrease.

The same effect is achieved by creating new financial assets with the distinguishing characteristic of tax-exempt bonds, that is, that provide interest income exempt from taxation. The competing asset has the effect of reducing the demand for tax-exempt bonds and shortening each investor's portion of the demand schedule. Depending upon the pre- and post-tax-change intersections of the demand and supply schedules, bonds may have to be marketed to lower tax bracket investors, the yield ratio will increase, and state and local borrowing costs will increase. The quantity of bonds issued will decrease.

Minimum Tax

Concern has long existed that an income tax rife with tax preferences for assorted types of capital income enables some individuals and corporations to avoid paying their fair share of taxes to support public services.

.... many individuals and corporations did not pay tax on a substantial part of their economic income as a result of the receipt of various kinds of tax-favored income or special deductions.... As a result, there were large variations in the tax burdens placed on individuals or corporations with similar economic incomes, depending upon the size of their preference income. (Joint Committee on Internal Revenue Taxation 1970, 104–5)

At various times, this problem has been dealt with by the introduction of a minimum tax on this preference income. The general idea is that all citizens should pay some tax, and if they are not paying it via the regular income tax, then at the least they should have to pay some (smaller) amount based upon the tax preferences used to reduce their taxable income. When a minimum tax is implemented, the effect on tax-exempt bonds depends upon what tax preferences are included in the minimum tax base.

If the base includes many tax preferences on assets competing with tax-exempt bonds, but does not include the interest income from tax-exempt bonds, then the degree of preferential taxation for tax-exempt bonds has been increased relative to other preferentially taxed assets. Those seeking to shelter their income from taxation will find tax-exempt bonds more attractive and will increase their demand for the bonds. In terms of figure 9.1, all segments of the demand curve would shift to the right if the minimum tax applies to both corporate and individual tax preferences. If the supply curve has not changed, and the shift has not simply moved the intersection of the demand and supply schedules along the CD segment of the demand curve, the implicit tax rate would rise, the yield ratio would decline, and state and local borrowing costs would decrease. The quantity of bonds issued would increase.

Nontax Factors Influencing Corporate Purchasers

The positioning of the demand curve is also affected by nontax factors, particularly those portions of the schedule representing the desired purchases of commercial banks and property and casualty insurance companies. These institutions hold state and local bonds to shield their income from federal taxation, and their purchases are determined primarily by expectations of profitability and loan demand. Commercial banks have short-term liabilities and tend to purchase short-term tax-exempt issues, while property and casualty insurance companies have long-term liabilities and tend to purchase long-term tax-exempt issues. When they expect to experience low profitability or high loan demand, they decrease their net purchases of tax-exempt bonds. In effect, this shortens the horizontal portion of the demand curve associated with their marginal tax rate and shifts down those portions of the demand curve associated with lower marginal tax rates. The CD segment is shortened and the DE segment shifts down. If prior to the change the supply curve intersected the demand curve in or to the right of the now-eliminated portion of the CD segment, the yield ratio and state and local borrowing costs are increased. The quantity of bonds issued is decreased. Commercial bank holdings may also be influenced by the desire to attract some of the state's demand deposit accounts. Some quid pro quo relationship may exist between a commercial bank's state demand deposit business and its willingness to hold bonds of the state and its local governments in its investment portfolios as security.

Notes

1. This downward sloping portion of the demand curve represents a smoothing of a series of horizontal segments, one for each marginal tax rate, with each tax rate's segment beginning at the quantity of bonds that ends the previous segment.

2. Numerous articles have estimated the effect of the supply of tax-exempt bonds on municipal interest rates and the yield ratio. See Kidwell and Koch (1983), Hendershott and Koch (1977), and Peek and Wilcox (1986).

3. The importance of the marginal rate structure as a determinant of the yield ratio has been demonstrated in three recent studies. See the article by Peek and Wilcox (1986) and two others by Poterba (1984, 1989).

Chapter Ten

ECONOMIC INCENTIVES AND SUPPLY

The issuance of tax-exempt bonds to fund public capital formation is derived from the desire of state and local taxpayers for public consumption. This desire is determined by such factors as the size of the population, the income of the citizens, the production characteristics (e.g., the capital/labor ratio) of publicly provided goods, the geography of the jurisdiction, and citizens' tastes and preferences. However, the primary emphasis of this book is not on the use of tax-exempt bonds for such traditional public capital formation, but on their use for nongovernmental purposes. Thus, this chapter focuses on those factors that provide incentives for the issuance of bonds to finance private activities.

Five factors are discussed in turn. The first factor is that economic theory has been unable to provide practical guidance on a case-by-case basis for determining what activities satisfy a public purpose, thus leaving the decision in the hands of state and local officials. These officials face four types of incentives to issue more than the socially desirable amount of tax-exempt bonds: the cost of the bonds to the state and local taxpayer is substantially understated; the benefits to the state and local taxpayer are substantially overstated compared to the benefits for the federal taxpayer; the private sector is aware that use of these bonds can reduce their cost of capital; and substantial electoral benefits may be garnered by state and local officials for providing subsidized financing to their constituents, both business and individual.

DEFINING PUBLIC PURPOSE

A major reason it was so difficult for Congress to control the use of tax-exempt bonds for private purposes was the difficulty of defining what constitutes a public purpose. In practice, determination of what activities satisfied a public purpose proceeded in two steps. State and local officials made the *initial* decision to finance a particular activity with tax-exempt bonds, and then issued bonds for that purpose. This decision established the activity as a public purpose or, at least, as an activity eligible for tax-exempt financing.

Such state and local initiative was supported on both economic and legal grounds. First, it was consistent with the view that state and local officials are better able to discern their constituents' preferences for public goods than are more geographically remote federal officials. Second, it was consistent with the now-rejected view that the United States Constitution protects state and local governments against all federal intrusion in their financial affairs. In this view, the theory of intergovernmental tax immunity precludes the federal government from taxing the interest income from state and local bonds, whatever their purpose.[1]

The second step in the definition of public purpose was the often-exercised congressional right to an after-the-fact review of these purposes. State and local officials tended to interpret these persistent efforts to limit the use of tax-exempt bonds for some activities as an assertion by Congress that it believes itself to be a better judge of citizens' preferences for public goods than are state and local officials, and that Congress rejects the constitutional justification for tax exemption.

These differing views of congressional actions reflected an important fact: although economic theory (as discussed in chapter 5) provides justification for federal subsidy of the state and local sector, it is not a practical tool for Congress to use to determine precisely what services should be subsidized. This point requires some explanation.

The economic justification for public goods provision suggests that the state and local sector should provide goods and services when external benefits or costs preclude the private sector from providing the socially desirable amount. This amounts to saying that goods provided publicly should have a substantial element of collective (or joint) consumption. Considerations of intergovernmental efficiency, however, suggest that not all collectively consumed goods provided by the state and local sector merit federal subsidy. This more restrictive view confines the federal subsidy to those collective consumption goods that are likely to be underprovided by state and local governments. And such underprovision often results from the spillover of benefits among jurisdictions.

The task of identifying those goods that possess externalities sufficiently large to merit state and local provision, but not provided in the proper quantities by the state and local sector owing to the presence of spillovers, is akin to untying the Gordian knot. One's perception of externalities and of state and local roles versus federal roles in the accommodation of externalities is undoubtedly influenced by all those noneconomic and nonquantifiable factors that determine our preferences, such as politics, religion, culture, and ethics.

A few examples are instructive in this regard, particularly because (as will be shown in chapter 11, on legislation) these examples have been the subject of congressional action attempting to define what satisfies a public purpose. Golf courses, tennis courts, and other recreational facilities would be considered by many to be essentially private goods. But some individuals perceive it to be unjust to withhold recreational goods from those incapable of paying for them. In effect, these individuals' sense of interdependence perceives benefits for all when those unable to pay gain access to the facilities. Should such individuals dominate the political process in a jurisdiction, golf courses and tennis courts become legitimate prospects for state and local provision. However, unless such preferences are representative of a fairly broad spectrum of voters in the United States, golf courses and tennis courts are probably not legitimate prospects for federal subsidy of state and local provision. In this instance, the case for federal subsidy fails owing to the absence of spillovers.

Conversely, pollution abatement is often cited as an activity whose collective consumption benefits require public provision. It may be, furthermore, that the external costs from pollution caused by manufacturing activity spill out of the community in which they are produced, being carried by rivers to downstream communities or by air currents to adjacent communities. The citizens in the producing community are unlikely to provide sufficient incentives for pollution abatement to satisfy the citizens of these downstream or adjacent communities. If this pattern of external cost spillovers is repeated in a sufficient number of locations throughout the country, federal subsidy of state and local pollution abatement is likely to receive the type of attention that has been devoted to acid rain and hazardous wastes.[2] Federal subsidy of such activities is, of course, but one alternative for control. Regulation and taxes are other policy instruments for achieving the public interest in adjusting outputs. These alternatives have different allocative and distributional effects than subsidies.

This discussion illustrates that there is no single answer to the questions of what goods and services the state and local sector should provide, and which of these should receive a federal subsidy. Economic theory was useful in explaining the conditions under which federal subsidy was desirable. But it was not easy to quantify these conditions in a manner that Congress could use to determine public purpose, as is made abundantly clear in chapter 11's description of congressional attempts to define public purpose.[3] The definition of public purpose is necessarily elastic and subject to continuous reexamination. In the political process this has proved to be conducive to the growth of private-purpose bond volume.

UNDERSTATEMENT OF COSTS TO THE STATE AND LOCAL SECTOR

Costs to state and local taxpayers for the issuance of tax-exempt bonds were understated in several respects: state and local taxpayers' financial responsibility for the payment of debt service was lacking; the taxpayers benefiting from the bond issuance bore little of the cost of reduced national income caused by directing scarce savings into less productive investments; arbitrage profits could be earned; and taxpayer approval was usually not required or was easily avoided by state and local officials. Standard economic theory suggests that any good priced at zero (or even at less than its marginal cost of production) will generate excess demand.

Absence of State and Local Taxpayer Financial Responsibility

The extent of state and local taxpayers' financial responsibility for tax-exempt revenue bonds had a direct effect on state and local officials' perception of the cost to their constituents. State and local officials tended to view tax-exempt revenue bonds as being costless to their taxpayers, and thus to themselves. To understand this thinking it is necessary to recall the distinction between a general obligation (GO) bond and a revenue bond. The GO bond pledges the tax revenues of the state or local government as payment for the debt service. A revenue bond usually pledges only the revenue stream generated by the project being built or revenue from other projects, but not the government's taxing power.[4] Almost all of the activities that have been the subject of congressional limitation efforts were financed with revenue bonds.

Beginning in 1968, the Internal Revenue Code did impose a financial responsibility test for tax-exempt status of private-purpose bonds. If more than 25 percent of the bond proceeds was used in a trade or business, then not more than 25 percent of the debt service could be secured by the property or revenues of an entity engaged in a trade or business. This seemed to suggest that bonds were eligible for tax exemption only if the issuing entity (frequently an agency or authority created by a government) pledged to repay 75 percent or more of the debt service with tax revenues or other government funds rather than with revenues generated from the project being built.

This financial responsibility test was short-circuited for a long list of private activities (see chapter 11 for the details) that were, in effect, granted tax exemption even if more than 25 percent of the debt service was secured by property used in a trade or business. This meant the government could pledge user charges or revenues from the project being built for payment of the debt service. The state or local government did not need to pledge to repay the debt service with tax revenues even if these pledged project revenues were inadequate to cover debt service.

For example, if a hospital built with revenue bond proceeds was underutilized and revenues were inadequate for full payment of debt service, the issuing government was under no obligation to use tax revenues for the shortfall. Thus, the cost of an unsuccessful project fell upon bondholders in the form of defaulted or delayed payments. Because the other major cost of the subsidy, the foregone tax revenues from nontaxable interest income, fell upon federal taxpayers, state and local government officials tended to act as though their middleman role generated no direct costs.

In discussing the reasons for the growth of mortgage revenue bonds for owner-occupied housing, the Congressional Budget Office (1979, 5) stated: ". . .these programs appeal strongly to local officials who believe that the programs provide them with an opportunity to give positive benefits to their constituents *with no expenditure of local or state tax revenues*" [emphasis added].

It is likely, however, that these tax-exempt revenue bonds imposed some indirect costs in the form of higher interest rates for general obligation financings. Economic theory suggests that these private-purpose issues increased the supply of tax-exempt bonds and, assuming the supply of savings seeking tax-exempt shelter did not increase, should have raised the interest cost for financing traditional public sector infrastructure. In fact, there is evidence to indicate that an increased supply of bonds did narrow the spread between tax-exempt and taxable bond yields (Peek and Wilcox 1986; Peterson, Tuccillo, and Weicher 1981). Despite the implications of the theory and the empirical evidence, state and local officials tended to reject or minimize the importance of these overall higher interest costs, perhaps because the amount of bonds each jurisdiction contributed to supply was too small by itself to have more than a tiny and imperceptible impact on interest costs.

Decreases in National Income Borne by Others

When scarce savings are diverted from investments that the market has determined provide a higher private return into investments that provide lower private returns, a reduction in national income occurs. This reduction imposes a cost because there is a smaller pie—fewer goods and services—to divide among the nation's citizens. The bottom two rows of table 7.1 in chapter 7 provided estimates of these reductions in 1982 and 1989 for private investments financed with 10 percent to 50 percent tax-exempt bonds. A private investment financed with 50 percent tax-exempt bonds imposed a loss of national income in 1982 that ranged up to 19.46 percent of the return available from the best alternative investment; this loss ranged up to 9.65 percent in 1989.

Most of this loss is not borne by the state and local taxpayers on whose behalf the tax-exempt bonds were issued, but by the entire population of the country. Unless state and local taxpayers are sufficiently astute to realize that they are bearing similar losses imposed by the bonds being issued by other state and local jurisdictions, they substantially underestimate the cost of bond issuance to themselves. There is little indication that state and local taxpayers are aware of these costs.

Arbitrage Profits

A third factor in reducing the state and local taxpayer's cost was the investment of tax-exempt bond proceeds in higher-yielding taxable securities. Since state and local governments do not pay taxes, they receive the full pretax return on the securities. The difference between the earnings on the taxable securities and the interest expense on the tax-exempt bonds is called arbitrage profits. These arbitrage profits were frequently sufficient to pay not only for issuance costs but also to further reduce the effective interest rate on the bonds below the stated tax-exempt rate. A few simple examples will help to illustrate this technique. The object is to demonstrate how valuable arbitrage possibilities were to bond issuers prior to the first restrictions enacted in 1969. The examples are by no means illustrative of the complexity introduced by the numerous laws and regulations enacted since 1969 to control the issuance of arbitrage bonds.[5]

Consider, first, a straightforward arbitrage transaction of the type available prior to the restrictions adopted in 1969, identified in table 10.1 as "Straight Arbitrage Deal." Assume that a governmental unit wanted to construct a $10 million building. If it issued $10 million of tax-exempt term bonds at a 5 percent interest rate, its annual interest cost would be $500,000. Absent any restrictions on arbitrage earnings, suppose the construction schedule enabled the governmental unit to invest a five-year average of $5 million of the proceeds in taxable securities yielding 7 percent, with all proceeds expended by the end of the fifth year. These interest earnings would amount to $350,000 each year, $1.75 million over five years. In effect, the governmental unit's actual interest expense each of those five years is only $150,000 ($500,000 interest expense minus $350,000 interest earnings), an effective interest rate of 1.5 percent over the five-year period.

The governmental unit will include these arbitrage earnings in its financial deliberations, and is free to do several different things with

Table 10.1 ARBITRAGE PROFITS AND ADVANCE REFUNDING: A SIMPLIFIED EXAMPLE FOR A $10 MILLION, 5 PERCENT TERM BOND ISSUE

	Straight Arbitrage Deal (Years 1 to 5)[a]	Advance Refunding Deal (Years 6 to 10)[b]
Annual interest expense on original bond issue	$500,000	$500,000
Annual earnings on taxable securities	$350,000	$550,000
Effective borrowing rate on original bond issue	1.5%	4.5%
Reduction in annual tax payment or service fee on refunding bond issue	NA[c]	$100,000

a. Assumes a tax-exempt rate of 5%, a taxable rate of 7%, and that the construction schedule allows five-year average taxable security holdings of $5 million.
b. Assumes advance refunding is motivated by a decline in tax-exempt rate after year five to 4%, and the taxable rate to 5.5%.
c. NA, not applicable.

the profits. Part of the project cost could be financed with the arbitrage earnings, and the amount borrowed could be reduced accordingly. The project could be expanded and a larger amount of bonds issued. The earnings could, for all intents and purposes, be included in the general fund and used to increase current expenditures or to reduce the governmental unit's tax rate and its taxpayers' tax bills. If the project were financed with revenue bonds, the earnings could be used to reduce the special assessments or fees charged to users of the facility being constructed.

Another potential arbitrage opportunity is created by interest rate fluctuations that make it advantageous for issuers to retire outstanding bonds prior to maturity with the proceeds of a new issue carrying a lower interest rate. In itself, this does not necessarily create an arbitrage opportunity that did not exist prior to refunding (presumably, arbitrage profits are being earned on the original issue). But the provisions of the original bond issue may preclude its refunding— a call date may be too far in the future, or a substantial premium may have to be paid to bondholders if the bonds are called. In this case, advance refunding can be utilized—a second bond issue is created without retiring the original bond issue, thereby supporting a capital facility with outstanding bonds worth twice its value.

Although there are many complicated variants of advance refunding, the basic technique is very simple. The refunding bond issue carries a lower tax-exempt interest rate than the original bond issue. The proceeds of the refunding bond issue are invested in taxable securities (yield higher than the yield on the original tax-exempt securities) with maturities that match the maturities on the original bond issue. As these taxable securities mature and provide interest payments, these principal and interest payments are used to make the principal and interest payments on the original issue, with a little left over because the interest receipts from the taxable securities are greater than the interest payments on the original issue. Since the original tax-exempt bond issue is now secured by the proceeds and interest from the taxable securities, the revenue source that formerly secured the original tax-exempt bond issue is available to secure the refunding bond issue.

Returning to the previous example, suppose tax-exempt rates decline to 4 percent after year five and the issuer wants to refund the bonds, but is prevented from doing so by the absence of a call provision or prohibitive penalties for exercising a call. The issuer markets $10 million of tax-exempt bonds at a 4 percent interest rate and invests all the proceeds in taxable securities at a 5.5 percent rate (assuming taxable rates have also fallen) with a maturity schedule identical to the original issue. This example is listed in table 10.1 as "Advance Refunding Deal." Each year the issuer earns $550,000 interest on the taxable securities and must pay $500,000 of interest on the original tax-exempt bonds (that carry a 5 percent interest rate). The issuer is earning $50,000 of arbitrage profits, and the effective interest rate on the original bond issue is 4.5 percent (based upon interest expense of $500,000 minus $50,000 of arbitrage profits). In addition, the revenue stream that had been designed to secure the original bonds carrying a 5 percent interest rate is now only required to secure refunding bonds carrying a 4 percent interest rate. The tax contribution (GO bonds) or service fee (revenue bonds) necessary to finance the debt service on these refunding bonds could be reduced.[6]

As laws and regulations began to restrict state and local access to arbitrage earnings, new opportunities were created by the move of state and local governments into the "social banker" function, whereby the stated purpose of the borrowing is for state and local governments to take the bond proceeds and lend them to private individuals and businesses. A good example is the mortgage revenue bond program that was developed in response to escalating mortgage interest rates for owner-occupied housing in the late 1970s. State and local governments issued bonds at tax-exempt interest rates and loaned the money to homebuyers at rates below prevailing (taxable) mortgage interest rates. In effect, they were using the bond proceeds to purchase taxable securities—a straight arbitrage deal. The question was just where the lending rate should be set on the spectrum between the taxable and tax-exempt rates. Should arbitrage profits be allowed to exceed the amount necessary to cover the program's administrative cost, and the excess be allowed to accumulate in reserves or be spent for other, perhaps unrelated, purposes?

Another example of such arbitrage earnings is the student loan bond programs adopted in many states in the 1960s and 1970s. State and local governments issue bonds at tax-exempt interest rates and use the proceeds to buy portfolios of federally guaranteed student loans originated by financial institutions at rates below the prevailing commercial rates but substantially above the tax-exempt rate. Until the student has left school, the federal government pays the holder of the loans (the state and local government that issued the bonds to buy the loans) annual interest of 7 percent, a rate substantially below the interest rate the student will pay when he or she finally assumes responsibility for debt service on the loan. In addition, the federal government makes a special allowance payment to the lender (in this case, the state and local government) equal to the interest rate on 91-day Treasury bills minus 3.5 percentage points. As interest rates rose in the late 1970s, the special allowance payment became very substantial. Although the tax law had by this time imposed restrictions on the arbitrage earnings allowed to state and local governments, the special allowance payment was excluded by statute from this restriction. Thus, it was possible for state and local governments to earn substantially larger arbitrage profits on their student loan programs, an activity classified as a private activity, that could not be earned on bonds issued for traditional public purposes

The Congressional Budget Office has analyzed the arbitrage earnings of the student loan bond programs and projected the likely arbitrage earnings of bonds issued by two states, North Dakota and Wisconsin. They calculated that the present value of arbitrage earnings on a 1979 North Dakota bond issue of $78 million would exceed program operating expenses by $8 million. Thus, North Dakota would earn arbitrage profits in excess of administrative costs equal to 10.25 percent of the principal. In Wisconsin, the comparable figure for a $40 million dollar bond issue was $8 million dollars in present-value terms, an arbitrage profit in excess of administrative costs equal to 20.0 percent of the principal (Congressional Budget Office 1980, 55–57).

Absence of Requirements for Taxpayer Approval

A final aspect bearing on the popularity and cost of revenue bonds was the absence of a requirement for state and local officials to seek the explicit approval of their constituents to issue these bonds. In many states, the constitutional and statutory restrictions imposed on bond issuance apply only to general obligation bonds, which pledge the taxing power of the jurisdiction to pay the debt service (see the tables in appendix 2A, chapter 2). A requirement to seek the approval of the general public implies that the public official must provide a justification for a bond issue, and is an obvious incentive to careful consideration of its costs and benefits.

OVERSTATEMENT OF PUBLIC BENEFITS

State and local officials clearly saw private-purpose bonds as beneficial. First, they maintained that these bonds increased aggregate investment and federal tax revenue, and were therefore beneficial national investments. Second, even if aggregate investment and federal tax revenue did not increase, state and local government officials saw the bond proceeds as generating increased investment and jobs in the community, thereby expanding the state and local tax base.

This section discusses these issues. First, it reviews the literature that evaluates the response of savings to an increased rate of return on investment caused by reductions in the taxation of income from capital. A positive response is necessary if private-purpose tax-exempt bonds are to increase aggregate investment, employment, and federal revenue. Second, it investigates whether a positive savings response necessarily implies that Congress need not be so concerned about the growth in tax-exempt bond volume. Finally, it draws on the discussion of public intervention in private markets presented in chapter 5 to suggest how the benefits from tax-exempt bonds should be evaluated.

Can Private-Purpose Bonds Increase Federal Tax Revenue?

Unless unutilized savings are lying about prior to bond issuance, the ability of private-purpose revenue bonds to stimulate economic activity for the nation as a whole depends to a significant extent upon the responsiveness of savers to an increase in the return to capital caused by a decrease in taxation of capital income.

The sensitivity of savings to an increase in the return to capital has long been a contentious issue in the economics literature. The most recent burst of activity in the area probably stems from an article by Boskin (1978) that found a substantial positive relationship between the savings rate and the rate of return on capital. This article was carefully analyzed by Howrey and Hymans (1980), who found that Boskin's substantial positive relationship was very sensitive to model specification—it was not robust, in statistical terms. Furthermore, the estimate was an uncompensated response, that is, it included both effects from a change in the rate of return to capital—the change in the relative price of saving (the substitution effect) and the change in the incomes of savers (the income effect). The two effects could not be separated in the results, but because the income effect is always expected to be positive, the substitution effect had to be considerably lower (and could conceivably be negative). Since most tax policy changes take place in an environment that in effect provides (for taxpayers as a group) a compensated change in the rate of return on capital (incomes are held constant), it is important to have an estimate that nets out the portion of the savings change induced by the associated change in income.

Part of the difficulty with the savings literature was that the models had not incorporated a long enough time horizon, being based on an unrealistically short two-period choice between saving and consumption. Summers (1981) then led the analysis of savings behavior into the context of an individual's life cycle. But the development of the life cycle model is in an early stage and suffers from both conceptual and measurement difficulties that may overestimate the likely savings response to tax changes. The models must ultimately incorporate such concerns as. the share of necessities in consumption that restrict the proportion of income that can be shuffled between saving and consumption; the lumpiness of consumption caused by big-ticket items such as a house, college tuition, and other consumer durables; the presence of liquidity constraints that put obstacles in the path of reallocating consumption across time; and the role of bequests. Starrett (1988) showed that savings response estimates in the life-cycle models are very sensitive to the assumptions made about these factors.

The preponderance of the empirical evidence on the sensitivity of savings to changes in tax policy has been summarized by Bosworth (1988, 267): "To date, the empirical evidence has been quite conclusive in discounting any substantial effect on overall private saving rates of changes in the return to capital. Tax incentives for saving, in short, have a very small bang for the buck."

A survey of the compensated response of savings to a change in the rate of return to capital (the substitution effect) by Kotlikoff and Auerbach (1987) found estimates ranging from 0.07 to 0.45. This means that a 1 percent increase in the rate of return would generate anywhere from a 0.07 percent to a 0.45 percent increase in savings. The simulations in Kotlikoff and Auerbach's book used a mid-range value of 0.25. Some observers have suggested that, given the uncertainty surrounding this relationship, the most certain method of raising national savings is not through tax policy but through raising government savings (reducing the deficit) (Bosworth 1988; Von Furstenburg and Malkiel 1977).

Is It Good Policy to Judge Private-Purpose Bonds by Their Effect on Investment, Employment, and Federal Tax Revenue?

Suppose for the sake of argument that tax-exempt bonds can increase savings, investment, employment, and federal tax revenue. Does this necessarily imply that it is good policy to provide funding for all tax-exempt bonds? The short answer is no. The somewhat longer explanation has two elements. First, as capital accumulates from the increased savings, the most productive investments are exhausted and the marginal rate of return on investment begins to decline. As the rate of return declines, the savings rate begins to decline. Thus, we want to maximize the returns earned from the increased savings. Second, there is nothing unique about the stimulation properties of private-purpose revenue bonds. Utilizing a different investment stimulus program to achieve the increase in economic activity makes no appreciable difference to the level of the federal budget and the economy.[7]

Thus, from an aggregate perspective, whether or not private-purpose revenue bonds stimulated savings and investment and generated a net increase in federal tax revenues is not important to an evaluation of the bonds. Any effect they had on investment and federal revenues could have been provided by other means. The choice of which type of subsidy instrument is to be used or which activities are to be subsidized to attain the goal should be determined using some other criterion. Perhaps the irrelevance of the revenue question to the policy debate can be more clearly understood by tracing the effects of the tax incentives.

One must ask What would the foregone federal revenue from the exempt interest income be used for if not to subsidize tax-exempt bonds? Either taxes would be lower and aftertax disposable incomes higher, or the federal government would use the money to subsidize some other activity. In any case, all the beneficial investment and employment ascribed to the tax-exempt bonds would occur in some other industry, activity, or location. These foregone benefits represent the costs from federal subsidy of tax-exempt bonds, and must be subtracted from bond benefits to arrive at a measure of net benefits. It does not appear likely that a net benefit will result from such a calculation.

Alternatively, suppose savings are not responsive to an increase in the rate of return. The answer does not change. The tax-exempt bond incentives can be expected to simply reallocate investment and employment among locations and investment activities. The revenues associated with the bond investment can be estimated, but it is still necessary to estimate the loss of revenue from investment and employment displaced by the bonds. The end result is that little or no net revenue gain is likely to occur.

Benefits from Private-Purpose Tax-Exempt Bonds

If an increase in federal tax revenue cannot be used to justify private-purpose tax-exempt bonds, how can they be justified? As discussed in chapter 5, the generation of social benefits is a conceptually sounder basis upon which to judge the desirability of the bonds. The argument is that guiding investment and employment to geographic areas or activities that generate significant external benefits provides benefits to society in excess of what would be obtained if the investment and employment were directed by the private market. One might say that society values the improvement in the allocation of resources or the resulting change in the distribution of income.

It is possible that those jurisdictions that used the bonds succeeded in generating more taxable economic activity than they would have received if, for example, liberalized depreciation rules were utilized to stimulate investment. Considerable effort has been expended to document such effects.[8] A few examples are instructive.

Ture (1983) showed that New York State's industrial development bond program produced many new jobs for the state. Although this may well have been the case, the jobs created or maintained in New York were offset by a reduction of jobs in other locations, as the previous discussion indicates. Dewar (1980) suggested that Massachusetts's industrial development bond program did not produce many new jobs, as bond users reported they simply substituted the tax-exempt bond financing for other sources of capital. In addition, Stutzer (1985) examined the proposition that small-issue industrial development bonds increased statewide employment or property tax base growth in Minnesota, and concluded that the bonds did not have a significant effect. Thus, the evaluation studies suggest that even the state and local governments issuing the bonds may not have received appreciable benefits in some cases; and in cases where they did, it is likely that the increased investment and employment did not represent net benefits for the nation as a whole.

What the search for "benefits" seems to come down to is that the allocation of resources or the distribution of investment and employment by location or socioeconomic group was affected.[9] Unless these allocational or distributional goals were articulated by the federal government as a policy goal, however, one is hard pressed to see the changes as a "benefit" to society.

Even if such goals were articulated, they could not be achieved if the subsidy was available for firms and individuals generally, regardless of activity, location, or socioeconomic group served, as was the case before 1969. In such circumstances, no tax-induced capital cost differential exists and investment choices are based on other factors. In fact, as will be seen in chapter 11, the congressional effort that began in 1969 to restrict the volume of some private-purpose bonds by making eligibility for tax exemption dependent upon a more careful targeting of specific activities, groups, and locations does seem to suggest that Congress sees these allocational and distributional effects as a national benefit.

REDUCTION OF THE PRIVATE COST OF CAPITAL

The only way a private firm or individual could obtain access to the low-cost financing provided by tax-exempt debt was through the cooperation of public officials. The greater the potential reduction in the firm's cost of capital provided by tax-exempt financing, the greater was the pressure on state and local officials to issue more bonds on behalf of the nongovernmental user.

The federal income tax law provided many incentives to stimulate investment. The incentive offered to the state and local sector was the low interest rate on its bonds (relative to the interest rate on taxable bonds) provided by the exclusion of interest income from federal taxation. Numerous incentives were offered directly to the private sector, but the most important were the investment tax credit and accelerated depreciation (depreciation deductions in excess of economic depreciation). All of these incentives lowered the firm's rental cost of capital (the annual cost for a dollar of capital).

The use of tax-exempt financing for the capital needs of private firms or individuals enabled these private entities to combine the benefits of tax incentives designed for public and for private investment. Table 7.1 presented estimates of the rental cost of capital for a firm making investments in 1982 and 1989 in which the breakdown between equipment and structures is representative of the United States capital stock. The first column (to the right of the stub) of the first two rows shows the rental cost for an investment financed with 50 percent taxable debt and 50 percent equity, which used the investment tax credit and accelerated depreciation allowances: the rental cost of capital was 13.18 cents per dollar in 1982 and 16.31 cents per dollar in 1989.

The remaining columns of rows 1 and 2 show what happens to

the rental cost of capital when tax-exempt debt is substituted for taxable debt. The lower interest cost for tax-exempt debt caused the rental cost of capital to decrease to 12.95 cents per dollar in 1982 and 16.15 cents per dollar in 1989, when tax-exempt debt was used to finance 10 percent of the investment, and to 12.07 cents per dollar in 1982 and 15.48 cents per dollar in 1989, when tax-exempt debt was used to finance 50 percent of the investment. Rows 3 and 4 calculate the percentage reduction in the cost of capital from this use of the tax-exemption privilege. A project that substituted tax-exempt for all taxable debt (0.50 share financed with tax-exempt bonds) had its rental cost of capital reduced by 8.42 percent in 1982 and 5.09 percent in 1989.

It is apparent from these estimates that the ability of a private entity to gain access to tax-exempt financing for the debt-financed portion of its investment significantly lowered its cost of capital. This provided a substantial incentive for the private sector to pressure public officials to act as conduits for such financing. Given the tendency of state and local officials to understate the costs and overstate the benefits to their taxpayers from issuing bonds on behalf of nongovernmental entities, this incentive probably helped to increase the supply of tax-exempt revenue bonds.

ELECTORAL BENEFITS FOR STATE AND LOCAL OFFICIALS

A belief has long existed concerning the way in which American society makes decisions about the public's business. In general, it has been suggested that the participants in the public decision-making process ought to act differently than they do when making private economic decisions; they should be motivated by altruism and some vision of the public interest, not by self-interest. The discussions of civics, government, and public policy that most of us were exposed to in secondary school assumed that the participants in the decision-making process did indeed act in this way. Then, when the results of political decision making ran counter to the outcome that obviously would serve the public interest, the preferred solution often was to alter the institutions to enable the altruistic and public interest motives of the participants to achieve their full expression.

This view of collective decisionmaking has been challenged by the public choice theorists. Among other areas of inquiry, those toiling in the public choice vineyard study the effect of the behavior of participants in the political process on collective decision making and choices (Mueller 1976; Russell 1979). One of the behavioral axioms that has been subjected to repeated testing in the public choice literature is that those involved in making public decisions act from different motivations than when they make private decisions (Mueller 1976; Tullock 1979). Numerous efforts have been made to determine whether public decision makers are also motivated by self-interest. Rather than master issues, do legislators and other elected officials attempt to assist constituents and contributors who are important to their reelection prospects? Do bureaucrats, with pay scales controlled, attempt to maximize their power via the size of budgets and staff? And do judges attempt to make decisions based upon original intent and precedent because it is in their self-interest to preserve the demand for (and value of) the skills needed for this task (and over which their profession has monopoly control)?

One would be hard pressed to design a subsidy system more perfectly configured to the self-interest motive of elected officials than the tax-exempt bond provision of the Internal Revenue Code that existed prior to 1969. Elected officials need votes and resources to run for election and reelection. Political support is likely to follow if the influential business community, homeowners, college students, nonprofit organizations and assorted other groups can be given access to low-cost capital through the effort of the elected official.[10] Even if some citizens might think the process unseemly, many jurisdictions required no public notice or approval prior to issuance of bonds for which the tax base was not responsible for debt service. And the federal government did not require notice or approval at the state and local levels. Thus, the entire process of issuing the bonds and transferring the proceeds to the private sector could usually be carried out with relatively little public participation and awareness.

In addition, even if the bond issuance was public knowledge, those constituents not receiving the low-cost financing were usually encouraged to believe they would receive indirect benefits from increased investment and employment. Balanced against these perceived benefits, constituents incurred no direct costs for providing this subsidy. True, all constituents paying federal income taxes incurred an indirect cost in the form of higher federal taxes or lower federal expenditures necessary to pay for the foregone tax revenue on the exempt interest income. But these costs were probably perceived as being very low, since they were being borne by all taxpayers in the United States. Only if state and local taxpayers accurately perceived the cost implications for themselves when all states and localities issued bonds in the same relative amounts as their own jurisdiction would they be likely to object to their officials' use of these bonds for private purposes. This type of financial insight—of federal tax increases and expenditure reductions, of increased tax-exempt interest rates for financing traditional public facilities, and of no net investment and employment—simply did not occur to the average state and local taxpayer.[11]

CONCLUSION

Several economic incentives influenced the rapid growth in the volume of tax-exempt bonds issued for private purposes that began in the 1960s. The inability of economic theory to provide practical guidance on a case-by-case basis for determining what activities satisfy a public purpose left the decision in the hands of state and local officials. These officials faced numerous incentives to issue bonds in excess of the socially desirable amounts. State and local taxpayers incurred almost no direct costs from the issuance of these bonds, and had to bear a very small share of the decreased national income that resulted from directing scarce savings into less productive investments. The benefits as perceived by state and local officials and taxpayers substantially exceeded the benefits to the nation, as net investment and employment did not increase but were simply reallocated among activities and redistributed geographically. The ability of private businesses and individuals to lower their cost of capital by using tax-exempt financing created increased pressure on state and local officials for bond issuance. And the interest of state and local officials in garnering votes and contributions for reelection gave them some incentive for seeking out and encouraging the use of tax-exempt bonds by the private sector.

All of these factors had the effect of causing the state and local sector to increase the amount of bonds issued at any given tax rate or yield ratio. In effect, the supply curve was shifted to the right. Referring to the diagram of the tax-exempt bond market in figure 9.1, chapter 9, one might say these incentives caused the supply curve to shift from S^{**} (public-purpose bonds) to S^* (public plus private-purpose bonds), increasing the volume of bonds from Q^{**} to Q^* and lowering the market-clearing tax rate from t^{**} to t^*. As illustrated in figure 8.1, this additional supply of private-purpose bonds raises the borrowing costs on all state and local bonds, including those for public purposes. The only way this would not occur would be if the supply of private-purpose bonds was not sufficient to shift the supply curve beyond the horizontal CD segment of the demand curve.[12]

If these economic incentives influenced private-activity bond issuance from 1968 to the present, why wasn't a large bond volume also observed in prior decades? After all, these economic incentives for issuance were also embedded in the tax code that prevailed prior to 1969, and, as noted in chapter 3, Mississippi issued the first industrial development bond in 1936.

Nobody seems too certain of the explanation, but Leonard (1986) has addressed this issue. He cited three factors. First, uncertainty existed as to whether a public purpose was served by bonds issued for the direct benefit of a private business with the expectation of indirect public benefits generated by economic development. Although the Mississippi Supreme Court ruled that the first industrial development bond (IDB) issue served a public purpose, the decision concerning public purpose was left to be decided in each state. The courts in many states issued unfavorable rulings concerning the public-purpose nature of such bonds, effectively denying their issuance. Second, Leonard pointed out that it took some time for the revenue bond financing technique to be developed and to effectively sever a government's tax base from financial responsibility for the bonds. Thus, the debt ceiling legacy from the 19th century acted to discourage issuance in many governmental units. And, third, Leonard suggested that the 1968 legislation acted, perversely, to legitimize these bonds for many states that had been reluctant issuers. It provided a list of approved private activities whose public purpose and tax-exempt status were officially sanctioned. In response, many state restrictions were relaxed and issuance began in earnest.

Notes

1. This issue was discussed in some detail in chapter 3. The doctrine of intergovernmental tax immunity was rejected in the *South Carolina* decision of April 1988.

2. Debate continues on the desirable policy instrument to increase private pollution abatement. Regulation and/or taxation can also increase pollution abatement, but they distribute the costs of abatement differently than a federal subsidy of capital costs. The Tax Refor Act of 1986 removed the tax-exempt status of bonds issued for private pollution control, but inserted a new exception for hazardous waste treatment facilities.

3. The difficulty of measuring externalities is reflected in the economics literature. Some appreciation of the analytical complexities and practical difficulties of developing good estimates of external costs and benefits can be obtained from Baumol and Oates (198), Gramlich (1990), and Cordes, Nicholson, and Sammartino (1990).

4. Recall from chapters 2 and 4 that revenue bonds were not developed primarily as a vehicle for diverting tax-exempt bond proceeds to the use of the private sector. The development of revenue bonds probably owes more to constitutional and legislative restrictions on state and local governments' ability to incur general obligation (GO) debt in relation to the size of their tax base. In fact, revenue bonds have often been used for such public infrastructure projects as highways and bridges.

5. A description of the arbitrage laws and regulations is presented by Ballard (1984).

6. In a sense, the debate over arbitrage abuses is a classic illustration of being unable to see the forest for the trees. Concern with arbitrage abuses seems to be confined to the technical case represented by those "black box" deals, where bond proceeds are directly invested in higher-yielding securities. the possibility that state and local governments may be earning arbitrage profits indirectly is never addressed. Some states seem to have adopted the practice of accumulating tax revenue or user fees as surpluses in various funds, issuing bonds to finance activities that would have been financed with these surpluses, and investing the surplus funds in higher-yielding securities. Metcalf (1989) reported that state holdings of taxable financial assets increase by $6.73 per capita for every basis point increase in the spread between tax-exempt interest rates and the rates on these taxable financial assets. This result is certainly consistent with states' manipulation of their funds to earn indirect arbitrage profits.

7. This federal budgetary posture argument is not strictly true. Different sources of revenue and different spending programs will produce different incentives for business and individuals. Different incentives generate different responses in terms of altered economic decisions. The allocation of resources will vary, and output, employment, and revenues may differ. However, these "output" effects are sufficiently obscure that they are largely ignored in the budgetary process.

8. Most of the nonadvocacy research investigating the effect of tax subsidies on economic activity has focused on state and local property and income tax subsidies. A good exposure to the fruits and frustrations of this research can be obtained from Carlton (1979), Ledebur and Hamilton (1986), Newman and Sullivan (1988), and Wasylenko (1981).

9. If the concern is with the distribution of income, such an approach contradicts a long-held belief that social welfare is higher when the needy are helped by making transfer payments (money), rather than by interfering in market investment and employment decisions to raise their incomes. But transfers increasingly have come to be viewed as harmful to recipients' work incentives and to long-term economic prospects. In a sense, this argument suggests that the "no leaf raking" school of thought is myopic because it seeks distributional justice and short-term efficiency at the expense of long-term efficiency and economic growth. This perspective is used to justify market interference targeted to help the poor.

10. An interesting question arises here. Tax-exemption places local officials in the position of being monopolistic providers of low-cost financing. The literature on rent-seeking behavior suggests that artificially contrived rents (usually created by some government regulation or tax policy) are dissipated by those seeking the rents, that is, by competition. In this case, the question here is whether this competition among those clamoring for the subsidy enables local officials to transfer all or a portion of the benefits of the tax subsidy to themselves. See Tollison (1982) for a survey of the literature on rent-seeking behavior, and Krueger (1974) for an application of the concept to international trade.

11. Some opposition to the use of these bonds did develop due to the capital cost distortions the bonds introduced among competitors within a political jurisdiction. An example is the complaints of store owners in declining central business districts of towns and cities when they discovered that tax-exempt financing provided by their elected officials was being used to subsidize the establishment of competitive business districts in outlying areas of the jurisdiction.

12. Some might argue that rates on public-purpose bonds need not rise if the tax-exempt bond market is segmented between its private and public-purpose components. This might be true for small changes in private-purpose bond volume where the necessary supply of savings can be attracted from alternative (nonbond) tax shelters by marginally higher rates than prevail on public-purpose debt. But it is unlikely that an expansion of private-purpose debt of the magnitude observed here could be accommodated without making public-purpose debt compete (pay higher rates) to maintain its access to the scarce supply of savings seeking tax-exempt shelter.

Chapter Eleven

TAX-EXEMPT BOND LEGISLATION, 1968-89

The first two chapters of this part of the book divided the incentives affecting tax-exempt bonds into those factors influencing demand (purchasers) and supply (issuers). This chapter is devoted to a fairly comprehensive discussion of the tax-exempt bond legislation adopted by Congress over the last 20 years, beginning with the Revenue and Expenditure Control Act of 1968 and ending with the Omnibus Budget Reconciliation Act of 1989.[1] Although most legislative histories proceed chronologically, I have modified that procedure by grouping legislation according to the incentive being adjusted. Thus, for example, there are sections on provisions designed to curb arbitrage profits, on provisions devoted to defining public purpose, and on provisions intended to curb the ability of commercial banks to deduct their interest expenses incurred in the purchase of tax-exempt bonds. In addition, sections are devoted to income tax changes that were not directed at tax-exempt bonds but had a substantial effect on the bond market, such as general tax rate reductions or substantial changes in the taxation of alternative tax shelters. Within each of these "incentive" sections the discussion proceeds chronologically.

This approach should prove useful in several ways. First, at the most basic level, it provides a fairly comprehensive history of tax-exempt bond legislation organized by subject area—arbitrage, bank deductibility, targeting, and so forth. This should assist those interested simply in knowing what happened and when it happened. Second, it establishes a context for provisions that at the time of enactment may have appeared to be a somewhat chaotic effort to control bond volume—that is, the enactment of provision "y" at this time can be seen as a logical extension of, support for, or counter to provision "x" that was adopted at an earlier time. And third, the student of public policy can see that for much of this 20-year legislative effort, whether or not one agrees with the underlying philosophy of controlling bond volume, a basic philosophy was being pursued (with the occasional inexplicable lapse into public policy anarchy)—if the objective is to control bond volume, one must attack the incentives that promote bond issuance.

Reader Alert: This summary of 20 years of federal income tax law and descriptions of that law on a topic-by-topic and year-by-year basis makes for tedious reading at best, and frustration with the author at worst. The chapter is designed to be consumed like a Whitman's Sampler of chocolates—in choice bites at different sittings. In effect, the chapter is a reference work that can stand alone from the remainder of the book. The best approach might be to begin with tables 11.2, 11.3, and 11.4, which are designed to summarize the major types of legislation on a chronological basis. Following that overview, the summaries should be read that appear throughout the chapter. Finally, after consulting the table of contents, one can delve into the various sections as need arises. An effort has been made to root out the worst examples of "legalese" that appear throughout the tax code and conference reports describing the tax legislation. It is hoped that the increased readability compensates for any loss of precision. One other note: After a first mention, the full name of a legislative act is not always repeated in subsequent sections of the chapter (e.g., Deficit Reduction Act of 1984; the 1984 act).

Before proceeding to this legislative history organized by economic incentive, the reader might profit by a chronology of the income tax legislation enacted during the 1968–89 period.

INCOME TAX ACTS, 1968–89

Between 1968 and 1989, Congress enacted 17 public laws that significantly changed the structure of the individual and/or corporate income tax. Two of these were enacted in the last two years of the 1960s, 5 during the decade of the 1970s, and 10 between 1980 and 1989. The popular name and public law number of these acts are listed in the first two columns of table 11.1. Note that three of the laws appeared as part of budget reconciliation acts rather than as separate pieces of tax legislation, one in 1980 (Title XI of the Omnibus Reconciliation Act of 1980 that included the Mortgage Subsidy Bond Tax Act of 1980) and the others in 1987 and 1989 (parts of the Omnibus Budget Reconciliation Acts of 1987 and 1989). The third column lists any significant provisions of the legislation that affected the tax-exempt bond market directly or indirectly. Clearly it was not

Table 11.1 INCOME TAX LEGISLATION FOR 1968–89, AND ITS MAJOR
CHANGES AFFECTING TAX-EXEMPT BONDS

Name of Legislation	Public Law Number	Major Changes Affecting Tax-Exempt Market
Revenue and Expenditure Control Act of 1968	90-364	Public purpose definition
Tax Reform Act of 1969	91-172	Arbitrage profits, minimum tax
Revenue Act of 1971	92-178	Public purpose, tax shelters
Tax Reduction Act of 1975	94-12	None
Tax Reform Act of 1976	94-455	Arbitrage profits, minimum tax
Tax Reduction and Simplification Act of 1977	95-30	None
Revenue Act of 1978	95-600	Public purpose, minimum tax
Crude Oil Windfall Profits Tax Act of 1980	96-223	Public purpose, private capital costs
Mortgage Subsidy Bond Tax Act of 1980[a]	96-449	Targeting benefits, arbitrage profits, volume caps
Economic Recovery Tax Act of 1981	97-34	Public purpose, individual rate reduction, minimum tax
Tax Equity and Fiscal Responsibility Act of 1982	97-248	Public purpose, targeting benefits, arbitrage profits, private capital costs, etc.
Social Security Amendments of 1983	98-21	Counting exempt interest income toward threshhold for taxing Social Security benefits
Deficit Reduction Act of 1984	98-369	Targeting benefits, private capital costs, volume caps
Tax Reform Act of 1986	99-514	Public purpose, targeting, arbitrage, tax shelters, rate reduction, minimum tax
Omnibus Budget Reconciliation Act of 1987	100-203	Public purpose
Technical and Miscellaneous Revenue Act of 1988	100-647	Targeting, arbitrage
Omnibus Budget Reconciliation Act of 1989	101-239	Public purpose, arbitrage, enforcement

a. The public law number actually refers to the Omnibus Reconciliation Act of 1980.

possible to summarize within the table all aspects of bond legislation in each act, but the major focus of each is included.

In trying to organize this large and complex amount of information, it became obvious that some items applied to more than one category. My most difficult choice in this regard was whether a legislative change defines a public purpose or is more targeted to program beneficiaries in order to reduce the overstatement of benefits. According to the rule followed here, legislation that permits or denies tax exemption for an activity (e.g., mass transit commuting facilities or sports stadiums) is classified as an effort to define public purpose. Legislation that broadens or narrows eligibility to use tax exemption for an activity, either by characteristics of individuals (e.g., income limits for residents of multifamily rental housing) or by location (e.g., restriction to "distressed" or "targeted" areas) is classified as an effort to reduce the overstatement of benefits by narrowing the gap between benefits from the state and local perspective and benefits from the federal perspective.

Choices also had to be made in several other areas. Restrictions on advance refunding are classified under the arbitrage category because the technique was frequently, but by no means always, associated with the earning of arbitrage profits. Federal guarantee of tax-exempt bonds is classified with the private capital costs category because it lowers the yield required on a bond and, therefore, the rental cost of capital for the firm. It is, of course, equally true that guarantees lower financing costs for public-purpose bonds as well as private-purpose bonds. Provisions such as registration, taxpayer approval, and reporting requirements are classified under a "good government" category on the theory that any information that could become available to the public enhances the likelihood of taxpayers demanding accountability.

DEFINING PUBLIC PURPOSE

The congressional effort to define public purpose for the use of tax-exempt bonds began in 1968 and continues to this day. This section endeavors not only to give readers an understanding of this legislation but also to develop their appreciation of the difficulty facing Congress in this task. To try to present an exhaustive account of every legislative detail that could be interpreted as defining public purpose would be an interminable exercise and would detract from this major purpose. Accordingly, the discussion focuses on the major changes in the tax law but includes, when they contribute to an understanding of the complexity of the definitional task, some of the minor changes as well.

Legislation

1968

In response to the growth of bonds issued for "private purposes," the Revenue and Expenditure Control Act of 1968 made the first effort to define public purpose, to sort out good (public purpose and tax exempt) and bad (private purpose and taxable) uses of the bonds. The definition of public purpose provided by this act was, in effect, expressed in the negative by defining the "bad" bonds, termed industrial development bonds (IDBs). Any nonbad bond was "good" so long as it was issued by a "state or political subdivision thereof."

The IDB test had two parts: more than 25 percent of the bond proceeds had to be used by a nongovernmental entity in a trade or business; and debt service on more than 25 percent of the proceeds had to be secured by (or derived from payments in respect to) property used in a trade or business.[2] If a bond issue failed to pass either of these tests, the bond issue was tax exempt. This test was fairly complicated and became a focal point of controversy over the alleged inhibition of infrastructure financing and privatization efforts attributed by state and local officials to tax-exempt bond legislation.

Figure 11.1 summarizes the possibilities facing state and local issuers upon adoption of this test. The lower right quadrant depicts those bonds that fail both parts of the IDB test—25 percent or less of the bond proceeds is used by a nongovernmental entity, and 25 percent or less of the debt service is secured by payments in any way related to property used in a trade or business. These bonds may be tax exempt. In effect, the governmental unit owns and manages the facility, and the bonds can be either general obligation (GO) or revenue bonds. Debt service on revenue bonds could be secured by user charges on the facility built with the proceeds, because this property is not being used in a trade or business. Examples of these traditional types of public infrastructure are public schools and toll roads managed by public authorities.

The upper right quadrant depicts those bonds that pass the use portion of the test but fail the security interest test. These bonds may also be tax exempt. A facility with these characteristics could not be financed with revenue bonds, because the security interest test would be passed and the bonds would be taxable. An example would be a privately managed sewage treatment plant financed with general obligation bonds.

The lower left quadrant depicts those bonds that fail the use portion of the test and pass the security interest test (more than 25

Figure 11.1 USE (U) AND SECURITY INTEREST (S) TESTS FOR INDUSTRIAL
DEVELOPMENT BONDS, 1968

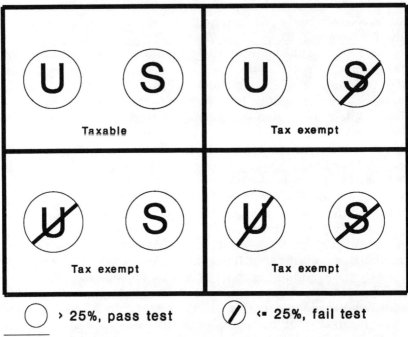

percent of proceeds secured by property used in a trade or business).
These bonds may be tax exempt. These facilities can be financed
with revenue bonds. It is hard to think of an example of this hy-
pothetical case, but it might occur when a store on the first floor of
a bond-financed five-story public office building made rent payments
equal to more than 25 percent of the debt service on the bonds used
to finance the whole building.

The upper left quadrant contains those bonds that are taxable. They
would, for example, include bonds for projects financed with revenue bonds and owned and/or managed by private firms. The list of
facilities frequently financed by state and local governments in this
fashion prior to the 1968 act is extensive—airports, harbor facilities,
solid waste disposal facilities, convention centers, sports stadiums,
parking garages, and so forth. Imposition of the IDB test would have
denied tax exemption to bonds issued for many activities that Congress deemed to be quasi-public in nature.[3] For this reason, a lengthy
list of exceptions to the tests was provided for specific activities,

turning what would be pumpkins under the general rule into carriages.

Excepted activities were: (1) residential real property; (2) sports facilities; (3) facilities for a convention or trade show; (4) airports, docks, wharves, mass-commuting facilities, parking facilities, or facilities for storage or training directly related to any of the foregoing; (5) sewage or solid waste disposal facilities, and facilities for the local furnishing of electric energy, gas, or water; (6) air or water pollution control facilities; and (7) acquisition or development of land for industrial parks. In addition, any IDB issue of $1 million or less was excepted if the proceeds were used for the acquisition, construction, or improvement of land or depreciable property. At the election of the issuer, the $1 million limit could be increased to $5 million if the aggregate amount of related capital expenditures made over a six-year period was not expected to exceed $5 million (including those financed with the IDBs).

Simply listing the exceptions does not do justice to the congressional effort to define public purpose. One must read the committee reports and explanation of the conference agreement to appreciate the degree of legislative specificity being applied to the question of an activity's eligibility for tax exemption. For example, the exception for residential real property was described as being for buildings containing one or more complete living facilities (whose components were defined) for nontransients, but which could include facilities for nonfamily purposes (such as a laundromat or other retail establishment); the sports facilities exception was to apply to both spectator and participation sports facilities, including such facilities as stadiums, ski slopes, golf courses, and facilities directly related to these exempt sports facilities (U.S. Congress 1968).

Table 11.2 is designed to help the reader keep track of the evolving federal definition of public purpose. The first section of the table tracks the IDB tests for businesses and individuals. Note that the 1968 legislation refers only to business usage (I return to this point later). The next section lists those business activities that pass the IDB test (and are therefore taxable) but have been provided with a special exception to enable bonds issued to be tax exempt. The activities are listed in the first column under two categories, exempt-activity and small-issue bonds. Activities listed under "exempt-activities" include those that received a specific exemption in the 1968 act. The second category is "small-issues," and includes virtually any activity (including, at times, those listed under "exempt-activities") using less than a $1 million bond issue or a $5 million issue

Table 11.2 DEFINING PUBLIC PURPOSE: CHRONOLOGY OF ACTIVITIES DESIGNATED TAX-EXEMPT INDUSTRIAL DEVELOPMENT (PRIVATE-ACTIVITY) BONDS, 1968–89

	1968	1971	1976	1978	1980	1981	1982	1984	1986	1987	1988	1989
Industrial Development Bond Tests												
Business	X[a]								T[c]			
Individual								T[b]				
Tax-Exempt Activities												
Exempt-Activity Bonds												
Residential rental property	X				T							
Sports facilities	X								T			
Skyboxes, luxury boxes[d]								T				
Health clubs[d]								T				
Gambling[d]								T				
Convention and trade shows	X								T			
Airports, docks, wharves	X								T[e]			
Mass commuting	X								T[e]			
Bus, subway, rail cars						X						
Ferryboats							X					
Parking	X								T			
Sewage and solid waste disposal	X				X							
Steam generation					X				T			
Alcohol production					X				T			
Electric energy production					X							
Local furnishing of electricity	X											
Expanded definition of local				X								
Local furnishing of gas	X											
Expanded definition of local							X					

Provision								
Local furnishing of water	X							
Expanded definition of local		X						
Include business uses			X					
Investor-owned utility			X					
Air and water pollution control, private	X						T	
Public purchase of private facilities						X		
Land for industrial park	X							
Hydroelectric generating					X			
Volunteer fire departments				X				
Local district heating and cooling with steam or water						X		
Intercity high-speed rail transit							X	X
Hazardous waste disposal							X	
Qualified redevelopment								
501(c)(3)							T[f]	
Takeover of investor-owned utilities							T[g]	
Small-Issue Bonds	X					*'87		
Auto sales and service						T		
Retail food and beverage						T		
Recreation or entertainment						T		
Golf and country clubs						T		
Massage parlors						T		
Hot tubs and suntan						T		
Racetracks						T		
Racquet sports						T		
Delete R&D spending from $10 million capital limit						X		

continued

Table 11.2 DEFINING PUBLIC PURPOSE: CHRONOLOGY OF ACTIVITIES DESIGNATED TAX-EXEMPT INDUSTRIAL DEVELOPMENT (PRIVATE-ACTIVITY) BONDS, 1968–89—(continued)

	1968	1971	1976	1978	1980	1981	1982	1984	1986	1987	1988	1989
Manufacturing								*'89				*'90
Airplanes[h]								T	T[f]			
Liquor stores[h]							T					
Acquisition of land and existing facilities								T				
First-time farmers								X				
Private Loan Bonds												
Mortgage revenue bonds					*'84			*'83			*'90	
Student loan bonds			X						*'89		*'90	

Notes: X, exception to IDB (private activity) test enacted; T, exception to IDB (private activity) test repealed or altered; asterisk (*) and year indicates exception to IDB (private activity) test repealed at the beginning of the year cited.

a. Twenty-five percent "use of proceeds" and "security interest" tests.

b. Five percent "use of proceeds" test.

c. Ten percent "use of proceeds" and "security interest" tests.

d. Applies to small-issue IDBs as well.

e. Applies to related facilities with private use.

f. Ninety-five percent use for exempt purposes; for nonprofits, 95% use and ownership by nonprofit organizations or governments.

g. Bonds for this purpose were tax exempt, but were made taxable unless they received an allocation from the private-activity volume cap.

h. Applies to exempt-activity IDBs as well.

with a six-year capital spending restriction. The final section of the table lists those activities for which loans were made to private individuals for purposes not related to a trade or business.

The remaining columns of table 11.2 represent the years in which tax-exempt bond legislation was enacted that affected the list of exempt activities. An *X* in a cell indicates that exempt status was granted in that year. A *T* in a cell indicates that tax-exempt status was removed in that year and bonds for the activity were made taxable.[4] An asterisk (*) in a cell with a date indicates termination (sunset) of the exemption to be effective in the year indicated (usually beginning on January 1).

1971

The Revenue Act of 1971 made minor adjustments to public purpose definition. The amount of expenditures for unforeseen circumstances to be disregarded in the determination of the $1 million small-issue exception was increased from $250,000 to $1 million. The act also changed the requirement that "local" water facilities means service within two contiguous counties. This definition was expanded to include service within a city and a contiguous county, provided the water is available to the general public.

1976

The Tax Reform Act of 1976 expanded the exceptions to the general eligibility restrictions. Tax exemption was extended to bonds issued by not-for-profit corporations organized by, or requested to act by, a state or local government for the purpose of acquiring student loan notes incurred under the Higher Education Act of 1965.

1978

The Revenue Act of 1978 continued the liberalization of eligibility for tax exemption. The $5 million limit on six-years capital expenditure for small-issue IDBs was increased to $10 million (that is, the bond issue can range up to $10 million, provided total capital expenditures inclusive of the tax-exempt bonds do not exceed $10 million for a six-year period). The act extended the exception for local furnishing of water to include agricultural, industrial, commercial, and electric utility users, provided all users in the service area (including residential) are granted access to the water. Investor-owned regulated utilities for furnishing water were granted similar access to tax-exempt financing.

1980

The Crude Oil Windfall Profit Tax Act of 1980 further broadened the types of projects eligible for tax-exempt financing. Eligibility was extended to solid waste disposal facilities that generate steam, produce alcohol, or produce electric energy. An exemption was also granted to hydroelectric generating facilities with less than 25 megawatts of generating capacity, with scaled-down tax-exempt financing available to facilities up to 125 megawatts. The Omnibus Reconciliation Act of 1980 established a sunset date of December 31, 1983, for mortgage revenue bonds.

1981

The Economic Recovery Tax Act of 1981 added to the list of exceptions by permitting issuance of tax-exempt bonds to finance mass commuting vehicles such as buses, subway cars, and rail cars. The act also granted an exemption to the debt obligations of volunteer fire departments, whose eligibility had previously been denied because they were not a properly constituted "on behalf of" issuer—they were not "constituted authorities" possessing the power to tax, the power of eminent domain, or the police power.[5]

1982

The Tax Equity and Fiscal Responsibility Act of 1982 was very active in defining activities that did not satisfy a sufficient public purpose to merit an exception to the IDB rules. It eliminated the use of small-issue IDBs beginning in 1983 if more than 25 percent of the proceeds were used for certain types of facilities—automobile sales or service, retail food and beverage service (other than grocery stores), or provision of recreation or entertainment. No proceeds of exempt small-issues could be used for such activities as golf courses, massage parlors, hot tubs, and racetracks. In addition, it imposed a sunset date for small-issue IDBs issued after 1986.

The act also expanded eligibility to some extent. Ferryboats were added to the list of privately owned mass-commuting vehicles eligible for tax-exempt financing. Tax exemption was also extended to facilities for local district heating and cooling through steam or water from a central source. Expenditures on research and development were eliminated from the six-year $10 million limit on capital expenditures for certain small-issue IDB projects.

1984

The Deficit Reduction Act (DRA) of 1984 continued the definition process. Tax exemption was denied if more than 25 percent of the proceeds of an exempt-activity or small-issue IDB was used to finance either land acquisition (50 percent for industrial parks) or existing facilities. An exception was allowed for first-time farmers. In addition, tax exemption was denied for bonds issued to finance any airplane, skybox or other private luxury box, health club facility, any facility primarily used for gambling, or any package liquor store. Additional restrictions were placed on student loan bonds.

In addition, the act altered two previous congressional decisions to terminate exemption for certain activities. The sunset date on small-issue IDBs for manufacturing facilities and first-time farmers was extended to December 31, 1988. The December 31, 1986, sunset date for nonmanufacturing facilities was allowed to remain in effect. In addition, the sunset date for qualified mortgage bonds was extended to December 31, 1987.

Finally, a substantial gap in the private-use restrictions was closed in 1984. The "use of proceeds" and "security interest" tests for IDBs enacted in 1968 referred to use of the proceeds in a trade or business or the securing of the debt service with property used in or derived from a trade or business. Proceeds used by individuals or secured by property of an individual did not pass these trade or business IDB tests and were therefore eligible for tax exemption. In effect, the federal tax law contained no restriction on the ability of state and local officials to issue bonds and lend the proceeds to individuals for any purpose.

This was rectified in the DRA of 1984. Consumer loan bonds were defined as obligations that are part of an issue of which 5 percent or more of the proceeds is to be used, directly or indirectly, to make or finance loans to persons other than exempt persons (governmental entities or nonprofit organizations). Exceptions to this rule were made for loans that finance activities previously granted exemption. These activities included IDBs, qualified mortgage revenue bonds and qualified veterans' mortgage bonds, and student loans. In effect, use of bond proceeds by a nonexempt person was prohibited unless the purpose has been specifically approved by Congress.

1986

The Tax Reform Act of 1986 made substantial changes in the definition of public purpose. The two-part IDB test and the consumer loan test are described here first. To begin with, IDB terminology was deleted and the term "private activity" was introduced to denote those bond issues that pass the two-part trade or business tests. Both the "use of proceeds" and the "security interest" tests were tightened by reducing the percentage of proceeds for both tests from 25 percent to 10 percent. Any use by nonprofit organizations or by any other persons (not including state and local governments) is counted toward the 10 percent limit. These changes made it considerably easier for bond issues to pass the IDB (now private activity) tests and become taxable. Second, the consumer loan test was renamed the private loan test. In addition, all bonds meeting the private loan test are classified as private-activity bonds, the same category that includes the formerly named IDBs.

The act also further narrowed the exceptions to the IDB rules. (1) The exempt-activity exceptions for sports facilities, convention and trade show facilities, parking facilities, and private pollution control facilities were eliminated. (2) The exceptions for airports, docks and wharves, and mass commuting facilities were considerably narrowed. Use of bond proceeds was denied for related facilities such as: hotels; retail facilities in the terminal in excess of the size necessary to serve passengers and employees, and for any such facilities outside the terminal; office facilities for nongovernment employees; and industrial parks and manufacturing facilities. (3) The exemptions for solid waste disposal to generate steam or to produce alcohol were repealed. And (4), small-issue IDBs were subjected to a requirement that 95 percent of the proceeds be used for the exempt purpose; and nonprofit bonds were subjected to requirements that the facility be owned and that 95 percent of the proceeds be used by nonprofit organizations or a governmental entity.

Finally, two new activities were added to the list that receive tax exemption even when they pass the private-activity tests. Eligibility was extended to facilities for hazardous waste disposal (land incineration or permanent entombment), provided the wastes are generated by the public rather than a single firm (and are not radioactive). And eligibility was extended to redevelopment activities in blighted areas: to acquire real property; to clear and prepare land for redevelopment; to rehabilitate real property; or to relocate occupants of structures on the acquired real property. These qualified redevelopment bonds are tax exempt if 95 percent of the proceeds are used for redevelopment in a locally designated blighted area, and the debt service is secured either by general tax revenue or incremental property tax revenue attributable to the redevelopment. In addition, the sunset date for mortgage revenue bonds was extended to December 31, 1988, and the sunset date for small-issue IDBs to December 31, 1989.

1987

Prior to adoption of the Omnibus Budget Reconciliation Act of 1987, state and local governments could issue tax-exempt bonds to finance the construction, acquisition, or operation of *governmentally owned* output facilities (essentially for the provision of electricity and gas). This authority encompassed the purchase of existing nongovernmental output facilities, thereby converting private utilities into publicly owned utilities and making them eligible for tax-exempt financing. This act restricts the ability of state and local governments to provide tax-exempt financing for utility customers through the purchase of output facilities owned by the private, nonprofit, or federal sectors. The bonds issued for the purchase of such facilities are now considered to be taxable private activity bonds. An exception is provided for bonds issued to acquire electric energy or gas facilities, provided part of the state private-activity bond volume cap is allotted to the bonds used to make the purchase.

Two exceptions allow the issuance of tax-exempt bonds to acquire nongovernmental output property without recourse to the private activity bond volume cap. First, tax-exempt bonds may be used to finance an acquisition designed to satisfy increased demand within an area that the acquiring governmental unit has served for at least 10 years. Increased demand caused by sales outside a utility's usual service area could not justify acquisition of nongovernmental output property financed with tax-exempt bonds not subject to the volume cap. Second, tax-exempt financing outside the volume cap is permitted to extend utility service to areas acquired through annexation for general governmental purposes (for example, by transfer of voting registration and property tax rolls) and the extension of general governmental services to the annexed area. The bond issue qualifies under this rule only if (1) the annexed area is no more than 10 percent of the governmental unit's previous geographic area or (2) the increased output capacity is no more than 10 percent of prior output capacity.

1988

The Technical and Miscellaneous Revenue Act of 1988 added another category to the list of activities that pass the private-activity test but remain eligible for tax-exempt financing. The new category is intercity high-speed rail facilities for trains whose average speed between stations exceeds 150 miles per hour. In addition, the sunset date for qualified mortgage revenue bonds was extended to December 31, 1989.

1989

The Omnibus Budget Reconciliation Act of 1989 again rescued small-issue IDBs and mortgage revenue bonds from the dead. Their sunset date was pushed back another nine months, to September 30, 1990.

Conclusion

In attempting to draw distinctions between private and public activities, Congress has chosen a decision rule that relies upon relatively easy to obtain information on the amount of private business or individual use of the tax-exempt bond proceeds, rather than upon relatively hard (at times impossible) to obtain estimates of the extent to which any given activity generates external benefits or reduces external costs that spill out of the political boundaries of the spending jurisdiction.[6] In fact, although economic theory tells us a great deal about which goods' production should be adjusted by the public sector and how the costs of that adjustment should be distributed among citizens, it has little to say about whether those goods should be produced *by* the public sector. The physical act of production of a good or service should probably be undertaken by the sector that can do it most efficiently (at the least cost). If that happens to be the private sector, so be it.

Of course, the deficiency of the rule was fairly obvious to the participants in the political process, and was violated before the rule was set in type. Thus arose the exempt-activity and small-issue exceptions to the use (and security interest) test. A quick review of table 11.2 provides eloquent testimony to the difficulties encountered by Congress in attempting to choose which activities possessed sufficient benefits for federal taxpayers to merit public subsidy of private provision (and profit). Use of the "use" rule is undoubtedly attributable in part to these difficulties. Congress has found it necessary to impose explicit restrictions on the use of tax-exempt bond proceeds for everything from hot tubs and massage parlors to the generation of steam and production of alcohol from solid waste disposal. As the perception of public problems changed, so did the list of exceptions. The energy-related subsidies for activities such as steam generation and alcohol production adopted in the beginning of the decade were rescinded late in the decade. These were replaced by subsidies for newly popular issues such as intercity high-speed rail transit and hazardous waste disposal.

In effect, the definition process will never end and will always be somewhat subjective, and the use rule will always be less than satisfactory as an arbiter of public purpose. Thus, short of requiring any adjustment of private market outcomes to be both financed and produced via the public sector (an undesirable option), it behooves the federal government to encourage its partners in this market-adjustment enterprise (state and local officials, the financial community, private businesses, and individuals) to pursue socially responsible behavior. This is done by trying to control the structure of the various incentives facing the participants in this market. The remainder of the chapter is devoted to a discussion of how the tax law has attempted to manipulate these incentives.

TARGETING BENEFICIARIES

Table 11.3 summarizes federal efforts to manipulate the incentives that contribute to bond volume. A *D* indicates enactment of legislation that decreased some incentive that existed prior to 1968; an *I* indicates enactment of legislation that increased some incentive that existed prior to 1968. Efforts to narrow the gap between benefits as perceived by state and local taxpayers and benefits as perceived by federal taxpayers have been concentrated in several areas, and are summarized in the first section of the table under "Targeting Beneficiaries."

Owner-Occupied Housing

As discussed previously, the IDB tests imposed by the Revenue and Expenditure Control Act of 1968 focused on trade and business involvement in the tax-exempt bond market. No restrictions existed to prevent state and local governments from issuing bonds and using the proceeds to make loans to private individuals for the large capital needs that crop up during one's lifetime, such as purchase of a home and a college education. And as nominal interest rates began to rise rapidly in the latter part of the 1970s, state and local governments began to issue tax-exempt bonds to finance mortgages for single-family owner-occupied housing. It is not as though the federal government is unaware of the social benefits to be gained from a broad

Table 11.3 CHRONOLOGY OF TAX LEGISLATION AFFECTING TAX-EXEMPT BONDS, BY TYPE OF INCENTIVE, 1969–89

	1969	1976	1978	1980	1981	1982	1984	1986	1988	1989
Targeting Beneficiaries										
Mortgage revenue bonds:										
Principal residence				D						
Purchase price				D		I		D	D	
First-time homebuyers				D		I		D		
Mortgage credit certificates							D	D	D	
Income limits								D		
Veterans' bonds							D			
Multifamily rental housing										
Income limits				D		D		D	D	
Duration requirements				D		D		D		
Small-issue bonds			I				D	D		
Redevelopment bonds										
Arbitrage and Advance Re-funding	D									I
Advance refunding			D	D			D	D		
Purpose arbitrage				D		D				
Nonpurpose arbitrage						D	D	D	D	
Term to maturity								D		

Provision							
Rebate	I				D	D	D
Student loan	I			D	D	D	
Annuity contracts					D		
Private Capital Cost							
Depreciation deductions					D	D	
Government owner-ship		D			D	D	
Federal guarantees					D	D	
Good Government							
Registration		D		D	D	D	
Information reports			D	D	D	D,I	
Public approval			D		D	D	
Electoral benefits			D	D	D	I	
Income Tax Rates							
Individual			D	D		D	
Corporate			D			D	
Minimum Tax							
Individual	I		D		I	D	
Corporate	I		D		I	D	
Alternative Tax Shelters				D	I		
Commercial Bank Interest				D	I		
Deductibility		D		D	D	D	
Volume Caps					D	D	D
Enforcement					D	D	D

Notes: D, a decreased incentive for greater bond volume; I, an increased incentive for greater bond volume.

base of home ownership in the nation. It provides numerous expenditure and tax incentives to promote home ownership, not the least of which is the deductibility of mortgage interest payments from the income tax base. Table 6.1 in chapter 6 indicated that this tax expenditure produced the fourth highest federal revenue loss in 1983. In addition, some of the revenue loss from the deductibility of state and local taxes (the second highest revenue loss) is attributable to the property taxes paid on homes and could just as easily be classified as a housing subsidy. Congress seemed to feel that these existing subsidies were more than sufficient to provide for the homeownership needs of middle- and upper-income taxpayers, and that additional subsidies provided to these individuals through tax-exempt bonds generated little in the way of benefits to federal taxpayers.

1980

Accordingly, the Mortgage Subsidy Bond Tax Act of 1980, enacted as part of the Omnibus Reconciliation Act of 1980, placed various restrictions on "qualified mortgage bonds" in order to target more of the funds to first-time moderate- and lower-income individuals. First, tax-exempt bond financing was restricted to principal residences financed with new mortgages (except for replacement of a construction period loan). Second, a restriction was imposed on the purchase price, which required substantially all mortgages provided from bond proceeds to be for residences whose cost did not exceed 90 percent (110 percent in targeted economically distressed areas) of the average area purchase price. At least 20 percent of the lendable proceeds had to be reserved for mortgages in targeted areas for a period of at least one year. A targeted area was defined as (1) a census tract in which 70 percent or more of the families have an income less than or equal to statewide median family income or (2) an area of chronic economic distress. A third requirement attempted to target the benefits to first-time homebuyers by restricting financing of mortgages to persons not having an ownership interest in a principal residence at any time in the three-year period prior to issuance of the bond-financed mortgage. Explicit limitations on the incomes of mortgage recipients were considered and rejected to enable state and local governments sufficient flexibility to meet their needs, but bond proceeds were expected to be used for low- and moderate-income persons.

1982

The 1982 tax act, in reaction to the distressed state of the housing market during the recession, relaxed some of these restrictions. The three-year nonownership requirement was changed to apply to 90 percent (rather than 100 percent) of the mortgages financed with bond proceeds.[7] The purchase price limitation was increased from 90 percent (110 percent in targeted areas) of the average area purchase price to 110 percent (120 percent in targeted areas).

1984

Although the 1984 act did not modify the eligibility requirements for mortgage revenue bonds, the general explanation of the act made crystal clear the congressional intent that the bond proceeds be directed to lower-income families. Several methods for accomplishing this goal were suggested: state adoption of more stringent income or purchase price limitations than are required by the federal tax law; increased state efforts to more widely publicize the availability of the loans; and the exchange of mortgage revenue bond issuance authority for the newly created mortgage credit certificates (MCCs) that permit state and local authorities to offer higher percentage credits for lower-income families.

Congress was aware that, because of the nature of tax-exempt financing, it may be difficult to target the subsidy provided by mortgage subsidy bonds to those most in need of housing assistance. Congress therefore decided to offer States and localities the alternative of distributing mortgage credit certificates (MCCs) in lieu of qualified mortgage bonds. . .[B]y varying the amount of individual credits, State and local issuing authorities may achieve greater flexibility in targeting the subsidy to those individuals who are considered most in need. (Joint Committee on Taxation 1984, 907)

These MCCs allowed governments to exchange all or a portion of their mortgage revenue bonds allowed by the state volume cap (see the discussion of the mortgage revenue bond cap later in this chapter) for authority to issue one-fifth the volume of mortgage credit certificates. This means that state and local governments can trade five dollars of mortgage revenue bond borrowing authority for one dollar of MCCs. These certificates enable homebuyers to receive nonrefundable income tax credits for a specified percentage of their mortgage interest payments. Eligibility is subject to the same requirements as for mortgage revenue bonds.

1986

The coverage of the three-year nonownership restriction was extended to 95 percent (up from 90 percent) of the mortgages financed with the net proceeds of the bond issue. The purchase price restriction was returned to its original 90 percent and 110 percent of average area purchase price. The rate at which mortgage credit certificates could be substituted for mortgage revenue bond volume was raised from 20 percent to 25 percent—a dollar of credits for every four dollars of bond volume.

An income limitation was imposed for the first time. The income of mortgage recipients could not exceed 115 percent of the higher of (1) median family income for the area in which the residence is located, or (2) the statewide median family income. In targeted areas, two-thirds of the mortgage financing must be provided for those whose family income does not exceed 140 percent of the higher of median family income for the area in which the residence is located or the statewide median family income. The remaining one-third of mortgage financing may be used without regard to income limitations.

1988

The Technical and Miscellaneous Revenue Act of 1988 made a concerted effort to deal with the targeting aspect of mortgage revenue bonds. The purchase price and income limits were tightened to deal with what were considered to be two undesirable aspects of the program's operation. First, an unacceptably large proportion of participants was single, young, and had an expected lifetime income profile that was markedly higher than the current income eligibility standard. Second, no provision was made for recapture of the subsidy when these purchasers' increasing incomes caused them to sell their houses in order to "buy up" (purchase more expensive homes). These facts suggested that the bonds were being used to subsidize citizens who did not really belong to the targeted group of lower-income citizens.[8]

Income limits were therefore revised and a recapture provision created to deal with these problems. The income limit was adjusted in those areas where housing costs are high relative to national standards. The income limit (absent an area cost adjustment) was changed to the higher of 115 percent of area median income, the adjusted median income limit for a high housing cost area, or 115 percent of state median income.

A recapture rule was adopted for loans made after December 31, 1990. Recapture applies to dispositions of assisted housing that occur within 10 years of purchase by people whose incomes have increased substantially since purchase of the home. The amount recaptured is the lesser of 1.25 percent of the original loan balance for each year the loan is outstanding or 50 percent of the gain realized on the disposition.

Veterans' Mortgage Bonds

The Omnibus Reconciliation Act of 1980 required that veterans' mortgage bonds must be general obligations of the state. The 1984 act restricted the issuance of veterans' mortgage bonds to those states that had qualified programs in existence prior to June 22, 1984. In addition, loans were restricted to veterans who served in active duty any time prior to 1977 and whose application for the mortgage financing occurred before the later of 30 years after leaving the service or January 31, 1985. Finally, these loans were restricted to principal residences.

Multifamily Rental Housing

1980

The Omnibus Reconciliation Act of 1980 restricted the issuance of tax-exempt bonds for residential rental housing to projects in which at least 20 percent of the units are to be occupied by individuals of low or moderate income, determined in a manner consistent with the Leased Housing Program under Section 8 of the United States Housing Act of 1937. The required percentage of units occupied by low- or moderate-income individuals fell to 15 percent if the project was located in a targeted area (qualified Census tract or area of chronic economic distress). These projects also had to satisfy the Section 8 duration constraint, requiring that the 20 percent (15 percent) targeting requirement had to be met for a 20-year period. This provision protects against renting to low-income tenants for a short period of time in order to achieve funding eligibility and then switching occupancy to higher-income residents.

1982

The 1982 act made two changes in the rules for targeting rental housing to low- and moderate-income families. Low and moderate income was defined as 80 percent of area median income (regardless of the percentage used under the Section 8 program). The duration requirement was also modified. The 20 percent and 15 percent low-income occupancy requirements were to apply from the date 10 percent of the project is first occupied until the latest of (1) 10 years after 50 percent of the project is occupied, (2) the date when 50 percent of the longest-maturity bonds have expired, or (3) the date Section 8 assistance terminates.

1986

The 1986 act altered the income targeting requirements. Eligibility for tax-exempt bond financing was restricted to projects satisfying one of two requirements: 40 percent or more of the units must be occupied by tenants whose incomes are 60 percent or less of the area median gross income; or 20 percent or more of the units are occupied by tenants whose incomes are 50 percent or less of the area median gross income. No differential treatment is provided for projects located in targeted areas. The act provides that this income requirement be satisfied on a continuing basis, such that if the income limit is surpassed the tenant may no longer be counted as a unit satisfying the percentage requirements.

The duration requirement was changed once again. The income targeting requirements must be satisfied for a period beginning on the date at least 10 percent of the units are first occupied and ending on the latest of: (1) the date that is 15 years after the date on which at least 50 percent of the units are first occupied; (2) the first date all tax-exempt bonds used to finance the project have been retired; or (3) the date on which Section 8 assistance is terminated.

1988

Residential rental housing financed with tax-exempt bonds issued by nonprofit organizations was not subject to the income targeting restrictions that applied to for-profit projects financed with other private-activity bonds. The 1988 act applied the same income targeting provisions to nonprofit bonds issued for the acquisition of for-profit residential rental housing property, but not for bonds issued to finance new construction or rehabilitation of nonprofit residential rental housing.

Small-Issue IDBs

Most of the changes to small-issue IDBs over the 20-year period have been previously classified under the public purpose definition part of the chapter. A few targeting provisions did, however, sneak through. The Revenue Act of 1978 increased the $5 million limit on six-year capital expenditures for small-issue IDBs to $10 million. But if the project being financed is an urban development action grant facility in an economically distressed area, the capital expenditure limit is set at $20 million financed from other than tax-exempt bond sources.

The Deficit Reduction Act of 1984 restricted any one beneficiary's use of small-issue bonds to a maximum of $40 million of outstanding bonds. An exception was also provided to the prohibition against bond use for land acquisition. A $250,000 exception was provided if the person acquiring the land is a first-time farmer. Additional targeting was provided by extending the sunset date on small-issue IDBs for manufacturing facilities to December 31, 1988, while leaving the sunset date of December 31, 1986, for bonds issued to finance nonmanufacturing facilities.

The Tax Reform Act of 1986 (Public Law 99-514) extended the sunset date for small-issue bonds to finance manufacturing facilities to December 31, 1989, and decreed that bonds issued on behalf of first-time farmers were to be treated as manufacturing facilities for purposes of the new sunset date.

Qualified Redevelopment Bonds

Congressional concern with targeting can also be seen in the evolving treatment of bonds issued for economic redevelopment that are secured by tax revenues generated by the redevelopment. A jurisdiction would issue bonds to clear land or rehabilitate structures, would rent or sell the redeveloped real property to the private sector, and would use the incremental property tax revenues to pay debt service on the bonds. Since these so-called tax increment bonds were secured by tax revenues, they qualified for tax exemption even though they passed the use test to be taxable IDBs.

The 1986 Tax Reform Act gave these bonds the name *qualified redevelopment bonds*, classified them as exempt private-activity bonds, and wasted no time in imposing targeting restrictions. All proceeds must now be used for redevelopment in blighted areas and must be used to finance activities in the blighted area for which the bonds were issued. A blighted area was defined as one possessing excessive amounts of such things as vacant land on which structures were previously located, abandoned or vacant buildings, substandard structures, vacancies, and delinquencies in the payment of real property taxes. Designation of a blighted area is made by units of general-purpose local government, based upon a state law authorizing redevelopment in blighted areas.

To protect against indiscriminate use of the bonds, designated blighted areas may not have real property whose value exceeds 20 percent of the assessed value of all real property located in the general government unit that includes the blighted area. In addition, to protect against use of bonds for specially designated beneficiaries, a blighted area must contain either a minimum of 100 contiguous and compact acres or between 10 and 100 contiguous and compact acres with a single beneficiary receiving no more than 25 percent of the bond financing.

None of the bond proceeds can be used to finance golf courses, country clubs, massage parlors, hot tub facilities, suntan facilities, racetracks or other gambling facilities, or stores whose major business is sale of alcoholic beverages. No more than 25 percent of the bond proceeds can be used to finance any other facility whose financing with the proceeds of small-issue or other private activity bonds is restricted or prohibited.

Conclusion

Federal efforts to decrease the gap between federal and state and local perceptions of the benefits from tax-exempt financing of private activities have taken the form of narrowing the list of eligible beneficiaries. One approach has been to restrict the use of the bonds to areas characterized as distressed or blighted, that is, toward areas with concentrations of low-income people or lagging economic development. The second approach has been to restrict use of the bonds by income of recipient, without regard to the economic characteristics of the area in which the recipient lived.

The targeting provisions seem to suggest that benefits to federal taxpayers from state and local provision of services that are often provided by the private sector (e.g., housing and student loans) are only present if the services are provided to lower-income citizens; or if from state and local economic development effort, only if the development occurs in an economically disadvantaged area. These targeting provisions seem to be consistent with the external benefits and spillover principles discussed in chapter 5, for most of the benefits from local government redistributional efforts accrue to nonresidents and are thus more likely to be underprovided.

ARBITRAGE PROFITS AND ADVANCE REFUNDING

Arbitrage bonds were originally defined in the Tax Reform Act of 1969 as bonds issued where all or a major portion of the proceeds are expected to be used to acquire securities with a yield materially higher than the yield on the municipal bonds. The initial question concerning the provision was how much of the proceeds invested at materially higher yields constituted a major portion. The U.S. Department of the Treasury initially set this major portion standard at an amount in excess of 5 percent of the available proceeds, but soon raised it to an amount in excess of 15 percent. Thus, an issue was not to be considered an arbitrage bond if no more than 15 percent of the proceeds, including a reasonably required reserve or replacement fund, is invested in higher-yielding securities with an unrestricted yield. The remainder of the proceeds were subject to the materially higher-yield restriction, generally interpreted as any yield differential in excess of one-eighth of a percentage point.

These provisions were not very effective because the regulations allowed for a temporary three-year period of unrestricted investment of bond proceeds if a three-part reasonable expectations test was met: the project is begun within six months or a binding obligation is entered into; work on the project proceeds with due diligence; and 85 percent of the net proceeds (less any amounts in a debt service fund) are spent on the project within three years.[9]

Even with these restrictions, it was profitable for issuers to engage in advance refunding motivated by arbitrage earnings. The proceeds representing the unrestricted portions of an advance refunding issue were invested in high-yielding securities to generate arbitrage profits for the issuer. The proceeds representing the arbitrage-restricted major portion were also invested in high-yielding securities, but were purchased at a price sufficiently above the market price to keep the arbitrage earnings within the materially higher-yield restriction. Of course, this meant that the underwriter, who paid market price for these high-yielding securities and sold them to the issuer at an inflated price, earned most of the arbitrage profits (Mumford 1977, 190–94).

In addition, state and local governments took to issuing term bonds rather than serial bonds. Sinking funds were created into which were placed tax or project revenues for repaying the principal of the term bonds at maturity. Since the regulations specified that it was the use of bond proceeds (not tax or project revenues) that was restricted for arbitrage purposes, the arbitrage regulations did not apply to these sinking funds. The monies in these funds were, therefore, free to be invested at unrestricted yield (Peaslee 1979, 432–42).

The regulations had also enabled substantial arbitrage profits to be earned on tax and revenue anticipation notes (TANs and RANs).

TANs and RANs were not considered to be arbitrage notes if they were sized not to exceed the accumulated cash flow deficit over the next year plus one month's expenditures. Although problems existed in determining the cash flow deficit, a major problem was the upsizing of the note issues to accommodate one month's expenditure. For a state like California or New York, this interpretation created the potential for substantial arbitrage earnings based upon literally billions of dollars of arbitrage notes.

By 1978, the Treasury had responded to these transactions in several ways. One approach was to adopt a regulation that a bond transaction whose only advantage to the issuer comes from the minor portion arbitrage earnings is in violation of the regulation that a bond issue cannot exceed by more than 5 percent the amount of proceeds necessary for its governmental purpose. A second approach required that calculation of the yield on the securities purchased with the yield-restricted major portion of the advance refunding issue be based upon the market price of the obligations. A third approach was for the Treasury to offer a special series of government bonds available only to state and local governments whose yield is commensurate with the yield on municipal securities. A fourth approach required that all amounts held in a sinking fund, regardless of source, be treated as proceeds of the issue. Finally, the Treasury simply prohibited the investment of the minor portion of the refunding bond proceeds in unrestricted higher-yielding securities. Nonetheless, issuers and financial advisors continued to find ways to structure refundings to earn arbitrage profits (Mumford 1977, 193–98).

Legislation

1976

The 1976 act exempted special allowance payments on student loans from inclusion in the determination of arbitrage profits, thereby permitting student loan authorities to earn very large arbitrage profits when interest rates rose rapidly in the late 1970s. The 1978 act clarified some uncertainty as to whether an advance refunding issue of a tax-exempt IDB is also tax exempt. Tax exemption was granted, provided that substantially all the proceeds of the refunded issue were used for a qualified public facility and the facility is available to the general public.

1978

The 1978 act denied advanced refunding to IDBs. An exception was made for proceeds used to finance convention and trade show facilities, airports, docks, wharves, mass-commuting facilities, and parking facilities.

1980

Several arbitrage restrictions were imposed on mortgage revenue bonds in 1980. The yield on mortgages was restricted to no more than 1.0 percentage point in excess of the yield on the tax-exempt bond issue. The dollar value of tax-exempt bonds earning unrestricted yields on nonmortgage investments, known more generally as nonpurpose obligations (obligations not acquired to carry out the purpose for which the bonds were issued), was restricted to 150 percent of the annual debt service payment on a bond issue. An exception was provided for proceeds invested for a temporary period until such proceeds were needed for mortgages. Any nonpurpose arbitrage profits have to be paid or credited to the mortgagors or rebated to the Federal government. And advance refunding was denied for mortgage revenue bonds.

1982

The 1982 act raised the allowable arbitrage profit on mortgage revenue bonds from 1.0 to 1.125 percentage points above the yield on the bond issue. It also imposed a limit on the amount of time by which an IDB issue's maturity can exceed the expected economic life of the asset being financed with the bonds (the "term to maturity" provision). The average maturity of the bond issue cannot exceed the expected asset life by more than 20 percent.

1984

The 1984 act eliminated the qualified-facilities exception to the prohibition on advanced refunding for IDBs instituted in the 1978 act. It also restricted the amount of IDB proceeds that can be invested in nonpurpose obligations at a yield above the bond yield to 150 percent of annual debt service. The 150 percent figure does not include amounts invested for temporary periods that are otherwise permitted by the tax law. These "temporary period" amounts are subject to the rebate requirement if the bond proceeds are not expended within six months.

The act also imposed a rebate requirement on IDBs that earn arbitrage profits on nonpurpose obligations, including obligations invested in a debt service reserve fund. Rebatable profits include the amount by which the yield on the nonpurpose obligations exceeds the yield on the IDB issue plus any income earned on the arbitrage itself. The calculation of arbitrage is not reduced by issuance costs on the IDBs or underwriter's discount on the nonpurpose obligations. And any reduction of arbitrage by purchase or sale of nonpurpose obligations at other than fair market value is prohibited.[10] Rebate of arbitrage profits is waived if all IDB proceeds are expended for the governmental purpose for which the bonds are issued within six months of the issue date. Rebate of a debt service fund's arbitrage profits is also waived if no more than $100,000 of profits are earned. Multifamily rental housing bonds were exempt from all of the additional arbitrage restrictions imposed by the 1984 act.

Finally, the act directed that the Congressional Budget Office and the General Accounting Office study student loan bonds and make recommendations on the appropriate arbitrage restrictions that should be applied. It directed the Treasury Department to adopt new arbitrage restrictions on student loan bonds if the Congress does not do so, which Treasury did effective January 1990.

1986

The 1986 act extended: (1) the IDB rebate requirement for arbitrage profits earned on nonpurpose obligations to all tax-exempt bonds (governmental and private-activity bonds), with the single exception of mortgage revenue bonds, which have their own rebate rule; and (2) the restriction of nonpurpose investments in debt service reserves to 150 percent of annual debt service to all private-activity bonds, with the single exception of 501(c)(3) bonds. As with IDBs, rebate is not required if all proceeds are expended for the governmental purpose within six months of the issue date, or if unspent proceeds do not exceed the lesser of 5 percent of the gross proceeds or $100,000 (in which case another six months is allowed for expenditure of the proceeds prior to rebate). In addition, no rebate is required for governmental bonds if the governmental unit expects to issue no more than $5 million in governmental bonds during the calendar year. A transitional exception was provided for student loan bonds while they find another source of financing for administrative (program) and issuance costs.

The act curbed the ability of governmental units to inflate the size of their tax and revenue anticipation notes (TRANs), through use of the one-month expenditure provision discussed previously. Arbitrage rebate is not required if the unit's cumulative cash-flow deficit exceeds 90 percent of the TRAN six months after issuance.

The act extended the restriction on types of property in which bond proceeds can be invested without regard to yield restrictions to the purchase of annuity contracts. Thus, purchase of an annuity contract designed to fund a pension plan is subject to the same restrictions as though the pension fund were directly funded with bond proceeds.

The 1986 act also extended the requirement for rebate of mortgage revenue bond nonpurpose arbitrage to qualified veterans' mortgage bonds. Advance refunding is denied to all private-activity bonds except for 501(c)(3) bonds, and is limited to one advance refunding issue for governmental and 501(c)(3) bonds. Finally, the act extended the term-to-maturity rule previously applied to IDBs (average maturity cannot exceed expected asset life by more than 20 percent) to all private-activity bonds except for mortgage revenue and student loan bonds.

1988

The 1988 act imposed a three-year limit on loan origination from a mortgage revenue bond issue, after which unspent proceeds must be used to redeem bonds within a six-month period. Restrictions were also placed on blind-pool financings of governmental bonds, in which borrowers were not identified and no time period for loan origination was imposed. The issuer must certify that 95 percent of the proceeds will be spent within three years, and must ensure that all legal and underwriting costs are not contingent upon making loans and are paid within 180 days of issuance.

Finally, the 1988 act addressed the practice whereby some governmental units purchased residential rental housing units outside their boundaries with tax-exempt bond proceeds. In effect, these jurisdictions were acting as landlords and earning rents or income on these investments. The question here was whether the arbitrage rules requiring rebate of earnings on nonpurpose investments applied to these projects—that is, did these projects satisfy a governmental purpose? It was decided that the projects did not satisfy a governmental purpose, and they were subjected to the nonpurpose arbitrage restrictions.

1989

The 1989 act exempted from the rebate requirements the portion of the proceeds of governmental bonds and 501(c)(3) private-activity bonds used for construction projects, provided certain spend-down requirements are met. Ten percent of the proceeds must be spent within 6 months, 45 percent within the first year, 75 percent within 18 months, 95 percent within two years, and 100 percent within three years. Issuers failing to comply must either rebate the arbitrage earnings or pay a penalty equal to 3 percent of the difference between the unexpended proceeds and the required expenditure amount.

Conclusion

Several techniques were utilized to restrict issuers' access to arbitrage profits. As has been true with much of tax-exempt bond legislation, the techniques were often introduced in exchange for granting exempt status to a particular activity that otherwise satisfied the conditions for taxable IDB status, were then extended to all IDBs, and eventually to all tax-exempt bonds.

A distinction was drawn between high-yielding securities acquired in pursuit of the purpose for which the bonds were issued, so-called "purpose" obligations such as mortgages and student loans, and those acquired that had no relationship to the purpose for which the bonds were issued, so-called "nonpurpose" obligations such as taxable federal government securities. The dollar value of bonds earning nonpurpose arbitrage was restricted to 150 percent of annual debt service. Use of these earnings as a source of general revenue was first denied, and eventually subject to rebate to the federal government. Rebate requirements in turn were eventually extended to all tax-exempt bonds, with an exception provided for construction project proceeds of governmental and nonprofit private-activity bonds that satisfied spend-down proportions beginning at six months and ending in three years. The length of time bonds can remain outstanding was restricted to 120 percent of the expected life of the facilities being financed with all private-activity bonds—the term-to-maturity provision.

THE PRIVATE COST OF CAPITAL

The ability of tax-exempt bonds to lower the cost of capital for private users has been attacked in two ways over the last 20 years. One approach has been to deny use of the tax benefits intended for private investment to assets financed with tax-exempt bonds. This has been done using two techniques: by imposing reduced depreciation and investment tax credit benefits on the tax-exempt bond financed portion of an asset; and by imposing government ownership requirements that are tantamount to denying depreciation and investment tax credit benefits on the property. The second approach to reducing the capital cost subsidy has been to deny tax-exempt status to any bond that possesses a federal guarantee of all or part of its debt service, thereby increasing the bond yield.

Accelerated Depreciation Benefits

Depreciation allowances for both equipment and structures historically have reflected a tax life that is shorter than the economic life of the asset, and a more rapid rate of deterioration within that life span than is consistent with experience. As of 1982, depreciation allowances for equipment and structures were calculated using 150 percent and 175 percent declining balance formulas, respectively, over relatively short time periods, with allowance for an optional switch to a straight-line formula. The 1982 act curtailed one of these accelerated depreciation benefits for the portion of an asset financed with tax-exempt bonds, requiring the tax-exempt financed portion of the asset to be depreciated using a straight-line formula. Several exceptions were made to these restrictions: multifamily residential rental projects; public sewage and solid waste disposal facilities; some air or water pollution control facilities; and bonds used in conjunction with Urban Development Action Grants. (See table 7.1 for estimates of the effect of this restriction on the private cost of capital.)

By 1986, the depreciation allowances for the average piece of equipment was based upon an asset life of 7 years and a 200 percent declining balance formula with an optional switch to a straight-line formula. Structures were using a straight-line formula and an asset life of 31.5 years. The 1986 act changed both the asset life and the depreciation formula for equipment financed with tax-exempt bonds, requiring depreciation allowances to be calculated using an average 13-year life and a straight-line formula; and it lengthened the asset life for structures. All exceptions to the restriction were eliminated except for multifamily rental housing. ((See table 7.1 for estimates of the effect of this restriction on the private cost of capital.)

Government Ownership Requirements

When the 1984 act imposed a volume cap on selected private-activity bonds (discussed in detail later in this chapter), it excluded some tax-exempt IDBs from the cap, provided the facilities were owned by or on behalf of a governmental unit. This did not, however, mean that the governmental unit had economic or tax ownership. Rather, it meant that no nongovernmental entity is considered an owner of the facilities for federal income tax purposes. Thus, exclusion from the volume cap depended upon no private operator (lessee) of the facilities claiming the tax benefits of depreciation deductions or the investment credit.[11]

This provision was repealed by the 1986 act and replaced with a three-part test of governmental ownership. Property leased by a governmental unit to a private user is considered to be governmentally owned if (1) the nongovernmental lessee elects not to claim depreciation or an investment tax credit, (2) the life of the lease does not exceed 80 percent of the property's expected economic life, and (3) any lessee purchase of the property is at fair market value. Alternative operating agreements and management contracts must conform to similar rules.

Federal Guarantees

A tax-exempt bond that carries a federal guarantee can be issued at a lower yield than can a nonguaranteed bond with otherwise similar characteristics. A lower yield on the portion of an asset financed with tax-exempt bonds has the effect of lowering the cost of capital for the asset. The first instance of restricting the joint use of tax-exempt financing and federal guarantee was introduced in the Crude Oil Windfall Profits Tax Act of 1980. In this act, the exemption to the IDB test for solid waste disposal facilities was extended to include facilities used to convert solid waste into steam or alcohol, unless any debt service on the bonds was guaranteed directly or indirectly by the federal government.

This provision illustrates the first use of a strategy that became standard operating procedure in congressional efforts to control private-activity bond volume. In exchange for expanding the list of exemptions to the taxable IDB rules to accommodate some new policy thrust, the new exemptions were subjected to a restriction that had not been applied previously—in this case, against joint use of a federal tax subsidy and a federal guarantee. Thus, precedent was established, and the provision could ultimately be extended to all private-activity bonds and sometimes to all tax-exempt bonds.

The 1984 act extended the prohibition against federal guarantee to all tax-exempt bonds, whether private activity or governmental. Furthermore, it broadened the definition of guarantee to any arrangement that transfers risk to the federal government. Four categories of guarantee were identified: (1) any outright guarantee of debt service, in whole or in part, by the United States or any of its agencies or instrumentalities; (2) use of the bond proceeds to make loans or other investments whose payments are guaranteed, in whole or in part, by the United States or any of its agencies or instrumentalities; (3) investment of the proceeds, directly or indirectly, in federally insured deposits or accounts in a financial institution; and (4) payment of debt service is otherwise indirectly guaranteed, in whole or in part, by the United States or any of its agencies or instrumentalities. Numerous exceptions were granted to such activities as mortgage revenue bonds, student loan bonds, and multifamily rental housing bonds, due to the pervasiveness of federal insurance programs in many program areas affected by tax-exempt bonds.

VOLUME CAPS

In spite of all the legislation enacted to reduce the incentives of state and local borrowers to issue and of investors to purchase tax-exempt bonds, the federal government was still not satisfied with the volume of bonds being issued each year. In response, a series of arbitrary (nonmarket-oriented) restrictions called volume caps were imposed on issuers. These volume caps are summarized in table 11.4. The first volume restriction was enacted in the Mortgage Subsidy Bond Act of 1980. The annual volume of qualified mortgage bonds in a state was limited to the greater of (1) 9 percent of the average annual aggregate principal amount of mortgages executed during the three preceding years for single-family owner-occupied residences located in the state, or (2) $200 million. In 1984, the Deficit Reduction Act extended the concept to qualified veterans' mortgage bonds, limiting their volume to an amount equal to (1) the aggregate amount of such bonds issued by the state during the period from January 1, 1979, and June 22, 1984, divided by (2) the number (not to exceed five) of calendar years after 1979 and before 1985 during which the state actually issued qualified veterans' bonds.

The 1984 act also extended volume caps beyond the housing area. It imposed a volume limitation on certain IDBs and student loan bonds set at the greater of $150 per state resident or $200 million. This represented an important step away from detailed congressional attention to public-purpose definition. The object was to reduce the growth of private-purpose bonds while allowing the state and local

Table 11.4 VOLUME CAPS ON PRIVATE-ACTIVITY BONDS, 1980–88

Activity	1980	1984	1986	1987	1988
Mortgage revenue bonds	X		Stop[a]		
Veterans' mortgage bonds		X			
Greater of $150 per person or $200 million		X	Stop		
Exempt private activities not included in the cap:					
Mortgage, revenue bonds					
Veterans' mortgage bonds					
501(c)(3) bonds					
Multifamily rental housing					
Airports, docks, wharves[b]					
Convention and trade show[b]					
Mass commuting[b]					
Greater of $50 per person or $150 million[c]			X		
Exempt private activities not included in the cap:					
Veterans' mortgage bonds					
501(c)(3) bonds					
Airports, docks, wharves[b]					
Solid waste disposal[b]					
Private activities subjected to the cap since 1986:					
Takeovers of investor-owned utilities				X	
High-speed intercity rail transit—25% of proceeds					X
Limitation on outstanding tax-exempt bonds					
$40 million for each beneficiary of small-issue IDBs		X			
$150 million for each 501(c)(3) organization			X		

a. Stop denotes year cap terminated.
b. Exception applies to facilities owned by or on behalf of governmental entities.
c. Effective 1988; through 1987, was greater of $75 per person or $250 million.

sector to make decisions concerning what types of activities best serve public purposes and should thus be allocated part of the scarce private-purpose volume cap. Congress, however, retained some allocative control, and exempted some IDBs from the cap including multifamily rental housing and, if owned or operated on behalf of a governmental entity, convention or trade show facilities, airports, docks, wharves, and mass commuting facilities.

The 1984 act also introduced the first cap based upon the out-standing stock of tax-exempt bonds rather than the annual volume of bond issues. Any one beneficiary's use of small-issue IDBs was limited to $40 million at any one time.

The 1986 act made the most important move away from public purpose definition by setting a volume cap for each state equal to the greater of $50 per capita or $150 million, effective in 1988 (for 1987 the cap was set temporarily at the greater of $75 per capita or $250 million). The only private-activity bonds not subject to the cap are those issued for nonprofit organizations; governmentally owned airports, docks, wharves, and solid waste disposal facilities; and qualified veterans' mortgages (which remain subject to their own cap). A cap of $150 million also was imposed on a nonprofit organization's outstanding stock of tax-exempt bonds, with an exception allowed for hospital facilities.

GOOD-GOVERNMENT PROVISIONS

All provisions that increase the amount of information available to taxpayers, federal or state and local, are placed in the "good-government" category on the theory that additional information increases the likelihood that state and local officials will have to consider carefully the benefits and costs of any bond issue. Thus, the category includes provisions requiring bond registration, public approval, and reporting requirements. This section also includes the only piece of legislation dealing with enforcement and penalties adopted since 1968.

The Crude Oil Windfall Profits Tax Act of 1980, in exchange for the extension of eligible solid waste projects to those configured for steam generation or alcohol production, introduced a second restriction on tax-exempt bonds (in addition to the no-federal-guarantee provision discussed earlier). Bonds issued to finance these newly approved IDB activities had to be issued in registered form. Thus, a paper trail of municipal bond owners and recipients of interest income was established.

The 1982 act placed unprecedented emphasis on the taxpayer approval area. First, it introduced the first federal requirements for public approval at the state and local level.

. . . . Congress believed that, in general, State and local governments are best suited to determine the appropriate uses of IDBs. Congress believed that providing tax exemption for the interest on certain IDBs may serve legitimate purposes in some instances provided that the elected representatives of the State or local governmental unit determine after public input that there will be substantial public benefit from issuance of the obligations and provided that the affected public has had an opportunity to comment on the use of tax-exempt financing for particular facilities. In order to achieve this goal, the Act requires notice and a public hearing and approval by an elected representative of the issuer before issuance of IDBs. (Joint Committee on Taxation 1982, 99)

The approval requirement took two forms. The first required that notice be given of the intent to issue bonds for a project and to hold a public hearing to discuss the merits of the proposed bond issue. After the hearing, the bond issue must be approved by an elected official or legislative body. Alternatively, the proposed bond issue could be approved by a voter referendum to be held at the jurisdiction's normal election time and following its normal procedures for referenda.

Second, the registration requirement introduced in 1980 for a few IDB activities was extended to all tax-exempt bonds by the 1982 act, and incited a constitutional challenge that culminated in *South Carolina v. Baker*, 485 U.S. 505 (1988). Second, most private-activity bond issuers were required to file information reports to the Treasury Department with respect to each issue. The requirement applied to all IDBs, student loan bonds, and 501(c)(3) bonds. The reports had to include such information as: (1) characteristics of the bond issue (e.g. stated interest rate, amount of lendable proceeds, etc.); (2) name of the elected official or legislative body that approved the issue, or a description of the enabling voter referendum; and (3) information to identify the principal users of the facilities financed with the proceeds.

The 1984 act continued the drive for acquiring information about private-activity bonds. Information-reporting requirements were imposed on mortgage revenue bonds, to include (but not necessarily limited to) characteristics of the bond issue (e.g. interest rate, amount of lendable proceeds, etc.) and its issuer. In addition, the issuer was required to submit an annual policy statement specifying how in the following year it intended to comply with the congressional intent to target the bonds to lower-income families.

The 1986 act extended both the taxpayer approval and information-reporting requirements that were applied to private-activity bonds to all tax-exempt bonds. In addition, operators of bond-financed multifamily rental housing projects were required to certify annually their compliance with applicable income targeting requirements. Finally, the annual policy statement requirement imposed on mortgage revenue bonds in 1984 was repealed.

One could say that these efforts to require taxpayer approval might reduce potential electoral benefits in the form of contributions if taxpayers were induced to reject projects where the balance of public and private benefits was weighted toward the private. But instances in which projects have been rejected after being subjected to taxpayer approval have been relatively few. Another approach was also tried. The 1984 act required that the public official responsible for a private-activity bond allocation under the volume cap certify that the allocation was not made in return for any bribe, gift, gratuity, or direct or indirect contribution to any political campaign. The provision did not last long, as it was repealed by the 1986 act.

The enforcement options available to the Internal Revenue Service (IRS) have been rather limited (see chapter 12 for more details on this issue). The IRS could attempt to persuade but was unable to prevent an issuer from marketing a bond issue even when prior knowledge was available that the issue was "abusive" with respect to the existing bond laws. After issuance, IRS options were either extreme (declaring the interest income to be taxable or blacklisting the issuer to prevent its subsequent access to the bond market) or time consuming (bargaining over a negotiated settlement to recapture some of the lost federal revenue). The 1989 act extended section 6700 of the Internal Revenue Code to tax-exempt bonds. This provision permits IRS to go to court to prevent an abusive or fraudulent bond deal from going to market, and allows seizure of all money earned by the participants in any abusive or fraudulent deals.

INCOME TAX RATE REDUCTIONS

The first substantial rate change in the 1968–88 period under discussion occurred in 1981. The maximum individual marginal tax rate was reduced from 70 percent to 50 percent, making the value of tax-exempt interest income considerably less valuable to taxpayers whose tax rate had formerly been 70 percent. Somewhat smaller reductions in the attractiveness of tax-exempt bonds as a tax shelter were imposed on those taxpayers whose rates had ranged between 50 percent and 70 percent.

The 1986 act made the last significant changes in the individual and corporate rate structures. The individual rate structure was compressed into two brackets of 15 percent for taxpayers with adjusted gross income (AGI) less than $29,750 (married) and $17,850 (single) and 28 percent for taxpayers with AGI above those levels, with an effective 33 percent marginal rate for joint returns with incomes between $71,900 and $149,250 ($43,150 and $89,560 for single returns), a rate that is attributable to the phaseout of the benefits of the 15 percent bracket. The corporate tax rate was reduced from 46 percent to 34 percent. Both of these changes made tax-exempt bonds less attractive investments.

The effect on the demand curve of the rate structure in force after 1986 compared to before 1986 is presented in figure 11.2. Essentially, this diagram is an adaptation of figure 9.1, with the demand curve

Figure 11.2 DEMAND AND SUPPLY OF TAX-EXEMPT BONDS (PRE- AND POST-
1986 TAX RATES)

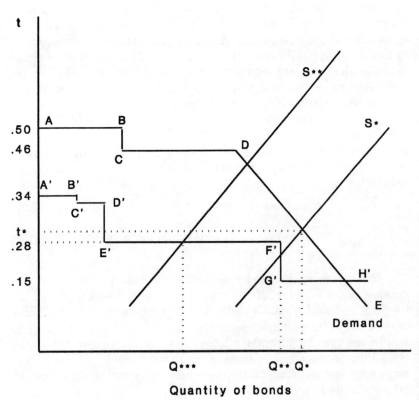

labeled *A* through *E* adjusted to reflect the corporate and individual tax rate reductions that occurred between 1968 and the 1986 act. Section *AB* now refers to all individual tax-exempt bond purchasers with a 50 percent marginal tax rate, and is considerably longer than the *AB* segment in figure 9.1, because it reflects all taxpayers who formerly had tax rates ranging from 50 percent to 70 percent. The corporate segment *CD* is drawn at the 46 percent marginal tax rate. The post-1986 demand curve for tax-exempt bonds is labeled *A'* through *H'*, and reflects the new corporate and individual rate schedules. Since the corporate sector has the highest marginal tax rate of 34 percent, segment *A'B'* represents corporate demand. Sections *C'D'*, *E'F'*, and *G'H'* refer to individuals with 33 percent, 28 percent, and 15 percent marginal tax rates respectively.[13] The corporate segment is shorter than previously drawn, to reflect the impact of the denial of commercial bank interest deductions on amounts borrowed to purchase tax-exempt bonds (discussed later in the chapter) and the decreased attractiveness of tax-exempt bonds as an investment relative to partially taxed assets. All individuals have been shuffled. The *C'D'* portion of the curve is relatively short because it contains the relatively few people with a 33 percent marginal tax rate (although they have a disproportionately large share of income). Most of the highest income purchasers of tax-exempt bonds appear on the relatively long *E'F'* portion of the curve, representing those taxpayers with a 28 percent rate.

If only the demand side of the market had been affected by the 1986 act, bond volume would have fallen slightly from Q^* to Q^{**}, leaving the market-clearing rate indeterminate between 28 percent and 15 percent. When combined with a shift of S^* to S^{**} that represents the effect of the 1986 Tax Reform Act on the supply of tax-exempt bonds, bond volume falls further to Q^{***}. The market clearing marginal tax rate is 28 percent.

MINIMUM TAX

1969 to 1982

The 1969 act introduced both individual and corporate add-on minimum taxes (AOMT) on preference income. The AOMT rate was set at 10 percent. Specified sources of preference income were included in the AOMT base. The minimum tax rate was applied to this AOMT base, adjusted by an offset equal to the sum of $30,000 plus any regular tax. The interest income on tax-exempt bonds was not included among the preference items included in the tax base, so the adoption of the minimum tax would tend to increase the demand for tax-exempt bonds.

An alternative minimum tax (AMT) with a top tax rate of 25 percent was added to the individual income tax system in 1978. These rates are applied to an AMT base equal to the sum of taxable income, adjusted itemized deductions, and capital gains. The individual pays the greater of AMT liability or the sum of the regular tax plus the add-on minimum tax. These changes were expected to reduce the taxation of preference income and, since tax-exempt interest is not part of the minimum tax base, would tend to decrease the demand for tax-exempt bonds.

The 1976, 1978, 1981, and 1982 acts adjusted the rates and/or coverage of the AOMT and AMT, thereby influencing the demand for tax shelters competing with tax-exempt bonds whose interest income was not included in the minimum tax base.

1983

The Social Security Amendments of 1983, although not a minimum tax, has a similar type of effect in that it imposes a tax on formerly tax-free interest income. This act included tax-exempt bond interest income in the calculation of the income threshold at which half of social security benefits are gradually taken into taxable income.

1986

The 1986 act created a corporate AMT, repealed the corporate AOMT tax, and expanded the individual AMT. The corporate AMT tax base is the corporation's taxable income increased by its tax preferences for the year. In general, the preference income included in the AMT base is substantially increased. Most important for tax-exempt bonds, all non-501(c)(3) private-activity tax-exempt bond interest income on new bond issues was included in the AMT tax base for the first time. This AMT base is reduced by $40,000 (minus 25 percent of AMT tax base in excess of $150,000, not to exceed $40,000) and taxed at a 20 percent rate. This amount is offset by the minimum foreign tax credit and investment tax credits to achieve the tentative AMT. The actual AMT is the amount by which the tentative AMT exceeds the regular tax.

The individual AMT rate was increased to 21 percent, and some adjustments were made to the AMT base. The exemption amounts ($40,000 for married and $30,000 for single) are reduced by 25 percent of the amount by which AMT taxable income exceeds $150,000 for married and $112,500 for single taxpayers. In general, the AMT tax base was expanded to include more preference income, particularly the interest income on non-501(c)(3) private-activity tax-exempt bonds. These changes would have the effect of reducing the demand for tax-exempt bonds, particularly because some of the tax-exempt interest income is included in the AMT base.

For corporations, tax-exempt bond interest income on both new and outstanding issues enters into the calculation of corporate excess book income. Until 1990, half of book income in excess of unadjusted alternative minimum taxable income is subject to the AMT rate of 20 percent, in effect a 10 percent tax on all tax-exempt interest income earned by corporations that are subject to the AMT. Beginning in 1990, 75 percent of adjusted current earnings (ACE) in excess of unadjusted alternative minimum taxable income is included in the alternative minimum income tax base. The calculation of ACE includes both tax-exempt bond interest income and any interest costs incurred in carrying the bonds.

DEDUCTIBILITY OF COMMERCIAL BANK INTEREST

The 1982 act disallowed 15 percent of the interest expenses incurred by commercial banks in borrowing funds used to purchase tax-exempt securities. The 1984 act increased this disallowance proportion to 20 percent. The 1986 act disallowed 100 percent of these interest expenses. An exception was made for the purchase of governmental and nonprofit organization tax-exempt bonds issued by governmental units that market less than $10 million of bonds annually. These bonds continued to be subject to a 20 percent disallowance. The reason for this exception was concern that small bond issues are less likely to be marketed through the existing national and regional financial networks, and historically have depended disproportionately on private placement with local financial institutions (commercial banks) for purchase of their bonds. The growth of mutual funds specializing in tax-exempt bonds, often focused on bonds issued within a particular state in order to avoid state and local income taxes, offers the possibility of an alternative market for private placement of these bonds.

ALTERNATIVE TAX SHELTERS

Each tax act from 1968 to 1989 influenced the effective tax rates of assets in competition with tax-exempt bonds for income seeking tax shelters. Prior to 1986, the effects of these changes on the demand for tax-exempt bonds were difficult to discern. But a motivating principle of the 1986 act was to pay for rate reduction by broadening the tax base. This act repealed the investment tax credit, scaled back depreciation allowances, taxed capital gains as ordinary income, curtailed the use of passive losses to shelter unrelated business income, imposed additional changes in accounting practices to make taxable income more closely approximate economic income, and reduced the preferences for such things as foreign income, pension plans, and employee benefits. Thus, the 1986 act served to increase the degree of preferential taxation of tax-exempt bonds relative to alternative investment choices. All other things being equal, these changes tend to shift the demand schedule for tax-exempt bonds to the right, thereby moving its intersection with the supply schedule farther to the left on the *EF* portion of the demand schedule in figure 11.2. This works to keep the yield ratio and borrowing costs from rising, should the supply of bonds rebound strongly from the relatively low volumes generated since the 1986 act.

CONCLUSIONS

This account indicates that federal legislation has focused on the economic factors that contributed to growth in the volume of tax-exempt bonds. The emphasis of this legislation has changed steadily from defining public purpose by identifying specific private-purpose activities to one in that these nontraditional private-purpose activities are subjected to a quantitative limit as a group. This may be seen by contrasting the list of excepted activities in the Revenue and Expenditure Control Act of 1968 with the imposition of a strict volume limit on most nontraditional activities in the Tax Reform Act of 1986.

This evolution in approach seems to make sense. When one looks carefully at the list of private-purpose activities financed with tax-exempt bonds, such as economic development, student loans, owner-occupied and multi-family rental housing, nonprofit organizations, and even "small-issue" assistance to private businesses, it is striking that most of these activities also receive federal support from the expenditure side of the budget or from other tax subsidies.[14] Congress has, by prior actions, implicitly certified some amount of most of these activities as serving public purposes. In fact, when one looks at the spectrum of activities in which the federal government is engaged (and ignores the specific individuals and areas that receive the assistance), the federal and state-local sectors' visions of public purpose seem markedly similar.

Attacking the growth problem with a fairly comprehensive volume limit accomplishes two goals simultaneously. First, it accommodates the diversity with which state and local governments divide responsibility between the public and private sectors. State and local officials can choose activities that best satisfy their vision of public purpose. Second, it enables the federal government to control its revenue loss.

Another evolution in legislative policy has been the increased use of targeting restrictions for activities such as housing. This reduces the dichotomy between federal and state-local officials' perceptions of public benefits and reduces the likelihood that the state and local sector will issue too many bonds because they overstate public benefits. Congress has essentially said that benefit spillovers exist and that federal financial support is merited for some types of activities, *provided* the benefits are targeted to people with certain income or demographic characteristics.

Even though the major source of cost understatement—the absence of a requirement that the debt service on failed projects be paid by tax revenues—has not been addressed, legislation has changed several of the financial incentives that contribute to the desire of state and local officials and private entities to use too many bonds. First, restrictions on arbitrage profits and advance refunding have decreased the ability of the state and local sector to reduce its interest cost below the stated interest rate on tax-exempt bonds and to use the bonds as a source of general revenue. Second, the subsidy provided to private capital costs has been reduced by restrictions on the use of private capital subsidies for the portion of an asset financed with tax-exempt bonds, termination of federal guarantees for tax-exempt bonds, and requirements for governmental ownership of facilities financed with tax-exempt bonds. And third, various good-government measures (taxpayer approval, reporting, etc.) may have increased the ability of taxpayers to evaluate their potential costs and benefits.

To the extent the supply of tax-exempt bonds is price sensitive (upward sloping), any reduction in the demand schedule has the effect of raising the interest cost of bond issuance and reducing the state and local sector's desired volume of bond issuance. The demand for tax-exempt bonds has been reduced by several changes in tax legislation that were not directed specifically toward controlling the volume of tax-exempt bonds. Foremost among these is the reduction of the individual and corporate income tax rate structures. The interest income on all non-501(c)(3) private-activity tax-exempt bonds was included in the individual and corporate alternative minimum income tax bases, and the interest income on all tax-exempt bonds was included in the calculation of excess corporate book income, which is a preference item. And commercial banks were denied the ability to deduct their interest expense incurred in borrowing funds used to purchase most tax-exempt bonds. Working against this downward shift in the demand for tax-exempt bonds was the elimination or reduction of tax preferences that had been enjoyed by many alternative tax shelters.

Notes

1. One can find more comprehensive treatments than are provided in this chapter of the tax-exempt bond provisions adopted by a single tax bill. The Joint Tax Committee provides a "General Explanation" document for most major tax legislation. These are all referenced in the bibliography and referred to repeatedly throughout the book. Two comprehensive treatments of the Tax Reform Act of 1986 that contain more commentary and analysis than are normally provided by the Joint Committee are available in Petersen (1987) and Livingston (1989).

2. Note the focus on use of the bond proceeds for commercial purposes that is implied by the words "trade or business." This emphasis would prove to be misguided when state and local governments began to develop programs to provide tax-exempt debt financing to individuals for their personal use. As discussed later in this chapter, this necessitated a second test to deal with nonbusiness private use.

3. These exceptions were, in effect, a recognition that some flexibility in who uses the proceeds is consistent with economic theory. Direct government provision is only one alternative for altering the amount of an activity. The government could use the proceeds to build a facility and contract for private-sector management. The government could also regulate or subsidize a privately owned and managed facility, or use the proceeds to subsidize private-sector capital formation. The important point is that any of these alternative types of intervention can use tax-exempt bonds to reduce the cost of capital and increase output of a good or service judged to serve a public purpose. It does not matter whether the proceeds are used directly by the government, or by businesses, individuals, and nonprofit entities. The choice among alternative agents (users of the proceeds) should depend on their relative cost in altering output. In principle, flexibility in who uses bond proceeds is desirable.

4. Because the effective dates of most tax legislation lag the adoption of the legislation, this means that tax exemption or removal of tax exemption was actually effective beginning in the year following that listed in table 11.2, or some period of months following the adoption of the legislation.

5. See the discussion in chapter 2 of public authorities.

6. Some appreciation of the analytical complexities and practical difficulties of developing good estimates of external costs and benefits can be obtained from Baumol and Oates (1988), Gramlich (1990), and Cordes et al. (1990).

7. The 90 percent test is computed excluding any financing used for targeted area residences, qualified home improvement loans, and qualified rehabilitation loans.

8. Two recent studies evaluated various aspects of the mortgage revenue bond program and came to different conclusions about its usefulness for federal policy purposes (see Wrightson 1988 and U.S. General Accounting Office 1988).

9. The temporary period could be five years if the project required a long construction period.

10. The issuer can reduce arbitrage earnings by paying an above-market price for the securities or by selling acquired securities at a below-market price. Either type of transaction will reduce the yield on the security.

11. This restriction applies equally to any lessees who operate the facility subsequent to the original operator.

12. The primary motivation for registration was compliance: to inhibit use of the bonds to evade estate and gift taxes; to enable tracking of capital gains on tax-exempt bonds (which is not tax exempt); and to inhibit use of the bonds in money laundering schemes.

13. This demand curve is drawn with no downward sloping portions because demand at each tax rate is large enough to be represented by more than a point (given the scale of the quantity axis). The downward sloping portions of the demand curve in figure 9.1 represent, in effect, a smoothing of very short horizontal segments representing many different marginal tax rates.

14. A concise summary of the financial assistance provided to these activities can be gleaned from any edition of the Office of Management and Budget's *Special Analyses: Budget of the United States Government* (Washington, D.C.: U.S. Government Printing Office). The chapters on federal credit programs, tax expenditures, and aid to state and local governments are of particular interest.

SELECTED ISSUES IN TAX-EXEMPT BOND POLICY: ENFORCEMENT, INFRASTRUCTURE, MUNICIPAL SOCIALISM, THE VOLUME CAP, AND ALTERNATIVE POLICIES

Chapter Twelve

ADMINISTRATION AND ENFORCEMENT

As detailed in chapter 11, the tax provisions devoted to tax-exempt bonds have increased dramatically in number and complexity over the last 20 years. The focus of this legislation has been to reduce the volume of tax-exempt debt issued each year and to target the debt that is issued to uses that satisfy a public purpose as perceived by the federal taxpayer. Of course, the effectiveness of laws depends upon oversight and enforcement; if these are lacking, the provisions eventually become a tax on honesty—a rather sandy base upon which to construct the foundation of an efficient and equitable tax system. The issuance of tax-exempt bonds is dominated by people whose financial and legal sophistication provide great ability to evaluate the trade-off between increased financial benefits and the risk of getting caught testing the limits of the tax law. The role of oversight and enforcement is particularly important for tax-exempt bonds, because until June 1989 their issuance and sale remained largely unregulated by Securities and Exchange Commission disclosure laws designed to protect the investor, and the new regulations will require time to become fully effective.

How does the Internal Revenue Service (IRS) administer and enforce the tax-exempt bond laws? Does it conduct a systematic effort to monitor compliance with the bond rules and to identify abusive bond issues that require some enforcement action? Or does it rely on a voluntary compliance system that activates its enforcement machinery only when instances of abuse are raised by sources of information external to the IRS? How does the IRS make its decisions about the allocation of scarce audit and enforcement resources among competing areas of the tax code? What kind of penalties does it have in its enforcement arsenal to provide an incentive for compliance with the tax-exempt bond law? Are they used? Are they effective?

My purpose here is not to allege that the IRS is derelict in its duty if it relies on voluntary compliance. If the objective of the tax collection agency is to maximize revenue collections, it is quite rational in an economic sense to rely on voluntary compliance for tax-exempt bonds if scarce enforcement resources are expected to collect more taxes when applied to a nonbond area. But Congress views the tax system as much more than a vehicle for collecting tax revenues. It also views the system as a vehicle for implementing various social policy objectives. Are these nonrevenue objectives being factored into IRS decisions about the allocation of audit and enforcement resources? Are the performances of IRS examination officials being evaluated and judged solely upon revenue collections, or do managers' marching orders also require them to meet various goals that reflect the social objectives of the tax legislation? If managers are judged solely upon revenue collections, is this the fault of the IRS or does the responsibility rest with the congressional propensity to legislate tax law with minimal attention to providing adequate resources and policy guidance for its administration?

This chapter discusses and evaluates how the tax-exempt bond legislation described in chapter 11 is administered and enforced. The IRS has no publicly available written material describing its enforcement of the tax-exempt bond laws. The contents of this chapter pertaining to the IRS are, therefore, the product of documents describing the overall administration and enforcement procedures of the IRS, as well as discussions with present and former IRS personnel and various bond counsel.

Some conclusions must necessarily be speculative, owing to the absence of relevant information or the reluctance of the IRS to acknowledge the existence of, let alone share, information it generates to make its decisions. If problems exist, it is the responsibility of the IRS to inform others of the difficulties and to suggest potential remedies; but adoption of solutions is clearly the responsibility of policymakers at the U.S. Department of the Treasury and in Congress, as well as at the IRS. It is hoped that some interesting issues are raised here about the explicit consideration of enforcement costs in the tax legislative process, the integration of the social objectives implicit in the tax code with the incentive structures currently in place at the system's revenue collection arm, and creation of new or more aggressive use of existing penalties to deter future abusive bond deals.

Administration and enforcement of a bond issue's compliance with the federal tax-exempt bond laws is a bit like a football team's defense against the run. The issue first encounters the defensive line, bond counsel, who check for compliance at the time the bond is being issued. Successful penetration of the line leads the issue to the linebackers, the state and local governments, who generally maintain some sort of administrative apparatus to check on the issue's continuing conformity with state constitutional and statutory restrictions as well as federal restrictions. The final defense rests with the safeties in the backfield, the IRS, who protect against the missed tackles of the other team members.

BOND COUNSEL

The bond counsel's function is "to provide an expert and objective legal opinion with respect to the validity of bonds and other subjects the opinion addresses. The opinion is an objective judgment rather than the partisan position of an advocate. It ordinarily is required by purchasers in order to provide assurance to investors" (National Association of Bond Lawyers 1987, 52).

The bond opinion usually addresses three major subjects: the status of the bonds as valid and binding obligations of the issuer; security and source of payment for the bonds; and the extent to which the bonds are exempt from federal and state income taxes. It is only the latter subject that is of interest here. A typical bond opinion contains some variant of the following phrases:

The interest on the Bonds is excluded from gross income for federal income tax purposes and is not an item of tax preference for purposes of the federal alternative minimum tax imposed on individuals and corporations; . . . *The opinions set forth in the preceding sentence are subject to the condition that the Issuer comply with all requirements of the Internal Revenue Code of 1986 that must be satisfied subsequent to the issuance of the Bonds in order that interest thereon be, or continue to be, excluded from gross income for federal income tax purposes. The Issuer has covenanted to comply with each such requirement.* Failure to comply with certain of such requirements may cause the inclusion of interest on the Bonds in gross income for federal income tax purposes to be retroactive to the date of issuance of the Bonds. . . [emphasis added]. (National Association of Bond Lawyers 1987, 6)[1]

This "unqualified" opinion as to the validity and tax exempt status of the bonds (in conjunction with the issuance of a nonarbitrage certificate)[2] essentially means that counsel has determined that a court would be unreasonable to hold to the contrary. Since the unreasonable can sometimes occur, the opinion really means that bond counsel thinks the risk of a contrary finding by a court is so small that the potential investor can safely ignore the possibility when calculating an appropriate price for the bond.

But note that the opinion on federal income tax exemption is conditional on the future behavior of the issuer (the part of the preceding quotation in italics). The opinion really says that all the documentation available to bond counsel at this moment as to the legal arrangements and future behavior of the issuer suggests that the issuer is now and will be in compliance with federal tax law: "The imposition of the condition of future compliance with such requirements is not intended to suggest that bond counsel need not consider the legality and practicability of such compliance, *but also is not intended to impose upon bond counsel any obligation of post-issuance monitoring*" [emphasis added] (National Association of Bond Lawyers 1987, 16).

One cannot get any more direct about bond counsel's responsibility for issuer compliance with the federal tax law after the bonds are issued and the fees collected. Responsibility does not exist, and I am not suggesting that it should exist—after all, nobody is paying bond counsel for this service. But think about the multitude of bond provisions that have been adopted over the last 20 years, as summarized in chapter 11. These provisions represent congressional efforts to direct the use of tax-exempt bonds for various purposes of social policy. Congress has said that many of these bonds are useful instruments of social policy only if they satisfy the rules as specified in the Internal Revenue Code.

For most bond issues, many of these tax provisions become germane well after the date on which the bonds are issued. For example, concerns about arbitrage earnings last as long as bond proceeds remain unspent and reserve and replacement funds exist; building a solid waste disposal plant and completing a contract to engage a manager take years; the recipient of a small-issue IDB is subject to capital spending restrictions that span a six-year period; and the average unit in a multifamily rental housing project is rented many times to people of varying income levels over a period of time that probably exceeds 20 years. These post-opinion actions must conform to the multitude of tax laws enacted by Congress. At the time these actions occur, compliance is assured only by the issuer's nonspecific promise extracted by the private legal profession months or years earlier.

STATE AND LOCAL GOVERNMENTS

With bond counsel out of the compliance loop once issuance has occurred, a heavy burden falls on the issuer to ensure continued compliance. According to the model bond opinion quoted previously, the issuer has "covenanted" itself to comply with each provision of the tax law. This section of the chapter examines how the issuer goes about living up to that pledge.

It is impossible to provide an exhaustive account of issuer efforts to monitor and enforce this pledge. There are no guidelines to direct the 50 states and the thousands of local governments and independent authorities on constructing procedures for this purpose. The account here is, therefore, of necessity, impressionistic and anecdotal. It focuses on efforts to monitor governmental bonds and two types of private-activity bonds.

Governmental Bonds

Most state and local governments issue and monitor governmental bonds through a treasurer's office, or perhaps a finance office. The issuer of a governmental bond must file IRS form 8038-G (reproduced in appendix 12A to this chapter). The form requests a considerable amount of information. The issue must be classified as a tax or revenue anticipation note, a lease or installment sale, or a bond for a selected list of purposes (e.g. education, transportation, housing, etc.). Financial characteristics of the issue are requested: maturity, yield, net interest cost, issue price, and so forth. Proceeds used for accrued interest, issuance costs, credit enhancement, reserve or replacement funds, and refundings must be identified. The weighted average maturity, last call date, and date of issuance of bonds to be refunded must be entered. A record must be made of any proceeds that require an allocation from the private-activity volume cap, that utilize the small governmental unit exceptions to the arbitrage rebate and interest cost deductibility rules, or are pooled financings.

Mortgage Revenue Bonds

Most private-activity bonds are not monitored by the treasurer or the finance office because the tax base of the political unit is not at risk. Compliance monitoring usually is done by the duly constituted authority (see chapter 2) that has borrowed on behalf of the state or local government. Private-activity bond issuers must submit IRS form 8038 shortly after the bond issue comes to market. This form (reproduced in appendix 12A to this chapter) requires information similar to that required on the 8038-G form filed for governmental bonds. In addition, more detailed information on the private-activity volume cap is required, including whether the authority is based on the current cap or carry forward of unused prior years' cap authority.

Each housing finance agency must submit periodically another report titled "Qualified Mortgage Bond Information Report." This report includes such information as: the number and volume of mortgage loans by income and acquisition cost; the number and volume of these loans within each income and acquisition cost class that satisfy the three-year requirement for targeted and nontargeted areas; and the number and volume of home improvement and qualified rehabilitation loans in targeted and nontargeted areas.

The U.S. General Accounting Office (GAO, 1988) conducted a survey in 1987 of 25 housing finance agencies that issue qualified mortgage revenue bonds. One of the subjects investigated in the GAO's discussions with the agencies was efforts to monitor compliance with the federal tax-exempt bond law. Of these agencies, 23 of 25 said they review the loans (made by private financial institutions) themselves or hire an outside reviewer to check on whether the loans satisfy the requirements of the tax law. The other two agencies said they rely on the lenders to ensure that loans comply with the tax law. Some agencies maintain that they have refused to purchase loans from lenders or have made lenders repurchase the loans when agency review suggested the loans did not comply with requirements of the tax law. In addition, 15 of the 25 agencies reported that their state and/or local audit agencies conduct reviews of their activities, although the reviews generally do not focus on compliance with Code provisions. The 40 percent of sample states that do not audit their housing agencies generally cite as justification the absence of state or local funds to finance agency activities.

The GAO checked on the quality of compliance using data on 177,786 loans made between 1983 and 1987 by 29 housing finance agencies. During this period, the purchase price of housing financed with mortgage revenue bonds was restricted to 120 percent of average area purchase price in targeted economically distressed areas and to 110 percent of average area purchase price in all other areas.[3] Table 12.1 presents the percentage distribution of loans by average area purchase price for those loans for which data on purchase price and the area average purchase price were available (about 61 percent of

Table 12.1 DISTRIBUTION BY AVERAGE AREA PURCHASE PRICE OF
MORTGAGES FINANCED WITH QUALIFIED MORTGAGE REVENUE
BONDS, 1983–87

	Purchase Price as Percentage of Area Average Purchase Price				
	0–90 %	91–110 %	111–120 %	121–150 %	>150 %
All agencies	84	11	2	2	1
State agencies	84	11	2	2	1
Local agencies	88	12	0	0	0

Source: U.S. General Accounting Office (1988), appendix III, table III.1.

the total loans). Eighty-four percent of all loans fell within 90 percent
of the area purchase price, and an additional 11 percent fell within
the 110 percent limit applicable to nontargeted areas. Thus, 95 percent of the loans satisfied the purchase price limitation without question. An additional 2 percent of the loans fell within the restrictions
for economically distressed areas, and satisfied the tax law if the
homes were indeed located in distressed areas. There is no way to
tell from these data whether another goal was met, the reservation
of at least 20 percent of the mortgage funds for targeted distressed
areas for at least one year.

These data tend to show that state and local governments have
done a good job of monitoring compliance in the mortgage revenue
bond area, although it would be desirable to know the status of the
40 percent of mortgages that lacked sufficient purchase price data
to be included in the table. The housing agencies seem to pay attention to the requirements of the federal tax law, although the state
and local governments themselves appear to practice little oversight
and monitoring of the financing authorities they have created. Some
bond trustees, banks designated by issuers to be the custodian of
funds and the official representative of bondholders, have recently
assumed a more active role in monitoring compliance. This increased
role is a response to a spate of abusive bond deals (not in the mortgage
revenue bond area) that caused the IRS to consider eliminating the
tax-exempt status of these bond issues and prompted bondholders
to inquire into the oversight efforts of the trustees.

Small-Issue IDBs

The picture is very different when the focus turns to small-issue
IDBs. The only federal reporting requirement is IRS form 8038. The

issuer, whether it be a state or local industrial development authority or a local general government unit, must report the same information as already discussed here for mortgage revenue bonds. In addition, information is reported about the industrial activity being financed, the type of property being financed (depreciation characteristics), and whether the issue claims the exception to the $1 million limit and accepts the six-year total capital expenditure limitation.

Unlike mortgage revenue bonds, the tax law requires no periodic follow-up report for small-issue IDBs. The development authority need not monitor compliance of these bond issues with the provisions of the tax law or prepare a periodic report to the IRS that does such things as identify bond issues by industrial activity or type of property, track the six-year total capital spending restriction for relevant issues, and check on the $40 million restriction on outstanding IDBs for one beneficiary.

This does not mean that some issuers may not monitor these provisions for their own purposes. The association representing industrial development authorities, the Council of IDB Issuers, has no information concerning the monitoring activities of its member agencies. To give readers a sense of the oversight applied to small-issue IDBs, a brief description is included here of perhaps the largest such agency, the New Jersey Economic Development Authority. The development authority has been in operation for 17 years and has issued bonds for over 4,000 projects. It currently has a portfolio of over 3,000 outstanding economic development bond issues. The authority has 12 full-time employees who review applications for bond financing and monitor outstanding bond issues for compliance. The application review process checks on the project's public purpose, that is, on the project's economic impact on New Jersey. This economic impact consists of the maintenance or provision of employment, the maintenance or enhancement of the tax base, or an expansion of the New Jersey economy. The applicant must specify how tax-exempt financing enhances the project's prospects, and what financing alternatives are available if the application is denied. If the $1 million limit is to be exceeded, the application must contain information on the project's capital spending history for the three prior years and three subsequent years. And the applicant must certify compliance with the $40 million limit on outstanding IDBs for any one beneficiary.

A sampling procedure is used by the New Jersey Development Authority to monitor continued compliance. A portion of outstanding issues is chosen for review. The focus of this review is to check on the success of the recipient in achieving its stated public purpose to affect jobs, the tax base, and the state's economy. The authority rescinds the loans of the very few projects that do not satisfy its criteria. The review does not monitor the project for compliance with the capital spending limits, because bond counsel are believed to have checked on that prior to issuance. In addition, violation of the limits is believed to be rare, because most of the projects are for $2 million or $3 million dollars and are unlikely to exceed a $10 million limit on total capital spending. Any recipient who desires to change the terms of the bond agreement must come to the authority for approval.

INTERNAL REVENUE SERVICE

IRS enforcement of the tax-exempt bond law is best understood within the context of the IRS enforcement program for the entire tax code. Accordingly, this section begins with a discussion of IRS goals, a brief history of the resources available to the IRS, some indication of the magnitude of the administrative task confronting the agency, and the decision-making techniques it has devised for allocating its scarce resources among many competing demands. This is followed by a more detailed discussion of the way the IRS monitors and enforces the tax-exempt bond laws.

Enforcement of the Tax Code

The primary function of the IRS is to maximize compliance with the tax law. If compliance were 100 percent, enforcement activities would collect no revenues. But compliance is not 100 percent, far from it. Underreporting of income and overreporting of exclusions, deductions, and credits exists. Steuerle (1986) reported that for 1981, the tax gap (the difference between tax liability reported on returns and true tax liability) amounted to $81 billion, 61.4 percent of which was attributable to underreporting of income receipts by individuals, 15.9 percent to overreporting of adjustments to income by individuals, and 7.8 percent to corporations.

Some noncompliance reflects taxpayer ignorance of or confusion with the tax law and some reflects a calculated decision on the part of taxpayers to maximize after-tax income by engaging in noncompliance. Some IRS activities are designed to increase compliance directly, so that revenue gains appear on the tax return as originally filed (better taxpayer information programs, for example). Enforcement programs are designed to have a direct effect on revenue collections, and may also have an indirect effect on compliance to the extent these efforts cause taxpayers to reassess the risk of having their noncompliance discovered. Enforcement of most areas of the tax code is characterized by two major activities. First, various sources of information returns filed by taxpayers (or their financial agents) are cross-checked with individual and corporate tax returns. Second, an ongoing audit presence is maintained in which selected returns are chosen for examination, often based upon statistical criteria that guide the selection of returns sampled from among the population of returns.

Table 12.2 provides a breakdown of IRS allocation of staff years among its many program units for 1972 and 1986, with the program units listed in order of their percentage increase over the period. Two points are noteworthy in these data. First, total staff years increased substantially over the period, from 66,982 to 93,724. Second, the great bulk of the increase was allocated to automated data processing (computerization), which experienced a 2,858 percent increase, and to information returns, which experienced a 1,008 percent increase. Examinations staff years rose from 24,075 to 28,431, an 18 percent increase. Such breakdowns are, of course, somewhat misleading, since some of the staff effort in computerization and information returns is obviously directed to enhancing the effectiveness of the examination program.

The work load facing the examinations staff grew substantially over this period. At the most basic level, there were 111.4 million filings in FY 1986 compared to 79.7 million in FY 1972, an increase of almost 40 percent. Filings per examinations staff year grew from 3,310 in 1972 to 3,918 in 1986, an increase of slightly more than 18 percent. But simply counting filings per unit of labor does not do justice to the extent of the increase in the work load. During this period, substantial revision of the tax code became a much more frequent occurrence than had previously been the case (see the enumeration of tax laws enacted between 1968 and 1986 in table 11.1). The use of exemptions, deductions, and credits to promote various social goals became quite common. Complex business arrangements were developed to take maximum advantage of many of these provisions, leading to widespread use of complex partnership arrangements and the burgeoning of the tax shelter industry. And more tax

Table 12.2 STAFF YEARS BY IRS PROGRAM UNIT, FISCAL YEARS 1972 AND
       1986

| | Staff Years | | Percentage |
Program Unit	1972	1986	Change
Automated data processing and information technology	161	4,762	2,858
Information returns program	448	4,962	1,008
Taxpayer service	2,078	4,578	120
Tax forms and publications	306	562	84
Appeals and tax litigation	2,217	3,578	61
Accounts receivable	7,895	12,201	55
Tax fraud investigations	3,214	4,346	35
Delinquent returns	2,066	2,688	30
Examinations	24,075	28,431	18
Employee plans	0	1,604	
Management services	0	1,237	
Exempt organizations	0	778	
Research initiative	0	102	
Returns processing	21,551	21,490	0
Internal audit	476	460	−3
Enforcement litigation and technical rulings	1,591	1,423	−11
Executive direction	147	127	−14
Statistics of income	667	395	−41
Total	66,892	93,724	40

Source: Steuerle (1986), table 2-1.

returns utilized these increasingly complex provisions as the tax
preparation industry grew.[4]

These trends—the work load growing much faster than agency
resources—placed a premium on the intelligent allocation of scarce
resources and led to the establishment of additional revenue collections as a primary criterion for distributing examination resources.
The IRS Examination office utilizes an examination resources allocation model (the Exam Model) to guide its allocation of enforcement
resources for many areas of the Internal Revenue Code. This Exam
Model estimates the likely revenue gains from directing enforcement
resources to certain types of returns and compares the revenue estimates to the average cost of the resources (staff years, equipment,

etc.) used to generate the revenue. Table 12.3 presents estimates for 1985 of the ratio of marginal yield to average enforcement cost for various classes of individuals, noncorporate business, and corporations. All marginal yield to average cost ratios are greater than 1, ranging as high as 7.2 for individuals with adjusted gross income (AGI) in excess of $50,000; 4.5 for noncorporate farms with income in excess of $100,000; and 7.1 for corporations with AGI between $50 million and $100 million. This means that, on the margin, an extra dollar of enforcement resources in 1985 could be expected to generate as much as $7 of additional revenue.

Table 12.3 YIELD AND COSTS OF EXAMINATION FOR VARIOUS CLASSES OF TAXPAYER, FISCAL YEAR 1985

Class of Taxpayer	Marginal Yield	Average Cost	Marginal Yield to Cost
Individuals			
Less than $10,000			
1040A	780	148	5.3
Non-1040A	1,087	225	4.8
$10,000–<$25,000			
Simple return	615	155	4.0
Complex return	633	226	2.8
$25,000–<$50,000	678	235	2.9
$50,000 and over	3,624	501	7.2
Noncorporate Business			
Nonfarm			
Under $25,000	1,818	575	3.2
$25,000–<$100,000	2,274	723	3.1
$100,000 and over	5,187	1,224	4.2
Farm			
Under $25,000	2,044	627	3.3
$25,000–<$100,000	1,226	746	1.6
$100,000 and over	5,598	1,242	4.5
Corporations			
No balance sheet	8,430	1,708	4.9
Under $50,000	2,578	1,443	1.8
$50,000–<$100,000	3,549	1,448	2.5
$100,000–<$250,000	5,425	1,573	3.4
$250,000–<$500,000	455	1,622	0.3
$500,000–<$1 million	7,345	1,903	3.9
$1 million to <$5 million	12,383	2,534	4.9
$5 million to <$10 million	18,876	3,214	5.9
$10 million to <$50 million	7,300	4,459	1.6
$50 million to $100 million	38,498	5,248	7.3

Source: Steuerle (1986), table 3-1.

Clearly, substantial revenue gains are possible from an increase in enforcement resources. The question of whether it is desirable to reallocate existing enforcement resources among classes of taxpayers is more difficult to answer. As noted, the objective of the IRS is to promote maximum compliance, which not only increases revenue but promotes equity among classes of taxpayers. In that regard, the IRS regards it as necessary to maintain some audit and enforcement presence among all classes of taxpayers, even if more revenue might be collected by reallocating enforcement activities from a relatively unproductive (in terms of revenue collections) class of taxpayers to a potentially more productive class.

Enforcement of Tax-Exempt Bond Laws

For some areas of the Code—such as pensions, charities, and tax-exempt bonds—the allocation of enforcement resources is not actually determined by this model, but seems to result from a "gut" estimate of what is needed for minimal enforcement effort. The enforcement effort for tax-exempt bonds rests primarily with two IRS offices—the Office of Chief Counsel, whose primary function is to write and issue regulations, and the Office of the Assistant Commissioner (Examination). The chief counsel's office has several responsibilities of an ongoing nature. First, it promulgates regulations to implement the statutory language adopted by Congress. Second, it makes revenue rulings to answer questions asked by bond counsel or raised by other bond market participants who are unclear about the applicability of the statutory language. And third, it makes letter rulings in response to specific requests for clarification on issues that must be settled before a particular bond deal can go to market. These letter rulings are not precedent setting in a legal sense, but tend to be followed by all other bond counsel.[5]

Prior to 1987, the IRS Examination office did not have an ongoing role in monitoring the tax-exempt bond area. It moved into action only upon receipt of information from the chief counsel that a previously marketed bond issue had some problems. This information did not come to the chief counsel as a result of any ongoing investigative program or sampling of existing bond issues, but rather from frustrated underwriters or bond counsel who felt that a competitor took liberties with the tax law in its structuring of a particular bond deal, or from the financial press (usually the *Daily Bond Buyer*) or some other publication that happened to discuss the details of a creative financing arrangement or the management of an existing project.

Upon receipt of this information, the national examination office would direct a field examination office to collect information on the deal. The field office would send the information collected to the national examination office, which would in turn convey the information to the chief counsel. The chief counsel would make a determination either to drop the allegation or to pursue it further. If the latter, the issuer or its bond counsel would be informed that the IRS believed the interest on the bond issue might not qualify for tax exemption. If the issuer disputed this allegation of the chief counsel, a meeting would be held at the national office. Based on this meeting, the issuer would request formal technical advice from IRS, and the field examination office would be directed to gather additional relevant information and submit it to the national office. Chief counsel would then made a final determination after additional consultation with the issuing authority (if they requested it).

At this point, the issuing authority and the IRS had several options. If the issuing authority accepted the IRS determination, the parties would enter into a closing agreement in which they bargain over the amount of money the issuing authority will pay to the IRS to compensate for unpaid taxes on the bonds' interest income. If no closing agreement were reached, the IRS could declare the bonds retroactively taxable and begin proceedings to tax the bondholders. This would undoubtedly provoke a lawsuit from the affected bondholders, and the dispute would wind up in court. A third alternative would be for the IRS to "blacklist" the issuer by informing the investment community that the certificates the issuer must have in order to issue tax-exempt bonds cannot be relied upon to ensure tax exemption.

Nowhere have I found any indication that the IRS makes any systematic effort to review the information that the current bond law requires issuers to provide. The 8038 forms are used by the Statistics of Income Division to prepare a report on the volume and uses of private-activity bonds by state, but there is no indication that the Office of Chief Counsel or the Examination office makes any use of these forms. The periodic reports made by housing finance agencies on the characteristics of their mortgage loans for owner-occupied housing are apparently never reviewed by the IRS. Nor does any IRS official seem to request or review the numerous reports that the states and local governments have devised for their own internal efforts to monitor compliance with state and federal laws.

RECENT ENFORCEMENT INITIATIVE

What this account tells us is that the IRS has relied almost entirely upon a system of voluntary compliance with respect to tax-exempt bonds. The agency has apparently felt that a small bond audit presence was sufficient to police the tax-exempt bond industry. This view has been emphatically challenged in recent years. In 1984 all private-activity bonds with the exception of multifamily rental housing bonds were subjected to arbitrage rebate restrictions. This provoked a surge in multifamily issues that the IRS ultimately came to suspect of possible arbitrage abuses. The scenario was repeated in 1985 and early 1986, as anticipation of legislation that would extend arbitrage restrictions to governmental issues caused a rush to market of numerous issues that ultimately came to have the taint of arbitrage abuse.

These activities have led to considerable press attention and demands for greater enforcement of the tax-exempt bond law.[6] Congressman Brian Donnelly wrote to Treasury Secretary Nicholas Brady on the subject.

The purpose of this letter is to urge Treasury to *aggressively* investigate transactions which occurred during that two-year period [between 1984 and conference action on the 1986 Act], especially those where no tangible projects have been constructed. Even where bonds have been redeemed, I would urge Treasury to investigate the potential for fraud on the part of parties to the bond deals. In the case of outstanding bonds which clearly are in violation of the law, Treasury should not hesitate to declare bonds taxable. Were Treasury to do this in just one instance, I'm confident that it would be a long time before another abusive deal came to market. (Donnelly 1989)

The National Association of Bond Lawyers also weighed in on the subject, although with a somewhat different focus, to Edward Roybal, chairman of the Subcommittee on Treasury, Postal Service, and General Government of the U.S. House of Representatives Committee on Appropriations.

During the past 10 years, there has been growing criticism of tax-exempt bond transactions that were considered to be in violation of the law or the spirit of the law as Congress intended it. While various new and complex laws have been enacted by Congress to respond to these criticisms, many practicing lawyers believe that *enforcement of existing law* [emphasis added] would have prevented most of these perceived abuses or so-called "bad deals." Much of this additional legislation, therefore, would not have been necessary had the IRS provided prompt and reasonable regulatory guidance and vigorous enforcement.

NABL recognizes that the delays and gaps in enforcement and regulatory guidance may be due to inadequate resources at Treasury and IRS . . . . We fully understand current budgetary constraints, but we believe it is "penny-wise and pound-foolish" to deny funds to the very agencies that can—without the enactment of new laws or the levy of new taxes—increase Federal revenues. We respectfully urge that your committee provide adequate funding for these branches of government to prevent abuses of the system. (National Association of Bond Lawyers 1989)

The IRS reacted to these concerns in 1988 by making its first tentative move into a proactive monitoring system for tax-exempt bonds. It established a small Information Gathering Programs Unit in the Examination office, to which 77 staff years were devoted in fiscal year 1989. This unit is responsible for gathering information concerning provisions of the tax law targeted by the chief counsel's office as being potentially troublesome. Provisions investigated in 1989 apparently included some in the tax-exempt bond area.[7] Such a mandate means that for the first time the IRS may focus on a class of all outstanding bond issues that utilized a tax-exempt bond provision targeted by the chief counsel, as opposed to gathering information on a specific bond issue because it already has been identified as having a potential problem.

In fact, the IRS is in the final stages of its first study of this kind, of multifamily housing deals, although it is not clear whether it was initiated prior to or after the establishment of the Information Gathering Programs Unit. The study was apparently motivated by a surge of issuances after passage of the 1984 arbitrage rebate rules that excluded multifamily housing projects. The study is based on a random sample and covers 85 projects. The results have not yet been made public, but IRS officials maintain that the error rate for compliance with the low-income targeting rules appears to be less than 5 percent.

POLICY ISSUES FOR PROACTIVE ENFORCEMENT

A proactive enforcement approach to monitoring compliance seems long overdue. A major question is, Why has the IRS waited so long to engage in such enforcement of tax-exempt bonds? Concern with maximizing compliance, as opposed to maximizing enforcement revenue, suggests that some proactive audit presence was called for—after all, a minimum audit presence has supposedly been agency policy. This section discusses several factors that may have contributed to the decision to use voluntary compliance, aside from the belief that state and local governments and agencies are basically honest in their tax-exempt bond dealings: a focus on maximizing enforcement revenue; the absence of explicit consideration of enforcement expenses in congressional tax legislation deliberations; the incentives provided for IRS managers; and the penalty structure in enforcement activities.

Maximizing Enforcement Revenue and Increased Work Load

Perhaps it was believed that the marginal yield ratio from tax-exempt bonds was so low (or so uncertain) that it outweighed any equity gains to be obtained from a minimum compliance effort. Unfortunately, no estimates are available of the marginal yield that can be expected from allocating enforcement resources to tax-exempt bonds. Tax-exempt bonds are a rather specialized area of the tax code, and are apparently not part of the Exam Model. But the fact that enforcement resources have been allocated to bonds only in reaction to outside information suggests that the IRS believed the marginal yield ratio to be considerably lower than is available in other areas.

Another contributing factor is raised in the NABL letter, which notes that the magnitude of the potential enforcement task has grown markedly in the last decade. The number of long-term bond issues in the late 1970s hovered around 5,000 per year. The number of issues exploded to more than 10,000 in 1985 in anticipation of the restrictions to be enacted in the 1986 Tax Reform Act. By 1987 the number of issues had receded to a more modest level of 6,534, an 18 percent increase over the 5,550 issues financed in 1980.

This current level is not that large an increase, and would represent an even smaller proportionate increase in the outstanding stock of bond issues. But here the NABL raises another important point, that the complexity of each issue is certainly much greater now than in 1968 when the tax system's attention to tax-exempt bonds was confined to one sentence in the Internal Revenue Code. At that time there were no private use and security interest tests; no list of exempt private activities; no arbitrage restrictions, replacement funds, and rebates; no targeting provisions relating to income, purchase price, first-time buyers, economic distress, and so forth; no registration and reporting requirements; no prohibitions against federal guarantees; no separate depreciation schedules for private assets financed with tax-exempt bonds; no advance refunding limitations; no volume caps;

no government ownership requirements; no small-issuer exceptions applied to arbitrage rebate and commercial bank deduction of interest costs; no taxpayer approval requirements; no capital restrictions; and no private-use portion of governmental bonds, to name just some of the many new wrinkles that must be considered if the IRS were to aggressively monitor compliance of the tax-exempt bond rules. If one could construct a "bond administration index" to reflect the time needed to audit these additional rules enacted between 1968 and 1988, it would undoubtedly have increased many hundreds of percent. Combined with the more modest increase in the number of issues, this more comprehensive index of work load would show that monitoring compliance is a very considerable task indeed.

Funding of Enforcement Activities

Now to the crux of the matter. What must be sacrificed if resources were reallocated from individual and corporate returns (based on the Exam Model data in table 12.3) to systematic monitoring of tax-exempt bond compliance? If history is to be our guide, the IRS clearly feels that enforcement revenue would decline. The NABL is straightforward about this issue, suggesting that additional resources are necessary to monitor the bond laws in the manner desired. The Donnelly letter ignores the funding issue, from which one might infer that the IRS can (should?) get more juice from the prune.

Steuerle (1986) commented extensively on the propensity of Congress to pass increasingly complex laws without making any allowance for the additional resources that may be required to effectively administer and enforce these laws. He suggests that administrative issues should receive much more attention during the tax legislative process. If two options for structuring a tax law present themselves— one administratively complex but very accurately targeted to achieve the desired purpose and the other administratively simple but less well targeted—the choice should be determined in part by our willingness or lack thereof to provide adequate funding for reasonable IRS enforcement. Absent proper enforcement funding, the choice of the complex alternative would be a triumph of form over substance, and less compliance might be achieved than would be obtained with the administratively simpler alternative.

Managers' Incentives

A related issue is the incentive structure provided to IRS managers. Two types of incentives are important. First, if examination personnel in field offices are evaluated based on revenues raised, it is important that revenues collected be assigned to the units responsible for their collection. Field examination of a bond issue occurs in the office located in proximity to the bond issuer. Should the bond issue be declared retroactively taxable, the actual collection of revenue will be spread all over the country in proportion to the location of bondholders. If these revenues are not counted as part of the examining field office's collections, the field manager has an incentive not to allocate resources to the tax-exempt bond area. Why allocate your scarce resources to an activity that will generate zero benefits to your job performance criterion (revenues collected)?

Second, Congress has turned the tax-exempt bond law into a very substantial program to achieve a variety of social goals—low-income housing, student loans, development funds for economically distressed areas, assistance for small businesses, and so on. If the success of the IRS manager responsible for allocation of enforcement resources is going to be judged by revenue collections, it is unavoidable that tax-exempt bonds will receive little attention. Many of the benefits from careful monitoring of tax-exempt bonds are not going to appear as greater enforcement revenue, but rather as a greater percentage of the benefits from the federal revenue loss being channeled to targeted individuals and communities. Thus, the achievement of social goals would need to be incorporated into the objective function of the IRS manager. He or she needs to be rewarded for achieving these goals.

Such reorientation of IRS incentives likely has to come from Congress, which would need to be willing to accept lower enforcement revenue in exchange for a higher percentage of the federal revenue loss reaching the targeted populations, and somehow incorporate this willingness into legislative language upon which the agency could act.

The Penalty Structure

Short of such a turnabout in congressional behavior, the remaining hope for improved enforcement rests with aggressive use of available penalties. The NABL letter refers to the need for "vigorous enforcement" and the Donnelly letter suggests that the IRS should declare an abusive issue to be retroactively taxable. The IRS has never declared the interest income from a publicly held bond issue to be retroactively taxable, although it has occasionally done so for a privately placed issue. This reluctance on publicly held issues may be partly due to the difficulties of identifying the bondholders when a substantial part of the stock of outstanding municipal bonds is held in bearer form. But all issues since 1982 have been issued in registered form, so locating the taxpayers for a relatively recent issue should be fairly easy.

The main source of IRS reluctance is probably concern as to whether their right to tax "innocent" bondholders would be upheld in court. This has recently been the subject of considerable speculation, with some lawyers maintaining that no judge is likely to require a bondholder to pay taxes on interest earnings when that bondholder entered into the contract in good faith that the issuer, underwriter, and bond counsel would also act in good faith. The violation of the tax law, the failure of one of the parties to act in good faith, is in no way attributable to any behavior on the part of the bondholder. One of the other three parties is responsible for having violated the law. After all, it is the issuer who has covenanted in the bond opinion to comply fully with the provisions of the tax law. Thus, the IRS seems disinclined to put its ultimate weapon to the test, preferring to use it as a club to force the parties into a negotiated settlement. Unfortunately, such behavior means the IRS cannot obtain maximum advantage from its most potent weapon—should declaration of retroactive taxability stand up in court, no investor would buy that issuer's bonds for a considerable period of time without receipt of a considerable interest premium. As suggested by Donnelly and implied by the NABL, such an occurrence would provide a formidable incentive to ensure that deals are not abusive.

The advantage of a negotiated settlement (closing agreement) is that any money collected by the IRS comes out of the pockets of the issuer, underwriter, or bond counsel. The problem with a negotiated settlement is that much of the revenue loss from the bonds is not recovered. In effect, the IRS and the alleged perpetrator (issuer, bond counsel, or underwriter) are each bargaining with the understanding that they might lose if the case ends up in the courts. Each party has an incentive to compromise that depends upon its convictions as to the strength of its case and the magnitude of its expected litigation costs. The IRS will settle for so many cents on the dollar. Unless this amount is sufficiently large to make the sum of the issuer's settlement and litigation costs at least as great as the benefits earned on the bond issue, an incentive remains to continue such behavior in the future. In fact, IRS closing agreements have generated only about $90 million on approximately 60 bond issues since 1982.[8]

Legislation was passed in the 101st Congress that drastically changes the financial incentives to engage in an abusive bond deal. This provision extends to tax-exempt bonds the section of the tax code (6700) that pertains to fraudulent tax shelters. It provides the IRS with the authority to recover 100 percent of the gross fees paid to all participants in an abusive bond deal. This penalty can be imposed retroactively or prior to delivery of bonds if a false or fraudulent statement were being used in the offering.

The final alternative is for the IRS to "blacklist" an issuer—refuse to provide the necessary certificates for bond issuance, in effect saying that their representations of tax exemption cannot be relied upon. This has never been done. In the case of special authorities, which are a dime a dozen, it is not clear that blacklisting would have any effect. A new authority could be created. The blacklisting would have to be extended to the sponsoring general governmental unit. Such a move would be fairly drastic for the IRS, since every issuer is represented in Congress by a congressman and two senators, and it is possible that the sponsoring unit is an innocent bystander to the transaction. But if the obvious political obstacles could be overcome and the sponsoring unit were knowledgeable with respect to the transaction, blacklisting the general government issuer for a period of time would undoubtedly provide a strong incentive for compliance and for careful monitoring of special authorities.

Congress appears ready to consider alternative penalties to the retroactive taxation of interest income, the theory being that a less draconian penalty would be used more often, and thus be more effective. The Joint Committee on Taxation has explored alternative penalty possibilities in its recent deliberations (in Pryde 1990).

CONCLUSION

Until very recently, the IRS has depended almost entirely upon a voluntary system of compliance for tax-exempt bonds. Several factors probably account for this decision. First, available data suggest that the magnitude of marginal revenues available from enforcement activities devoted to corporate and high-income individual returns is high. Second, both bond counsel and state and local governments have some responsibility and incentive to assure that tax-exempt bonds comply with the tax law. And third, the IRS has access to penalties for noncompliance that could act as very substantial deterrents to such behavior.

Nonetheless, one cannot help but be somewhat uneasy about a voluntary compliance system. The responsibility of bond counsel ends once its fees are paid and the bonds are issued. State and local efforts to monitor compliance for their own purposes vary greatly among types of activities and are often focused on whether the proceeds are used in a fashion to satisfy state and local public purposes, rather than investigating targeting provisions in the tax law. Some discussion has occurred in recent years about the responsibility of bond trustees to monitor compliance and to inform bondholders of difficulties, but little action has resulted. The IRS apparently makes no effort to utilize either the few reports required by federal law or the reports prepared by state and local authorities for their own purpose. And the experience at the U.S. Department of Housing and Urban Development with employee misuse of appropriations in the 1980s is an object lesson that reports offer protection only to the degree that the people responsible for preparing them are honest and competent.

Although the few available analyses of compliance with the targeting provisions of the tax-exempt bond law suggest a relatively low error rate, the IRS clearly recognizes the need to increase its enforcement efforts in the tax-exempt bond area, and seems to have assigned the task to the newly formed Information Gathering Programs Unit. But it is not clear what this unit will do in the bond area, or even whether bonds will receive a continuing share of the unit's budget. It would be far better to establish a modest four- or five-person Bond Unit whose responsibilities are entirely focused on tax-exempt bonds. The unit would concentrate not on raising revenue, since it seems that the vast majority of bond deals are not abusive or fraudulent, but on enhancing the tools available to achieve the social objectives for which the bonds are issued. In a world of zero budgetary growth, this requires that we be willing to trade off revenue collections for nonpecuniary social benefits. It hardly seems too much to ask that the spending of billions of dollars every year be accompanied by some minimum systematic effort to assure that the spending objectives are being met.

The Bond Unit would prepare a list of priority areas in which enforcement would be enhanced with adequate information. In some cases this information might already be available but unusable, due to an absence of summary and analysis. In other cases, new sources of information might need to be developed, primarily through sampling procedures. The unit could then proceed to work on these issues in order of priority. Clearly, a systematic information and evaluation system for tax-exempt bonds will take time to construct. The unit could be required to make annual reports on its activities to the Treasury Department and to Congress, focusing on the art of the possible. If the unit found it to be impossible, or too costly, to generate the information necessary to enforce existing Code provisions, it could suggest alternatives that might range from substitute provisions to conversion to a direct spending program. If it found no compliance problems in an area, it might suggest simplification and streamlining. Such recommendations might force the Treasury Department and Congress to undertake explicit consideration of enforcement in the tax legislative process.

Notes

1. Alternative language to the emphasized portion of this quotation is used in many opinions: for example, "For the purpose of rendering the opinions set forth in this paragraph, we have assumed compliance by the Issuer with requirements of the Internal Revenue Code of 1986 that must be satisfied subsequent to the issuance of the Bonds" (National Association of Bond Lawyers 1987, 16).

   Other aspects of the tax treatment of tax-exempt bonds (beyond the alternative minimum tax) are addressed in an "Official Statement," rather than the bond opinion. These include such issues as inclusion of tax-exempt interest as passive loss income for certain corporations or as part of the threshold calculation for taxation of social security benefits, and bank deductibility of interest expenses.

2. This certificate is issued on the basis of a "reasonable expectations" test set forth in IRS regulation section 1.103-13(a)(2) that the proceeds will be expended in a timely manner to build the project for which the bonds were issued. It is the interpretation of this "reasonable expectations" phrase that has caused much of the uncertainty in enforcement of the arbitrage restriction.

3. Prior to 1983 and after 1986, these purchase price limits were 90 percent for economically distressed areas and 110 percent in all other areas.

4. The growth and allocation of IRS resources is discussed in considerable detail in Steuerle (1986).

5. The staffs of the Joint Committee on Taxation and the Treasury Department's Office of Tax Policy also receive requests to comment on the legality of proposed bond deals.

6. These "black box" deals, in which funds issued to build housing or some other facility disappeared into complex financial structures from which they never returned except occasionally for bond redemption, were reported in great detail in numerous 1988 and 1989 issues of the *Daily Bond Buyer*, the financial daily that covers the

municipal market. The IRS has become embroiled in lengthy settlement negotiations with many of the issuers, underwriters, and bond counsel involved in these deals.

7. The IRS could not provide (or would not provide—it is hard to identify motivation when dealing with an institution as inherently cautious as the IRS) any estimate of the share of the 77 staff years that were to be devoted to tax-exempt bond provisions.

8. Based upon estimates provided to me by IRS officials during an interview November 16, 1989.

BOND REPORTING FORMS

10-31-89

8038   1

Form **8038** (Rev. May 1989) Department of the Treasury Internal Revenue Service	**Information Return for Tax-Exempt Private Activity Bond Issues** (Under Section 149(e)) ▶ See separate Instructions.	OMB No. 1545-0720 Expires 5/31/92

Part I   Reporting Authority   Check box if **Amended Return** ▶ ☐

1 Issuer's name	2 Issuer's employer identification number
3 Number and street	4 Report number PA19 _____ - _____
5 City or town, state, and ZIP code	6 Date of issue
7 Name of issue	8 CUSIP number

Part II   Type of Issue (check box(es) that applies and enter the Issue Price for each)   Issue Price

9   Exempt facility bond:
a ☐ Airport (sections 142(a)(1) and 142(c)) **9a**
b ☐ Docks and wharves (sections 142(a)(2)and 142(c)) **9b**
c ☐ Mass commuting facilities (sections 142(a)(3)and 142(c)) **9c**
d ☐ Water furnishing facilities (sections 142(a)(4)and 142(e)) **9d**
e ☐ Sewage facilities (section 142(a)(5)) **9e**
f ☐ Solid waste disposal facilities (section 142(a)(6)) **9f**
g ☐ Qualified residential rental projects (sections 142(a)(7) and 142(d)), as follows: **9g**
     Meeting 20–50 test (section 142(d)(1)(A)) . . . . ☐
     Meeting 40–60 test (section 142(d)(1)(B)) . . . . ☐
     Meeting 25–60 test (NYC only) (section 142(d)(6)) . . . . ☐
     Has an election been made for deep rent skewing, (section 142(d)(4)(B))? ☐ Yes ☐ No
h ☐ Facilities for the local furnishing of electric energy or gas (sections 142(a)(8)and 142(f)). **9h**
i ☐ Local district heating or cooling facilities (sections 142(a)(9) and 142(g)). **9i**
j ☐ Qualified hazardous waste facilities (sections 142(a)(10) and 142(h)). **9j**
k ☐ High-speed intercity rail facilities (sections 142(a)(11), 142(c), and 142(i)). **9k**
     Check box if you elected not to claim depreciation or any tax credit (see instructions) . . . ▶ ☐
l ☐ Facilities allowed under a transitional rule of the Tax Reform Act of 1986 (see instructions) **9l**
     Facility type . . . .
     1986 Act section . . . .
10 ☐ Qualified mortgage bond (section 143(a)) **10**
     Check box if you elect to rebate arbitrage profits to the U.S. . . . . ▶ ☐
11 ☐ Qualified veterans' mortgage bond (section 143(b)) **11**
     Check box if you elect to rebate arbitrage profits to the U.S. . . . . ▶ ☐
12 ☐ Qualified small issue bond (section 144(a)). Check box for $10 million small issue exemption ▶ ☐   **12**
13 ☐ Qualified student loan bond (section 144(b)) **13**
14 ☐ Qualified redevelopment bond (section 144(c)) **14**
15 ☐ Qualified hospital bond (section 145(c)) **15**
16 ☐ Qualified 501(c)(3) bond other than a qualified hospital bond (section 145) **16**
     Employer identification number (EIN) of qualifying 501(c)(3) organization _____
17 ☐ Nongovernmental output property bond (treated as private activity bond)(section 141(d)) **17**
18 ☐ Other. Describe (see instructions) ▶ **18**

Part III   Description of Bonds

	(a) Maturity date	(b) Interest rate	(c) Issue price	(d) Stated redemption price at maturity	(e) Weighted average maturity	(f) Yield	(g) Net interest cost
19 Final maturity . .		%	$	$			
20 Entire issue . .			$	$	years	%	%

▶r Paperwork Reduction Act Notice, see page 1 of the Instructions.   Form **8038** (Rev. 5–89)

8038 2   10-31-89

Form 8038 (Rev. 5-89)   Page **2**

Part IV Uses of Original Proceeds of Issue (Including underwriters' discount)		Amount
21	Proceeds used for accrued interest **21**	
22	Issue price of entire issue (enter amount from line 20, column c) **22**	
23	Proceeds used for bond issuance costs (including underwriters' discount) . . **23**	
24	Proceeds used for credit enhancement **24**	
25	Proceeds allocated to reasonably required reserve or replacement fund . . **25**	
26	Proceeds used to refund prior issues (complete Part VI) **26**	
27	Total (add lines 23, 24, 25, and 26) **27**	
28	Nonrefunding proceeds of the issue (subtract line 27 from line 22 and enter amount here) **28**	

Part V Description of Property Financed by Nonrefunding Proceeds
(Do not complete for qualified student loan bonds, qualified mortgage bonds, or qualified veterans' mortgage bonds.)

29	Type of Property Financed by Nonrefunding Proceeds:	Amount
a	Land **29a**	
b	Buildings and structures **29b**	
c	Equipment with recovery period of more than 5 years **29c**	
d	Equipment with recovery period of 5 years or less **29d**	
e	Other (describe) **29e**	
30	Standard industrial classification (SIC) of nonrefunding proceeds for the financed projects.	

	SIC Code	Nonrefunding proceeds $		SIC Code	Nonrefunding proceeds $
a			**c**		
b			**d**		

Part VI Description of Refunded Bonds (complete this part only for refunding bonds)

31	Enter the remaining weighted average maturity of the bonds to be refunded . . . . ▶ _____ years
32	Enter the last date on which the refunded bonds will be called . . . . ▶ _____
33	Enter the date(s) the refunded bonds were issued ▶

Part VII Miscellaneous

34 Name of governmental unit(s) approving issue (see instructions) ▶ ....

35 Enter the amount of the bonds designated by the issuer under section 265(b)(3)(B)(i)(III) . . . . . ▶ _____

Part VIII Volume Cap		Amount
36	Amount of volume cap allocated to the issuer. **Attach state certification** **36**	
37	Amount of issue subject to the unified state volume cap **37**	
38	Amount of issue not subject to the unified state volume cap or other volume limitations:	
a	Of bonds for governmentally owned solid waste facilities, airports, docks, wharves or high-speed intercity rail facilities **38a**	
b	Under a carryforward election. Attach copy of Form 8328 to this return **38b**	
c	Under transitional rules of the Tax Reform Act of 1986 . . . . **38c**	
	Enter the Act section of the applicable transitional rule . . . . . ▶	
d	Under the exception for current refunding (section 1313(a) of the Tax Reform Act of 1986) **38d**	
39	Amount of issue of qualified 501(c)(3) bonds:	
a	Qualified hospital bonds **39a**	
b	Qualified nonhospital bonds **39b**	
c	Outstanding tax-exempt nonhospital bonds **39c**	
40a	Amount of issue of qualified veteran's mortgage bonds **40a**	
b	Enter the amount of the state veterans' limit **40b**	

Part IX Arbitrage Rebate (see Instructions)

41	Method of payment ▶ . . . . ☐ Check ☐ Other
42	Amount being rebated ▶ $ _____
43	CUSIP number ▶

Under penalties of perjury, I declare that I have examined this return, and accompanying schedules and statements, and to the best of my knowledge and belief, they are true, correct, and complete.

**Please
Sign
Here**

▶ _____   ▶ Date _____
   Signature of officer

_____   _____
Type or print name of above officer   Title (type or print) of officer

✶U.S. Government Printing Office: 1989-242-473/80122

12-26-89   **8038-G** 1

| Form **8038-G** (Rev. October 1989) Department of the Treasury Internal Revenue Service | **Information Return for Tax-Exempt Governmental Obligations** ► **Under Section 149(e)** ► **See separate Instructions** (Use Form 8038-GC if the issue price is under $100,000) | OMB No. 1545-0720 Expires 5-31-92 |

Part I   Reporting Authority   Check box if **Amended Return** ► ☐

1 Issuer's name	2 Issuer's employer identification number
3 Number and street	4 Report number G19 –
5 City or town, state, and ZIP code	6 Date of issue
7 Name of Issue	8 CUSIP Number

Part II   Type of Issue (check box(es) that applies and enter the Issue Price)

9   Check box if obligations are tax or other revenue anticipation bonds ► ☐
10 Check box if obligations are in the form of a lease or installment sale ► ☐

		Issue price
11 ☐	Education	$
12 ☐	Health and hospital	
13 ☐	Transportation	
14 ☐	Public safety	
15 ☐	Environment (including sewage bonds)	
16 ☐	Housing	
17 ☐	Utilities	
18 ☐	Other. Describe (see Instructions) ► _____	

Part III   Description of Obligations

	(a) Maturity date	(b) Interest rate	(c) Issue price	(d) Stated redemption price at maturity	(e) Weighted average maturity	(f) Yield	(g) Net interest cost
19 Final maturity .		%					
20 Entire issue . .					years	%	%

Part IV   Uses of Original Proceeds of Bond Issues (including underwriters' discount)

21	Proceeds used for accrued interest		21
22	Issue price of entire issue (enter line 20c)		22
23	Proceeds used for bond issuance costs (including underwriters' discount) . .	23	
24	Proceeds used for credit enhancement	24	
25	Proceeds allocated to reasonably required reserve or replacement fund . .	25	
26	Proceeds used to refund prior issues	26	
27	Total (add lines 23, 24, 25, and 26)		27
28	Nonrefunding proceeds of the issue (subtract line 27 from line 22 and enter amount here)		28

Part V   Description of Refunded Bonds (complete this part only for refunding bonds)

29	Enter the remaining weighted average maturity of the bonds to be refunded . . . . ► _____ years
30	Enter the last date on which the refunded bonds will be called . . . . ► _____
31	Enter the date(s) the refunded bonds were issued ►

Part VI   Miscellaneous

32	Enter the amount of the state volume cap allocated to the issue . . . . ► _____
33	Enter the amount of the bonds designated by the issuer under section 265(b)(3)(B)(i)(III) (small issuer exception) . . . . ► _____
34	Pooled financings:
a	Enter the amount of the proceeds of this issue that are to be used to make loans to other governmental units ► _____
b	Check box if this issue is a loan made from the proceeds of another tax-exempt issue ► ☐ and enter the name of the issuer ► _____ and the date of the issue ► _____

Under penalties of perjury, I declare that I have examined this return and accompanying schedules and statements, and to the best of my knowledge and belief, they are true, correct, and complete.

Please Sign Here

► Signature of officer	Date	► Type or print name and title

For Paperwork Reduction Act Notice, see page 1 of the Instructions.   Form **8038-G** (Rev. 10-89)

12-26-89   8038-GC 1

Form **8038-GC**	Consolidated Information Return for Small Tax-Exempt Governmental Bond Issues, Leases and Installment Sales	
(Rev. October 1989)	▶ Under Section 149(e) ▶ For calendar year ending 19	OMB No. 1545-0720 Expires 05/31/92
Department of the Treasury Internal Revenue Service	(Use Form 8038-G if the issue price of the issue is $100,000 or more.)	

Part I   Reporting Authority   Check box if **Amended Return** ▶ ☐

1 Issuer's name	2 Issuer's employer identification number

3 Number and street

4 City or town, state, and ZIP code

Part II   Description of Obligations

5 Total issue price of all small tax-exempt governmental obligations issued during the calendar year . . . | **5** |

6 Check the box that most nearly approximates the weighted average maturity of the obligations:
a ☐ Less than 5 years
b ☐ From 5 to 10 years
c ☐ More than 10 years

7 Check the box that most nearly approximates the weighted average interest rate on the obligations:
a ☐ Less than 5%
b ☐ From 5% to 10%
c ☐ More than 10%

8 Total issue price of the obligations reported on line 5 that are:

a Obligations issued in the form of a lease or installment sale . . . . | **8a** |

b Obligations designated by the issuer under section 265(b)(3)(B)(i)(III) . . . . | **8b** |

| | **8c** |

c Obligations issued to refund prior issues . . . .

d Loans made from the proceeds of another tax-exempt obligation . . . . | **8d** |

Please Sign Here   Under penalties of perjury, I declare that I have examined this return and accompanying schedules and statements, and to the best of my knowledge and belief, they are true, correct, and complete.

▶ _____   _____ ▶ _____
Signature of officer   Date   Type or print name and title

General Instructions

(Section references are to the Internal Revenue Code unless otherwise noted.)

Paperwork Reduction Act Notice

We ask for this information to carry out the Internal Revenue laws of the United States. We need it to ensure that you are complying with these laws. You are required to give us this information.

The time needed to complete and file this form varies depending on individual circumstances. The estimated average time is:

Recordkeeping . . . . 3 hrs., 21 min.
Learning about the
law or the form . . . . .1 hr., 34 min.
Preparing the form . . . 2 hrs., 37 min.
Copying, assembling, and
sending the form to IRS . . . .16 min.

If you have comments concerning the accuracy of this time estimate or suggestions for making this form more simple, we would be happy to hear from you. You can write to either the **Internal Revenue Service**, Washington, DC 20224, Attention: IRS Reports Clearance Officer, T:FP; or the **Office of Management and Budget,** Paperwork Reduction Project (1545-0720), Washington, DC 20503.

Item You Should Note

A governmental unit is required to file this form for all small tax-exempt governmental obligations on which it pays interest. These obligations include bonds, leases and installment sales.

Purpose of Form

Form 8038-GC is to be used by issuers of tax-exempt governmental obligations to provide IRS with the information required by section 149(e) and to monitor the requirements of sections 141 through 150.

Who Must File

Each issuer must file Form 8038-GC for all tax-exempt governmental bonds, leases and installment sales issued during the calender year, with an issue price of less than $100,000. Form 8038-G is filed to report each issue of governmental obligations with issue prices of $100,000 or more.

When To File

File Form 8038-GC on or before February 15th after the close of the calendar year in which the issue is issued. Form 8038-GC must be completed based on the facts as of the close of the calendar year.

Late filing.—A Form 8038-GC filed after the due date may be granted an extension of time to file under section 3 of Rev. Proc. 88-10, 1988-1 C.B. 635, if it is determined that the failure to file in a timely manner is not due to willful neglect. A late Form

Form **8038-GC** (Rev. 10-89)

Chapter Thirteen

INFRASTRUCTURE
AND TAX-EXEMPT BONDS

During the 1980s, the word *infrastructure* became a Washington buzzword, supplanting the well-known *industrial policy* of the late 1970s, and in turn being supplanted by the *competitiveness* concerns of the late 1980s. The necessary condition for a term's ascension to buzzword status is fairly clear: its definition must be sufficiently elastic that supporters of conflicting policies can march comfortably under its banner. *Infrastructure* fits this condition admirably.

The 1980s saw considerable effort devoted to studying infrastructure (Congressional Budget Office 1988a, 1985, 1983; National Council on Public Works Improvement 1988). The consensus seemed to be that the nation's infrastructure "needs" were growing rapidly— the existing stock of it was deteriorating too quickly, investment in it was proceeding too slowly, and corrective policies were far too tardy in formulation and adoption. It was suggested that declining infrastructure spending was an important contributor to declining productivity and the nation's standard of living (Aschauer 1989; Munnell 1990). And of utmost importance from the perspective of this book, it was alleged that the congressional tax-writing committees, in their effort to reduce tax preferences and reduce the deficit, were worsening the problem by continually imposing restrictions on state and local governments' ability to issue the tax-exempt bonds necessary to finance the infrastructure so badly needed for the rebuilding of America.

Such was the mindset of the country's concern with infrastructure financing. The focus of discussion in this chapter is on whether the tax-exempt bond policies detailed in chapter 11 are in fact inhibiting state and local governments' ability to finance infrastructure. This is not an easy question to answer. True, Congress and the U.S. Department of the Treasury have spent the last 20 years trying to restrict tax-exempt bond issuance. But was state and local infrastructure financing really in such bad shape, and was it infrastructure financing that was being restricted?

The first section of this chapter asks, What is infrastructure? It examines attempts made by studies of infrastructure spending to justify their decisions as to which types of capital spending to include in the infrastructure definition. The second section presents two sets of data relating to the infrastructure problem. Set one is based on "needs" studies that attempted to determine how much would have to be invested to bring the existing public stock of capital up to fixed standards. Set two comes from Census Bureau data and tracks changes in public spending on physical capital, paying particular attention to the distinction between the experience of the federal government and that of the state and local sector.

The third section imparts some perspective to the state and local infrastructure problem. It discusses the extent to which these data may overstate the infrastructure problem, and estimates the extent to which private-activity bonds used for infrastructure are not counted in the Census data as state and local capital outlays. The fourth section investigates the impact of tax-exempt bond policy on the infrastructure problem. It estimates the increased interest costs imposed on state and local infrastructure financing by the use of private-activity tax-exempt bonds for noninfrastructure financings. Estimates are then made of the amount of infrastructure financing not undertaken because of these interest cost increases. This analysis suggests that federal restrictions on the use of tax-exempt bonds for private activities, rather than inhibiting the formation of infrastructure, have actually worked to increase infrastructure spending.

WHAT IS INFRASTRUCTURE?

As commonly used, the term *infrastructure* applies to facilities with high fixed costs and a long physical life. This definition is inadequate because it encompasses all spending for the provision of physical capital projects. In fact, the term is often applied only to that portion of the capital stock provided by the public sector, what some refer to as public works.

This restriction to the public sector's capital stock seems consistent with the definition found in *Webster's New Collegiate Dictionary*, 1975, which defines *infrastructure* as the "*underlying foundation* [emphasis added] or basic framework (as of a system or organization)." This hints at the basic requirement for infrastructure (public works), that it be capital spending that for some reason the private sector either does not provide or underprovides, but is nevertheless necessary for private capital formation. But this begs the question as to what types of capital spending form this underlying foundation.

This question has been addressed in various ways by those studies completed in the 1980s that investigated the infrastructure issue. The Congressional Budget Office (1983, 1) stated:

The concept of infrastructure can be applied broadly to include such social facilities as schools, hospitals, and prisons, and it often includes industrial capacity as well. The seven systems considered in this study share the common characteristics of capital intensiveness and high public investment at all levels of government. *They are, moreover, directly critical to activity in the nation's economy* [emphasis added].

This provides some help, but it still does not tell us how we are to determine which capital spending is critical and should be considered infrastructure suitable for federal provision.

Vaughan and Pollard (1984, 1) also leave the issue up in the air.

The term infrastructure includes a wide array of public facilities and equipment required to provide social services and support private sector economic activity. Among the types of public service and production facilities commonly included in infrastructure are roads, bridges, water and sewer systems, airports, ports and public buildings. . . .A jurisdiction, however, may choose a broader or narrower definition for capital facilities planning and management activities, depending on what is practical, feasible, or necessary.

The report on infrastructure by the National Council on Public Works Improvement (1988, 33) appears at first glance to be equally obscure in specifying a definition of *infrastructure*.

The Council chose to study nine categories of public works infrastructure. . . .These categories have strong links to economic development and, except for the last, a tradition of direct public-sector involvement. The facilities have high fixed costs and long economic lives. . . .The nation's infrastructure comprises far more than the categories studied directly by the Council. . . .Taken as a whole, the services they provide form the underpinnings of our nation's defense, a strong economy and our health and safety.

This does not really provide much guidance. All capital has strong links to economic development and is characterized by high fixed costs and long economic lives. Using "a tradition of direct public sector involvement" as justification borders on being a circular def-

inition. But the glimmer of a justification for the council's choices
then appears in the form of a quotation from the venerable Adam
Smith (1976):

The third and last duty of the sovereign or commonwealth is that of erect-
ing and maintaining those public institutions and those public works,
which, though they may be in the highest degree advantageous to a great
society, are, however, of such a nature, that the profit could never repay
the expense to any individual or small number of individuals, and which
it therefore cannot be expected that any individual or small number of
individuals should erect or maintain. . . .[T]he works and institutions of
this kind are chiefly those for facilitating the commerce of the society,
and those for promoting the instruction of the people. (34)

What is being suggested here is that the public sector might want
to get involved if the physical capital cannot be profitably produced
by the private sector. Since Adam Smith's time, such goods have
come to be known as pure public goods (as discussed in chapter 5).
To reiterate, such goods are identifiable by two characteristics: once
the good is provided, no one can be excluded from its consumption;
and one person's consumption of the good in no way diminishes the
amount of the good available for others to consume. Goods with
these characteristics will not be provided by the public sector because a profit cannot be made from their production.

Unfortunately, infrastructure activities in which the public sector
is engaged are not accurately described by the characteristics of pure
public goods. Many of these activities can (and sometimes are) also
provided by the private sector, such as electricity, irrigation, recreational facilities, hospital facilities, and so forth. To justify these
activities, one must turn to the external costs and benefits discussed
in chapter 5.

Vaughan (1983, 40) said: "The basic guideline for state and local
officials to follow in deciding "who does what" is that the public
sector should only intervene if market-determined outcomes are neither efficient nor equitable." In other words, the public sector may
want to get involved in providing infrastructure if the private sector
does not provide the proper amount or if the distributional consequences of private provision prove unacceptable.

The Congressional Budget Office (1983, 5) goes somewhat further
in specifying circumstances in which private provision may prove
to be unacceptable.

In making infrastructure investments, each level of government has its
own unique role to play. State or local governments subsidize facilities

that serve their own residents, but they do not always have incentives to make investments that also serve the best interests of the economy at large. The federal government is in the best position to ensure that infrastructure investments simultaneously advance national goals of efficiency and fairness. Over the years, federal involvement in the provision of public works has grown in response to several specific concerns:

Underdeveloped regions. States in less developed regions may lack the resources to finance the construction of infrastructure projects needed for regional development.

External costs and benefits. Individual states may lack the incentives to supply certain facilities and services in sufficient quantity, since the costs and benefits of some public works cross state borders.

Centralized planning. Some infrastructure services are provided most effectively when coordinated by central administrative bodies.

Inequities and hardship. Some population groups, such as the poor and the handicapped, may need federal intervention to assure their access to certain public services.

Thus, the Congressional Budget Office identifies four primary justifications for the federal government to intervene in the production of infrastructure, in effect suggesting that infrastructure can be found along most of the "publicness" spectrum.

In another report on infrastructure two years later, the Congressional Budget Office (1985) alluded again to these principles. Notice that whereas the definition following contains no direct reference to these four criteria, it justifies infrastructure selection on the basis that these activities *require* a high level of public investment, which, given the 1983 report, seems to suggest that the correct amount of the capital spending will not result without federal financial support.

This report defines public works infrastructure to include highways, aviation, mass transit, wastewater treatment, water resources (ports, inland waterways, and multipurpose dams), water supply, and railroads. These systems have been selected for analysis because the services they provide directly support the nation's economy, they are characterized by facilities with high fixed costs and a long physical life, and they require a high level of public investment. (1)

Nonetheless, the task of identifying infrastructure that is deserving of public support is difficult. External effects are hard to identify, their magnitude is difficult to measure, and their geographic dispersion almost impossible to discern. As a result, decisions about infrastructure are inherently subjective within the broad bounds imposed by the economic criteria discussed in chapter 5. What is notable, however, is that all of the studies seem to indicate that infrastructure consists of physical capital whose services are characterized by a substantial element of collective consumption. When tracking in the next section what happened to infrastructure spending at the state and local levels from 1966–67 to 1986–87, reliance is placed upon the usual Census data on capital spending. When adjusting these data to incorporate capital facilities provided via tax-exempt financing, the collective consumption with spillovers criterion is applied.

SPENDING ON INFRASTRUCTURE

Whatever infrastructure may be, an important question for tax-exempt bond policy is whether it is being underprovided by state and local governments. All levels of government build capital facilities and contribute to the nation's infrastructure. Federal outlays for capital facilities in 1987 for the national defense amounted to $89.5 billion (71.1 percent of total federal capital outlays). Nondefense capital outlays were divided between direct spending on federal programs ($12.5 billion—10.0 percent of total capital outlays), and indirect spending channeled through state and local governments as matching grants-in-aid ($23.8 billion—18.9 percent of total capital outlays). From 1977 to 1987, federal nondefense capital outlays declined from 1.10 percent to 0.80 percent of the gross national product (GNP), not a pretty picture for those concerned with infrastructure.

Comparisons of infrastructure "needs" with current levels of infrastructure investment also raised concerns. The results of three "needs" assessments are presented in table 13.1, and show annual infrastructure "needs" in 1982 dollars ranging from a high of $118.2 billion to a low of $52.6 billion. Since 1986 spending (in 1982 dollars) on the types of infrastructure included in the table amounted to only $46 billion, the data suggest the existence of a substantial shortfall.

The numbers in table 13.2 paint a somewhat different picture for the state and local sector. The table contains state and local governments' capital outlays for selected functions for a 21-year period, 1966–77 to 1986–87. Note that total capital outlays grew over this period by 51.5 percent in constant dollars, with the rate varying widely among functions—336.4 percent for transit and −13.2 percent for higher education. As a share of GNP, capital outlays declined substantially between 1966–77 and 1976–77, from 2.7 to 1.8 percent,

Table 13.1   ANNUAL INFRASTRUCTURE INVESTMENT "NEEDS" FOR
SELECTED FUNCTIONS (1982 DOLLARS, BILLIONS)

	Association of General Contractors	Joint Economic Committee	Congressional Budget Office
Function			
Highways and bridges	62.8[a]	40.0	27.2
Other transportation (mass transit, railroads, airports, ports, locks, waterways)[b]	17.5	9.9	11.1
Drinking Water	6.9	5.3	7.7
Wastewater Treatment	25.4	9.1	6.6
Drainage	5.6	[c]	NA[d]
Total	118.2	64.3	52.6

Source: Congressional Budget Office (1988a), appendix table.

a. Highways only. Bridges were estimated separately at an additional one-time repair cost of $51.7 billion.

b. The Joint Economic Committee study excluded needs for locks and waterways; the Congressional Budget Office study excluded needs for railroads.

c. Included under wastewater treatment.

d. NA, not available.

but rebounded somewhat to 2.2 percent of GNP by 1986–87. This recovery occurred in spite of Reagan administration policies (see chapter 5) that caused federal grants-in-aid for capital outlays (see the numbers near the bottom of table 13.2) to decline in real terms by 2.9 percent over the 10-year period. This decrease in federal support during the decade was more than counterbalanced by state and local spending from their own resources, which grew sufficiently in real terms to raise state and local own-source capital spending from 1.02 percent of GNP in 1976–77 to 1.65 percent in 1986–87.[1] This reversed the trend of the preceding 10 years that had seen state and local own-source capital spending decline from 2.3 to 1.0 percent of GNP.

PUTTING THE STATE AND LOCAL INFRASTRUCTURE PROBLEM IN PERSPECTIVE

Both the needs data and the capital outlays data seem to suggest that state and local infrastructure investment lagged over the last two decades. This was particularly true during the 1967–77 decade, with

Table 13.2 STATE AND LOCAL EXPENDITURES FOR CAPITAL FACILITIES IN
CURRENT DOLLARS, BY FUNCTION AND SOURCE OF REVENUE
(OWN-SOURCE OR GRANTS-IN-AID), 1976–77 TO 1986–87
($ BILLIONS)

	1986–87 ($)	1976–77 ($)	1966–67 ($)	Percentage change, constant dollars 1976–77 to 1986–87 (%)
All Functions	98.3	36.3	22.2	51.5
As percentage of GNP	2.2	1.8	2.7	
Higher education	6.2	1.8	2.4	10.0
Elementary and secondary-education	11.6	3.9	4.0	0.5
Other education		0.3	0.2	
Highways	28.6	11.2	9.4	3.8
Health and hospitals	3.1	1.7	0.6	71.6
Natural resources, parks and recreation	4.8	1.6	1.3	27.4
Housing and community development	3.5	1.1	0.9	29.3
Air transportation	—	0.5	0.3	NAª
Water transport and terminals	—	0.3	0.2	NA
Sewerage	7.3	4.4	1.1	134.2
Utilities				
Water supply	6.0	1.8	1.1	95.5
Electric power	5.0	2.6	0.6	206.9
Transit	4.1	1.3	0.3	336.4
Gas supply	0.3	0.0	0.0	144.6
Other and unallocable	17.7	3.6	1.8	230.8
Federal grants-in-aid, physical capital investment	23.7	16.1	3.2	151.1
State and local physical capital investment financed with own revenue sources	74.5	20.2	19.0	34.5
As percentage of GNP	1.6	1.0	2.3	

Sources: U.S. Bureau of the Census (1985, 1988a); Office of Management and Budget (1989).
a. NA, not applicable, because 1986–87 data are missing for this category.

spending recovering (measured by state and local capital outlays as a share of GNP) during the next decade but still falling short of the mid-1960s level. The picture painted by these data must, however, be qualitatively adjusted in several ways.

It is likely that the "needs" numbers cited in table 13.1 are overstated. The National Council on Public Works Improvement (1988), the Congressional Budget Office (1988a), and the Office of Management and Budget (1988a) have all critiqued the various infrastructure "needs" analyses. Their most important criticism is that the studies assume the economy's underlying production relationships have been unchanged over time—that public infrastructure's relative importance to the production process has been maintained. But the optimal level of infrastructure investment relative to GNP depends upon several factors that may be moving in favor of a less infrastructure-intensive economy. First, infrastructure needs depend upon the efficiency with which the infrastructure is utilized. Policies to improve this efficiency have been adopted and others are being actively pursued. Examples cited by the Congressional Budget Office include reducing the unit cost of drinking water by consolidation of small water-supply systems into regional systems; and designation of high-occupancy vehicle lanes on highways to increase capacity during commuting hours.

This point is akin to saying that our focus should be on the services from capital spending rather than on capital spending. Unfortunately, no series on infrastructure services exists. But we do know that the services generated by a capital facility are dependent to a great extent on the maintenance of the facility. Interestingly, in a study for the National Council on Public Works Improvement, the U. S. Department of Commerce (1987, 51) found that while spending on capital facilities was declining in real terms from 1960 to 1980, spending on operations and maintenance was climbing in real terms from $120 to $240 per capita.

Second, in the study just cited, the Department of Commerce (1987) illustrated that all types of economic activity do not utilize infrastructure equally. Since manufacturing may be a relatively heavy user per dollar of GNP generated compared to the service and financial industries, continuation of the trend for the economy to become less manufacturing intensive could reduce the infrastructure requirement per dollar of GNP. Third, it is also likely that the "needs" studies have overstated the magnitude of the problem because they assume prior infrastructure was necessary and must therefore all be replaced. But it is not clear whether or not replacement of all existing facilities is a wise investment decision, particularly when the benefits from the original investment may have fallen short of its costs or produced a relatively low rate of return compared to other uses of the funds. All of these considerations suggest that a lower ratio of state and local infrastructure spending to GNP may be desirable for today's world compared to the mid-1960s.

Turning to the Census data in table 13.2, the statistics overstate the problem (as measured by capital spending rather than services) by understating the infrastructure put in place by state and local governments over the 1977 to 1987 period. This tends to understate the current ratio of state and local infrastructure spending to GNP in comparison to the mid-1960s ratio. The forces that led to this conclusion are summarized well by Vaughan (1983) in his comments on public policies toward infrastructure investment.

Even if public intervention is required, it does not have to involve spending public funds or public ownership of facilities. Regulation of private suppliers—of drinking water prices, for example—can lead to the desired supply of services without full public ownership. The task is by no means easy, but without cutting back on some public services, there will not be enough tax revenues to pay for those services that properly belong in the domain of state and local government. (40)

* * *

Assigning priorities for public spending will require a rigorous questioning of traditional practices. If a convention center is a demonstrable boon to a local economy, why is it not financed privately? . . . Is public ownership of the water supply system necessary when electricity and gas are privately provided? Does an airport need to be owned by the county? Some economists have proposed radical measures such as the outright sale of subway systems and toll bridges to private firms, replacing public schools with education vouchers, privatizing garbage collection, and selling off state parks. The economics and politics of these proposals are complex and will require careful research and analysis by all levels of government. (39–40)

This plea for privatization of infrastructure financing was not ignored in the 1980s (perhaps "privatization" did not quite achieve buzzword status, but it came close). As discussed in chapter 5, the Reagan administration made privatization a focal point of its economic policy. The state and local sector began gnawing on this bone even earlier. The passage in 1978 of California's Proposition 13 kicked off the tax revolt in the state and local sector, which led inexorably to privatization efforts. State and local governments have been scrambling ever since to find alternative ways to finance public services.

Part of these efforts involve requirements for developers of both residential and commercial structures to include as part of their development plan such essential, and previously publicly financed, capital facilities as roads, sewerage, water supply, etc. These costs were often paid by having the developers incorporate the costs into their pricing strategies. Such privately built capital facilities do not appear in the capital spending numbers in table 13.2.

This privatization trend extended to state and local use of tax-exempt bonds. Chapter 5 documented the growth in private-activity tax-exempt bonds beginning in the mid-1970s. For certain activities that might be considered infrastructure, state and local governments had the option of issuing bonds on behalf of a private business, which would in turn use the proceeds to build the capital facility. The private firm would make payments to the issuing government through some sort of lease/rental arrangement sufficient to pay the principal and interest on the bonds. The Census data in table 13.2 do not reflect such capital spending in the totals. Unless a public authority builds and operates the facility, Census does not count the bond-financed capital expenditures in the totals. The transaction is treated entirely as a financial transaction. The issuing government is assigned a liability (the principal and interest on the bonds) and an asset of equal value (the future stream of lease or rental payments). Receipt of the lease or rental payments triggers payment of principal and interest, and both the asset and the liability are written down. But nothing appears in the public capital spending data.

Although much has been written concerning the potential of private developers to provide public capital infrastructure, evidence of its use seems to be primarily anecdotal. If the privately provided share of spending in the latter decade covered by table 13.2 exceeds the share provided in the former decade, the infrastructure problem would be overstated. The magnitude of any such effect is unknown because no estimates of privately provided infrastructure are available.

The picture is brighter for private-activity tax-exempt bonds. We know that private use of tax-exempt bonds was very low in the mid-1960s compared to today. From the Treasury data on private-activity bond volume, it is possible to obtain an estimate of the mid-1980s volume issued for those activities that might be characterized as infrastructure.

Assuming that bond proceeds are expended within three years, the private-activity bond financing for infrastructure is calculated as an average of 1984 to 1986 new bond issues. Bonds issued for student loans, single-family mortgages, multifamily rental housing, nonprofit entities, small-issue IDBs, and pollution control are deleted from the private-activity volume data, leaving issues from the following categories: airports, docks, and wharves; sewage and waste disposal; and other (see table 11.2 for a list of the activities included in this "other" category). This yields an estimate of $6.5 billion (from average new issues of $61 billion) to be added to state and local capital expenditures for 1987.[2] State and local own-source outlays are increased from $74.5 billion to $81.0 billion, raising the state and local share of GNP from 1.6 to 1.8 percent and edging it closer to the mid-1960s level of 2.3 percent. A considerable gap of 0.5 percent remains, however, unless one believes that it is likely to be closed by the possibility that the optimal share of infrastructure in GNP is lower today than in the mid-1960s, and that the growth of operation and maintenance expenditures suggests that capital services have fared much better than capital facilities.

IMPACT OF "NON-INFRASTRUCTURE" BONDS ON INFRASTRUCTURE BONDS

The preceding discussion suggests that a portion of private-activity tax-exempt bonds has played a positive role in state and local financing of infrastructure. This portion has been adapted to assist the private sector in providing infrastructure to the tune of an annual average $6.5 billion from 1984 to 1986. But take a look at the bond volume issued for those activities I deleted from the private-activity bond totals to arrive at that $6.5 billion. Recall that these deleted activities included student loans, single-family mortgages, multifamily rental housing, nonprofit entities, small-issue IDBs, and pollution control. These activities were deleted because they did not fit the criteria for infrastructure established by the infrastructure studies. The annual average bond volume issued for these activities from 1984 to 1986 was $60.9 billion.[3]

What does economic theory tell us about the effect this "non-infrastructure" financing had on the ability of state and local governments to issue bonds for infrastructure? The reader can follow this discussion by referring to figure 11.2 in chapter 11. A downward sloping demand schedule such as the one denoted by *ABCDE* in figure 11.2 reflects the fact that investors are only willing to purchase larger amounts of bonds in exchange for higher interest rates. The

$60.9 billion of non-infrastructure bonds represents more than half (55 percent) of average annual new long-term tax-exempt issues from 1984 to 1986, an amount sufficiently large to shift supply along the demand curve from S** to S* in figure 11.2. The bottom line is that these non-infrastructure bonds were issued in sufficient volume to move the market-clearing marginal tax rate down and the yield ratio up, thereby raising the interest cost on infrastructure bonds.

Table 13.3 provides a range of estimates of the present value of state and local taxpayers' increased interest costs on the $49.7 billion of infrastructure bonds issued by state and local governments that was caused by the issuance of non-infrastructure bonds. Depending on the elasticity of the demand schedule (the sensitivity of investors' demand for tax-exempt bonds to a price change), this supply increase might have been accommodated with a variety of price responses. The table provides estimates assuming the tax-exempt interest rate increased between 25 and 125 basis points (about 0.4 to 2 basis points per billion dollars of non-infrastructure financing). The present value of these increased interest costs on $49.7 billion of infrastructure bonds lies somewhere between $1.427 billion for a 25-basis-point rise and $7.135 billion for a 125-basis-point rise.

These are substantial costs. State and local taxpayers would undoubtedly have been willing to issue more bonds for infrastructure financing if borrowing costs had been lower. Suppose taxpayers' price elasticity of demand for infrastructure financing (thinking now in terms of state and local demand for tax-exempt savings and investors' supply of savings) were one, meaning that a 10 percent decrease in interest costs would generate a 10 percent increase in infrastructure financing. That 25-basis-point increase in table 13.3 represents an almost 3 percent increase in the average Aa tax-exempt borrowing rate from 1984 to 1986 (see table 4.3, chapter 4). A 3

Table 13.3 PRESENT VALUE OF STATE AND LOCAL TAXPAYERS' INCREASED INTEREST COSTS ON INFRASTRUCTURE BONDS CAUSED BY ISSUANCE OF NON-INFRASTRUCTURE BONDS ($ BILLIONS)

Average Infrastructure Volume, 1984–86	Increase in Basis Points				
	25	50	75	100	125
$49.705	$1.427	$2.854	$4.281	$5.708	$7.135

Sources: Volume data from table 4.2 and discussion in the text; see table 4.7 for assumptions used for present value calculations.

percent increase in $49.7 billion average infrastructure financing would have generated another $1.5 billion of infrastructure. A 125-basis-point increase represents a 16.9 percent increase in the Aa tax-exempt borrowing rate, which might have meant an additional $8.4 billion of infrastructure financing. If we were to add that $8.4 billion to the 1987 state and local own-source capital outlays in table 13.2 and the $6.5 billion of private-activity bond issues classified as infra-structure, outlays would rise to $89.4 billion. State and local infra-structure spending would rise to 1.98 percent of GNP.

Thus, tax-exempt bond policies favoring private-activity bonds have influenced the infrastructure problem in two ways. First, any "privatized" infrastructure financed with private-activity tax-exempt bonds is not included in estimates of state and local capital spending, thereby overstating infrastructure deficiencies. Second, the large amount of non-infrastructure tax-exempt financings raises the interest costs of infrastructure financings, thereby discouraging infrastructure formation.

CONCLUSIONS

Many studies have suggested that spending on infrastructure has lagged over the last two decades. The "needs" studies suggest that annual investment in infrastructure might have to rise as much as 100 percent to bring the existing public capital stock up to fixed standards. Census data indicate that state and local own-source spending on physical capital as a percentage of GNP has decreased since the mid-1960s, moving from 2.3 percent in 1967 to 1.0 percent in 1977, then rebounding somewhat to 1.6 percent by 1987. This deterioration of the public capital stock has been identified as a major contributor to the decline in productivity that eats away at the na-tion's standard of living.

Census data do understate state and local own-source capital out-lays as a share of GNP, because the data do not count the increase in infrastructure put in place by the private sector (the privatization effort) in the last decade: the efforts made by state and local govern-ments after the Proposition 13-induced tax revolt in the late 1970s to force developers of residential and commercial property to in-corporate infrastructure in their projects; and the growing use of private-activity tax-exempt bonds to finance some infrastructure. If the infrastructure financed with these tax-exempt bonds (an average of $6.5 billion from 1984 to 1986) is added to state and local capital spending, its share of GNP rises from 1.6 to 1.8 percent, still considerably short of the 2.3 percent in 1966–67.

Part of this gap is attributable to tax-exempt bond policy. The volume of new issue long-term private-activity bonds not generally considered to be financing infrastructure averaged $60.9 billion from 1984 to 1986. This volume was sufficiently large to influence the interest cost on tax-exempt infrastructure financings. The present value of state and local taxpayers' estimated increased interest cost on infrastructure financings that was imposed by these non-infrastructure financings ranged between $1.4 billion for a 25-basis-point increase in the interest rate and $7.1 billion for a 125-basis-point increase. If the 125-basis-point increase prevailed (certainly possible when 55 percent of the new issue long-term market was non-infrastructure financings), $8.4 billion of tax-exempt infrastructure financing might have been discouraged. If these financings are added to the Census data on state and local capital spending, their 1987 share of GNP would rise to 1.98 percent. The importance of the Tax Reform Act of 1986 in reducing the volume of non-infrastructure financings is apparent. It should save state and local taxpayers a considerable amount of money and add to the stock of state and local infrastructure.

Notes

1. The own-source data are calculated by subtracting the amount for federal grants-in-aid (which comes from federal budget data) from state and local spending on all functions at the top of table 13.2 (from Census data). The calculation is not entirely accurate for two reasons. First, grants-in-aid are received by state and local governments in the year indicated, but actually spent over a period of years. Grants-in-aid for the preceding three years were $22.7, $24.9, and $26.3 billion. So it is likely that the 1987 number somewhat underestimates the actual grant dollars expended in 1987. Second, the data cover slightly different time periods. The grants-in-aid are based upon the federal fiscal year from October through September, whereas the state and local data are based upon state and local fiscal years that usually run from July through June.

2. Again, this calculation is not a perfect representation of expenditures, because the bond proceeds will be spent over a period of several years.

3. In fact, $60.9 billion probably understates non-infrastructure tax-exempt bond financing. The next chapter discusses the encouragement tax-exempt bonds provide

to the state and local sector to provide services that essentially are private in nature and would be likely to be provided adequately by the private sector if the public sector ended its provision. The primary example discussed is public power. Tax-exempt bonds issued for public gas and electric averaged $20.3 billion from 1984 to 1986. If these bonds were included, noninfrastructure tax-exempt bond financing would be $81.2 billion.

Chapter Fourteen

TAX-EXEMPT BONDS AND MUNICIPAL SOCIALISM: THE CASE OF PUBLIC POWER

The appropriate division of production responsibilities between the public and private (and more recently the nonprofit) sectors has always been a subject of debate in the United States. Political rhetoric to the contrary, socialism in its classic sense—public ownership of the means of production—has long been present. Government activities were even decried as "creeping socialism" earlier in the 20th century.[1] The U.S. House of Representatives was sufficiently concerned with government competition in 1933 to hold hearings and issue a report on the subject (U.S. Congress 1933). Some in the private sector complained in the 1980s of unfair competition from both the public sector and nonprofit organizations, and emphasized that the private sector's perceived competitive disadvantage was due in no small part to the preferential federal income tax treatment enjoyed by the other two sectors (Small Business Administration 1983). These claims found a champion when the Reagan administration stated its intention to promote "privatization" by moving the production of some public services from the federal sector to the private sector.

The juxtaposition of the terms "tax-exempt bonds" and "socialism" in the title of this chapter may seem to be unnecessarily provocative. But tax-exempt bonds do play a part in encouraging public ownership of the means of production, and it is this role that is emphasized in this chapter. Much of the legislation discussed in chapter 11 restricts the issuance of those tax-exempt bonds that enlist the support of the private sector in providing public goods. In other words, this legislation keeps a close eye on tax-exempt bond-financed "privatization" efforts in order to ensure that public goods are being provided along with the benefits that inevitably accrue to private participants. But who makes certain that public benefits for the federal taxpayer are also provided by bond issues that do not involve any private-sector participation? The short answer is, nobody does—there is almost no federal constraint on the ability of state and local governments to market private goods through bond-financed publicly owned business enterprises.[2]

It was inevitable, however, that the Reagan administration's focus on privatization would be extended to include federal government support of state and local services provided through bond-financed publicly owned business enterprises. This finally occurred in 1987, when legislation was adopted prohibiting local government use of tax-exempt bonds to finance acquisition of rental housing located outside the boundaries of the jurisdiction, restricting tax-exempt bond-financed takeovers of investor-owned electric and natural gas utilities, and restricting bond-financed business enterprises of Indian tribal governments. This chapter begins by contrasting (1) the extensive legislative attention devoted to the public-purpose content of tax-exempt bond issues that involve private participation with (2) the paucity of attention devoted to those bond issues that finance publicly owned facilities. It concludes with a detailed analysis of the policy issues raised by the investor-owned utility takeover restriction.

BONDS THAT HAVE PRIVATE PARTICIPATION

Consider an activity that a state or local government wishes to finance in cooperation with the private sector, using tax-exempt private-activity bonds. Behind those four words—*tax-exempt private-activity*—lies a considerable amount of judgment sifted through the legislative sieve concerning how the federal government spends the taxpayers' money. When a proposed bond issue passes the tests indicating the existence of private use and private security interest, Congress imposes constraints on state and local behavior. The only activities judged to merit federal subsidy are those that have a sufficient element of public goods provision (usually in the form of external benefits provided or external costs curtailed) included in the totality of the activity. In recent years, for example, the externality problem has been clearly recognized for waste water treatment facilities. Many localities would devote insufficient resources to waste water treatment if left to make their own allocative decision, because they would undervalue the costs imposed on downstream localities.

Although it may be impossible to measure the externalities involved in waste water treatment with sufficient precision to design just the right subsidy to produce the optimal level of local spending, the case has been made clearly enough to stimulate the political process to respond. Even with private sector involvement, the external benefits to federal taxpayers are sufficient to merit federal subsidy. A substantial portion of chapter 11 is devoted to describing those activities that Congress has decided merit tax-exempt bond support. But the central point here is that Congress sees the need to consider federal taxpayer benefits carefully when private participation is contemplated.

PUBLIC BUSINESS ENTERPRISES

In contrast, almost any activity characterized by public ownership is eligible for tax-exempt financing, and the private-activity bond rules never come into play. The absence of any requirement to pass every bond issue through the public-purpose sieve is generally not a problem, because most publicly owned facilities have a large element of public goods consumption (e.g., a toll highway or a public school). But this is not the case for public business enterprises.

Three factors distinguish these public enterprises from publicly owned facilities that provide "public goods." First, their output is sold in the same way that output from private enterprises is sold: at prices designed to cover the total cost of the enterprise; and with consumption limited to those citizens who pay for the good—those who don't pay for it don't get it. Second, the price of the output is not subsidized by the jurisdiction in question. The institutional arrangements may even go the other way. A public power system or a state liquor store may be expected to price in such a way that excess revenue is generated to support other public expenditures.[3] And third, the enterprise is not ancillary to the production of some public good. Even though the school cafeteria may exhibit the first two characteristics of a public enterprise (although in many instances there may well be a local subsidy), it is not a public enterprise in the sense the term is used here, because the cafeteria is ancillary to the production of public education.

Citizens have an incentive to lobby their local governments to expand their activities into the private sector's realm through the formation of tax-exempt, bond-financed, publicly owned business enterprises. Chapter 7 illustrated how tax-exempt debt financing lowers capital costs, which can in turn be converted into a lower product price.[4] Whether local governments act on this incentive also depends upon other economic factors. The "nondistribution" constraint prohibits public enterprises from distributing profits to its managers.[5] Without this monetary incentive, the public sector manager presumably is less motivated to pursue efficient production methods and may produce the good or service with higher noncapital factor costs than a privately organized firm. But if the public manager is able to disguise the extraction of profits in the form of higher wages or fringe benefits, or is motivated by nonpecuniary benefits that accrue from serving the public interest, efficiency losses may not be very great.[6]

Whatever may be the ultimate effect of these competing influences in a specific locality, local government provision of activities also provided by the private sector has been substantial. Table 14.1 presents data on the number of nonfederal government units that owned and operated or owned and contracted out four services in 1987— over 14,000 water supply systems, over 4,000 public transit systems, almost 4,000 electric power facilities, and about 2,000 gas supply systems.[7]

Other services that would seem suitable for private provision are also provided by state and local governments, although less extensively than utilities. For instance, 17 state governments operate liquor stores, as do counties or municipalities in several states; West Virginia owns and operates lodges in its public parks; North Dakota has its own commercial bank. Numerous other examples could be listed. A municipal hospital recently proposed to solve its financial difficulties by financing the acquisition of privately owned, and profitable, nursing homes with tax-exempt bonds. In theory, there is nothing in federal law to prevent local governments from going into

Table 14.1 NUMBER OF GOVERNMENTAL UNITS OWNING AND OPERATING OR OWNING AND CONTRACTING SELECTED PUBLIC SERVICES, 1987

	Counties	Munici-palities	Townships	Special Districts	Total
Electric power	68	3,321	457	a	3,846
Gas supply	63	1,938	203	a	2,204
Water supply	398	12,807	1,162	a	14,367
Public transit	246	798	269	3,060	4,373
Total	775	18,864	2,091	3,471[a]	

Source: Bureau of the Census (1988b).
a. Special districts having electric, gas, and water utilities are grouped together by the Census data. They total 411, and are included in the special district total.

the automobile business or the computer business. In reality, the ability of state and local governments to issue bonds to finance public enterprises, or, in the language of this chapter, to extend municipal socialism, has been limited primarily by public-purpose doctrines in state constitutions and general public aversion to public ownership of businesses.

PUBLIC POWER

The numerous federal restrictions on issuance of tax-exempt bonds enacted in the last 20 years do not, with the exception of the three small provisions adopted in 1987, limit the use of tax-exempt bonds to finance municipal enterprises.[8] The most important of these three provisions was targeted to the best-known example of a private good that has been provided by public business enterprise, output facilities that provide electric power and natural gas to homes and businesses. The volume of tax-exempt bonds issued for these facilities from 1978 to 1987 appears in figure 14.1. The low point occurred in 1979 when about $4.8 billion was issued; volume peaked in 1985 at almost $28 billion. Gas and electric's share of total tax-exempt volume has been much more stable, hovering in the 11 percent to 13 percent range most of the time.

The Omnibus Budget Reconciliation Act (OBRA) of 1987 restricted the authority of state and local governments to issue tax-exempt bonds to finance the purchase (takeover) of nongovernmentally owned output facilities. Although this output-facilities restriction was supported by the private utility industry, it was adamantly opposed by the public power industry and many state and local officials. Three policy issues fueled the 1987 debate: the potential federal revenue loss from tax-exempt bonds issued to finance takeovers; whether state and local provision of utility services generates benefits for federal taxpayers, thereby satisfying a public purpose; and whether tax-exempt financing is necessary to preserve a takeover threat that inhibits monopolistic pricing by private utilities.

Legislation Restricting Takeovers of Investor-Owned Utilities

Prior to OBRA 1987, state and local governments could issue tax-exempt bonds to finance the construction, acquisition, or operation of governmentally owned output facilities. This authority encom-

Figure 14.1 GAS AND ELECTRIC TAX-EXEMPT BOND VOLUME AND SHARE OF
TOTAL BOND VOLUME, 1973–87

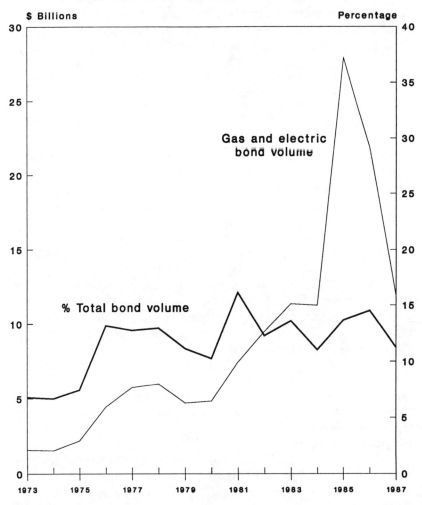

Source: *The Bond Buyer Yearbook*, various issues.

passed the purchase of existing nongovernmental output facilities,
thereby converting private utilities into publicly owned facilities and
making them eligible for tax-exempt financing. The only restrictions
on this authority were limitations on the amount of the proceeds
devoted to private use (referred to as nonqualified proceeds, see
Internal Revenue Code section 141(b)(4)).

The 1987 act narrowed the ability of state and local governments to provide tax-exempt financing for utility customers through the purchase of output facilities owned by the private, nonprofit, or federal sectors. The bonds issued for the purchase of such facilities (generating, transmission, distribution, and other related facilities) are now considered to be taxable private-activity bonds.

An exception is provided if the bonds are issued to acquire electric energy or gas facilities, provided part of the state private-activity bond volume cap is allotted to the bonds in question. Since 1988, these annual volume caps are the greater of $150 million or $50 per capita per year for each state. Given the cost of most utility takeovers, a significant portion of the volume cap would have to be allocated for a utility takeover. State and local government officials must now decide whether their taxpayers value the benefits of utility takeover more than they value the benefits of using the allotted bond volume for other activities.[9]

In addition, two exceptions allow the issuance of tax-exempt bonds to acquire nongovernmental output property without recourse to the private-activity bond volume cap. First, tax-exempt bonds may be used to finance an acquisition designed to satisfy increased demand *within* an area that the acquiring governmental unit has served for at least 10 years. Increased demand caused by sales outside a utility's usual service area could not justify acquisition of nongovernmental output property financed with tax-exempt bonds not subject to the volume cap.

Second, tax-exempt financing outside the volume cap is permitted to extend utility service to areas acquired through annexation for general governmental purposes (for example, by transfer of voting registration and property tax rolls) and the extension of general governmental services to the annexed area. The bond issue qualifies under this rule only if (1) the annexed area is no more than 10 percent of the governmental unit's previous geographic area or (2) the increased output capacity is no more than 10 percent of prior output capacity.

Federal Revenue Loss

Many state and local officials believe that the legislation passed in 1982, 1984, and 1986 that restricted tax-exempt bond volume was motivated primarily by the desire of the federal government to reduce federal revenue losses and reduce the deficit. The American Public Power Association (APPA) argued that rather than costing the federal government revenues, takeovers would actually increase federal revenues.

... reduced electric rates lead to increased discretionary income for consumers and additional capital for new investment in plants and equipment. The resulting increased payrolls (and thus, increased tax revenue)
and reduced Federal welfare and unemployment costs more than compensate for the revenue loss from further issuance of tax-exempt bonds for
even a large public takeover. (American Public Power Association n.d., 2)

This type of argument is used repeatedly by those seeking a wide
variety of federal subsidies. The concept may even be true in the
limited context in which it is presented, because lower utility prices
will increase the real incomes of utility consumers and may even
lead to some of the effects discussed by the APPA. But in a broader
context, this argument is, to be blunt, incorrect and misleading because it ignores the part of the calculation that is detrimental to the
public utilities' case. When the argument is placed in the context of
the entire economy, a very different result emerges.

One must ask what the foregone federal revenues (that make the
price reduction possible) would have been used for if they had not
subsidized a utility takeover. Would they have lain idle? Of course
not. Either taxes would have been lower and after-tax disposable
incomes higher, or the federal government would have used the
money for some direct spending program. In either case, the benefits
cited by the APPA would have occurred in some other industry or
activity. These foregone benefits represent the costs from federal
subsidy of a takeover, and must be subtracted from the benefits discussed by the APPA to arrive at a measure of net benefits. It is highly
unlikely that a net benefit would result from such a calculation.

Do Output Facilities Serve a Public Purpose?

More fundamental issues of public policy are at work here, such as
whether the output-facilities provision is consistent with the developing federal view of what activities satisfy a public purpose and
which activities might be considered for privatization. First, it is
necessary to decide whether an economic case exists for public sector
production of electricity (or gas). In economic terms, electric and gas
utility services do not possess the characteristics that require provision by the public sector.[10] Clearly, electricity or gas can be produced and distributed by the private sector.

A second issue is whether the private sector produces the proper
amount of electricity at the correct price. Several factors may lead
to an incorrect result: (1) the decisions of private producers and

consumers may not account for social costs such as pollution of various sorts or the potential benefits of conservation efforts; (2) reliance on a sole provider for a geographic area (as a cost-minimizing strategy) may enable the provider to engage in monopolistic pricing; and (3) a private producer may not find it profitable to provide the universal service that society deems fair at a cost that is affordable to geographically isolated consumers.

It is certainly true that all of these considerations are relevant for the electric utility industry. Pollution costs are significant, and the long-run consequences of energy-intensive production and consumption on the U.S. economy and security could be profound. Private producers have no incentive to internalize the costs of pollution in their rate structure, and efforts to curtail demand through conservation efforts may be inconsistent with efforts to maximize profits. This is a necessary but not sufficient reason to adopt public production. A market-oriented economy ought to accomplish its social goals with the least intrusive policy instrument. Society's politically bartered pollution and conservation goals can be achieved far less intrusively with a judicious mixture of tax and regulatory policies that alter the incentives of private producers than is possible with resort to public production that arrives at the same result. It is not even true that public ownership necessarily will pursue these goals as an expression of the public interest. Public managers are subject to cost pressures from their customers, most of whom will be as upset at higher rates as would the customers of a private utility. Wilson and Richardson (1985) even suggest that regulation of private utilities has been more successful at promoting conservation than has public ownership.

The second rationale for public ownership, monopolistic pricing, is also a very real consideration. Generation, transmission, and distribution of electricity all lend themselves to monopoly (Braman 1989a). Again, regulation of the private sector may be a preferred alternative to public ownership, particularly because access to tax-exempt financing may lead to inefficient decisions. This issue is discussed more completely in the next section.

The third rationale is universal service. This was an important reason for the development of publicly owned utilities. Private utilities in the early part of the 20th century often considered it unprofitable to extend service to rural areas, giving rise to the creation of publicly owned electric utilities and rural electric cooperatives (that enjoy tax preferences, but not tax-exempt financing) (Wilcox

1955). But universal service is no longer an issue, and certainly not an issue when discussing tax-exempt financing of takeovers of privately owned utilities.

This discussion suggests that the three market imperfections do not require public provision but can, in principle, be accommodated by regulation of private industry. But we also know that regulation is itself an imperfect art,[11] and that the definition of what is a public service (as opposed to a private good) is sufficiently subjective that it cannot be precisely specified. Thus, the subjective judgment of taxpayers in a state or local region may be that public provision of electricity is justified. This does not, however, necessarily imply that it makes sense for the federal government to tax the country to help pay for this state or local decision. Economic theory suggests that federal subsidy would be justified only if taxpayers who reside outside the state or local area providing the service receive a portion of the social benefits resulting from this service. If a spillover of benefits does not exist, then a federal subsidy effectively redistributes income geographically, which may or may not be the intent of the subsidy.

Well, one might ask, is it not true that electricity historically has been provided by both the private and public sectors, even though it is obvious that utility services are amenable to private provision? The answer, clearly, is yes. And the 1987 OBRA legislation continues to provide federal financial support for most such public activities.

First, those governments that have a tradition of public provision of utility services can continue to finance the purchase of privately owned electric and gas output facilities with tax-exempt bonds. Allowances were made for those governments to expand their capacities as demand grows because of population growth or political annexation. Second, the legislation does not prohibit the use of tax-exempt bonds by any jurisdiction for the construction of new output facilities that are to be publicly owned and may compete with privately owned facilities.

But at the same time, Congress seems reluctant to extend federal financial support to those parts of the country that have historically had private-sector utility services. As a small step in that direction, the 1987 legislation says that if a state or local government in an area where utilities are typically provided by private sources wants to provide electricity or gas by purchasing privately owned output facilities (rather than constructing new facilities), the federal government will not provide any financial support unless state and local taxpayers agree to use part of their allowable private-activity bond volume. Note that Congress did not prohibit state and local officials from deciding that electricity or gas generation is a legitimate public activity for the state and local sector; Congress simply said that the federal taxpayer receives inadequate benefits to justify unrestricted access to a federal subsidy.

Monopolistic Pricing

Interested consumer groups and some in the public power industry complain that the output-facilities legislation eliminates the threat of public takeover as an incentive for investor-owned utilities to avoid monopolistic pricing. This premise suggests that without tax-exempt financing, the takeover by municipalities of some investor-owned output facilities would be economically infeasible. However, it is not clear why the takeover of an investor-owned utility practicing monopolistic pricing depends on the use of tax-exempt bonds. After all, a public authority can go to the taxable market for capital, and it still has a cost advantage by virtue of the fact that a public utility is, when all is said and done, not subject to income taxation.[12]

An examination of possible municipal behavior upon removal of the capital cost advantage provided by tax-exempt bonds can help to clarify the issue. A takeover decision financed with taxable bonds implies that the takeover remains advantageous to all local taxpayers, which implies the existence of monopolistic pricing (assuming neither the public nor private sector possesses operating cost advantages). All taxpayers would benefit from the lower prices a takeover would bring. In contrast, a decision not to take over a privately owned output facility implies that the investor-owned utility threatened with municipal takeover is not engaging in monopolistic pricing. In such circumstances, a decision not to take over is precisely the conclusion that Congress is hoping will be reached.

It is, of course, possible that a local government might still decide in favor of a takeover even if monopolistic pricing is not present. This takeover is, however, less likely without tax-exempt financing, because it cannot be advantageous to all local taxpayers. Such a takeover would subsidize local taxpayers as a function of their utility consumption and tax local taxpayers as a function of the tax structure. Who knows which citizens would be the winners and which citizens the losers? In contrast, with tax-exempt financing, local officials still have a powerful incentive for a takeover because all local taxpayers can benefit from the lower price made possible by the tax-exempt financing. Federal taxpayers are placed in the position of paying for lower utility prices for select groups of local taxpayers, without the compensatory social gain of monopolistic price elimination.

Even if investor-owned utilities are practicing monopolistic pricing behavior, it is not clear that public takeovers financed with tax-exempt bonds are the reasonable policy response. First, aren't regulators supposed to keep track of utility pricing? If regulation is not working to prevent monopolistic pricing, isn't this a state and local problem? Second, does it make sense to solve one problem (an artificially high price caused by monopolistic price setting) by creating another problem (federal subsidy of selected groups of local taxpayers without compensatory benefits to federal taxpayers)?

CONCLUSIONS

OBRA 1987 included a provision that, in effect, denied the use of tax-exempt bonds to finance public takeover of investor-owned utilities, thereby intervening for the first time in the freedom of local governments to form public business enterprises and foster municipal socialism. Additional congressional efforts to restrict the use of tax-exempt bonds to finance other essentially private activities may arise in the future.

The three categories of policy issues that were debated in this electric and gas utility case provide insight into the nature of the forthcoming battles the tax-exempt bond community may find itself fighting with increasing frequency. The assertion that tax-exempt bonds for almost any activity generate more federal revenue from increased economic activity than they cost in foregone tax revenue is fundamentally flawed. The argument ignores the alternative uses to which the federal subsidy could be put, thereby seriously overstating the net gain to federal revenues. This "let's subsidize ourselves to prosperity" argument has been made innumerable times. Perhaps it is time to impose a moratorium on its use in the policy process. The key members of Congress who confront this argument, the members of the Senate Committee on Finance and the House Committee on Ways and Means, are well positioned to evaluate it critically.

The public service and national benefit issue may provide somewhat more fertile ground for defending tax exemption for some activities. The economic theory of public goods is sound, but the precision with which one can determine the necessity for public provision of most activities and the presence or magnitude of national benefits is limited. Subjectivity creeps into the analysis, and arguments can be made on both sides of the issue.

Using this utility case as an example, the economic characteristics of electricity and gas provision happen to be consistent with private provision. It is, however, possible that the private sector may not provide the proper amounts at the correct price due to pollution costs, monopolistic pricing, or unwillingness to provide universal service. All of these difficulties could be more easily handled through a well-managed regulatory process, however, rather than through public provision. And a decision by local government to provide utility services (whether due to historical precedent or because the regulatory process is not working) does not necessarily imply that there are national benefits to justify federal subsidy.

This lack of certainty concerning federal support for utility services is reflected in the legislation. The output-facilities provision in the 1987 act is consistent with congressional efforts over the last 20 years to restrict the use of tax-exempt bonds to activities whose public benefits spill over state and local political boundaries. But the provision is not as restrictive as it could be—tax-exempt bonds can still be issued for construction of new facilities without restriction, and allowance is made for jurisdictions that already provide utility services to use tax-exempt bonds to purchase facilities to satisfy increased demand due to population growth or annexation. The qualitative nature of the public goods evaluation produces policies that appear to be inconsistent but may actually reflect the uncertainty of congressional judgment.

Finally, any activity whose access to tax-exempt bonds is considered for restriction will raise other policy issues that bear on the desirability of tax-exempt financing. These issues will be as varied as are the activities facing restriction, so the specific details of this monopolistic pricing discussion are not relevant. But the discussion does illustrate how easy it is to challenge the often rather glib assertions of subsidy proponents by using economic theory and common sense to illuminate the subsidy's effects on economic efficiency and the income distribution.

In this utility case, for example, it is argued that the use of tax-exempt bonds is not essential to preserve the threat of a public takeover as an incentive for investor-owned utilities to avoid monopolistic pricing. Taxable-financed takeovers are also effective and are far less likely to encourage inefficient economic decisions. If a takeover is economically infeasible without tax-exempt bonds, this suggests that monopolistic pricing is not a problem. If this is true, allowing tax-exempt financing for such takeovers means that federal taxpayers are paying for the lower utility prices of consumers in a select local area and, presumably, receiving no benefits in return.

Notes

1. A summary of U.S. experience with public enterprise is available in Wilcox (1955), chapter 21. More theoretical discussions of the principles on which such decisions should be made are available in any standard public finance textbook such as Musgrave (1959) or Browning and Browning (1979), and in chapter 5 of this book. Recent books by Rose-Ackerman (1986) and Weisbrod (1988) expand the analysis to include the role of a nonprofit sector.

2. What the federal government gives (with tax-exempt financing) it can also take away by taxing the public enterprise's income if a nonessential governmental service is being provided. Section 115 of the Internal Revenue Code addresses the issue: "Gross income does not include—(1) income derived from any public utility or the exercise of any essential governmental function and accruing to a State or any political subdivision thereof, or the District of Columbia; . . . (Internal Revenue Code 1989).

Whether this is ever enforced is a good question. For instance, income from state liquor stores is not taxed, and these institutions are certainly not essential governmental functions. Chaper 5 discusses the difficulty of discerning essential governmental functions and public purposes.

3. In a study of the 1973 financial performance of 58 municipally owned North Carolina electric utilities, Strauss and Wertz (1976) found that all reported positive net income, and that this "profit" was used to substitute for own-source revenue, particularly property taxes.

4. Of course, state and local business enterprises are not subject to federal income taxes, which also can be converted into lower product prices.

5. The term *nondistribution constraint* was coined by Henry Hansmann (1980) when discussing the incentives facing nonprofit organizations.

6. The comparative economic incentives facing governments, nonprofit organizations, and for-profit firms are discussed and evaluated in great depth by Weisbrod (1988), primarily in chapters 3, 4, and 9.

7. The number of water supply systems for special districts is understated in table 14.1 because it does not include multifunction special districts that combine water supply with sewerage services or natural resource services.

8. Much of the discussion in this part of the chapter comes from Zimmerman (1989).

9. New Orleans is in the process of negotiating a taxable debt-financed takeover of private gas and electric utilities for $716 million.

10. As discussed in chapter 5, a good that requires public provision possesses two essential characteristics: (1) consumption cannot be denied to those unwilling to pay for the good (like national defense, which once provided can be consumed whether or not an individual pays for it); and (2) one family's consumption of a unit of the good does not prevent another family from using that unit (again like national defense).

11. This does not mean that regulation is always successful at its task. See the analysis of electric utility regulation, both public and private, in Hyman (1989).

12. It has been argued by proponents of public power that tax-exempt financing is a necessary counterweight to the tax preferences enjoyed by investor-owned utilities. But these tax preferences only reduce tax liability, providing the private firm with a portion of the much larger preference enjoyed by public utilities, tax exemption.

Chapter Fifteen

THE VOLUME CAP AND PRIVATE-ACTIVITY BONDS IN 1989

The volume cap on private-activity tax-exempt bonds is supposed to achieve three objectives. First, bonds having the taint of private use are targeted to a list of approved activities that Congress believes provide some public benefits to federal taxpayers. Second, the federal revenue loss is controlled by limiting the volume of such private-activity bonds that can be issued in any one year. And third, state and local decision makers are given the flexibility to allocate the volume cap among the list of approved activities in accordance with the desires of their constituents.

The cap provides another benefit to all parties. It reduces the amount of time and effort that must be invested in the bargaining between Congress and state and local officials as changing economic conditions and public tastes and preferences cause state and local decision makers to alter the allocation of the cap. If the changing preferences involve only a reallocation among already-approved activities, it is nobody's business but state and local officials and their constituents. If the changing preferences lead to a desire to issue bonds for non-exempt activities C and D rather than for exempt activities A and B, the task of convincing Congress of the desirability of expanding the list of exempt activities to include C and D is greatly eased by congressional knowledge that the maximum federal revenue loss will not change (assuming the existing volume cap is fully utilized).

Prior to the adoption of the volume cap, local governments and their various authorities issued private-activity bonds independently of state control (most of the constitutional and statutory restrictions discussed in chapter 2 apply only to general obligation bonds). Considerable concern was expressed by local officials that, under the volume cap, local governments would lose their independence in issuing private-activity bonds and would be required to petition the state for every private-activity bond allocation. Proponents of the various private activities subject to the volume cap were also concerned that their activities would not receive a fair share of the available cap.

Three full years after implementation, little is known about the states' operation of the volume cap or about their allocation priorities. Nor is much known about the volume of private-activity bonds issued in each state. The Deficit Reduction Act of 1984 required that a form must be filed with the U.S. Treasury Department for every private-activity tax-exempt bond issue (see chapter 11 for more information about form 8038), although no requirement was imposed on the Treasury to summarize and publish this information. Nonetheless, the information on these forms appears in a report published periodically in *SOI Bulletin*, a quarterly report of the Internal Revenue Service. Unfortunately, no report has been published since the data on 1986 bond issues were summarized in the summer 1988 issue.

This chapter presents the results of a survey by the Advisory Commission on Intergovernmental Relations and the Urban Institute of state and local government experience with the 1989 private-activity bond volume cap. The survey form is reproduced in appendix 15A to this chapter. This survey was designed to close some of the information gaps just noted. Three types of information were obtained. One set of questions asked about the priorities established to allocate the cap, that is, the priorities used to allocate the cap between state government and local governmental units; the priorities used to allocate the state and local shares by types of activities; and pending or proposed changes in these priorities.

The second set of questions requested data on: (1) the total volume of bonds issued in 1989 requiring a volume cap allocation; (2) the division of this total volume between issues using an allocation from the 1989 cap and those using an allocation carried forward from volume cap authority unused in previous years; (3) the division of these two categories by type of private activity; and (4) bond volume by type of activity that had to be denied or delayed due to the unavailability of volume cap. These data are useful for assessing the decrease in private-activity bond volume since the cap's adoption in 1986, and the presence, in some states, of unused volume cap available to finance exempt private-activity bonds in 1989 and, in other states, of insufficient volume cap to finance all requests for volume cap allocations in 1989. No information was collected on the total amount of prior years' unused volume cap *available* to finance bond issues in 1989.

A final survey question asked for suggestions for reform of the existing volume cap rules imposed by the federal government.

Survey responses were received from all 50 states; only the District of Columbia failed to respond. The numerical data from Alabama could not be reconciled and are not included in the numerical tables, although Alabama's information on priorities is included in the tables explaining allocation priorities. Thus, the numerical data in this chapter cover 49 states.

Before discussing the survey results, it is useful to summarize the operation of the volume cap.

HOW THE UNIFIED VOLUME CAP WORKS

Under current law, each state has the authority to issue tax-exempt private-activity bonds in an amount equal to $50 per resident of the state, calculated using the most recently released U.S. Bureau of the Census state population estimates. If a state's population results in the authority to issue less than $150 million, the state allocation is automatically raised to $150 million.[1]

As a spur to state legislation, the volume cap legislation imposed a 50/50 split of the volume cap between state issuing authorities and local issuing authorities that was to prevail until the governor issued a proclamation or the state legislature passed a statute concerning an alternative allocation. No restrictions were placed on the states' latitude in changing this 50/50 allocation between state and local units of government or reserving a portion for various types of private activity.

Volume cap that is not used during the year in which it is received may be carried forward for a period of three years. At the time of carry-forward, the state must make an irrevocable election of the type of activity (but not the specific project) for which the unused volume cap will be used, such as qualified mortgage revenue bonds or student loans. Small-issue industrial development bonds may not be financed with carry-forward authority, nor may any of the portion of governmental bonds used for private purposes (10 percent governmental bond proceeds). Any carry-forward assigned to mortgage revenue bonds had to be used before the exemption for mortgage revenue bonds expired in September 1990.

The states are not required to report to the Internal Revenue Service on their compliance with the volume cap. As with most aspects of the tax-exempt bond law, the IRS relies primarily on voluntary compliance implemented by bond counsel, who offer opinions that a proposed bond issue conforms to the provisions of the tax code. If the volume cap is exceeded and it comes to the attention of the tax authorities, those bond issues that placed the state's volume over the cap are deemed to be taxable.

WHO ADMINISTERS THE VOLUME CAP?

"Diverse" is an apt characterization of the state agencies responsible for allocating the volume cap. A few states have retained total control of the volume cap within the governor's office. Some states have placed the responsibility with the state offices dealing with budget and finance or with issuance of public debt, usually the treasurer's office. Other states have given the responsibility to the agency whose mandate most closely approximates the purpose for which the bonds are issued, usually a department of commerce or a department of economic and community development. And a few states have created an entirely new entity to allocate the cap, usually giving it a title such as "bond allocation committee." A list of the responsible state agencies is presented in table 15.1.

These agencies are responsible for keeping track of private-activity bond issues that draw on the cap, and most also prepare an annual report on their activities. Some of these agencies are also responsible for processing applications for cap allocations and making decisions about which applications will receive a cap allocation based upon priorities enacted by legislative statute or proclamation of the governor; the remaining agencies seem to perform primarily a pass-through function in which they allocate the year's allowable bond volume to other agencies or authorities according to predetermined amounts (such as housing, education, or development finance authorities). These recipient agencies or authorities then assume the responsibility for choosing among the requesters for shares of the volume cap.

ALLOCATION PRIORITIES

Two types of priorities have been established. Some states set aside fixed proportions or dollar amounts of the cap for state authorities and local authorities. Some states also dedicate a fixed proportion

Table 15.1 STATE AGENCIES RESPONSIBLE FOR ADMINISTERING THE ALLOCATION OF THE PRIVATE-ACTIVITY BOND VOLUME CAP, 1989

State	Agency
Alabama	Industrial Development Authority
Alaska	State Bond Committee
Arizona	Department of Commerce
Arkansas	Development Finance Authority
California	Debt Limit Allocation Committee
Colorado	Department of Local Affairs, Division of Local Government
Connecticut	Private Activity Bond Commission
Delaware	Department of Finance
Florida	Department of General Services, Division of Bond Finance
Georgia	Department of Community Affairs
Hawaii	Department of Budget & Finance, Finance Division
Idaho	Department of Commerce
Illinois	Office of the Governor
Indiana	Employment Development Commission
Iowa	Iowa Finance Authority
Kansas	Department of Commerce
Kentucky	Private Activity Bond Allocation Committee and Office of Financial Management & Economic Analysis
Louisiana	State Bond Commission and Office of the Governor
Maine	Finance Authority of Maine
Maryland	Department of Economic & Employment Development
Massachusetts	Executive Office for Administration & Finance
Michigan	Department of Treasury
Minnesota	Department of Finance, Cash & Debt Management Division
Mississippi	Department of Economic Development
Missouri	Department of Economic Development
Montana	Department of Administration, Office of the Director
Nebraska	Investment Finance Authority

continued

Table 15.1   STATE AGENCIES RESPONSIBLE FOR ADMINISTERING THE ALLOCATION OF THE PRIVATE-ACTIVITY BOND
VOLUME CAP, 1989 (continued)

Nevada	Department of Commerce
New Hampshire	Housing Finance Authority and Industrial Development Authority
New Jersey	Department of the Treasury
New Mexico	State Board of Finance, Department of Finance & Administration
New York	State Budget Division
North Carolina	Federal Tax Reform Allocation Committee
North Dakota	Governor's Office
Ohio	Director of the Department of Development
Oklahoma	Department of Commerce
Oregon	State Treasury and Private Activity Bond Committee
Pennsylvania	Department of Commerce, Bureau of Bonds
Rhode Island	Public Finance Management Board
South Carolina	State Budget & Control Board
South Dakota	Office of the Governor
Tennessee	Department of Economic & Community Development, Division of Community Development
Texas	Department of Commerce
Utah	Department of Community & Economic Development, Division of Community Development
Vermont	Emergency Board
Virginia	Department of Housing & Community Development
Washington	Department of Community Development
West Virginia	Community & Industrial Development
Wisconsin	Department of Development, Housing & Economic Development Authority, and Building Commission
Wyoming	Governor's Office

Source: Advisory Commission on Intergovernmental Relations (ACIR)-Urban Institute Private-Activity Bond Survey 1989.

or dollar amount of the cap for a particular type of activity. The material presented here is based entirely upon the information provided by the survey respondents, so it is subject to the range of errors common in responses to such instruments.

Division between State and Local Issuing Authorities

The results of state legislation to allocate the cap are divided into two categories in table 15.2. The "All to State" category lists those states reporting that 100 percent of the cap is nominally in state hands. Local governments in these states must ask the state for cap allocations and compete with state usage in all cases. Some states in this category are explicit in stating that the cap is available to all state or local issuers on an equal basis, subject, of course, to any priorities established for favored activities, which are discussed in the next section. Others are not explicit about equal access for state and local issuers, but the implication seems to be that the cap is available to both state and local issuers on an equal basis.

The "Divided between State and Local" category lists those states that divide the cap into portions for state use and for local use and describes the allocations. The divisions are not absolute, however. The usual procedure is to reserve an allocation for at least nine months of the calendar year. It is not even clear in all cases that a portion reserved for the state is necessarily used by the state. For example, a portion allocated to a state housing finance agency may simply mean that its share of the cap is protected from local development or student loan authorities but is available to be allocated by the state housing finance agency to local governments seeking funding for multifamily rental housing. Consequently, the allocation listed in the "Divided between State and Local" column is very likely not an accurate reflection of which government actually issues the bonds that use the cap.

The allocation among governmental units in most states is further muddied if the reserved allocation is not used by a set date during the year, which for most states lies somewhere between September 1 and December 21. When this date arrives, any unused cap usually reverts to a central pool available to other issuers, sometimes restricted to issuers at the same level of government that has not used the cap, but often including both state and local issuing authorities.

Illinois's allocation between the state and its local governments is unique. The Tax Reform Act of 1986 established a system of direct allocations to units of home-rule government in states that have a

Table 15.2 ALLOCATION PRIORITIES FOR THE VOLUME CAP ON TAX-EXEMPT PRIVATE-ACTIVITY BONDS IN 1989: DIVISION BETWEEN STATE AND LOCAL GOVERNMENTS ($ MILLIONS)

All to State[a]	Divided between State and Local[b]
Alabama	Alaska: At least 25% to municipalities.
Arkansas	Arizona: 20% to state, 42% to nonurban areas, and 38% to urban areas.
California	Colorado: 50% to state, 25% to larger local governments based on population, 25% available to other local issuers.
	Connecticut: 72% to state, 18% to municipalities and their authorities.
	Delaware: $75 to state, $26.25 to New Castle County, $18.75 to City of Wilmington, $15 each to Kent and Sussex Counties.
	Florida: 40% to state, 60% to 16 regions (groups of counties) in proportion to their share of state population.
Georgia	Hawaii: 50% to state, 37.55% to city and county of Honolulu, 5.03% to county of Hawaii, 2.41% to county of Kauai, 5.01% to county of Maui.
Idaho	Illinois: 50% of 5/11 of cap to state, 50% of 5/11 to nonhome-rule local governments; 6/11 to home-rule local governments.
	Indiana: 38% to state, 62% to local.
	Iowa: 53% to state, 5% to local, remainder open.
Kansas	Kentucky: At least 60% to local.
	Louisiana: 70% to state.
Maine	Maryland: 47.5% to state, 40% to counties in proportion to population, 2.5% to municipalities.
Massachusetts	Michigan: 40% to state, 60% to local.
Minnesota	
Mississippi	Montana: $105 to state, $45 to local.
Missouri	
Nebraska	Nevada: 50% to state, 50% to local as proportion of population.
New Hampshire	
New Jersey	New Mexico: 60% to state, 40% to local.
North Carolina	

North Dakota	New York: 1/3 to state, 1/3 to local, 1/3 reserved for all issuers. Ohio: $225 to state, $130 to local. Oklahoma: 24% to state, 56% to local. Oregon: $127.5 to state, $22.5 to local.
Rhode Island	Pennsylvania: After a set-aside for housing and small issues, 50% of remainder is given to counties for small issues.
South Dakota	South Carolina: 40% to state, 60% to local. Tennessee: $25 to state, rest to counties in proportion to population. Texas: 15% reserved for state, remainder available to all issuers. Utah: 25% to state, 50% to cities and counties with 30,000 population and 4-year total bond issuance of $12 million, 25% to other cities and counties.
Vermont Washington West Virginia Wyoming	Virginia: 86% to state, 14% to local. Wisconsin: $115 to state, rest to local.

Source: ACIR–Urban Institute Private-Activity Bond Survey 1989.
a. All to State: no set asides for local governments.
b. Divided between State and Local: set asides for local governments for at least part of the year.

home-rule unit system. The only state to which this system applies is Illinois. This "home-rule" rule has the effect of bypassing any allocation system established by state legislation or proclamation. The resulting allocation gives $\frac{6}{11}$ of the Illinois volume cap to the 109 home-rule units of local government (because these home-rule governments comprise $\frac{6}{11}$ of the state population), and $\frac{5}{11}$ to the state. Half of the state's share is reserved for the state, and half is reserved for nonhome-rule units of local government. Needless to say, since the 109 home-rule governments act entirely independently of the state allocation system, the data on cap allocations in the remainder of this chapter include only the portion of the Illinois cap controlled by the state (which happens to include a small portion of the home-rule allocation that a few home-rule local governments return to the state).

Table 15.2 indicates that 28 of the 50 states have reserved portions of the cap for local issuers. The allocation is nonspecific in most states, usually saying that no more than X% goes to the state and Y% goes to local governments. But a few states get very specific. Tennessee divides the nonstate share among counties in proportion to their population, and Utah reserves 50% of the cap allocation for cities and counties having at least 30,000 population and a four-year total bond issuance of at least $12 million.

Division between Types of Exempt Activities and Selection Criteria

The Tax Reform Act of 1986 subjected most exempt private activities to the volume cap, and many states decided to set aside a portion of the cap to be used exclusively for a subset of these activities. The states also had to establish criteria for selecting among competing projects. These priorities and criteria are summarized in table 15.3. States that report no priorities among competing activities and allocate the cap on a first-come first-served basis, with an occasional restriction on the maximum size of the allocation for a project, are listed under the "No Priorities" column. Only 18 states fall into this category. The remaining 32 states have either established priorities among activities or have allocated the cap among competing projects according to some set of economic criteria, most often the number of jobs created or number of low-income persons benefited.

A statement of intent to use the private-activity bond volume to promote economic growth and job creation is nearly universal in the states' enabling legislation or proclamations that established the pri-

Table 15.3 ALLOCATION PRIORITIES FOR THE VOLUME CAP ON TAX-EXEMPT PRIVATE-ACTIVITY BONDS IN 1989: DIVISION AMONG TYPES OF ACTIVITIES AND USE OF ECONOMIC MEASURES AS SELECTION CRITERIA ($ MILLIONS)

No Priorities[a]	Priorities[b]
Alaska	Alabama: 25% to housing, 10% to student loans, 35% for small issues, 15% for exempt facilities.
Arizona	Arkansas: $15 for multifamily housing, $50 for industrial development, $25 for single-family housing, $15 for student loans, balance for all other bonds. Allocated in chronological order.
Delaware	California: Top priority is multifamily and single-family housing for low-income people; small issues ranked by number of new jobs created (relocated jobs receive lower priority); priority of all other activities depends upon benefits to lower-income households.
	Colorado: Focus on housing, agricultural development, postsecondary education facilities, health facilities, and student loans. Choices made based upon job creation or retention.
	Connecticut: 40% of state share to housing, 32% to economic development.
	Florida: 62.5% of state share for housing.
Hawaii	Georgia: 40% to housing, 40% to economic development (must have one job created per $125,000 of bonds).
	Idaho: 28% of state share to housing, 1% to student loans, 8% to economic development; local share not specified by activity.
	Illinois: 30% to single-family housing, 12% to economic development, 16% to student loans, 5% to small issues for first-time farmers; all other activities on a chronological basis.
	Iowa:
	Kansas: $5 to student loans, $25 to small issues, $5 for private-use portion; approved in chronological order.
	Kentucky:
	Louisiana: Maine: Priority order is small issues, housing, student loans, all others; small issues allocated based upon economic impact.

continued

Table 15.3   ALLOCATION PRIORITIES FOR THE VOLUME CAP ON TAX-EXEMPT PRIVATE-ACTIVITY BONDS IN 1989: DIVISION AMONG TYPES OF ACTIVITIES AND USE OF ECONOMIC MEASURES AS SELECTION CRITERIA ($ MILLIONS) (continued)

No Priorities[a]	Priorities[b]
Massachusetts	Maryland: 60% to housing (35% to counties on a per capital basis), 5% for nonhousing (to counties on a per capita basis).
	Michigan: Chronological, but can adjust based upon impact on state economy and leverage of other sources of capital.
	Minnesota: Priority to manufacturing and housing, public facilities; Minneapolis and St. Paul and other first class cities guaranteed percentage of cap; choices by lot if insufficient cap.
Mississippi	Missouri: No activity favored, but priority of projects based upon ability of beneficiary to locate project outside state, impact upon local businesses, number of persons families, or businesses that benefit from project.
	Montana: 40% of state share housing, 25% to student loans, remainder for all other activities on chronological basis.
Nevada	Nebraska: 30% to housing, 20% to student loans, 20% to all other activities, 30% to governor's discretion; choice among projects in category based upon job creation and retention.
New Mexico	New Hampshire: 1/3 housing, 2/3 all other activities.
New York	
North Carolina	New Jersey: Largest shares usually go to housing and economic development; small amount to environmental protection activities; $20 set aside for private-use portion.
	Ohio: Single-family housing, small issues; chronological basis.
	Oklahoma: 20% to small issues.
	Oregon: $60 of state share to housing, $60 to economic development, $7.5 to energy.
Rhode Island	Pennsylvania: First priorities are housing and student loans, 50% of remainder for small issues, other 50% for exempt facilities.

South Dakota	South Carolina: Chronological order, with some discrimination by job creation. Tennessee: Priority 1—manufacturing and other activities that export more than half their output, or produce goods more than half of which are used to produce exported products, or more than half their output substitutes for imports into Tennessee. Priority 2—single-family housing, multifamily housing, and other activities that have a secondary impact on Tennessee economy. Priority 3—other eligible areas. Texas: 33% to single-family housing, 10% to small issues. Utah: State share for single-family housing and student loans. Vermont: Housing, industrial development, student loans. Virginia: 41% to housing, 41% to industrial development, 8% to student loans, 10% to governor's discretion; chronological order.
West Virginia	Washington: Apportioned for housing, student loans, exempt facilities (sewage treatment, mass transit, local utilities, etc.), public utility districts, and small issues. Wisconsin: In decreasig order of priority, single-family housing, small issues, multifamily housing, all other activities; chronological order. Wyoming: $90 million for single-family housing.

Source: ACIR–Urban Institute Private-Activity Bond Survey 1989.
a. No Priorities: no set asides for specific activities or allocation based on economic criteria.
b. Priorities: set asides for specific activities or allocation based on economic criteria.

vate-activity bond programs. Unless these economic growth and job creation criteria have some element that is unique, they are not included in the description in table 15.3. Several of the priority systems are described next.

California makes low-income multifamily rental housing its top priority, followed by single-family housing with special emphasis on low-income applicants. Small-issue industrial development bonds (IDBs) are the next priority, with the choice among competing projects based upon the number of jobs created; within the jobs criterion, preference is granted to new jobs over relocated jobs, and to jobs created in enterprise zones over other locations. The choice among all other types of activities is based upon the extent to which low-income households are benefited. Thus, California stands almost alone among the states in the extent to which it attempts to focus its private-activity bond volume on low-income households.

Tennessee claims to choose among competing projects entirely on the basis of the impact on the Tennessee economy. The first priority goes to manufacturing and other activities that: (1) export more than half their output; (2) produce goods more than half of which are used to produce exported products; or (3) produce goods more than half of which substitute for imports into Tennessee. The second priority is for single-family housing, multifamily housing, and other activities that have a secondary impact on the Tennessee economy. The third priority is all other eligible uses.

Georgia takes a numerical approach. It requires that private-activity bonds issued for economic development generate at least one job for every $125,000 of bonds issued.

STATE INITIATIVES TO REFORM PRIORITIES

Seven states report some degree of interest in changing their allocation priorities in response to their experience with the volume cap. Arkansas is considering changing from a first-come first-served basis to a system of as yet unspecified priorities. Nevada has recently introduced criteria for allocating the state share of the cap, among them the number of new jobs created and jobs retained, and any known environmental impact from the project. Minnesota is also considering changes in its priority system, but the changes are not yet public information. Oklahoma is increasing its share to small issues, and adding shares for student loans and exempt facilities.

South Carolina may shift from a predominantly first-come first-served basis to a more explicit consideration of economic impact than now takes place. Wisconsin reports some legislative interest in setting more explicit shares for the activities currently considered priorities. Illinois plans to set an earlier date (July 15) for when the unused volume cap of home-rule units (except for Chicago) reverts to a common pool available for all issuers.

BONDS ISSUED BY TYPE OF ACTIVITY AND YEAR OF VOLUME CAP

The 49 states that provided internally consistent survey data issued $15.182 billion in private-activity bonds in 1989 that were subject to a unified volume cap. Note that advance and current refundings are not included in the data. The division of this bond volume among eligible private activities is presented in table 15.4, column 2. Each activity's share of the total is presented in column 3. By far the largest volume, $5.606 billion (36.9 percent of the total), was issued for mortgage revenue bonds, followed by small-issue IDBs with $3.228 billion (21.3 percent), solid waste disposal, $1.633 billion (10.8 percent), multifamily rental housing, $1.292 billion (8.5 percent), and student loans with $1.250 billion (8.2 percent). Very small or zero amounts of bonds were issued in 1989 for four exempt activities: mass commuting vehicles ($1 million), local district heating and cooling ($4.3 million), high-speed rail transit ($0), and takeover of investor-owned utilities ($0). The "Other" category includes bonds for which survey respondents were uncertain as to activity classification or that were issued for activities whose exemption has been removed but for which a few transition rules continue to generate some bond issuance. By far the most important of these transition-rule activities is pollution control. It is included as a separate category in this table ($309 million of bonds were issued in 1989).

Not all tax-exempt private-activity bonds issued in 1989 used borrowing authority from the 1989 volume cap. The Tax Reform Act of 1986 allows unused volume cap to be carried forward for a period of three years. Due to these rules, many bonds issued in 1989 used volume cap authority from as far back as 1986. Columns 4 and 6 in table 15.4 divide the $15.182 billion of bond volume in column 2 between those bonds using 1989 volume cap and those using volume cap carried forward into 1989. Of the total volume, $9.773 billion

Table 15.4 NEW-ISSUE TAX-EXEMPT PRIVATE-ACTIVITY BONDS ISSUED IN 1989 THAT WERE SUBJECT TO THE VOLUME CAP: BY TYPE OF EXEMPT ACTIVITY AND YEAR OF VOLUME CAP AUTHORITY ($ MILLIONS)

Activity	Total Volume ($)	(%)	1989 Cap ($)	(%)	Carry Forward ($)	(%)
Mortgage revenue bonds	5606	36.9	3491	35.7	2115	39.1
Student loans	1250	8.2	592	6.1	658	12.2
Small issues	3228	21.3	3228	33.0	0	0.0
Multifamily housing	1292	8.5	817	8.4	475	8.8
Qualified redevelopment	173	1.1	45	0.5	128	2.4
Mass-commuting vehicles	1	0.0	1	0.0	0	0.0
Furnishing of water	162	1.1	34	0.3	128	2.4
Local furnishing of electric/gas	777	5.1	389	4.0	388	7.2

Local district heating and cooling	4	0.0	4	0.0	0	0.0
Hazardous waste disposal	85	0.6	81	0.8	3	0.1
Sewage disposal	422	2.8	250	2.6	173	3.2
Solid waste disposal	1633	10.8	463	4.7	1170	21.6
Takeover of IOUs[a]	0	0.0	0	0.0	0	0.0
High-speed rail transit	0	0.0	0	0.0	0	0.0
Pollution control	309	2.0	153	1.6	156	2.9
Private-use portion[b]	137	0.9	137	1.4		0.0
Other categories	104	0.7	88	0.9	16	0.3
All activities	15,182	100.0	9,773	100.0	5,409	100.0

Source: ACIR–Urban Institute Private-Activity Bond Survey, 1989.
Note: Columns may not sum to totals, owing to rounding.
a. IOUs, investor-owned utilities.
b. Proceeds of governmental electric utility bonds used for a private purpose.

used 1989 volume cap and $5.409 billion used prior years' volume cap. Each activity's share of the 1989 and prior years' volume cap issuance is presented in columns 5 and 7 of the table.

HAS THE CAP REDUCED USE OF PRIVATE-ACTIVITY BONDS?

The question of whether the cap has reduced the use of private-activity bonds is somewhat more complicated than it appears. The normal approach would be to compare the estimates in table 15.4 with the bond volume issued in 1986, the year prior to the volume cap instituted by the Tax Reform Act of 1986. New-issue private-activity bond volume in 1986 was only $17.2 billion, a 75 percent decrease from the preceding year. Reason exists to suggest that this 1986 volume does not accurately reflect demand for pre-volume cap private-activity bond issuance. Auten and Chung (1988) asserted that this volume reflected: the issuance in 1985 of many bond issues that were originally planned for 1986, in anticipation of restrictions included in the House bill that were to go into effect on December 31, 1985; and delay of bond issues originally planned for 1986 due to uncertainty during the first nine months of 1986 about passage of the 1986 act and in the last three months about regulations to implement the new law. For these reasons, the comparison in this section uses an average of new private-activity bond issues for the three years preceding the 1986 act, 1984–86.

New issues of private-activity bonds in 1984–86 were $65.8 billion, $99.8 billion, and $17.2 billion, respectively. But these totals include bonds issued for nonprofit entities and for airports, docks, and wharves, all of which are exempt from the volume cap imposed in 1986.[2] After deducting bonds issued for these activities, the average private-activity bond volume from 1984 to 1986 was $45.9 billion. In contrast, the volume cap for all 50 states and the District of Columbia was a mere $13.899 billion in 1989. If $45.9 billion is a fair representation of what unconstrained demand for private-activity financings would have been in 1989, the volume cap in 1989 was restrictive indeed, imposing a 69.7 percent decrease in private-activity bond volume (assuming the entire volume cap was used).

Table 15.5 provides some insight into how the states spread the pain among private activities. It compares average new issue volume for 1984–86 and 1989 by type of activity. The 1989 volume totals

Table 15.5 EFFECT OF VOLUME CAP ON NEW-ISSUE PRIVATE-ACTIVITY
BONDS: 1989 VOLUME COMPARED TO AVERAGE VOLUME FOR
1984–86 ($ MILLIONS)

Activity	Average 1984–86	1989	Percentage Change
Student loans	1,956	1,250	−36.1
Mortgage revenue bonds	9,593	5,606	−41.6
Small issues	13,602	3,228	−76.3
Multifamily housing	10,688	1,292	−87.9
Sewage and waste disposal	4,231	2,140	−49.4
Pollution control	4,701	309	−93.4
Other	1,146	1,357	18.5
Total	45,918	15,182	−66.9

Sources: ACIR-Urban Institute Private-Activity Bond Survey, 1989; and Auten and
Chung (1988).

$15.182 billion, an amount greater than the $13.899 billion volume
cap due to carry-forward authority from prior years. It is not clear
how much of this carry-forward-based volume would have been issued using 1989 authority if carry-forwards were not permitted. Ideally,
one would want to scale the $15.182 billion of 1989 issues back to
the total dollar value of the volume cap, but it is not clear how the
scaling back should be shared among eligible activities. Instead, table
15.5 uses all 1989 issues, in effect understating the magnitude of the
decrease caused by the volume cap. It is hoped that this makes little
difference, since it is the relative decrease among activities that is
of interest here. It is also important to note that the percentage changes
in the last column of the table reflect more changes than simply
imposition of the volume cap. Some of the activities that remained
exempt over the period have been subjected to targeting and definitional changes. Some activities have been removed from the list
of exempt activities while others have been added; all are included
in these figures in the "Other" category, with the exception of bonds
issued for nonprofit organizations and airports, docks, and wharves.
And many transition rules were enacted in 1986 that grandfathered
projects in the planning stage that might otherwise have required a
volume cap allocation.

Table 15.5 shows that private-activity bond volume subject to the
volume cap has declined by 66.9 percent. The activities experiencing
the least reduction are student loans, 36.1 percent, and mortgage
revenue bonds, 41.6 percent. The activity suffering the biggest hit
(that remains eligible for an exemption) seems to be multifamily

housing, with a reduction of 87.9 percent. The multifamily housing number may be overstated, however, for two reasons: (1) the arbitrage-driven multifamily housing deals uncovered in the Matthews-Wright and related scandals suggest that a significant portion of this pre–Tax Reform Act volume may not have been housing deals at all;[3] and (2) tax-exempt bond-financed housing projects became considerably less attractive due to the restrictions imposed in 1986 on the ability of taxpayers to offset income from one economic activity with losses generated from another activity, the so-called passive loss restrictions.

BONDS ISSUED BY STATE

The total volume of bonds issued in 1989 for each type of private activity (table 15.4, column 2) is disaggregated by state in table 15.6. Several activities are supported by most of the states. Forty-three states issued private-activity bonds for single-family housing (mortgage revenue bonds), 43 for small-issue IDBs, 26 for multifamily housing, and 19 for student loans. The number of states issuing other types of bonds declines substantially.

Figure 15.1 separates each state's total volume according to whether its borrowing authority came from the 1989 volume cap or unused authority carried forward from prior years. Eighteen states used prior years's authority to fund more than 50 percent of their private-activity bond issues. Clearly, the ability to use carry-forward authority substantially reduced many states' need to use the 1989 volume cap.

IS THERE UNUSED VOLUME CAP?

The matter of whether there is unused volume cap is also difficult to answer. First, if volume cap were to be unused, it must be understood that this unused cap would be smaller or even nonexistent without the restrictions on the list of activities for which state and local governments can issue bonds. Second, the three-year carry-forward provision suggests that large capital projects occur irregularly, and use of the cap should be averaged over several years. Unfortunately, the data here are for 1989 issues only. Using these data, figure 15.2 shows that, in 41 of the 49 states, bonds issued in

Table 15.6 TAX-EXEMPT PRIVATE-ACTIVITY BONDS ISSUED IN 1989: BY STATE BY TYPE OF ACTIVITY ($ MILLIONS)

	Mortgage Revenue	Student Loans	Small Issues	Multi-family	Qualified Re-development	Furnish-ing of water	Local Furnish-ing	Hazard-ous Waste	Sewage Disposal	Solid Waste	Private Use	Other	Total
AK	77.2	31.2											108.4 AK
AZ	96.2	25.0	21.7	8.1									151.0 AZ
AR	50.0	50.0	78.7			2.0				46.7			227.4 AR
CA	642.4		151.3	467.7					147.0				1408.4 CA
CO	101.5	80.2	23.5	6.7									211.8 CO
CT	184.0		17.4	52.0						55.3		4.0	312.7 CT
DE	85.4		12.0				20.0						117.4 DE
FL	419.2		67.1	201.1					29.0	523.9	67.1	26.5	1333.9 FL
GA	92.1		164.7	27.2					87.0		10.1		381.1 GA
HI				120.1									120.1 HI
ID	147.9		31.2										179.1 ID
IL	104.6	85.1	63.0	10.0				16.0	31.9				310.6 IL
IN		50.0	170.8	0.6		40.5	23.5	20.0					305.3 IN
IA	99.0		48.2						1.3		3.2	16.3	168.1 IA
KS	104.9		36.0					7.8					148.7 KS
KY	119.0		119.0										119.0 KY
LA	159.0	75.0	12.5	1.0									247.5 LA
ME	24.5		37.2										81.9 ME
MD	129.7		32.9	20.2		20.0			0.7				183.3 MD

continued

Table 15.6 TAX-EXEMPT PRIVATE-ACTIVITY BONDS ISSUED IN 1989: BY STATE BY TYPE OF ACTIVITY ($ MILLIONS)
(continued)

	Mortgage Revenue	Student Loans	Small Issues	Multi-family	Qualified Re-development	Furnishing of water	Local Furnishing	Hazardous Waste	Sewage Disposal	Solid Waste	Private Use	Other	Total
MA	59.0	30.0	43.0	108.5				2.5				6.0	246.5
MI	69.9		240.4	14.9					22.9	5.0		224.9	581.5
MN	94.7		90.4	17.1					18.9			0.5	221.7
MS	52.4		60.8							21.5			134.7
MO	215.0	8.7	98.7	19.6									341.9
MT	25.0	105.8								65.0			195.8
NE	1.5	8.0	18.5										28.0
NV	73.0		22.6	6.1			75.0						176.7
NH	150.4		10.6	12.5		1.6				90.3		84.3	349.7
NJ	268.0		112.0		30.5	25.6				275.0	20.0		731.1
NM	35.0		18.0				2.2						55.2
NY	200.0		213.1	64.3	7.1	20.0	350		79.2	9.4		9.9	952.7
NC	106.0		163.0			12.0				124.0			405.0
ND	100.0	100.0		0.9			59.4			50.9			311.2
OH	462.2	65.3	217.2		10.0	0.8	47.5		4.2				771.3
OK	119.6	9.0	37.3					6.2					172.1
OR	69.9		55.1	7.0		5.4						0.3	137.7
PA	113.0		113.0	4.0						150.0			380.0
RI	19.5		8.4										27.9
SC		47.2	147.3										194.5
SD		224.0									7.4		231.4

TN	141.0		122.3					7.0			28.0		298.2 TN
TX	349.0	197.0	32.0	1.0				25.0		200.0		45.0	857.0 TX
UT	89.9		8.6	18.9	25.0	34.0	18.8						168.3 UT
VT	111.4	24.0	5.0										135.3 VT
VA	49.2		98.1		100.0		12.0			15.0			286.3 VA
WA	63.7		68.8	12.4									156.8 WA
WV			11.1	50.0			168.9						230.0 WV
WI	71.5		125.2	40.1							0.7		237.5 WI
WY	14.8	35.0											49.8 WY
U.S.	5606.2	1250.4	3227.6	1291.9	172.6	161.8	777.0	84.5	422.2	1633.0	136.5	417.8	15181.5 US

Source: ACIR–Urban Institute Private-Activity Bond Survey, 1989.

Note: "Other" in this table includes the following categories from table 15.4: mass-commuting vehicles, local district heating and cooling, high-speed rail transit, takeover of investor-owned utilities, pollution control, and "other."

Figure 15.1 EXEMPT PRIVATE-ACTIVITY BONDS ISSUED IN 1989 USING 1989
AND PRIOR YEARS' VOLUME CAP AUTHORITY: RANKED BY
VOLUME OF ISSUES USING 1989 AUTHORITY

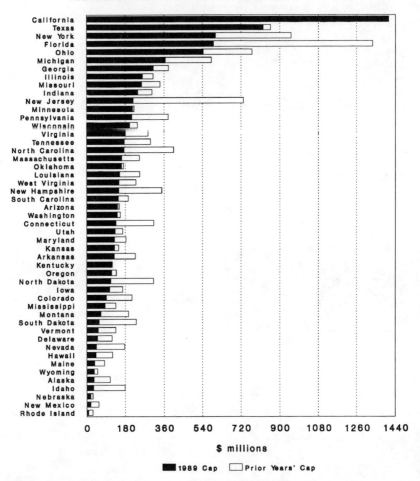

Source: ACIR–Urban Institute Private-Activity Bond Survey, 1989.

1989 that were subject to the 1989 volume cap did not use all of the
volume cap.[4] The unused share of volume cap ranged from 94.4
percent in Rhode Island to 1.9 percent in Texas. These shares represent each state's 1989 volume cap that has been carried forward
to finance bond issuance through 1992. Total unused 1989 volume
cap for these 41 states amounted to $3.741 billion—36.3 percent of

Figure 15.2 PERCENTAGE OF 1989 PRIVATE-ACTIVITY VOLUME CAP NOT
USED IN 1989 BY BONDS CLAIMING 1989 AUTHORITY

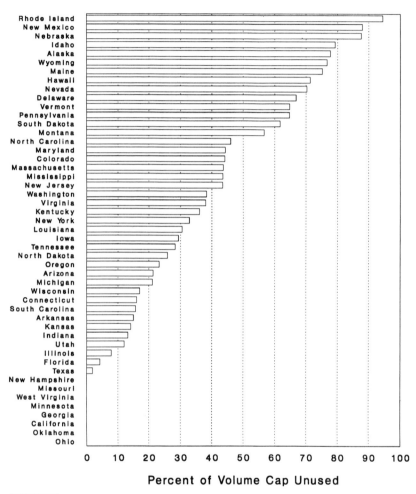

Percent of Volume Cap Unused

Source: ACIR–Urban Institute Private-Activity Bond Survey, 1989.

their volume cap and 27.7 percent of the volume cap available to all
49 states.

Unused Volume Cap and Carry-forward Authority

These numbers probably represent an upper bound on unused 1989
volume cap authority. Some of the projects funded in 1989 with

unused prior years' volume cap would have been funded with 1989 volume cap had the carry-forward authority not existed. This 1989 issuance from carry-forward authority can be used to set a lower bound on excess 1989 volume cap. Suppose that no carry-forward of unused prior years' volume cap existed, and that all projects funded with carry-forward authority requested allocations from the 1989 volume cap. Unused volume cap would then equal the 1989 volume cap minus all private-activity bonds issued in 1989. Figure 15.3 uses this estimate of unused cap to calculate for each state the percentage of volume cap that would have been unused in 1989.

States whose volume cap would not have been exhausted if all of their 1989 tax-exempt private-activity bond issues (under cap authority from 1986 through 1989) had been funded from the 1989 cap decrease in number from 41 (figure 15.2) to 20 (figure 15.3). Rhode Island again has the greatest share unutilized, 81.4 percent. The average unused cap for all states declines from $91.2 million to $57.7 million. The total dollar value of unused cap decreases by more than two-thirds, to $1.154 billion from the $3.741 billion when only issues using 1989 cap authority were included. This unused cap represents 28.4 percent of the cap available to these 20 states, and only 8.5 percent of the cap available to all 49 states.

Unused Volume Cap and Spending Priorities

The true picture of volume cap utilization probably lies somewhere between the data summarized in figures 15.2 and 15.3. It is clear that, as of 1989, the use of private-activity bond issues (constrained to those activities allowed by law) fell short of volume cap availability in some states.

Two other factors should be considered when assessing the extent to which unused volume cap exists in any given year. First, as noted in tables 15.2 and 15.3, most states establish priorities by allocating set shares of the cap for state versus local governments and for selected activities. These shares are reserved for those governments and activities for a portion of the year, ranging from 9 to 11 months, after which any unused cap allocation usually becomes available for all types of exempt activities for any issuer. This is a relatively short planning horizon, which undoubtedly frustrates some efforts to take advantage of the unutilized capacity that crops up at the end of the year. Absent these reserved set asides, some of this unused volume cap probably would have been used in 1989, so that the unused

Figure 15.3 PERCENTAGE OF 1989 PRIVATE-ACTIVITY VOLUME CAP NOT
USED IN 1989 BY BONDS CLAIMING 1989 OR PRIOR YEARS' CAP
AUTHORITY

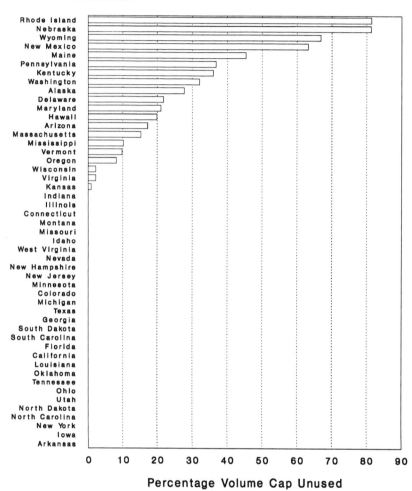

Percentage Volume Cap Unused

Source: ACIR–Urban Institute Private-Activity Bond Survey, 1989.

volume cap supply suggested in figure 15.2 would be overstated.
Second, states must elect the activity on which to spend unused
volume cap at the time it is carried forward. It is possible that some
of this available carry-forward authority was not used in 1989 because the state's carry-forward election did not conform to the activities for which it needed the authority in 1989.

The last column of table 15.7 contains the total number of states with unused volume cap and the amount of their unused volume cap. The top half of the table is based on 1989 issues using 1989 cap authority. In the column labeled "Thirty," suppose that up to 30 percent of unused volume cap were attributable entirely to the short planning horizons that are the inevitable side effect of establishing spending priorities; that is, the desire to use exempt private-activity bond financing was actually 30 percent higher during 1989 than actual issues. If it is assumed that, with better planning or a more flexible allocation system, this unused cap would otherwise have been used, the number of states with unused caps would decline from 41 to 25 (eliminating the 16 states whose unused cap was less than 30 percent). The dollar value of unused cap would decline from $3.741 to $2.618 billion (calculated as 70 percent of total unused cap in the last column, since the 30 percent planning penalty also applies to the states with unused caps above 30 percent). Now look at the column labeled "Ten." If 10 percent is considered to be a more reasonable threshold for the amount of activity inhibited by the bond

Table 15.7 NUMBER OF STATES WITH UNUSED VOLUME CAP AND TOTAL UNUSED VOLUME CAP AFTER ADJUSTMENT FOR SHORT PLANNING HORIZON AND IRREVOCABLE CARRY-FORWARD ELECTION ($ MILLION)

	Percentage of Volume Cap Adjusted			Total for States with Unused Cap
	Ten	Twenty	Thirty	
Calculated using 1989 authority				
Number states	38	31	25	41
Dollars of unused cap—adjusted for short planning horizon	3366.6	2992.6	2618.5	3740.7
Calculated using 1989 + carry-forward authority				
Number states	15	11	8	20
Dollars of unused cap—adjusted for short planning horizon and carry-forward election	1038.8	0.923	0.808	1154.2

Source: ACIR-Urban Institute Private-Activity Bond Survey, 1989.

allocation priorities, the number of states with unused cap would decline only to 38 (eliminating the three states whose unused cap was less than 10 percent). Unused cap would decline only to $3.367 billion (calculated as 90 percent of total unused cap in the last column).

The second panel of table 15.7 repeats these calculations using the same method employed for figure 15.3—unused volume cap based on all 1989 issues, whatever the source of their volume cap authority. In this case, the source of the frustrated use of volume cap is both the short planning horizon and the requirement to make an irrevocable election of private-activity use at the time unused cap was carried forward. If 30 percent of the unused cap is attributable to these factors, the number of states with unused cap would decline from 20 to 8 and the dollar value of unused cap would decline from $1.154 billion to $808 million. If 10 percent is considered to be a more reasonable threshold, the number of states with unused cap would decline only to 15 and the unused cap would decline only to $1.039 billion.

Volume Caps and the $150 Million Cap for Small States

It is possible that this picture of unused volume cap is somewhat skewed by the special treatment the 1986 act provided for small states, which are guaranteed at least $150 million of volume cap even if the product of $50 times their population produced a smaller cap allocation. If the demand for tax-exempt private-activity bond usage is a constant function of population, as is implied by the per capita allocation applied to most states, these small states would be expected to have a greater amount of unused volume cap on average than would other states. Indeed, this turns out to be the case.

Table 15.8 decomposes the unused volume cap data by type of cap allocation—per capita and $150 million. The first four columns of the first row array the states with unused volume cap by the percentage of volume cap unused. Columns 6 and 7 record the number of states with unused cap and all states. The last two rows separate the states into those with a per capita volume cap and those with a $150 million cap. Forty-one of the 49 states have unused volume cap. Of the per capita allocation states, 21 of the 27 have unused volume cap. Eleven of these 21 states have unused capacity that exceeds 30 percent of the volume cap (52.3 percent of per capita states with unused cap). Eighteen have unused capacity that exceeds 10 percent of the volume cap.

Table 15.8 STATES WITH UNUSED VOLUME CAP IN 1989 ARRAYED BY TYPED
OF CAP ALLOCATION: NUMBER OF STATES AND PERCENTAGE OF
CAP UNUSED

	Percentage of Volume Cap Unsued				Total States with Unused Cap	All States	Percentage of Cap Unused
	< 10	10 to 20	20 to 30	> 30			
States with unused cap	3	7	6	25	41	49	36.3
Per capita allocation	3	4	3	11	21	27	27.9
$150 million allocation	0	3	3	14	20	22	56.7

Source: ACIR–Urban Institute Private-Activity Bond Survey, 1989.

Of the 22 states with a $150 million cap, 20 have unused borrowing authority. Fourteen of these 20 have unused borrowing authority that exceeds 30 percent of the cap (70 percent of $150 million states with unused cap). All 20 states have unused capacity that exceeds 10 percent of the volume cap.

The last column of table 15.8 presents the average percentage of unused volume cap for states with unused volume cap. The 36.3 percent unused cap for all 41 states overstates the magnitude of the unused volume cap for those states receiving a per capita allocation. When disaggregated by type of allocation, the unused volume cap share for the 20 states with a $150 million allocation, 56.7 percent, is double the 27.9 percent share for the 21 states with a per capita allocation.

DENIED OR DELAYED PROJECTS

States were asked about requests for volume cap allocations that had to be denied or delayed to a subsequent year owing to unavailability of volume cap. Respondents in a few states were questioned about the methodology and procedures used in preparing the numbers. The answers to these queries indicated two things: (1) states excluded from the data projects unlikely to be funded no matter how much funding was available; and (2) projects not even proposed to the bond allocation agency because of prior knowledge of inadequate volume cap are not included in these data—nobody seemed to have a good feel for their magnitude. Nonetheless, these are undoubtedly the least reliable data from the survey.

Twenty-seven states reported the existence of denied or delayed projects. The first column of table 15.9 to the right of the stub lists $6.015 billion of such projects by type of activity. The largest amounts were $2.147 billion for mortgage revenue bonds and $2.109 billion for solid waste disposal. The amount for the next largest activity, small issues, was considerably smaller at $518.5 million.

The next four columns in table 15.9 divide these amounts between states using all their volume cap and those reporting unused volume cap. Columns 3 and 4 are based on unused volume cap calculated using only 1989 authority (see figure 15.2). States that did not use all their volume cap account for 62.9 percent of these denied or delayed projects ($3.783 billion), and they account for more than 50 percent of it in all but 4 of the 11 categories for which unsatisfied

Table 15.9 DENIED OR DELAYED REQUESTS FOR VOLUME CAP IN 1989, DIVIDED BETWEEN STATES REPORTING EXHAUSTED AND UNUSED VOLUME CAP ($ MILLION)

| | | Unused Cap Status of States | | | |
| | | Calculated Using 1989 Authority | | Calculated Using 1986–89 Authority | |
Private Activity	Excess Demand ($)	All Used (%)	Some Unused (%)	All Used (%)	Some Unused (%)
Mortgage revenue bonds	2146.9	64.3	35.7	82.5	17.5
Student loans	404.0	0.0	100.0	28.5	71.5
Small issues	518.5	28.2	71.8	83.1	16.9
Solid waste disposal	2109.0	22.5	77.5	56.7	43.3
Multifamily housing	222.8	59.6	40.4	72.8	27.2
Qualified redevelopment	20.0	0.0	100.0	100.0	0.0
Furnishing of water	157.1	0.0	100.0	89.8	10.2
Local furnishing of electricity/gas	315.6	0.0	100.0	50.6	49.4
Hazardous waste disposal	8.0	0.0	100.0	100.0	0.0
Sewage disposal	112.3	89.1	10.9	100.0	0.0
Private-use portion	0.5	100.0	0.0	100.0	0.0
Total	6014.7	37.1	62.9	68.5	31.5

Source: ACIR–Urban Institute Private-Activity Bond Survey, 1989.

allocations are reported. The last two columns of the table are based on unused volume cap calculated using both 1989 and prior years' carry-forward authority (see figure 15.3). The share of denied or delayed projects reported by states that have not used all their volume cap declines to a still hefty 31.5 percent ($1.895 billion), but now these states account for more than 50 percent of unallocated projects in only one category (student loans).

How can it be that somewhere between $3.783 and $1.895 billion of denied or delayed tax-exempt private-activity bond financing exists in states that have between $3.741 and $1.154 billion of unused volume cap available for funding? Several explanations come to mind, First, the survey is an imperfect instrument for collecting data. Some of the states undoubtedly overreported excess demand by assigning projects to 1989 that might not have been ready for funding until 1990, or by including some projects that might not have been eligible for the tax exemption, or simply by making unrealistically high estimates.

Second, the states' priority systems and the need to make irrevocable elections for the use of unused volume cap at the time of carry-forward often make it difficult to switch unused volume cap from one level of government or activity whose priority allocation is high compared to demand for financing to another level of government or activity whose priority allocation either was too low or nonexistent. Third, some of the unused volume cap from priority allocations is actually pledged as a carry-forward to high-ranking projects whose timing did not quite coincide with the allocation cycle. As a result, less-preferred projects get rejected. It is not clear why the less-preferred projects did not receive the 1989 allocation and the most-preferred simply got assigned part of the 1990 allocation. It may be that projects that take a long time to develop, such as a resource recovery plant, seek a pledge of current-year cap in the initial phase of development planning that will then be carried forward to be used some time during the next three years.

STATE SUGGESTIONS FOR REFORM OF THE VOLUME CAP

The states were asked if they had suggestions for improving the way in which the volume cap functions. They were not asked whether the volume cap should be retained. Responses were received from 22 states. These responses focused on the following issues.

Problems with Cap Allocation among States

Concern was expressed that the allocation of the volume cap among the states is unfair. The cap is allocated by population (except for the small states that receive $150 million). It was noted that the distribution of demand for the various private activities included under the cap is affected by factors in addition to population. Mortgage revenue bonds were cited as an example—states with high housing costs cannot provide as much housing for a given population as states with low housing costs. It was suggested that the cap formula be adjusted to take economic and demographic factors into account.

Problems with Sunset

The continual debate over sunset of mortgage revenue bonds and small-issue IDBs has caused allocation problems. Survey respondents claimed that the uncertainty created by postdated sunsets causes demand that would have been expressed some time after the sunset date to be accelerated and expressed in the year prior to the sunset date, creating problems in the allocation of the volume cap. With many states having assigned a fixed proportion of the cap to small issues and mortgage revenue bonds, this forces projects for other activities to do without an allocation until a later year.

Problems with Carry-forward

It was suggested that the way carry-forwards are handled should be changed. Requiring carry-forwards to be allocated to a particular issuer or activity reduces the state's flexibility to adjust to annual changes in demand among eligible activities. Respondents suggested that the carry-forward should reside with the state administering agency without allocation to specific users or activities, thereby increasing flexibility. Another respondent also claimed that the time frame for reporting to IRS on the allocation of the carry-forward was too short.

Problems with Activity Definition

The major concern in this area is investment for environmental and conservation purposes. Many states believe that activities such as solid waste disposal, hazardous waste disposal, sewage treatment plants, and similar facilities that are not governmentally owned should not be included in the volume cap, because they have a large component of public consumption no matter the form of ownership employed. They report substantial backlogs of projects in this area, and expect the backlog to continue to grow at a rapid rate. One state expressed concern that should mortgage revenue bonds and small-issue IDBs ever be allowed to sunset, the volume cap might be reduced. It was suggested that this cap will be needed to fund these rapidly growing environmental and conservation projects.

Two other suggestions were related to environmental issues. One proposed that pollution control bonds should again be made an exempt activity. Another complained that the restriction of land acquisition costs to 25 percent of bond proceeds is too low for some projects such as sanitary landfills.

Several small and primarily rural and agricultural states suggested that restriction of the eligibility for small-issue IDBs to manufacturing facilities is unfair. Since these states have little in the way of manufacturing, the economic engines of their states receive little of this low-cost debt financing. They wonder what is so magical about manufacturing activity. In contrast, a large urban state suggested that the restriction of small issues to manufacturing was most desirable, and should not be extended to other types of economic activity.

Another state considers the 10 percent use of proceeds and security interest tests to be unrealistic with respect to the presence of public benefits. This state feels that governmental bonds should be allowed to have more than 10 percent private use and security interest.

Miscellaneous Suggestions

Although responses seemed to indicate some acceptance of the need for the federal government to set a cap on private-activity bond volume, no such positive views were expressed about the second part of the volume cap program—the creation of a list of exempt activities to be included under the cap. It was suggested that the list be eliminated, thereby allowing the states to determine the activities on which to allocate the cap.

One state objected not so much to the adoption of a volume cap, but, rather, to the administrative costs of complying it. It considers the cap to be one more example of mandates imposed by the federal government without compensation to help implement the federal goals.

CONCLUSIONS

As of 1989, the volume cap has succeeded in reducing private-activity bond volume by two thirds relative to the volume issued in 1984–86. Responsibility for allocating this reduced bond volume is spread among a diverse assortment of state agencies, ranging from governors' offices to specially created bond allocation committees. The majority of states have created set-asides for local governments and for favored exempt activities.

The volume cap appears to be sufficiently large (or the list of exempt activities has been sufficiently restricted) that unused volume cap is available in 41 of the 49 states in the survey, and amounted to 36.3 percent of their available volume cap. This masks considerable variation between the large states, whose volume cap is determined on a per capita basis, and the small states, whose volume cap is set at $150 million. Twenty of the 22 small states in the survey reported unused cap, while 21 of the 27 large states reported unused cap. The average share of unused cap was much higher in the small states, averaging 56.7 percent compared to 27.9 percent for the large states. These estimates of unused cap would be lower if the bond issues financed from volume cap carried forward from prior years represent demand that would otherwise have been financed out of the 1989 cap. If all of these carry-forward financings represent 1989 demand, the number of states with unused volume cap would have declined to 20, with unused volume cap equal to 28.4 percent of the cap.

In spite of the prevalence of unused cap, the states reported excess demand for financing a variety of exempt activities. A considerable portion of this demand was reported by states that also reported unused 1989 volume cap. To some extent, this may reflect the difficulties of making rapid transfers of unused cap between levels of government and among exempt activities that had received priority allocations, as well as the requirement for making an irrevocable election about the activity to be financed at the time of carry-forward. It may also reflect a desire to allow high-priority projects whose timing does not quite coincide with the calendar year accounting for the volume cap to carry a current-year allocation forward, rather than reassign the unused volume cap to a lower priority project and make the higher priority project return for a new allocation the next year.

The states had several suggestions for changing the operation of the volume cap. These included allocating the volume cap among the states with criteria that reflect need more accurately than does population; removing projects that foster environmental objectives from the cap; making a final decision on small-issue and mortgage revenue bonds; allowing the carry-forward allocations to remain with the state for future allocation; and enabling small rural states to use small issues for a broader range of activities than manufacturing.

The results of this survey suggest several things. First, adding new activities to the list of exempt private activities is likely to increase the federal revenue loss. Many states at the present time do not have adequate demand for the list of eligible activities to fully utilize the existing volume cap. This is particularly true for those states that receive cap allocations in excess of $50 per person residing in the state. The share of their volume cap unused is almost 57 percent, about 30 percentage points higher than for the large states receiving $50 per person.

Second, the majority of states (28) have established local set-asides from the volume cap to allay the fears of the local governments that adoption of a state-administered system would deny them a fair share of allowable private-activity bond volume. In most of the remaining 21 states, projects are awarded volume cap based upon a first-come first-served basis, with no hint in the administrative guidelines of state preference. The suggestions for reform included none for federally mandated local shares, but since the survey was completed by state officials, any such desires that may exist are unlikely to have been represented.

Finally, single-family housing and small-issue IDBs seem to be the activities most likely to receive priority volume cap allocations. If these two activities are allowed to sunset in September 1990 as provided in current law, it would seem to be an opportune time to consider at least two options. The first option is appealing only to federal policymakers. The size of the volume cap could be reduced with a resulting reduction in the long-term potential for federal revenue loss. The volume of issues in 1989 indicates that demand (as constrained by tax law) is likely to fall far short of the current cap levels for quite some time, particularly without the demand from users of mortgage revenue bonds and small-issue IDBs.

If that option is not feasible or desirable, it might be the time to reallocate any volume cap vacated by mortgage revenue bonds and small-issue IDBs, probably to environmentally oriented projects. This would have four advantages: (1) such projects do have a substantial element of collective consumption that meets this text's criterion for federal subsidy (spillovers across jurisdictions), unlike small-issue IDBs; (2) the federal subsidy would be redirected to state and local infrastructure, unlike housing and the private capital formation stimulated by small-issue IDBs, and, it is hoped, would help to arrest the slide in the nation's productivity; (3) state and local officials are likely to be supportive of (or less hostile to) such a change, since they seem to sense a substantial increased demand in the environmental area; and (4) it would constitute a positive federal response to state and local complaints about the imposition of federal mandates (including in the environmental area) without any corresponding federal financial support.

Notes

1. Because some U.S. possessions have such small populations, the allocation of those with populations less than the least populous state are restricted to the per capita amount actually received by the least populous state.

2. Nongovernmentally owned airports, docks, and wharves were subject to the volume cap in 1989, but table 15.3 indicates that no bonds were issued for these purposes in 1989.

3. Arbitrage bonds are issued primarily to generate interest earnings rather than to build capital facilities. The proceeds of the bond issue are invested by the state or local government in taxable securities that earn a higher yield than the tax-exempt yield that must be paid by the state or local government on its tax-exempt bonds. Arbitrage bonds were first restricted in 1969, and were subjected to increasingly more comprehensive rebate requirements beginning in 1984 (and modified in 1989). An account of the multifamily housing arbitrage deals that occurred prior to the Tax Reform Act of 1986 is available in numerous issues of the *Daily Bond Buyer* from 1987 through 1989.

4. Any state that had less than $500,000 of volume cap remaining was considered to have exhausted its cap.

PRIVATE-ACTIVITY BONDS

Table 15A.1 PRIVATE-ACTIVITY BONDS

SURVEY OF STATE EXPERIENCE WITH PRIVATE-ACTIVITY BOND VOLUME CAP

For purposes of follow-up, please provide the name and phone number of the person completing the survey:

Name: _____

Phone number: (   ) _____

I. RULES TO ALLOCATE THE VOLUME CAP

According to federal law, bonds that pass nongovernmental (private) use and security interest tests are taxable unless the activity being financed is on a list of exempt activities. Most of these exempt activities are subject to a volume cap. Each state's exempt private-activity bond volume is to be allocated among the various governmental units within the state that are authorized to issue tax-exempt private-activity bonds. This allocation can either be done via the statutory method dictated by the federal government (one-half of the bond volume to the state and its agencies and one-half to local governmental units having bond issuing authority) or by state legislation that can allocate the volume cap in any way desired.

A. What agency administers the allocation of the volume cap in your state?
B. What rule is used to allocate the share of the volume cap dedicated to the state and its agencies versus the share dedicated to local governmental units having issuing authority? (If a statute, handbook, or document describing the rules is available, a copy would be sufficient.)
C. What rules are used to allocate the volume cap among the eligible private activities? (If a statute, handbook, or document describing the rules is available, a copy would be sufficient.)

II. AMOUNT TO BE ALLOCATED

A. What was the 1989 volume cap for allocation within your state?
B. According to federal law, all private-activity bonds issued in 1989 are subject to the 1989 volume cap except for: (1) those private-

activity bonds issued in 1989 that utilized unused volume cap
carried forward from any of the three preceding years; and (2)
501(c)(3) bonds (for nonprofit organizations), veterans' mortgages, and governmentally owned airports, docks, wharves, and
solid waste disposal facilities. In addition, the private-use portion
(in excess of $15 million) of governmental bonds for output fa-
cilities is also subject to the cap.

1. What was the *total volume of private-activity bonds* issued
   within your state in 1989 subject to the volume cap? (*Include*
   in this total those bonds issued under 1989 volume cap authority, those issued under unused volume cap carried forward from previous years, and the private-use portion of
   governmental bonds; *do not* include in this total bonds issued
   for nonprofit organizations, veterans' mortgages, and governmentally owned airports, docks, wharves, and solid waste disposal facilities.)
2. What was the total volume of private-activity bonds issued
   within your state in 1989 *based upon carry-forward authority*
   (using unused volume cap borrowing authority carried forward from previous years)?
3. If you have such information, what was the total volume of
   private activity bonds issued within your state in 1989 for
   nonprofit organizations, veterans' mortgages, and governmentally owned airports, docks, wharves, and solid waste disposal
   facilities?

III. BREAKDOWN BY TYPE OF ACTIVITY

Please complete the accompanying private-activity bond volume table. The list includes all activities classified as exempt private activities by the Tax Reform Act of 1986 and subsequent additions to
the list, even those few private activities that are not subject to the
volume cap. Note that the sum of the numbers entered in column
(1) for private activities subject to the volume cap should equal the
number entered in question II.B.1. Columns (2) and (3) separate bonds
reported in question II.B.1 between those issued under the 1989 cap
allocation from those issued under prior years' cap allocations that
have been carried forward. The sum of column (3) for activities
included in the cap should equal the number you recorded in question II.B.2. The sum of the numbers you record in column (4) for
private activities not included in the cap should equal the number
you recorded in question II.B.3.

Example: Suppose $100 million of bonds were issued for nonprofit organizations (501(c)(3)s). For the "nonprofit organizations" category, enter $100 million in column 4.

Example: Suppose $100 million of bonds were issued for multifamily rental housing during 1989, of which $24 million was from carry-forward authority. Enter $100 million in column 1, $76 million in column 2, and $24 million in column 3.

Example: Suppose $2 billion of *governmental* bonds were issued, and $75 million of the proceeds were used for *private* purposes under the 10 percent rule. Enter $75 million in column 1 and $75 million in column 2.

Note: A string of Xs indicates "not relevant" for that private activity.

Private-Activity Bond Volume in 1989
(enter numbers in $ millions)

Activity	(1) Total volume	(2) 1989 Authority Included in Cap	(3) Carry-Forward Authority	(4) Private Activity but Excluded from Cap
Under Volume Cap:				
Qualified mortgage revenue				XXXXXXXXX
Student loans				XXXXXXXXX
Small-issues				XXXXXXXXX
Multifamily rental housing				XXXXXXXXX
Qualified redevelopment				XXXXXXXXX
Mass commuting				XXXXXXXXX
Furnishing of water				XXXXXXXXX
Local furnishing of electricity and gas				XXXXXXXXX
Local district heating and cooling				XXXXXXXXX
Hazardous waste disposal				XXXXXXXXX
Sewage disposal				XXXXXXXXX
Airports, docks, wharves, solid waste				
Takeover of investor-owned utilities				XXXXXXXXX
High-speed intercity rail transit				XXXXXXXXX
Private use portion of governmental bonds			XXXXXXXXX	XXXXXXXXX
Not Subject to Cap:				
Veterans' mortgages	XXXXXXX	XXXXXXXXX	XXXXXXXXX	
Nonprofit organizations	XXXXXX	XXXXXXXXX	XXXXXXXXX	

IV. DEMAND FOR PRIVATE-ACTIVITY BONDS

Did you have to deny or delay requests for bond issues due to insufficient volume cap? Yes _____ No _____ . If you did, please list the volume of bonds affected by private-activity category. If you have reason to believe these numbers understate demand (for example, if knowledge of exhausted volume caps kept issuers from requesting allocations), please make a note of this understatement beside the numbers entered.

Activity	Volume Denied or Delayed
Qualified mortgage revenue bond	
Veterans'mortgage bonds (has its own cap)	_____
Student loans	_____
Small-issues	_____
Airports, docks, wharves	_____
Solid waste disposal	_____
Multifamily rental housing	_____
Qualified redevelopment	_____
Mass commuting	_____
Furnishing of water	_____
Local furnishing of electricity and gas	_____
Local district heating and cooling	_____
Hazardous waste disposal	_____
Sewage disposal	_____
Takeover of investor-owned utilities	_____
High-speed intercity rail transit	_____
Private-use portion of governmental bonds	_____

Questions V and VI elicit opinions about what may occur with respect to the volume and allocation of the private-activity bond cap in your state, as well as solicit suggestions for federal government policy changes. If a different office or agency in the state is responsible for such issues, please do not hesitate to share this survey with them.

V. LOOKING AHEAD

A. How do you expect 1990 volume to compare to 1989 volume?

B. Do you expect to consider a change in allocation method or priorities? If so, please describe the options being considered.

VI. SUGGESTIONS FOR CHANGE

Please provide any suggestions you may have for restructuring the cap at the federal level (e.g., size of the cap, activities to be deleted from the cap or added to the cap, etc). Please note that any discussion of these suggestions in the survey results will maintain respondent anonymity.

Chapter Sixteen

ALTERNATIVE POLICIES: REDEFINING PUBLIC PURPOSE AND THE VOLUME CAP

The *South Carolina* decision (see chapter 3) made it clear that the federal government possesses the authority to tax state and local bonds, or, to put this thought in a more realistic policy context, to deny tax exemption for some activities state and local governments hold dear. This decision removed the threat of a constitutional roll-back of some or all of the bond legislation adopted in the last 20 years that taxes some state and local bonds. An opportunity is presented to rethink the existing approach to limiting tax-exempt bond volume and preventing abusive uses of bond proceeds, an approach that amounts to taxing some state and local debt. The current rules have evolved in a series of ad hoc steps over the past 20 years. Quite possibly, a fresh approach would satisfy federal policy concerns as well as enhance the ability of state and local officials to finance capital expenditures that benefit not only their own constituents but also serve broader national interests.

This chapter uses the insights gained from the earlier parts of this book to discuss alternative approaches to controlling bond volume and allocating the volume cap.

DEFINING PUBLIC PURPOSE

Discussion in earlier parts of this book has suggested several things about the private business test. The first part of the test (the use of proceeds test or simply the use test) works well to identify and make ineligible for tax-exempt financing the vast bulk of private commercial and industrial activity. But because the test is not based on a theory of public interference in private markets like that outlined in chapter 5, it renders ineligible for tax-exempt financing privately owned and operated facilities, such as a jail, that might pass muster for a federal capital subsidy on theoretical grounds. Conversely, as discussed in chapter 14, it renders eligible for tax-exempt financing municipally owned and operated facilities, such as those for providing electricity, that might not pass muster. State and local officials have complained about the restrictions of the private-business use test, arguing that it prevents "privatization" arrangements that allow public services to be provided at least cost. Not much attention is given to the permissiveness of present law, which puts no limits on federal subsidies for what might be called municipal socialism.

The second part of the private-business test (the security interest test) implies that state and local taxpayers are required to assume financial responsibility for projects that do not meet the test and that such responsibility is a precondition for issuance of tax-exempt bonds. This is not the case. Many projects that do not involve private business use are financed with revenue bonds where debt service is paid only from user fees. If the fees prove to be inadequate, bondholders rather than taxpayers are at risk. Thus, the private-business test seems deficient on two grounds. First, it hampers legitimate public-private partnerships. Second, it encourages excessive issuance of bonds in cases where local citizens would not support their issuance but for the indirect interest subsidy.

Scant attention has been devoted to the search for alternative mechanisms that would work better from both a federal and a state-local perspective? I am aware of only two discussions of alternative definitional approaches, plus the existence of several bills introduced in the 101st Congress.

The Anthony Commission on Public Finance

The bond community's unhappiness with the bond provisions of the Tax Reform Act of 1986 found expression through the Anthony Commission on Public Finance, a group formed by Congressman Beryl Anthony of Arkansas, a member of the House Committee on Ways and Means. The commission was established in 1987

... to (1) consider the effect of the current federal tax law on the ability of state and local governments to carry out their responsibilities to their citizens and (2) recommend appropriate changes in that law consistent with both financial prudence and the respective rights of the national, state and local governments in our federal system. (Anthony Commission on Public Finance 1989, 1)

The commission members consisted of "governors, mayors, county officials, state treasurers, other government officials and other experts involved in tax-exempt financing." These "other experts" were representatives of the underwriting and bond counsel communities, and did not include any public finance or tax economists.

A major part of the Anthony Commission's final report, issued in October 1989, dealt with recommendations for an alternative definition of public purpose. The report's primary concern was that the current rules unnecessarily discourage private participation in providing public service when that private participation would result in more efficient (less costly) provision of public services. In other words, the current rules discourage public/private partnerships. It recommended that two broad categories of tax-exempt bonds be created: public-purpose bonds and private-activity bonds.

A facility would be classified as public-purpose if it is governmentally owned and operated or, if privately provided and privately managed, the primary benefits accrue to the community as a whole rather than to private parties. Thus, we can see right away that the commission wants certain types of bonds now classified as private-activity bonds to be reclassified as governmental bonds. Rutledge (1990) emphasized the importance of this reclassification by noting that "miscategorization" of governmental facilities as private activities has costly consequences, subjecting the bonds to: the alternative minimum tax; the denial of the small-issuer arbitrage rebate and bank interest deduction exceptions; the volume cap; advance refunding; and issuance cost limitations. The commission's suggested framework for accomplishing this goal involves establishing three types of public-purpose bonds: governmental bonds, public activity bonds, and exempt-purpose bonds.

Governmental Bonds

Governmental bonds would be determined by application of the current private business test (what this book refers to as the use and security interest tests). But the criteria that determine what constitutes private use would be adjusted. At present, private use results from four types of arrangements with a private person: a lease; an output purchase contract; a management or operating contract lasting longer than five years; or an ownership interest. The commission would have the Internal Revenue Service (IRS) ignore these contractual arrangements in determining eligibility for tax exemption if: the arrangements are entered into through arm's-length negotiations; private use and operation of the facility occurs at market prices; and the benefits of the tax-exempt financing that accrue to the private user are shared with the general public.

The example cited by the commission is the renting of surplus office space in a government office building to the private sector at a rate arrived at with arm's-length negotiations. Evaluating this example against the suggested framework raises two distinct problems. The first problem relates to the focus of the commission's (and the Internal Revenue Code's) concern, the possibility of private benefit from tax-exempt financing. Is the rental rate charged the private user supposed to be identical to what the private user would have paid for comparable quarters in a private building financed with taxable debt, or to a rate in a building financed with tax-exempt debt? Presumably, what is being referred to here is rental rates that incorporate taxable financing; otherwise tax benefits are being passed on to private users. But the commission's proposal is not clear on this point.

Even if the acceptable rental rate incorporates taxable financing, adoption of this approach would constitute a quantum leap in complexity. Eligibility decisions that under current law are based upon simple institutional arrangements as stated in contracts would be supplanted by an interpretation as to the reasonableness of the financial terms of those institutional arrangements. Who is to monitor what constitutes arm's-length negotiations and market rates? As the system now works, bond counsel would pass judgment as to the appropriateness of these arrangements, and lawyers are not well equipped to pass judgment on what is essentially an economic issue.[1] As discussed in chapter 12, the capacity of the Internal Revenue Service to monitor the decisions of bond counsel and enforce the economic intent of such proposed tax-exempt bond rules is limited, and the likelihood of significant additional resources being allocated to tax-exempt bond enforcement is remote. This type of change might very likely change the nature of the errors committed by the test, from errors rejecting projects for tax-exempt financing that do have a public-purpose component to errors accepting projects for tax-exempt financing that do not have a public-purpose component.[2]

Finally, what does it mean in the example involving rental of surplus office space to require that the benefits received by the private entity must be shared with the general public? If the rental rate incorporates taxable debt financing in its cost structure, there are no private benefits attributable to tax-exempt debt financing.[3] If the rental rate incorporates tax-exempt debt financing, there are private benefits attributable to tax-exempt debt financing. The only sharing going on in the latter case is that the private beneficiary and the general public share access to the same below-market-rate office building. But one would need to stretch the normal interpretation of the word "sharing" to suggest that the private beneficiary's tax benefits are being shared with the general public.

The second concern with this proposal may be more important. Even if the rental rates for the surplus office space do incorporate taxable debt financing in their determination, doesn't this type of framework open the door for what was characterized in chapter 14 as municipal socialism? What is to prevent local governments from building office space far in excess of governmental needs, renting the surplus space at market rates to the private sector in competition with the private real estate industry, and earning revenue for the general fund? Why write something into the Code that says the federal government is willing to subsidize any activity of state and local governments with low-cost debt financing, provided a market rate is charged to the users of the service?

Public-Activity Bonds

The second type of public-purpose bonds, public-activity bonds, fail at least one of the stated three criteria that determine private use for governmental bonds. These criteria are repeated here for emphasis: the arrangements are entered into through arm's length negotiations; private use and operation of the facility occur at market prices; and the benefits of the tax-exempt financing that accrue to the private user are shared with the general public. A select set of activities would remain eligible for tax-exempt financing in spite of failing these tests because they are believed to provide important benefits to the general public. These public-activity bonds would be subject to several alternative private-use criteria, the most important of which include: private owners or managers could not receive tax benefits from accelerated depreciation or investment tax credits; purchase of the facility by private managers would have to be made at fair market value; management contracts could not exceed the useful life of the facility; the facility would have to be designed to serve the general public, using current tax law criteria.

The activities mentioned by the Anthony Commission as eligible for this exemption include solid waste disposal, hazardous waste disposal, wastewater treatment and collection facilities, community development, and certain multifamily housing projects. One can discern the logic behind the commission's choice of activities. All of these activities, with the exception of community development, are ones that might reasonably be considered to have external benefits that spill over the boundaries of existing political jurisdictions. The benefits are concentrated in the environmental area or targeted to lower-income households. The commission recommends careful scrutiny of eligibility for this category to ensure meaningful public benefits.

Nonetheless, it is hard to discern the meaningful differences between the eligibility criteria for these public-activity bonds and the criteria for governmental bonds. Since the criteria only deny private users the tax benefits of accelerated depreciation and tax credits, private users presumably could receive benefits in the form of lower rental or lease payments that reflect tax-exempt rather than taxable borrowing rates, benefits that are denied to governmental bonds.

Exempt-Purpose Bonds

The third public-purpose category includes bonds issued on behalf of nonprofit organizations, the section 501(c)(3) organizations. The commission believes that these organizations do not need to satisfy the government ownership and operation criteria, since they provide services that governments would otherwise have to provide. In effect, if bonds issued on behalf of these organizations do not satisfy a public purpose, the problem is with the part of the code dealing with charitable organizations rather than the tax-exempt bond rules.

Projects that do not qualify under one of the three categories of public-purpose bonds would be classified as a private activity. In general, these projects would be characterized by private ownership and operation that realize some of the tax benefits of ownership. No expansion of the current list of activities that qualify as exempt private activities is advocated, and all other restrictions would remain in effect, including targeting restrictions and the volume cap.

Requiring Financial Responsibility

An entirely different approach to defining public purpose was suggested by Zimmerman (1987). He discussed the possibility of substituting a meaningful financial responsibility requirement for the private business test. First, all bonds issued by state and local governments (or their duly created agencies or authorities) that guarantee state and local government financial responsibility for debt service would be tax exempt. These bonds could be labeled either general obligation (GO) or revenue bonds, so long as a revenue stream inadequate to service the bonds triggered state and local government payment from their own resources, including tax revenue if necessary. Second, all bonds assuming such financial responsibility would be free of any restrictions on types of activities and on who uses the proceeds.

This alternative formulation gives something to and takes something away from both the federal and state-local governments. First, in exchange for state and local governments placing their tax base at risk for what they regard as public-purpose projects, these governments are given the right to define public purpose and provide public services in what they consider to be the most efficient manner, which might well include private provision. Second, in exchange for the federal government's withdrawal from defining public purpose and specifying who can use bond proceeds, the federal government knows that state and local taxpayers must balance the risk of future potential tax payments with the benefits they expect to obtain from bond issues.

The proposal has three major problems, one institutional in nature, one economic, and one practical. The institutional problem concerns the prevalence of state constitutional and statutory restrictions on the issuance of general obligation debt. The tables 2A.1 and 2A.2 in the appendix to chapter 2 indicate that in 1986, 40 states limited state borrowing in some manner beyond requiring that each bond issue receive legislative approval; and every state imposed some restriction on local governments, most often in the form of a ceiling as a percentage of property values or as a requirement that capital facilities be built with the proceeds. These limitations would have to be changed before more bonds backed by tax revenues could be issued. Resistance to changing these limitations is likely to be considerable. In fact, the limitations are at least in part responsible for the development of the revenue bond, whose use in many jurisdictions was a response to debt limit levels that were inadequate to enable issuance of bonds even for some traditional infrastructure. Although caution is called for when changing the rules of the game, consideration of such a federal policy change should not be precluded by current institutional arrangements.

The point of this proposal is, after all, to require state and local governments to carefully balance benefits and costs of bond issuance. This balancing does not occur with the revenue bond. If the "private-purpose" bonds now being issued are actually providing public services comparable in value to their potential claim on the state and local tax base, the political will to alter the institutional rules of the game would be present. This discussion suggests that such a scheme, if adopted, might be phased in over time. This would allow the state and local sector time for the necessary institutional adjustments.

The economic and practical problems with the proposal were discussed by Davie and Zimmerman (1988). The economic problem is that a financial responsibility requirement may not assure a sufficient federal interest in the project to merit a subsidy. If a general obligation gloss on a revenue bond is all it takes to make a bad bond good, the rule could be easily circumvented by using letters of credit and bond insurance to put distance between bonds and taxpayer responsibility. And even if such insulating mechanisms were denied, conduit financing still would be widely used in cases where taxpayers can reasonably expect never to be called upon to support the bond issue.

This latter difficulty is illustrated by what occurred following adoption of the only mention of general obligation bonds in present law. Veterans' mortgage bonds were required by the Mortgage Subsidy Bond Tax Act of 1980 to be issued as general obligations of the states that issue them. The provision was designed to give limited grandfather relief to three states that had historically issued tax-exempt general obligation bonds to provide veterans with cheap mortgage money. It was thought at the time that the general obligation requirement would prevent other states from engaging in the practice. In fact, two other states did develop similar programs (and additional states were considering them), precisely because taxpayers could be convinced that mortgage payments and prepayments would always be sufficient to pay debt service on the bonds and that their obligation would never be called upon. Subsequent legislation was required to limit issuance of veterans' mortgage bonds to five grandfathered states. In light of this experience, is it likely that a community will deny tax-exempt debt financing to a blue chip private firm such as International Business Machines or General Motors when it is making a choice about facilities location, or to wealthy individuals seeking mortgage or student loan financing?

The practical problem is that it is hard to argue that revenue bonds without a GO backup, such as those for a toll road or a waste treatment plant, are bad in every conceivable case. For example, the division of general obligation responsibility among states in a multistate port or airport authority might create very difficult problems that conceivably could preclude the use of tax-exempt bonds viewed to be reasonable on all other grounds. Specifying the type of government whose general obligation bonds are acceptable is another problem. As noted in chapter 4, special authorities and districts have proliferated over the years. Should these units of government be able to issue GO bonds even if they have limited tax capacity? How, for example, should bonds issued by an irrigation district covering the land of only six farmers be treated?

Despite these problems, Davie and Zimmerman (1988) suggested that the concept of preconditioning tax exemption on state or local fiscal responsibility, particularly for single-jurisdiction projects, merits consideration as part of a revised limitation policy. They proposed that it could be combined with a decision to specify in the Internal Revenue Code good or acceptable uses of the bonds, rather than defining bad uses and allowing exceptions. Two lists might be needed, one for facilities owned and operated by state and local governments (e.g., schools) and another where the facilities could be either publicly or privately owned and operated (e.g., sewer plants). Such a positive approach would allow Congress to focus on the question of uses of bond proceeds that merit a federal subsidy (not unlike the public-activity part of the Anthony Commission's three-part public-purpose bond proposal). If the items on the list are specified in broad terms or the list gets too long, a volume cap covering some or all of the items could be added to limit federal revenue losses.

Davie and Zimmerman (1988) contended that such an approach would allow state and local officials to pursue public-private partnerships in order to provide many types of public services,[4] but that defining the individual items on a list of good uses of bond proceeds could be nettlesome. Some regional and local differences might have to be recognized. For example, small airfields in Alaska may be as worthy of federal subsidy as highways in Ohio, but small airports elsewhere might not make the list. Fixed-dollar per capita volume caps may treat rapidly growing areas unfairly. A cap shifts power from localities that now have free access to bond issuance to states that would have the power to allocate a fixed volume of issuance among supplicant jurisdictions.

Current Legislative Proposals

The 101st Congress has been active in making suggestions for revision of the public purpose definition. H.R. 4100 and S. 700 would implement the Environmental Infrastructure Act of 1990. This act would define infrastructure bonds as

. . . any State or local bond which is issued as part of an issue 95 percent or more of the proceeds of which are to be used to provide infrastructure facilities which are available for the ultimate use of the general public (including electric utility, industrial, agricultural, commercial, nonprofit, or governmental users).

Infrastructure facilities would include those for sewage, solid waste disposal, hazardous waste disposal, furnishing of water, or any others needed to comply with federal statutes and regulations administered by the U.S. Environmental Protection Agency. Infrastructure bonds would not be subject to the private business tests and would not be private activity bonds.

Two things are noteworthy about this proposal. First, bonds issued for these activities would be tax exempt whether or not a private person receives direct benefit. This means a privately owned water or solid waste disposal company could finance its capital facilities with tax-exempt bonds even if the output from these facilities were entirely consumed on a contractual basis by other private businesses. Second, unlike current tax-exempt private-activity bonds that must sacrifice some of the tax advantages of accelerated depreciation in exchange for the tax exemption privilege (see chapter 11), these facilities would be eligible to take full advantage of accelerated depreciation. Furthermore, all infrastructure facilities would be reclassified to the 7-Year Accelerated Cost Recovery Class, thereby considerably shortening the depreciation period and increasing the value of the tax benefits. In effect, bonds for infrastructure facilities used by private entities would be more preferentially taxed than governmental bonds.

The underlying logic of this proposal seems to be that the external benefits to society from these environmentally sensitive activities are more than adequate to compensate for direct private use and benefit. It is interesting to note that the activities included in this proposal are fairly consistent with the activities that respondents to the volume cap survey (see chapter 15) wanted removed from the cap.

This approach to environmental control raises an interesting issue. The object here is to cope with the effects of pollution. There are several market-oriented approaches from which to choose. The first is to impose a tax on the goods that are the source of pollution production. This raises the price of these goods and provides an incentive to switch the production process to less pollution-intensive methods. A by-product of this approach is that the costs are shared by the people responsible for producing the pollution, consumers of the product, and the capital and labor involved in its production. A second approach is a variant of the first, but is more flexible in how the costs are shared among the market participants. A judgment is made about the total amount of pollution to be allowed. Each existing producer of the pollution is given the right to produce some portion of the allowable pollution. Producers of the pollution can then buy and sell these pollution rights in response to their differing efficiencies in reducing pollution.

A third approach is to subsidize the cost of processing the pollution after it is produced, the route chosen by the proposed Environmental Infrastructure Act. In this case, more pollution is produced because those producing and benefiting from the pollution are not confronted with the full higher price of its abatement. Many of the costs are borne by society in general, rather than targeted to the responsible industry participants (both producers and consumers). Thus, the mix of output and the distribution of disposable income in society differs depending on the method of pollution control chosen. This proposed act chooses a higher pollution level and spreads the costs across society.

Two other proposed pieces of legislation, H.R. 3663 and S. 1885, would enact the National Recyclable Commodities Financing Act of 1989. This act would add recycling facilities to the list of private activities eligible for tax-exempt financing. Recycling facilities would be treated similarly to those for solid waste disposal, in that they would not be subject to the volume cap if the facilities are governmentally owned. Again, Congress seems to be sensitized to the states' concern with environmental needs indicated in the volume cap survey.

Two other definitional changes have been proposed. First, S. 1221 would make permanent the provision that small-issue loans for first-time farmers are an exempt private activity. This change also reflects concerns expressed in the volume cap survey, that small-issue industrial development bonds (IDBs) had been restricted too much to be useful to rural agricultural states. Second, S. 1627 would adopt the Anthony Commission's recommendation that bonds issued on behalf of a nonprofit organization be considered governmental bonds rather than private activity bonds.

ALLOCATING THE VOLUME CAP AMONG THE STATES

As noted in chapter 15, the survey of state experience with the volume cap indicated some concern with the use of population as the sole factor for allocating the volume cap among the states. It was felt that population might not be a good measure of the states' relative financing needs for exempt private activities or their ability to finance these needs. If that is the case, and the marginal benefits to society from tax-exempt private-activity bonds are directly related to the magnitude of these needs or inversely related to financing abilities, then allocation by population is not maximizing benefits from the federal revenue loss. Activities financed in some states provide smaller benefits than are available from projects not financed in other states.

Table 16.1 presents estimates of how the 1987 volume cap allocation might have differed if it had been distributed on the basis of three measures of state fiscal capacity rather than on the basis of population. The three measures are personal income (PI), the representative tax system (RTS), and total taxable resources (TTR).[5] Personal income has been used frequently in federal grant formulas as a measure of state revenue-raising ability. It is considered inadequate because it fails to incorporate fully: (1) the earnings of commuters who cross state boundaries; (2) the tax base for severance taxes and related energy taxes; (3) access to large amounts of tourist income from another state; and (4) the relatively high concentration of corporate profits or other returns to capital not fully reflected in personal income.

The RTS deals with these problems by calculating average national tax rates for all tax bases used by the states. These average rates are then applied to each state's base for every tax base utilized in the 50 states, whether or not the state uses the tax base. The RTS has been criticized because it narrows the tax base to those already chosen by the 50 states, it ignores interdependence among the various bases and its potential effect on their revenue-raising abilities, and it places heavy demands on data generation.

TTR is an adjusted version of gross state product, the state counterpart to gross national product. It includes the returns to capital and adjusts for personal income's problems with incorporating residence and place-of-work-based income flows. It also suffers from heavy data requirements and a few unsettled conceptual problems.

Two adjustments were made in making the calculations: (1) the per capita allocation was set at $50 rather than the $75 that prevailed in 1987; and (2) the $150 million floor was replaced by a $50 million floor, a compromise between the congressional desire to provide disproportionate assistance to the small states and knowledge that a floor distorts any conceivable measure of need or fiscal capacity.

Table 16.1 TAX-EXEMPT PRIVATE-ACTIVITY BOND VOLUME CAPS
MEASURED ON PER CAPITA BASIS: CURRENT LAW ALLOCATION
COMPARED WITH ALLOCATION BY THREE MEASURES OF FISCAL
CAPACITY

| | Per Capita Allocations | | | Maximum Cap Difference among Three Fiscal Capacity Allocators |
	Current Law	Personal Income (k = 1.4)	Representative Tax System (k = 1.5)	Total Taxable Resources (k = 1.4)	
United States	$58	$58	$58	$58	8
Alabama	50	100	96	99	4
Alaska	286	95	95	95	0
Arizona	50	69	61	71	10
Arkansas	63	104	97	101	7
California	50	34	38	37	3
Colorado	50	54	36	49	18
Connecticut	50	16	16	16	0
Delware	233	78	78	78	0
District of Columbia	241	80	80	80	0
Florida	50	53	51	65	14
Georgia	50	74	71	73	3
Hawaii	139	49	46	48	3
Idaho	150	95	87	94	8
Illinois	50	46	58	46	12
Indiana	50	69	70	70	0
Iowa	53	66	72	67	6
Kansas	61	60	61	56	4
Kentucky	50	95	89	92	6
Louisiana	50	100	71	80	29
Maine	126	69	62	75	13
Maryland	50	30	45	45	15
Massachusetts	50	20	26	27	7
Michigan	50	58	61	59	3
Minnesota	50	50	51	50	1
Mississippi	57	126	115	122	10
Missouri	50	64	65	65	1
Montana	185	92	74	84	18
Nebraska	94	67	65	63	4
Nevada	149	50	50	50	0
New Hamshire	142	47	47	47	1
New Jersey	50	11	29	22	19
New Mexico	100	103	77	91	26
New York	50	31	45	29	16
North Carolina	50	79	73	76	6
North Dakota	223	87	73	78	14
Ohio	50	62	64	61	3
Oklahoma	50	88	60	79	28
Oregon	55	68	63	70	7

Table 16.1 TAX-EXEMPT PRIVATE-ACTIVITY BOND VOLUME CAPS
MEASURED ON PER CAPITA BASIS: CURRENT LAW ALLOCATION
COMPARED WITH ALLOCATION BY THREE MEASURES OF FISCAL
CAPACITY (continued)

	Per Capita Allocations			Maximum Cap
	Current Law	Personal Income (k = 1.4)	Representative Tax System (k = 1.5)	Total Taxable Resources (k = 1.4)	Difference among Three Fiscal Capacity Allocators
Pennsylvania	50	53	61	59	8
Rhode Island	152	51	58	56	7
South Carolina	50	96	88	98	10
South Dakota	212	96	93	96	3
Tennessee	50	85	80	84	5
Texas	50	76	56	63	20
Utah	89	100	84	92	16
Vermont	274	91	91	91	0
Virginia	50	46	56	51	10
Washington	50	53	58	53	4
West Virginia	79	102	85	98	16
Wisconsin	50	59	68	61	8
Wyoming	306	102	102	102	0
Range	256	115	100	106	
Standard deviation	73	26	20	23	

Source: Aten and Zimmerman (1990).

Notes: No state is permitted an allocation of less than $150 million for the allocation under current law; $50 million for the three fiscal capacity measure. The parameter k reflects the degree of equalization provided by an allocation formula. A low k of 0.1 or 0.2 would provide a high degree of equalization, and only a few states would receive bond allocations. Since Congress is likely to desire some private-activity bond authority for all states, k was chosen such that every state would receive a positive allocation from the formula.

This latter point is borne out by the results in chapter 15 that showed that the $150 million floor apparently is much too large for most small states to use. The total volume cap allocation in 1987 used in this table was $14.1 billion (only $12.2 billion without the $150 million floor). The total amount to be allocated was kept at $14.1 billion.

Column 2 of table 16.1 provides the current-law volume cap allocation in 1987, calculated in per capita terms. The average for the United States is $58 (higher than $50 due to the $150 million minimum). Some states and areas with relatively high per capita incomes and small populations are rewarded with large per capita allocations (e.g., Alaska—$286; District of Columbia—$241) because of this large minimum. The range for these current volume cap allocations is a staggering $256 per capita, and the standard deviation is $73.

Columns 3, 4, and 5 of table 16.1 present the per capita amounts that would be provided were that same $14.1 billion bond volume allocated to the states using the measures of fiscal capacity. Note that the U.S. average remains at $58 per person for every allocation system; only the distribution among the states changes. The range drops dramatically for all three of the fiscal capacity allocators, to $115 for the personal-income allocator, $106 for the total-taxable-resources allocator, and $100 for the representative-tax-system allocator. The standard deviations also fall, to a low of $20 for the RTS.

Figure 16.1 highlights the winners and losers for the RTS allocation in table 16.1. It displays the difference between each state's bond volume allocations from the RTS allocator and the current-law allocator. The states are ranked from the largest decrease to the largest increase (ascending order of positive change). Energy-rich and small-population states experience the largest declines. Wyoming and Alaska, which have both characteristics, experience the largest decrease of $204 and $190 per capita, respectively. Eight states have allocation decreases in excess of $100. All the states with large reductions are states with small populations that significantly benefit from the $150 million guaranteed to such states.

Mississippi and Alabama, near-universally recognized as among the poorest states, experience the largest increases of $58 and $46 per capita in their volume caps (see figure 16.1). Six states experience increases in excess of $30. Relatively well-to-do states, such as New York and Pennsylvania, neither gain nor lose much, as the loss they experience because they are well to do appears to be offset by their share of the cap relinquished by the smaller states (owing to the smaller floor). Energy-rich Louisiana would obtain a significant increase in authority to issue bonds. However, its energy reserves are rapidly becoming depleted.

These results lead to two general conclusions about the current formula for distributing authority to issue bonds: (1) the large minimum payment disproportionately benefits states with small populations; and (2) the failure to include a fiscal capacity measure benefits energy-rich states and penalizes poor states.

It is interesting to note the similarity in the allocations among the three fiscal capacity measures. The difference between each state's largest and smallest volume-cap allocation for the three fiscal ca-

Figure 16.1 CHANGE IN STATE PER CAPITA VOLUME CAP: ALLOCATION BY
POPULATION AND THE REPRESENTATIVE TAX SYSTEM

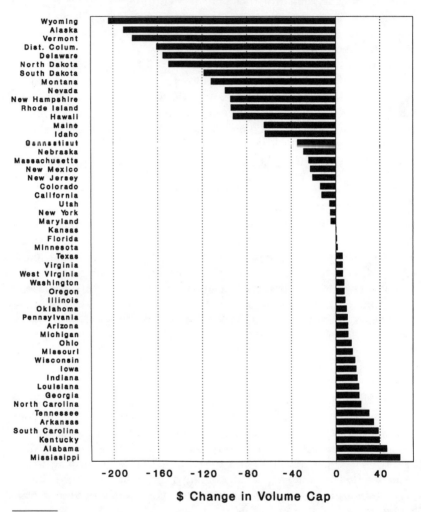

$ Change in Volume Cap

Source: Aten and Zimmerman (1990).

pacity allocators appears in the last column of table 16.1. The average
for the 50 states and the District of Columbia is $8. Only 4 states, all
energy-rich states whose allocations are biased under the personal-
income measure because personal income fails to measure their energy capacities correctly, had volume cap differences greater than or
equal to $20—Louisiana ($29), Oklahoma ($28), New Mexico ($26),

and Texas ($20). With a few exceptions, it does not seem to make much difference which fiscal capacity measure is used to make the allocation.

TAXABLE BOND OPTION

A discussion of alternative policies for tax-exempt bonds would not be complete without some mention of the taxable bond option (TBO), the perennial favorite in the 1960s and 1970s of those wishing to reform the market for tax-exempt bonds. The TBO would substitute a direct federal subsidy of the interest costs on taxable state and local debt for the exemption of interest income on tax-exempt state and local debt (U.S. Congress 1976).

The use of tax-exempt bonds for private purposes was not a significant issue during the TBO's heyday, and in fact, the TBO does not have much to contribute to a solution of the primary issue raised in this book—controlling private use. It would contribute nothing to the definition of public purpose. All the rules adopted in the last 20 years, with the notable exception of those dealing with arbitrage earnings, would still be necessary to determine which state and local bonds satisfy a public purpose and are eligible for the interest subsidy. Thus, the TBO appears to have no role to play in discussions of this policy issue, and is likely to be further from adoption than ever.

The proposal was designed to achieve two other objectives. First, it was expected to broaden the market for state and local debt by raising its interest rate and making the debt attractive to purchasers of taxable corporate and federal debt. Second, it was expected to direct a larger portion of the federal revenue loss to state and local governments by eliminating the windfall gains earned by purchasers of tax-exempt debt whose marginal tax rates were higher than the break-even marginal tax rate (see the discussion in chapter 5).

The latter objective was largely eliminated by the individual and corporate rate reductions enacted in 1981 and 1986. The narrowing of the marginal rate structure from a range of 14 percent to 70 percent to a range of 15 percent to 34 percent has substantially reduced the windfall gains for the inframarginal purchasers of tax exempts. The first objective would still have some merit by attracting individuals in the 15 percent bracket who currently purchase taxable debt instruments for reasons other than tax considerations.

CONCLUSIONS

Allowing the private sector to be an active participant in producing public services is at the heart of the dispute over tax-exempt bonds. The benefits to be gained are that the private sector may be able to produce the service at least cost. Fewer federal dollars would be required to achieve any given change in output. Set against this benefit is the unavoidable fact that some portion of the federal subsidy benefits private persons, which, if not carefully controlled, creates an incentive for bond issuance to exceed the optimal amount. This excess bond volume can easily cost more than the benefits gained from private participation.

The current system of controls errs on the side of rejecting some projects with private participation that probably would serve a primarily public purpose. The proposals of the Anthony Commission would err on the side of accepting some projects with private participation that probably would serve a significant private purpose. The problem with switching to the commission's more permissive set of controls is the difficulty of administering and enforcing the rules that are devised to implement the controls. The current enforcement system is relatively mechanical and relies primarily on voluntary compliance. The proposed system would rely on interpretations of legally ambiguous economic terms such as arm's-length negotiations and market prices, and the potential gains to the private sector almost guarantee that considerable efforts would be expended to frustrate the intent of the legislation and tilt the system toward private gain.

If a more permissive set of rules should be adopted, some protection of the federal purse could be provided by severely constraining the types of activities for which private participation is allowed. First, the subsidy could be concentrated on infrastructure. Although difficult to identify, it certainly does not include single-family housing and student loans. Public goods theory also provides some guidance in further whittling down the list of eligible activities, and suggests the elimination of small-issue IDBs and qualified redevelopment bonds. It might also be possible to eliminate various utility services that can easily (and eagerly) be supplied by the private sector in the desired amounts, particularly gas and electric utility services. In areas where the infrastructure issue is ambiguous, perhaps tax exemption could be made to depend upon issuing the bonds as general obligations of the taxpayers, with a restriction on the ability of taxpayers to use bond insurance to insulate themselves against the risk of default. And inclusion in the approved list should be near automatic for any facilities whose provision the federal government feels so strongly about that it is willing to mandate provision by state and local governments.

These suggestions should not be taken to mean that activities such as single-family housing, student loans, industrial development, and some public utility services do not serve important public purposes. The issues here are twofold. First, infrastructure serves a more basic public purpose in contributing to the nation's productivity and the size of the pie we all have to eat. If we use the scarce supply of tax-exempt savings on these other activities, we are settling for a smaller pie. Second, the public benefits generated by industrial development and some public utility activities do not spill over political boundaries, and thus according to economic theory do not deserve subsidy at the federal as opposed to the state and local levels of government.

The allocation of the volume cap among the states could reflect more accurately the needs and fiscal capacities of the states. Reallocation among the states might even be accompanied by a reduction in the national total of private-activity bonds, particularly if those activities not classified as infrastructure were eliminated from tax exemption. In fact, if the cap were sufficiently small and sufficiently targeted to infrastructure activities, state and local officials would have more incentive to allocate the scarce funds to those partnerships weighted most heavily in the public sector's favor. The costs of more permissive rules for public/private partnerships would be much less, and some federal control might be relinquished.

Notes

1. Legislation that mandates market rates or fair market value for transactions is notoriously difficult to administer. A good example of this is the interminable haggling over the bids that have been received in the federal government's coal leasing program on its western coal lands. Regulations duly prescribe the procedures to be followed to ensure arm's-length negotiations and the receipt of fair market value, but Congress often disputes the reasonableness of the bids accepted by the U.S. Department of the Interior. The dispute became so acrimonious in the early 1980s that a commission was appointed to investigate charges of inadequate bids. See Linowes et al. (1984).

2. Statisticians might say that this proposal moves from a system with a substantial type I error, in which we have an unacceptably large chance of rejecting true null hypotheses, to a system with a substantial type II error, in which we have an unac-

ceptably large chance of accepting false null hypotheses. The federal government prefers to err on the side of a large type I error; state and local governments prefer to err on the side of a large type II error.

3. This would not be true if a government built sufficient office space to affect market rental rates. In effect, a large infusion would shift the supply of office rental space to the right, driving down market rates on all rental property, both public and private. In this case, lessees would benefit from lower rental rates and lessors would suffer from a lower rate of return on their property.

4. Of course, public-private partnerships could be used with taxable financing for projects that provide parochial benefits only.

5. The relative strengths and weaknesses of these measures of fiscal capacity and the procedures used to make the estimates of cap allocations are discussed in Aten and Zimmerman (1990). A more detailed discussion of the RTS is available in Advisory Commission on Intergovernmental Relations (1983); for a discussion of TTR, see Aten (1986).

6. Some might argue that human capital is sorely underfinanced, and that subsidies directed to education would contribute at least as much to the nation's productivity as subsidies directed to infrastructure. But student loans are for higher education, and the debate over underinvestment in education seems to be focused on elementary and secondary education. One might argue that directing scarce tax-exempt funds to student loans detracts from the funds available for elementary and secondary education.

BIBLIOGRAPHY

Advisory Commission on Intergovernmental Relations. 1989. *Significant Features of Fiscal Federalism, 1989 Edition,* vol. 1, no. M-163. Washington, D.C.: Advisory Commission on Intergovernmental Relations, January.

————. 1987. *A Catalog of Federal Grant-in-Aid Programs to State and Local Governments,* no. 153. Washington, D.C.: Advisory Commission on Intergovernmental Relations, August.

————. 1983. *1981 Tax Capacity of the Fifty States,* no. A-93. Washington, D.C.: Advisory Commission on Intergovernmental Relations.

American Public Power Association. n.d. "Talking Points on Section 10173." Washington, D.C.: American Public Power Association.

Anthony Commission on Public Finance. 1989. *Preserving the Federal-State-Local Partnership: The Role of Tax-Exempt Financing.* Washington, D.C.: Anthony Commission on Public Finance, October.

Aschauer, David Alan. 1989. "Is Public Expenditure Productive?" *Journal of Monetary Economics* 23 (2, March): 177–200.

Aten, Robert H. 1986. "Gross State Product: A Measure of Fiscal Capacity." In *Measuring Fiscal Capacity,* edited by Clyde H. Reeves. Boston: Oelgeschlager, Gunn, & Hain, 97–140.

Aten, Robert H., and Dennis Zimmerman. 1990. "Allocating Private-Activity Tax-Exempt Bonds among States Using Three Measures of Fiscal Capacity." *Proceedings of the Eighty-Second Annual Conference, 1989, National Tax Association–Tax Institute of America.*

Auten, Gerald, and Edward Chung. 1988. "Private Activity Tax-Exempt Bonds, 1986." *Statistics of Income Bulletin* (Internal Revenue Service) 8 (1, Summer): 65–75.

Avery, Robert B., Gregory E. Elliehausen, and Arthur B. Kennickell. 1988. "Measuring Wealth with Survey Data: An Evaluation of the 1983 Survey of Consumer Finances," *Review of Income and Wealth,* 34 (December).

Bailey, Martin J. 1974. "Progressivity and Investment Yields under U.S. Income Taxation." *Journal of Political Economy* 84 (November): 1157–75.

Ballard, Frederic L., Jr. 1984. *ABC's of Arbitrage*. Washington, D.C.: Packard Press.

Baumol, William, and Wallace Oates. 1988. *The Theory of Environmental Policy*. Cambridge, England: Cambridge University Press.

Bell, Michael E. 1989. "The Electric Power Industry and the Nation's Infrastructure." Research Paper. Washington, D.C.: Urban Institute, October 20.

Bond Buyer. 1989. *1989 Yearbook*. New York: Bond Buyer.

Boskin, Michael J. 1978. "Taxation, Saving, and the Rate of Interest." *Journal of Political Economy* 86 (April): S3–S27.

Bosworth, Barry. 1988. "Comments." In *Uneasy Compromise: Problems of a Hybrid Income-Consumption Tax*, edited by Henry J. Aaron et al. Washington, D.C.: Brookings Institution, 265–68.

Bowers, J.L. Jr. 1951. "Limitations on Municipal Indebtedness." *Vanderbilt Law Review*: 37–52.

Bradbury, Katharine, Karl E. Case, and Constance R. Dunham. 1989. "Geographic Patterns of Mortgage Lending in Boston, 1982–1987." *New England Economic Review* (Federal Reserve Bank of Boston) (September/October): 3–30.

Braman, Susan. 1989a. "Economic Rationale for Federal Government Involvement in the Electric Power Industry." Research Paper. Washington, D.C.: Urban Institute, October 20.

———. 1989b. "Exploring Economic Rationales for Federal Support of Publicly-Owned Electric Utilities." Research Paper. Washington, D.C.: Urban Institute, October 20.

Brazer, Harvey E. 1959. "The Deductibility of State and Local Taxes under the Individual Income Tax." In *Tax Revision Compendium: Compendium of Papers on Broadening the Tax Base*, vol. 1 Report prepared for House Committee on Ways and Means, 86th Cong., 1st Sess. November 16.

Break, George. 1967. *Intergovernmental Fiscal Relations in the United States*. Washington, D.C.: Brookings Institution.

Browing, Edgar K. and Jacquelene M. Browning. 1979. *Public Finance and the Price System*. New York: Macmillan Publishing Co., Inc.

Buenker, John D. 1964. "The Adoption of the Income Tax Amendment: Case Study of a Progressive Reform." Ph.D. diss., Georgetown University, Washington, D.C.

Carlton, Dennis. 1979. "Why New Firms Locate Where They Do: An Econometric Model." In *Interregional Movements and Regional Growth*, edited by William Wheaton. Washington, D.C.: Urban Institute.

Clark, Phil, and Tom Neubig. 1984. "Private Activity Tax-Exempt Bonds, 1983." *Statistics of Income Bulletin* (Internal Revenue Service) (Summer): 97–107.

Congressional Budget Office. 1988a. *New Directions for the Nation's Public*

Works. Washington, D.C.: U.S. Government Printing Office, September.

———. 1988b. *The Changing Distribution of Federal Taxes: A Closer Look at 1980.* Washington, D.C.: U.S. Government Printing Office, July.

———. 1987. *The Changing Distribution of Federal Taxes: 1975–1990.* Washington, D.C.: U.S. Government Printing Office, October.

———. 1985. *The Federal Budget for Public Works Infrastructure.* Washington, D.C.: U.S. Government Printing Office, July.

———. 1983. *Public Works Infrastructure: Policy Considerations for the 1980s.* Washington, D.C.: U.S. Government Printing Office, April.

———. 1980. *State Profits on Tax-Exempt Student Loan Bonds: Analysis and Options.* Washington, D.C.: U.S. Government Printing Office, March.

———. 1979. *Tax-Exempt Bonds for Single-Family Housing.* Study prepared for the Subcommittee on the City of the House Committee on Banking, Finance and Urban Affairs. April. 96th Cong., 1st. Sess. Committee Print 96-2.

Cordes, Joseph, Eric Nicholson, and Frank Sammartino. 1990. "Raising Revenue by Taxing Activities with Social Costs." *National Tax Journal* 63, September.

Council of Economic Advisers. 1990. *Economic Report of the President.* Washington, D.C.: U.S. Government Printing Office, February.

Courant, Paul, Edward Gramlich, and Daniel Rubinfeld. 1979. "The Stimulative Effects of Intergovernmental Grants: Or Why Money Sticks Where It Hits." In *Fiscal Federalism and Grants-in-Aid,* edited by Peter Mieszkowski and Wallace E. Oates. Washington, D.C.: Urban Institute.

Davie, Bruce F. 1989. "Rostenkowski's Minimum-Tax Plan Merits Support from Issuers." *Muni Week* (July 10): 3.

———. 1963. "State and Local Government Bond Issues, before 1913: A Study of Increased Market Perfection". Ph.D. diss., Harvard University, Cambridge.

Davie, Bruce F., and Dennis Zimmerman. 1988. "Tax-Exempt Bonds after the *South Carolina* Decision." *Tax Notes* 39 (13, June 27): 1573–80.

Day, Donald, ed. 1949. *The Autobiography of Will Rogers.* Boston: Houghton Mifflin Co.

Dewar, Margaret E. 1980. "The Usefulness of Industrial Revenue Bond Programs for State Economic Development: Some Evidence from Massachusetts." Working Paper 63. Cambridge: Joint Center for Urban Studies of the Massachusetts Institute of Technology and Harvard University, March.

Donnelly, Brian. 1989. Letter to The Honorable Nicholas Brady. March 31.

Executive Office of the President. 1985. *The President's Tax Proposals to* the Congress for Fairness, Growth, and Simplicity. Washington, D.C.: U.S. Government Printing Office, May.

Federal Reserve System. 1988. Flow of Funds Accounts: Financial Assets and Liabilities Year End, 1964–87. Washington, D.C.: Board of Governors, September.

————. 1983. Survey of Consumer Finances. Washington, D.C.: Federal Reserve System.

Financial Markets Research Center. 1989. Costs of Issuance on Tax-Exempt Debt: An Initial Report on the FMRC 1988 Survey. Albany: State University of New York at Albany, School of Business, April.

FMRC. See Financial Markets Research Center.

Galper, Harvey, and Eric Toder. 1981. "Modelling Revenue and Allocation Effects of the Use of Tax Exempt Bonds for Private Purposes." In Efficiency in the Municipal Bond Market, edited by George Kaufman. Greenwich, Conn. JAI Press.

GAO. See U.S. General Accounting Office.

Gramlich, Edward M. 1990. A Guide to Benefit-Cost Analysis. Englewood Cliffs, N.J.: Prentice-Hall.

————. 1982. "An Econometric Examination of New Federalism," Brookings Papers on Economic Activity, no. 2. Washington, D.C.: Brookings Institution.

————. 1977. "Intergovernmental Grants: A Review of the Empirical Literature." In The Political Economy of Fiscal Federalism, edited by Wallace E. Oates. Lexington, Mass.: Lexington Books.

Gravelle, Jane G., and Dennis Zimmerman. 1984. "Tax Progressivity and the Design of Tax Incentives for Investment." Public Finance Quarterly 12 (July): 251–89.

Grossman, Hyman C. 1990. "Tax Reform's Effect on Municipal Issues." Credit Week (February 26).

Hansmann, Henry. 1980. "The Role of Nonprofit Enterprise," Yale Law Review (April): 835–99.

Harberger, Arnold C., and Martin J. Bailey. 1969. The Taxation of Income from Capital. Washington, D.C.: Brookings Institution.

Heins, A. James. 1963. Constitutional Restrictions against State Debt. Madison, Wis.: University of Wisconsin Press.

Hendershott, Patric, and Timothy W. Koch. 1977. "An Empirical Analysis of the Market for Tax Exempt Securities." Research Paper. New York: New York University.

Hillhouse, Albert M. 1936. Municipal Bonds: A Century of Experience. New York: Prentice-Hall.

Howrey, E. Philip, and Saul H. Hymans. 1980. "The Measurement and Determination of Loanable-Funds Saving." In What Should Be Taxed: Income or Expenditure? edited by Joseph A. Pechman. Washington, D.C.: Brookings Institution.

Huckins, Larry E. 1986. "Tax Exemption of Municipal Bond Interest: Revenue and Resource Allocation Effects." In *Federal-State-Local Fiscal Relations, Volume I.* Washington, D.C.: U.S. Department of the Treasury, Office of State and Local Finance, September.

Hyman, William A. 1989. "Regulation of Electric Utilities." Research Paper. Washington, D.C.: Urban Institute, October 20.

Inman, Robert P. 1979. "The Fiscal Performance of Local Governments: An Interpretative Review." In *Current Issues in Urban Economics,* edited by Peter Mieszkowski, and Mahlon Straszheim. Baltimore: Johns Hopkins University Press.

Internal Revenue Code, 1988: Complete Text with Index. St. Paul: West Publishing Co.

Internal Revenue Service. 1989. *Statistics of Income Bulletin.* Washington, D.C.: U.S. Government Printing Office. Spring.

———. 1985. *Annual Report: Commissioner of Internal Revenue and Chief Counsel for the Internal Revenue Service.* Washington, D.C.: U.S. Government Printing Office.

Joint Committee on Internal Revenue Taxation. 1972. *General Explanation of the Revenue Act of 1971.* December 15. Joint Committee Print.

———. 1970. *General Explanation of the Tax Reform Act of 1969.* December 3. Joint Committee Print.

Joint Committee on Taxation. 1987a. *Description of the Technical Corrections Act of 1987.* June 15.

———. 1987b. *General Explanation of the Revenue Provisions of the Tax Reform Act of 1986.* May 4. Joint Committee Print.

———. 1984. *General Explanation of the Revenue Provisions of the Deficit Reduction Act of 1984.* December 31. Joint Committee Print.

———. 1983. *Trends in the Use of Tax-Exempt Bonds to Finance Private Activities, Including a Description of H.R. 1176 and H.R. 1635.* June 13. Joint Committee Print.

———. 1982. *General Explanation of the Revenue Provisions of the Tax Equity and Fiscal Responsibility Act of 1982.* December 31. Joint Committee Print.

———. 1981. *General Explanation of the Economic Recovery Tax Act of 1981.* December 29. Joint Committee Print.

———. 1976. *Summary of the Tax Reform Act of 1976.* October 4.

Kenyon, Daphne A. 1989. "Estimating the Federal Revenue Loss from Issuance of Tax-Exempt Bonds." Research Paper. Washington, D.C.: Urban Institute. October 20.

———. 1988. "Implicit Aid to State and Local Governments through Federal Tax Deductibility." In *Intergovernmental Fiscal Relations in an Era of New Federalism,* edited by Michael Bell. Greenwich, Conn. JAI Press.

———. 1984. "Federal Income Tax Deductibility of State and Local Taxes:

What Are Its Effects? Should It Be Modified or Eliminated?" In *Strengthening the Federal Revenue System*, 37–66. Washington, D.C.: Advisory Commission on Intergovernmental Relations, October.

Keynes, John Maynard. 1936. *The General Theory of Employment, Interest, and Money*. New York: Harcourt, Brace & Co.

Kidwell, David S., and Timothy W. Koch. W. 1983. "Market Segmentation and the Term Structure of Municipal Yields." *Journal of Money, Credit and Banking* 15 (1, February): 40–55.

Kormendi, Roger C., and Thomas T. Nagle. 1981. "The Interest Rate and Tax Revenue Effects of Mortgage Revenue Bonds." In *Efficiency in the Municipal Bond Market*, edited by George Kaufman. Greenwich, Conn.: JAI Press.

Kotlikoff, Laurence J., and Alan J. Auerbach. 1987. *Dynamic Fiscal Policy*. New York: Cambridge University Press.

Krueger, Anne O. 1974. "The Political Economy of the Rent-Seeking Society." *American Economic Review* 64 (June): 291–303.

Lamb, Robert, and Stephen P. Rappaport. 1987. *Municipal Bonds*. New York: McGraw-Hill Book Co.

Ledebur, Larry, and William Hamilton. 1986. "The Failure of Tax Concessions as Economic Development Incentives." In *Reforming State Tax Systems*, edited by Steve Gold. National Conference of State Legislatures.

Leonard, Herman B. 1986. *Checks Unbalanced: The Quiet Side of Public Spending*. New York: Basic Books.

Lind, Robert C., et al. 1982. *Discounting for Time and Risk in Energy Policy*. Washington, D.C.: Resources for the Future.

Linowes, David F., et al. 1984. *Report of the Commission: Fair Market Value Policy for Federal Coal Leasing*. February. Washington, D.C.

Livingston, Michael. 1989. "Reform or Revolution? Tax-Exempt Bonds, The Legislative Process, and the Meaning of Tax Reform." *U.C. Davis Law Review* 22 (Summer): 1165–1237.

Maxwell, James A. 1946. *The Fiscal Impact of Federalism in the United States*. Cambridge: Harvard University Press.

Maxwell, James A., and Richard J. Aronson. 1977. *Financing State and Local Governments*. Washington, D.C.: Brookings Institution.

McBride, William H. 1988. *Bond Attorneys' Workshop*. Hinsdale, Ill.: National Association of Bond Lawyers.

Mellon, Andrew W. 1924. *Taxation: The People's Business*. New York: MacMillan Co.

Metcalf, Gilbert. 1989. "Arbitrage and the Savings Behavior of State Governments." Working Paper 3017. Cambridge: National Bureau of Economic Research.

Miller, Victor J. 1988. "A History of Federal Grants-in-Aid to State and Local

Governments." Federal Funds Information for States, Special Analysis. Washington, D.C.: Federal Funds Information for States. June.

Minarik, Joseph J., and Rudolph G. Penner. 1988. "Fiscal Choices." In *Challenge to Leadership: Economic and Social Issues for the Next Decade*, edited by Isabel V. Sawhill. Washington, D.C.: Urban Institute Press.

Moak, Lennox L. 1970. *Administration of Local Government Debt*. Chicago: Municipal Finance Officers Association.

Moody's Investors Service. 1990. *Moody's Bond Record*. New York: Moody's Investors Service. June.

――――. 1987. *Moody's on Municipals: An Introduction to Issuing Debt*. New York: Moody's Investors Service.

Morris, C.R., Jr. 1958. "Evading Debt Limitations with Public Building Authorities: Costly Subversion of State Constitutions." *Yale Law Journal*: 234–68.

Mueller, Dennis C. 1976. "Public Choice: A Survey." *Journal of Economic Literature* 14 (2, June): 395–433.

Mumford, Manly. 1977. "Arbitrage and Advance Refunding." *Municipal Finance: The Duke Law Journal Symposium*. Cambridge, Mass.: Ballinger Publishing Co.

Munnell, Alicia H. 1990. "Why Has Productivity Growth Declined? Productivity and Public Investment." *New England Economic Review* (January/February): 3–22.

Musgrave, Richard A. 1959. *The Theory of Public Finance: A Study in Public Economy*. New York: McGraw-Hill Book Co.

Mussa, Michael L., and Roger C. Kormendi. 1979. *The Taxation of Municipal Bonds: An Economic Appraisal*. Washington, D.C.: American Enterprise Institute.

Nathan, Richard P., F.C. Doolittle, et al. 1987. *Reagan and the States*. Princeton, N.J.: Princeton University Press.

National Association of Bond Lawyers. 1989. Letter to Honorable Edward R. Roybal. April 20.

――――. 1988. *Fundamentals of Municipal Bond Law*. Hinsdale, Ill.: National Association of Bond Lawyers.

――――. 1987. *Model Bond Opinion Project (1987 Revision) and The Function and Professional Responsibiliities of Bond Counsel*. Hinsdale, Ill.: National Association of Bond Lawyers.

National Council on Public Works Improvement. 1988. *Fragile Foundations: A Report on America's Public Works*. Final Report to the President. Washington, D.C.: National Council on Public Works Improvement, February.

Neubig, Thomas S. 1989. "The Current Role of the Tax Expenditure Budget in U.S. Policymaking." In *Proceedings of John Deutsch Conference* on *Tax Expenditures and Government Policy*, edited by Neil Bruce. Kingston, Ontario: Queens University.

Newman, Robert, and Dennis Sullivan. 1988. "Econometric Analysis of Business Tax Impacts and Industrial Location: What Do We Know and How Do We Know It? " *Journal of Urban Economics* (March):

Noto, Nonna A., and Dennis Zimmerman. 1984. "Limiting State-Local Tax Deductibility: Effects among the States." *National Tax Journal* 57 (December): 539–49.

————. 1983. "Limiting State-Local Tax Deductibility in Exchange for Increased General Revenue Sharing: An Analysis of the Economic Effects." Report prepared for Subcommittee on Intergovernmental Relations of the Senate Committee on Governmental Affairs, S. 98-77. 98th Cong., 1st Sess. August.

Oates, Wallace E. 1979. "Lump Sum Intergovernmental Grants Have Price Effects." In *Fiscal Federalism and Grants-in-Aid*, edited by Peter Mieszkowski and Wallace Oates. Washington, D.C.: Urban Institute.

Office of Management and Budget. 1989. *Historical Tables: Budget of the United States Government, Fiscal Year 1990*. Washington, D.C.: U.S. Government Printing Office.

————. 1988a. "Supplement to Special Analysis D." Washington, D.C.: U.S. Government Printing Office, May.

————. 1988b. *Special Analyses: Budget of the United States Government, Fiscal Year 1989*. Washington, D.C.: U.S. Government Printing Office.

Osbourn, Sandra S. 1981. *Block Grants: The Administrative Costs Issue*. Washington, D.C.: Congressional Research Service, Library of Congress, April 1.

Ott, David J., and Allan H. Meltzer. 1963. *Federal Tax Treatment of State and Local Securities*. Washington, D.C.: Brookings Institution.

Peaslee, James M. 1979. "The Limits of Section 103(c): Municipal Bond Arbitrage after the Invested Sinking Fund." *Tax Law Review* 34 (3, Spring): 421–71.

Pechman, Joseph A. 1977. *Federal Tax Policy*. Washington, D.C.: Brookings Institution.

Peek, Joe, and James A. Wilcox. 1986. "Tax Rates and Interest Rates on Tax-Exempt Securities." *New England Economic Review* (Federal Reserve Bank of Boston) (January/February): 29–41.

Petersen, John E. 1989a. "The New SEC Rule on Municipal Disclosure: Implications for Issuers of Municipal Securities." *Government Finance Review* 5 (October): 17–20.

————. 1989b. "Questions and Answers Regarding SEC Rule 15c2-12." Washington, D.C.: Government Finance Officers Association, October.

————. 1987. *Tax-Exempts and Tax Reform: Assessing the Consequences of the Tax Reform Act of 1986 for the Municipal Securities Market.* Washington, D.C.: Government Finance Officers Association/Academy for Contemporary Problems.

Petersen, John E., and Ronald Forbes. 1985. *Innovative Capital Financing.* Chicago: American Planning Association.

Peterson, George. 1984. "Federalism and the States." In *The Reagan Record,* edited by John L. Palmer and Isabel V. Sawhill. Washington, D.C.: Urban Institute Press.

Peterson, G.E., J.A. Tuccillo, and J.C. Weicher. 1981. "The Impact of Local Mortgage Revenue Bonds on Securities, Markets, and Housing Policy Objectives." In *Efficiency in the Municipal Bond Market,* edited by George C. Kaufman. Greenwich, Conn.: JAI Press.

Poterba, James M. 1989. "Tax Reform and the Market for Tax-Exempt Debt." *Regional Science and Urban Economics* 19: 537–62.

————. 1984. "Explaining the Yield Spread between Taxable and Tax-Exempt Bonds: The Role of Expected Tax Policy." In *Studies in State and Local Public Finance,* edited by Harvey Rosen. Chicago: University of Chicago Press.

Public Securities Association. 1987. *Fundamentals of Municipal Bonds.* New York: Public Securities Association.

Pryde, Joan. 1990. "Congress Seen Studying Alternative Penalties for Tax Code Abuses by Municipal Issuers." *Muni Week* (May 7): 1.

Rabinowitz, Alan. 1969. *Municipal Bond Finance and Administration.* New York: John Wiley & Sons.

Rose-Ackerman, Susan, ed. 1986. *The Non-Profit Sector: Economic Theory and Public Policy.* New York: Oxford University Press.

Russell, Clifford S. 1979. "Applications of Public Choice Theory: An Introduction." In *Collective Decision Making: Applications from Public Choice Theory,* edited by Clifford S. Russell, 1-25. Baltimore: Johns Hopkins University Press.

Rutledge, Virginia B. 1990. Before House Committee on Ways and Means. 101st Cong., 2d Sess. March 5.

Rymarowicz, Lillian, and Dennis Zimmerman. 1988. "Federal Budget and Tax Policy and the State-Local Sector: Retrenchment in the 1980s." Washington, D.C.: Congressional Research Service, Library of Congress, September 9.

Samuelson, Paul. 1954. "The Pure Theory of Public Expenditures." *Review of Economics and Statistics* 36 (4, November): 387–89.

Sbragia, Alberta M. 1983. "Politics, Local Government, and the Municipal Bond Market." In *The Municipal Money Chase: The Politics of Local Government Finance,* edited by Alberta M. Sbragia, 67-111. Boulder, Colo.: Westview Press.

Small Business Administration. 1983. *Unfair Competition by Nonprofit Organizations with Small Business: An Issue for the 1980s.* Washington, D.C.: U.S. Government Printing Office, November.

Smith, Adam. [1776] 1976. An Inquiry into the Nature and Causes of the
    Wealth of Nations. Chicago: University of Chicago Press.
Smith, Dan Throop. 1961. Federal Tax Reform: The Issues and a Program.
    New York: McGraw-Hill Book Co.
Starrett, David A. 1988. "Effects of Taxes on Saving." In Uneasy Compro-
    mise: Problems of a Hybrid Income-Consumption Tax, edited by
    Henry J. Aaron et al., 237–59. Washington, D.C.: Brookings Insti-
    tution.
Steuerle, Eugene C. 1986. Who Should Pay for Collecting Taxes? Financing
    the IRS. Washington, D.C.: American Enterprise Institute.
Strauss, Robert P., and Kenneth I. Wertz. 1976. "The Impact of Municipal
    Electric Profits on Local Public Finance." National Tax Journal 29
    (March): 22–30.
Studenski, Paul, and Herman E. Krooss. 1952. Financial History of the United
    States. New York: McGraw-Hill Book Co.
Stutzer, Michael J. 1985. "The Statewide Economic Impact of Small-Issue
    Industrial Revenue Bonds." Federal Reserve Bank of Minneapolis
    Quarterly Review, 9 (Spring): 2–13.
Summers, Lawrence H. 1981. "Capital Taxation and Accumulation in a Life
    Cycle Growth Model." American Economic Review 71 (September):
    533–44.
Toder, Eric, and Thomas S. Neubig. 1985. "Revenue Cost Estimates of Tax
    Expenditures: The Case of Tax-Exempt Bonds." National Tax Jour-
    nal 38 (3, September): 395–414.
Tollison, Robert D. 1982. "Rent Seeking: A Survey." Kyklos 35 (4): 575–
    602.
Trujillo, Patricia A. 1989. "Municipal Bond Financing after South Carolina
    v. Baker and the Tax Reform Act of 1986: Can State Sovereignty
    Reemerge?" Tax Lawyer 42 (1): 147–171.
Tullock, Gordon. 1979. "Public Choice in Practice." In Collective Decision
    Making: Applications from Public Choice Theory, edited by Clifford
    S. Russell. Baltimore: Johns Hopkins University Press.
Ture, Norman B. 1983. "Industrial Revenue Bonds: Estimates of Employment
    Effects and Size of Benefitting Companies." New York: New York
    State Economic Development Council.
U.S. Bureau of the Census. 1988a. Government Finances in 1986–87, ser.
    GF-87-5. Washington, D.C.: U.S. Government Printing Office, No-
    vember.
———. 1988b. "Government Organization: 1987." In Census of Govern-
    ments, ser. GC87(1)-1. Washington, D.C.: U.S. Government Printing
    Office, August.
———. 1985. "Historical Statistics on Governmental Finances and Em-
    ployment." In 1982 Census of Governments, ser. GC82(6)-4. Wash-
    ington, D.C.: U.S. Government Printing Office, January.

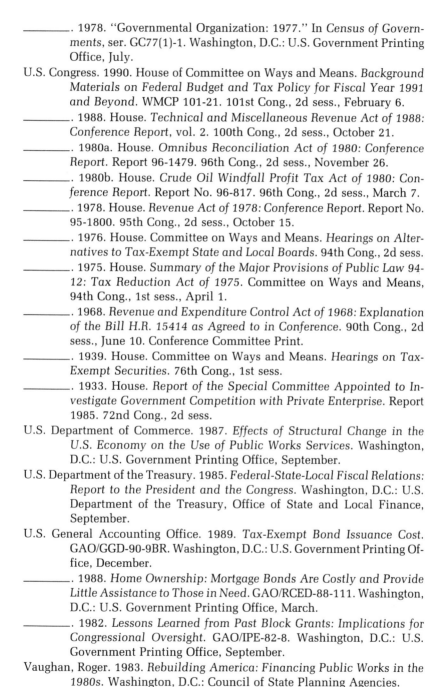

————. 1978. "Governmental Organization: 1977." In *Census of Governments*, ser. GC77(1)-1. Washington, D.C.: U.S. Government Printing Office, July.

U.S. Congress. 1990. House of Committee on Ways and Means. *Background Materials on Federal Budget and Tax Policy for Fiscal Year 1991 and Beyond.* WMCP 101-21. 101st Cong., 2d sess., February 6.

————. 1988. House. *Technical and Miscellaneous Revenue Act of 1988: Conference Report*, vol. 2. 100th Cong., 2d sess., October 21.

————. 1980a. House. *Omnibus Reconciliation Act of 1980: Conference Report.* Report 96-1479. 96th Cong., 2d sess., November 26.

————. 1980b. House. *Crude Oil Windfall Profit Tax Act of 1980: Conference Report.* Report No. 96-817. 96th Cong., 2d sess., March 7.

————. 1978. House. *Revenue Act of 1978: Conference Report.* Report No. 95-1800. 95th Cong., 2d sess., October 15.

————. 1976. House. Committee on Ways and Means. *Hearings on Alternatives to Tax-Exempt State and Local Boards.* 94th Cong., 2d sess.

————. 1975. House. *Summary of the Major Provisions of Public Law 94-12: Tax Reduction Act of 1975.* Committee on Ways and Means, 94th Cong., 1st sess., April 1.

————. 1968. *Revenue and Expenditure Control Act of 1968: Explanation of the Bill H.R. 15414 as Agreed to in Conference.* 90th Cong., 2d sess., June 10. Conference Committee Print.

————. 1939. House. Committee on Ways and Means. *Hearings on Tax-Exempt Securities.* 76th Cong., 1st sess.

————. 1933. House. *Report of the Special Committee Appointed to Investigate Government Competition with Private Enterprise.* Report 1985. 72nd Cong., 2d sess.

U.S. Department of Commerce. 1987. *Effects of Structural Change in the U.S. Economy on the Use of Public Works Services.* Washington, D.C.: U.S. Government Printing Office, September.

U.S. Department of the Treasury. 1985. *Federal-State-Local Fiscal Relations: Report to the President and the Congress.* Washington, D.C.: U.S. Department of the Treasury, Office of State and Local Finance, September.

U.S. General Accounting Office. 1989. *Tax-Exempt Bond Issuance Cost.* GAO/GGD-90-9BR. Washington, D.C.: U.S. Government Printing Office, December.

————. 1988. *Home Ownership: Mortgage Bonds Are Costly and Provide Little Assistance to Those in Need.* GAO/RCED-88-111. Washington, D.C.: U.S. Government Printing Office, March.

————. 1982. *Lessons Learned from Past Block Grants: Implications for Congressional Oversight.* GAO/IPE-82-8. Washington, D.C.: U.S. Government Printing Office, September.

Vaughan, Roger. 1983. *Rebuilding America: Financing Public Works in the 1980s.* Washington, D.C.: Council of State Planning Agencies.

Vaughan, Roger, and Roger Pollard. 1984. *Rebuilding America: Planning and Managing Public Works in the 1980s.* Washington, D.C.: Council of State Planning Agencies.

Vehorn, Charles L., and Edward Nannenhorn. 1990. "Setting Limits on the Tax-Exempt Bond Market: Where Do We Go From Here?" *Tax Notes* 47 (9, May 28): 1111–7.

Vogt, Jack, and Lisa Cole. eds. 1983. *A Guide to Municipal Leasing.* Chicago: Municipal Finance Officers Association.

Von Furstenburg, George M., and Burton C. Malkiel. 1977. "The Government and Capital Formation, A Survey of Recent Issues." *Journal of Economic Literature* 15 (September): 835–78.

Walsh, Annmarie Hauck. 1978. *The Public's Business: The Politics and Practices of Government Corporations.* Cambridge: MIT Press.

Washington Post. 1988. Sec. C, May 17.

Wasylenko, Michael. 1981. "The Location of Firms: The Role of Taxes and Fiscal Incentives." In *Urban Government Finance: Emerging Trends,* edited by Roy Bahl. Beverly Hills, Calif.: Sage Publications.

Weisbrod, Burton A. 1988. *The Nonprofit Economy.* Cambridge: Harvard University Press.

Wilcox, Clair. 1955. *Public Policies toward Business.* Homewood, Ill.: Richard D. Irwin.

Wilson, J., and L. Richardson. 1985. "Public Ownership vs. Energy Conservation: A Paradox of Utility Regulation." *Regulation,* (September/October).

Wrightson, Margaret T. 1989. "The Road to *South Carolina*: Intergovernmental Tax Immunity and the Constitutional Status of Federalism." *Publius: The Journal of Federalism* (Summer): 39–55.

_____. 1988. *Who Benefits from Single-Family Housing Bonds?: History, Development and Current Experience of State-Administered Mortgage Revenue Bond Programs.* Washington, D.C.: Georgetown University, Public Policy Program, April 28.

Zimmerman, Dennis. 1989. "Privatization, Unfair Competition, and Future Restrictions on Tax-Exempt Bonds." *Municipal Finance Journal* 10 (2).

_____. 1988. "The Intergovernmental Struggle over Tax-Exempt Bond Reform." In *Intergovernmental Fiscal Relations in an Era of New Federalism,* edited by Michael Bell. Greenwich, Conn.: JAI Press.

_____. 1987. "Separating Public and Private-Purpose Tax-Exempt Bonds." *Tax Notes* 31 (5, May 5): 509–12.

ABOUT THE AUTHOR

Dennis Zimmerman is a specialist in public finance at the Congressional Research Service of the Library of Congress. His primary research interests are federal tax policy, intergovernmental fiscal relations, and energy policy, topics on which he has published many articles and written many reports for Congress. He has served as a consultant on tax-exempt bonds to the Advisory Commission on Intergovernmental Relations, and in the mid-1980s as a technical advisor to the U.S. Department of Treasury's study of federal-state-local fiscal relations. He has taught at Wayne State University and American University, spent a year as an Economic Policy Fellow at the Brookings Institution, and a year as a Visiting Fellow at the Urban Institute, where he wrote this book.